# Praise for The

"An accessible, engrossing account of the [...] that Mr. Bernanke, with Mervyn A. King of the Bank of England and Jean-Claude Trichet of the European Central Bank, endured in pulling the world financial system back from collapse."  
—*The New York Times*

"A detailed and fast-moving account of these perilous years. This is the crisis as told through e-mails, phone calls, meetings, and one very fateful walk along the beach in Deauville, France."  
—*The Wall Street Journal*

"Mr. Irwin's sweep is impressive. He uses anecdotes from the main historic crises to explain financial jargon which is not only thick, but changes over time. . . . [Irwin] is good at describing the deeper power shifts as well as the personality clashes."  
—*The Economist*

"An excellent account . . . scrupulously reported and full of clear explanations of events and economic concepts. . . . An incredibly valuable book for all economically concerned non-economists. As someone who knows well the three central bankers that the book features . . . I can attest that the narrative has more than just a ring of truth. It gets the individuals, the circumstances surrounding their decisions, and their motivations right and also presents them fairly. Irwin's volume will have lasting value for a wide range of audiences, including students and elected officials, but it will make its greatest contribution as a corrective to the many unfounded or simply crazy ideas about monetary policymakers' intentions and impact."  
—Adam S. Posen, *Foreign Affairs*

"*The Alchemists* is a deeply researched and painstakingly reported account of what went wrong, and how the world's top three central bankers . . . struggled to keep the global financial system from capsizing."  
—*Strategy+Business*

"A highly readable account of central banking in a time of crisis." —*USA Today*

## ABOUT THE AUTHOR

Neil Irwin is senior economic correspondent at *The New York Times*. He was previously a columnist at the *Washington Post*, where he led coverage of the global financial crisis and response of the Federal Reserve and other central banks. He has an MBA from Columbia University, where he was a Knight-Bagehot Fellow in Economic and Business Journalism. Irwin appears regularly on television analyzing economic topics, including on MSNBC, CNBC, and the PBS *NewsHour*. He lives in Washington, D.C.

# The Alchemists

THREE CENTRAL BANKERS
AND A WORLD ON FIRE

# NEIL IRWIN

PENGUIN BOOKS

PENGUIN BOOKS
Published by the Penguin Group
Penguin Group (USA) LLC
375 Hudson Street
New York, New York 10014

USA | Canada | UK | Ireland | Australia | New Zealand | India | South Africa | China
penguin.com
A Penguin Random House Company

First published in the United States of America by The Penguin Press,
a member of Penguin Group (USA) Inc., 2013
Published in Penguin Books 2014

Photograph credits appear on pages 415–16.

ISBN 978-1-59420-462-3 (hc.)
ISBN 978-0-14-312499-3 (pbk.)

Printed in the United States of America
1  3  5  7  9  10  8  6  4  2

BOOK DESIGN BY AMANDA DEWEY

*To my parents, Co and Nancy Irwin*

# Contents

*Part II:*

# PANIC, 2007–2008

*Part III:*

# AFTERMATH, 2009–2010

*Part IV:*

# THE SECOND WAVE, 2011–2012

# Time Line

**November 30, 1656**—Johan Palmstruch's Stockholms Banco is chartered by Swedish king Karl X Gustav.

**1661**—Stockholms Banco issues the first paper banknotes in Europe.

**September 17, 1668**—After Stockholms Banco collapses, the Swedish Riksbank is created. It remains the country's central bank until this day.

**July 27, 1694**—King William III charters the Bank of England.

**May 10, 1866**—British bank Overend, Gurney & Co. fails, sparking a panic in the London money markets. The Bank of England floods the banking system with liquidity, acting as lender of last resort.

**Fall, 1907**—A banking panic in New York sparks a global economic downturn, crystallizing the need for a central bank in the United States.

**December 23, 1913**—The Federal Reserve Act passes, setting up a central bank for the United States, albeit one with a complicated structure of twelve powerful regional branches.

**1923**—The German Reichsbank, led by Rudolf von Havenstein, prints massive amounts of money, resulting in hyperinflation. Price increases of thousands of percent per month destabilize the war-ravaged nation and spark uprisings by the Nazis and other insurgent groups.

**November 16, 1923**—Hjalmar Schacht introduces a new and more stable German currency, the rentenmark. Its value is set at one rentenmark per trillion reichsmarks.

**October 29, 1929**—The U.S. stock market crashes on "Black Tuesday."

**May 11, 1931**—Credit-Anstalt, a leading Austrian bank, fails, prompting a ripple effect of withdrawals and more bank failures in Germany and elsewhere in Europe.

**July 9, 1931**—Hans Luther, head of the German Reichsbank, travels to European capitals and then to meet fellow central bankers in Basel, looking in vain for international relief from the growing banking crisis.

**September 21, 1931**—Britain leaves the gold standard, facing economic collapse should it try to maintain the peg of the pound to the price of gold.

**July 22, 1944**—Global economic leaders finish a conference in Bretton Woods, New Hampshire, where they agree to a world economic order for the post–World War II globe.

**August 15, 1971**—With the United States struggling to maintain the peg of the dollar to gold as mandated by the Bretton Woods system, President Richard Nixon suspends the gold window. His advisers include Federal Reserve chairman Arthur Burns and Treasury official Paul Volcker.

**1978**—In Arthur Burns's final year as Federal Reserve chair, inflation reaches 9 percent.

**October 6, 1979**—In an unscheduled Saturday meeting of Fed policymakers, new chairman Paul Volcker engineers an interest rate hike and a new strategy to tighten the money supply, aiming to bring down inflation. These rate hikes lead to a deep recession, but eventually end the inflation that took root under Burns.

**December 10, 1991**—European leaders agree to the Maastricht Treaty, pledging to create a common currency.

**June 1, 1998**—The European Central Bank is created to administer the euro.

**March 19, 2001**—Suffering economic stagnation in the wake of a real estate and banking system collapse, the Bank of Japan begins a program of buying assets, known as quantitative easing.

**July 1, 2003**—Mervyn King takes office as 119th governor of the Bank of England.

**November 1, 2003**—Jean-Claude Trichet takes office as second president of the European Central Bank.

**February 1, 2006**—Ben Bernanke takes office as the fourteenth chairman of the Board of Governors of the Federal Reserve System.

## 2007

**August 9**—BNP Paribas announces it is unable to value mortgage-related assets on the books of three funds it manages, sparking a freeze-up in money markets and a €95 billion intervention by the ECB.

**September 14**—The Bank of England intervenes to aid Northern Rock, a British bank on the verge of failure.

**December 12**—The Federal Reserve, Bank of England, ECB, and central banks of Canada and Switzerland announce "liquidity swap lines" to provide up to $24 billion to help ease a freeze-up of the banking system. The first joint international effort of the global central banks during the crisis, it is a tool to channel dollars from the Fed to European banks that are facing shortages of dollars.

## 2008

**March 14**—The Fed rescues investment bank Bear Stearns by putting up $30 billion toward its acquisition by J.P. Morgan. It is the first bailout by the Fed in the crisis.

**September 15**—Lehman Brothers files for bankruptcy.

**September 16**—The Fed rescues insurer AIG with an $85 billion emergency loan.

**September 18**—The Fed, ECB, and central banks of Britain, Canada, Japan, and Switzerland expand swap lines by $180 billion, a move that enables the global central banks to lend dollars into their domestic banking systems.

**September 24**—Fed swap lines are extended to the central banks of Australia, Sweden, Denmark, and Norway.

**September 29**—Swap lines are expanded by another $330 billion.

**September 30**—The Irish government announces it is guaranteeing the liabilities of the nation's major banks, sparking a run on banks in European nations without such guarantees.

**October 7**—The Fed announces the "Commercial Paper Funding Facility" to backstop the multitrillion-dollar market for short-term corporate lending.

**October 8**—In the first ever globally coordinated monetary policy action, the central banks of the United States, eurozone, Britain, Canada, Sweden, and Switzerland announce that they are all cutting interest rates.

**October 29**—Fed swap lines are extended to the central banks of Brazil, Mexico, South Korea, and Singapore.

**November 6**—Bank of England cuts target interest rate by 150 basis points.

**December 16**—The Fed cuts its target interest rate to near zero and says it expects conditions will warrant "exceptionally low" rates for "some time."

## 2009

**March 5**—The Bank of England slashes its target interest rate to 0.5 percent and announces £75 billion of bond purchases, or quantitative easing.

**March 9**—Global stock markets reach their lowest levels in over a decade, with the Standard & Poor's 500 off 57 percent from its 2007 peak.

**March 18**—The Fed expands its own quantitative easing, to a total of $1.75 trillion in purchases of a variety of securities.

**March 24**—Bernanke and Timothy Geithner, the treasury secretary and former New York Fed chief, are pilloried in a House committee hearing for bailing out AIG.

**May 13**—The ECB cuts its main interest rate to a record low 1 percent.

**June 17**—Mervyn King delivers the annual Mansion House speech in London, blindsiding Chancellor Alistair Darling with criticism of British bank regulation.

**August 6**—King is outvoted on the Bank of England's monetary policy committee, favoring a larger expansion of quantitative easing than the majority.

**August 25**—President Barack Obama announces that he is reappointing Bernanke to a second term as Fed chair.

**October 4**—The socialist PASOK party prevails in Greek elections, bringing Prime Minister George Papandreou to power. His government encounters massive deficits.

## 2010

**January 28**—The Senate confirms Bernanke for a second term as Fed chair by the narrowest margin in history.

**February 7**—Finance ministers and central bankers of the Group of Seven leading industrialized powers meet in the Iqaluit, Canada. In the frigid Arctic air, a consensus emerges toward austerity and tighter money.

**February 11**—European leaders hold an emergency summit on Greece and pledge to aid the cash-strapped nation.

**April 23**—Papandreou asks for a €45 billion bailout from European nations and the IMF.

**May 2**—European leaders agree to a €110 billion Greek aid package, which markets quickly decide is inadequate.

**May 5**—Protests of Greek austerity measures turn violent in Athens, as three people die in a firebombed bank.

**May 6**—The ECB holds a monetary policy meeting in Lisbon and makes no change to interest rate policies. Markets decline as Trichet suggests no move toward ECB aid for Greece. U.S. markets experience what becomes known as the Flash Crash, plummeting briefly. That evening, ECB governing council members discuss the possibility of buying bonds to ease pressure on Greece and other nations facing high borrowing costs. British elections are held, resulting in a swing in power toward the conservatives but no outright majority, necessitating negotiations to form a coalition with the Liberal Democrats.

**May 7**—Axel Weber, president of the German Bundesbank, sends an e-mail to colleagues retracting his open-mindedness of the night before to ECB bond purchases. Trichet travels to Brussels to impress upon European government heads the urgency of a eurozone rescue fund, implicitly dangling the possibility that if they act, the ECB could take action as well.

**May 9**—Eurozone finance ministers negotiate in Brussels to create a €750 billion rescue fund, known as the European Financial Stability Facility, as ECB officials in Basel, Frankfurt, and elsewhere agree to begin buying bonds to allay pressure from the bond markets. Weber votes against the move and holds a secret conference call of the Bundesbank board to consider whether to comply with the ECB's directive. The Fed reopens swap lines with the ECB and other international central banks.

**May 11**—A crucial amendment to the Dodd-Frank Act aiming to increase transparency at the Fed—but maintain independence of monetary policy—passes the Senate. David Cameron becomes British prime minister after successfully forming a coalition with the Liberal Democrats.

**May 12**—An amendment to keep the Fed in place as regulator of large and small banks passes the Senate.

**July 21**—Obama signs the Dodd-Frank Act into law, increasing the powers of the Fed.

**August 27**—Bernanke gives a speech at the Jackson Hole economic symposium, raising the possibility of a new round of quantitative easing to address a slowdown in the U.S. economy.

**October 18**—In Deauville, France, German chancellor Angela Merkel and French president Nicolas Sarkozy walk on a seaside promenade and agree that private creditors must take losses in future bailouts. Trichet is stridently opposed to this approach, which causes a new wave of disruption in financial markets.

**October 23**—Finance ministers and central bankers of the Group of 20 major world powers meet in Gyeongju, South Korea, where Bernanke explains the Fed's expected new policy of quantitative easing to skeptical international policymakers.

**November 3**—The Fed announces it will buy $600 billion in Treasury bonds in a second round of quantitative easing that will be widely known as QE2. It draws intensive criticism from American conservatives and the German, Chinese, and Brazilian governments.

**November 21**—Ireland, under post-Deauville pressure from bond markets, requests a bailout.

## 2011

**February 11**—Axel Weber resigns from the Bundesbank. His opposition to ECB bond purchases makes his possible ascent to the presidency of the central bank untenable.

**April 6**—Portugal requests a bailout, becoming the third European country to do so.

**April 8**—The ECB elects to hike interest rates, the first of two quarter-point increases, seeing a risk of inflation even as much of the continent falls into depression.

**May 6**—Trichet leaves a secret meeting of European officials in Luxembourg where the possibility of Greece leaving the eurozone is to be discussed, angry that the existence of the meeting has leaked to the press.

**May 11**—Merkel indicates that she supports Mario Draghi, Italy's top central banker, to replace Trichet as ECB president when Trichet's term is to end.

**May 14**—Dominique Strauss-Kahn, the managing director of the IMF, is arrested in New York for sexual assault against a hotel maid. He had been a crucial voice in negotiations over Greek aid to take into account the damage that rapid austerity could cause to the Greek economy.

**May 17**—European finance ministers instigate talks over Greek bondholders taking losses, against Trichet's vociferous objections.

**June 16**—Mervyn King and new chancellor George Osborne deliver a coordinated message at the Mansion House Dinner in London, announcing plans to bring down budget deficits and to shift far greater control over the financial system to the Bank of England.

**June 30**—Papandreou narrowly clings to power in Greece as he wins passage of a €78 billion package of austerity measures. Violence continues in the streets as the Greek economy falls into depression.

**July 21**—After lengthy negotiations, a group representing banks and other Greek bondholders agrees to take a loss.

**August 5**—With borrowing costs spiking for the Italian and Spanish governments amid a loss of confidence in European resolve, Trichet sends letters to the Italian and Spanish finance ministers outlining the steps they must take to receive help from the ECB.

**August 7**—The ECB resumes buying bonds, now including those from Spain and Italy.

**September 9**—Jürgen Stark, a German member of the ECB executive board, resigns, joining Weber as the second German to leave in protest of bond buying by the central bank.

**September 21**—Responding to another wave of weakness in the U.S. economy, the Fed announces its Maturity Extension Program, known as Operation Twist, aimed at replacing $400 billion in shorter-term bonds the Fed owned with a comparable amount of longer-term bonds, achieving some of the effects of new QE with less political blowback.

**October 6**—Concerned about the ripple effects of the eurozone crisis on the British economy, the Bank of England policy committee unanimously agrees to an additional £75 billion of quantitative easing.

**October 19**—At a farewell celebration for Trichet at the Frankfurt opera house, key players including Trichet, Draghi, Merkel, Sarkozy, and IMF chief Christine Lagarde meet to plot a path forward, amid worries that neither Papandreou nor Italian prime minister Silvio Berlusconi have the credibility to continue leading their nations.

**October 27**—European leaders, in yet another summit, negotiate for Greek bondholders to take further losses and extend a new aid package to Greece.

**October 31**—Papandreou calls for a referendum on the Greek bailout agreement, creating a situation in which a no vote would mean his nation's leaving the eurozone.

**November 1**—Draghi takes office as the third president of the European Central Bank.

**November 3**—The ECB cuts its interest rate target a quarter percent at Draghi's first policy meeting as president, and follows suit the next month, reversing the Trichet rate hikes from the spring of 2011 and reacting to a rapidly deteriorating European economy.

**November 4**—At the Group of 20 summit in Cannes, Merkel, Sarkozy, and other heads of state pressure Papandreou and Berlusconi to fulfill their obligations or stand down.

**November 6**—Papandreou steps down, to be replaced as prime minister by Lucas Papademos, a former ECB vice president.

**November 12**—Berlusconi steps down, to be replaced by Mario Monti, a former European commissioner.

**November 30**—The Fed, ECB, and other leading central banks again announce swap lines to try to funnel dollars toward ailing European banks.

**December 21**—The ECB institutes a "long-term refinancing operation" (LTRO), which pumps €489 billion into European banks for a three-year term.

## 2012

**February 29**—The ECB holds a second LTRO, pumping an additional €529 billion into European banks.

**May 6**—Greek parliamentary elections lead to no decisive result, as extreme parties of the left and right see major gains.

**July 26**—In a speech in London, Draghi pledges that the ECB will do "whatever it takes to preserve the euro."

**September 6**—The ECB announces a new program of Outright Monetary Transactions, a pledge to buy bonds in unlimited amounts to combat market bets against the survival of the eurozone.

**September 13**—The Fed announces a resumption of quantitative easing, pledging to continue buying bonds indefinitely unless the outlook for the job market in the United States improves or inflation becomes a threat.

**October 23**—Mervyn King delivers a speech saying that "printing money is not... simply manna from heaven." He also says that "there are no shortcuts to the necessary adjustments in our economy," as the Bank of England largely sits on its hands amid the new activism from the Fed and ECB.

**December 12**—The Fed announces it expects to keep low-interest-rate policies in place until either the U.S. unemployment rate falls to 6.5 percent or inflation is poised to exceed 2.5 percent.

# Introduction:
# Opening the Spigot

On August 9, 2007, Jean-Claude Trichet awoke at his childhood home of Saint-Malo, on the coast of Brittany, ready for a day puttering about in his motorboat and enjoying the company of his grandchildren. It was time for his summer respite after a busy year as president of the European Central Bank. Mervyn King, the governor of the Bank of England, had also planned a leisurely Thursday: He would make his way from his flat in London's Notting Hill neighborhood to the Kennington Oval, on the city's south side, to watch the British national cricket team play India. Ben Bernanke, the chairman of the U.S. Federal Reserve, was alone among the three men who would guide the world through the convulsions of the half decade to come in having scheduled a regular workday. His security detail was to drive him from his Capitol Hill row house to the Treasury Department, where he had an early breakfast with Secretary Henry Paulson. Bernanke would eat oatmeal. For the three men, the day would not go quite as planned.

At about 7:30 a.m., Trichet's phone rang. Francesco Papadia, the head of the ECB's markets desk, was on the line from the central bank's headquarters in Frankfurt. "We have a problem," Papadia said.

Gigantic French bank BNP Paribas had announced that it was suspending withdrawals from three investment funds it managed. The funds were invested heavily in U.S. home-mortgage-backed securities that had become nearly impossible to value. Customers' money would be locked up until the bank could figure out exactly how much the investments were worth. In itself, it was a tiny development: The three relatively obscure funds held only €1.6 billion in assets.

But the announcement confirmed the worst fears of bankers across Europe. They'd been worried for weeks about the losses they were facing on U.S. home loans. Supposedly ultrasecure mortgage bonds that had traded freely earlier in 2007 had by late July hardly been trading at all. As more and more people who'd taken out risky loans to buy a house in Tampa or Cleveland or Phoenix found themselves unable to pay them back, all the assumptions on which those loans had been made started to be called into question. Maybe all those AAA-rated securities weren't really AAA after all. Had the banks poured vast sums into bonds that weren't worth what they'd seemed to be? And if BNP Paribas couldn't figure out how much its own funds were worth, how could any other bank know its real exposure to mortgage-backed securities?

It's not for nothing that the word "credit" derives from the Latin *creditus*, "trusted." Banks use highly rated securities as almost the equivalent of cash—whenever they need more dollars or euros, they hand the bonds over to another bank as collateral. It's one of the basic ways they ensure they have exactly the amount of money they need to meet their obligations on any given day. But when it came to those mortgage-backed securities in early August 2007, that simple exchange suddenly became complicated. The problem wasn't just that the securities were worth less than they'd been before—after all, banks can deal with losses. It's that no one knew just how much less—and whether, if one bank had lent money to another down the street in exchange for mortgage-backed securities, it would ever get paid back.

Papadia and his staff spoke regularly with treasurers at twenty major European banks known as the money market contact group, and its members had been warning for days that, as one ECB official put it, an "infarction" was imminent. That Thursday morning, it hit: After the BNP Paribas announcement, with each bank out only for itself, the usual supply of cash was fast evaporating. "Trust was shaken today," Deutsche Bank chief european economist Thomas Mayer told the *New York Times*. As one executive of a major global bank said later, "It was something none of us had experienced. It was as if your entire life you had turned the spigot and water came out. And now there was no water."

It's a more precise metaphor than it may seem, for liquidity is exactly what was disappearing in the banking system that day. No longer were euros, dollars, and pounds as easy to come by as water. History has taught again and again that when banks shut down and hoard their money, so too do the economies they serve. A banker who's unwilling to lend to other bankers is likely also to be unwilling to lend to the businesses and households that need money to build a factory or buy a house. If unchecked, the banking crisis in Europe could inflict untold damage on the world economy. Suddenly, the European habit of taking a lengthy late summer vacation had become very inconvenient.

Gather the Executive Board, Trichet instructed Papadia. He needed to talk to the six officials from across Europe who share the collective authority to deploy the resources of the central bank—including the ability to create euros from thin air. ECB staff in Frankfurt began calling around to various villas and retreats in Spain, Italy, and Greece to arrange an emergency conference call. Trichet normally used the walled medieval port town of Saint-Malo as a retreat from the world, a place where he could enjoy the water and read poetry and philosophy. But now it would become the nerve center from which he would manage the first phase of the first great financial crisis of the twenty-first century.

By 10 a.m., the full Executive Board was on the line. Trichet was emphatic: "There is only one thing we can do, which is to give liquidity." The ECB, he insisted, must flood the banking system with euros. He was proposing that the central bank fulfill its traditional role as "lender of last resort," stepping in when private banks were pulling back, and using a novel means to do so. The ECB would abandon its usual practice of pumping some fixed amount of money into the banking system and instead make an unlimited number of euros available to the banks that needed them. The technical term for what Trichet and the Executive Board did at 12:30 p.m. central European time is to offer a "fixed-rate tender with full allotment."

Translation: Come and get it, guys. We'll give you as many euros as you need at 4 percent. Some forty-nine banks took €95 billion.


The Federal Reserve Bank of New York maintains a markets desk to monitor what's going on across the world of finance, but during the early hours of the morning on the East Coast that Thursday, only a handful of young staffers were on duty to monitor overnight activity. It would take hours for the news to make its way to New York Fed president Timothy Geithner, who was on vacation on Cape Cod, and Bernanke, who was getting ready for his breakfast with Secretary Paulson.

At 6:49 a.m., Bernanke received an e-mail from Brian Madigan, head of the Fed's monetary affairs division, explaining that "as you've probably seen, markets have sold off again overnight" and updating him on activity in the European bond and stock markets. But Madigan hadn't yet received word of the ECB's action. It was nearly half an hour later, as Bernanke's black Cadillac sped along Independence Avenue, driven by an officer of the Federal Reserve's own police force, before the chairman received the first word that the ECB had done something unusual. A 7:16, an e-mail arrived from David Skidmore, an official in the Fed's press office: "Apparently Deutsche Bank had two money market funds fail and the ECB is making tender offers for dollar-denominated assets. Glenn Somerville of Reuters, who I've been talking to, is heading to the Treasury press room early."

The details were wrong: It was BNP Paribas, not Deutsche Bank, three funds, not two, and the tender offers were denominated in euros, not dollars. But the gist was right: The ECB had intervened in markets in a way it never had before. And the most powerful man at the Fed was finding out about it through garbled rumors from a Reuters reporter. By the time he sat down for oatmeal with Paulson at 7:30, it was clear that something big had happened, even if no one seemed to be sure exactly what it was.

It wasn't until 8:52 a.m. that Bernanke got a more accurate update, in the form of an e-mail from Kevin Warsh, a Fed governor who often acted as the chairman's emissary to people in financial markets and at other central banks. "This action by the ECB sends two signals," wrote Warsh, who had been working the phones all morning. "First, they are ready to provide liquidity to ensure the smooth operation of European money markets. Second, they are providing liquidity at their policy rate, and thus far not viewing a liquidity squeeze as a more fundamental reason to adjust its policy stance." The Americans quickly understood that Trichet was trying to draw a bright line between what the ECB was doing for the financial system and what it was doing to address any underlying weakness in the European economy as a whole.

After breakfast, Bernanke went to his office at the white marble Eccles

Building in Washington's Foggy Bottom neighborhood. At 11 a.m., he met with a man named Lewis Ranieri, looking to pick his brain. In the 1980s, as a bond trader at investment bank Salomon Brothers, Ranieri had played a crucial role in developing the very concept of mortgage-backed securities. In other words, he'd more or less invented the markets that were now imploding. At 2 p.m., Bernanke met with Raymond Dalio and others from the world of finance. Dalio managed the world's largest hedge fund, Bridgewater Associates, with $120 billion under its control. He'd developed a sophisticated model for understanding what was happening with credit extension in the economy, and Bernanke hoped to learn from Dalio's analysis and perhaps incorporate it into the Fed's own understanding of what was causing the financial and economic upheaval.

Later that afternoon, Bernanke's inner circle of advisers, including both Warsh and Madigan, gathered on the leather couch and chairs in the chairman's ornate workspace overlooking the National Mall. Geithner dialed in from Cape Cod, where he kept his cell phone to his ear as he paced in and out of his old family retreat. Fed vice chairman Don Kohn called in from his car en route to a wedding in New Hampshire. Market specialists were on speakerphone from New York, whose Federal Reserve branch had pumped $24 billion into the markets that morning as part of its routine efforts to keep short-term interest rates at the Fed's official target. American banks weren't having the same liquidity problems that their European counterparts were, so there was no apparent need for an intervention along the lines of what Trichet had done. It had been a brutal day in the U.S. markets, though, with the Dow Jones Industrial Average down 387 points, nearly 3 percent.

Bernanke was eager to signal to the world that the Fed was on the same page as the ECB, ready to stand behind the financial system as needed. Perhaps a statement saying as much was in order, he argued. Geithner, who often favored taking the most aggressive steps possible to bolster markets in crisis, wanted to begin discussing cutting interest rates to try to counteract the tightening of credit in the economy. But on that day at least, the group agreed that such an action was premature. A statement it would be.

Bernanke and his advisers talked about its language, and his communications aide, Michelle Smith, typed it up back at her office. She e-mailed him at 5:37 p.m. with a draft of what the Fed would tell the world the next morning at 8 a.m. It was a mere seventy-eight words, and stated that "in current circumstances, depository institutions may experience unusual funding needs because of dislocations in money and credit markets," and that "the Federal Reserve is providing liquidity to facilitate the orderly functioning of financial markets."

Bernanke and the Fed, in other words, were ready to open the spigot as well.

A t the Kennington Oval that Thursday, it was an up-and-down day for England that ended poorly for the home team. India scored 316 runs and lost four wickets on the first day of a five-day match. Mervyn King had left instructions with his staff that he not be disturbed except in an emergency, which created an interesting dilemma for the markets staff of the Bank of England, ensconced in its fortresslike headquarters on Threadneedle Street in the City of London. Was the ECB's surprising injection of money into the banking system in fact an emergency?

When staffers finally decided that the answer was yes and called him, King was less worried about any action the Bank of England might take than whether the ECB was generating more panic by intervening instead of simply standing by. Just the day before, in a press conference, he'd described the tightening of the credit markets as "a welcome development, as a more realistic appraisal of risks is being seen." He was privately dismissive of Trichet's action, telling confidants that his old friend Jean-Claude had overreacted. The intervention, King argued, could prevent a necessary and overdue market correction. The banking system was simply counteracting years of excess, and Britain could easily weather whatever came next.

Among the leaders of the world's great central banks, King would remain the deepest skeptic of the severity of the emerging crisis for more than a year to come. One of the most accomplished British economists of his generation, he believed in the purity of markets and was reluctant to intervene even when they seemed to be going haywire. The so-called King of Threadneedle Street was also supremely confident of his own views and analysis and quick to challenge anyone who disagreed—even when that someone was the most powerful central banker in continental Europe. A son of the working class in a country acutely sensitive to class divisions, King had used his extraordinary intellect and deep-seated competitive streak to claw his way into the nation's ruling class. After joining the Bank of England as chief economist in the early 1990s, a time when the credibility of the institution was at a low point, he reshaped it in his image: rigorous in its analysis, theoretical in its approach, unsparing in its dismissiveness toward employees or departments that didn't meet his high standards or share his predispositions.

In previous years, King had deemphasized regulating the banks, which he viewed as a messy, legalistic business compared to the elegant, intellectual work of shaping monetary policy. He even seemed to disdain bankers personally, and was privately contemptuous of their views. "Financial stability became a downplayed part of the institution," said Kate Barker, a member of the Bank of England's Monetary Policy Committee from 2001 to 2010. "[King predecessor] Eddie [George] was sorry to lose the financial-stability role, but I don't think Mervyn was initially very interested in it."

Indeed, on that chaotic Thursday, King left it to Deputy Governor Rachel Lomax to represent the bank in conference calls with his counterparts across the world. Later on, King would put himself as close to the front lines of the battle against panic as anyone. But on day one, his arrogance left him in the grandstands.

The leaders of the three major Western central banks were in different worlds—far apart physically, as was usually the case, but also disconnected in their analysis of the problem facing the world economy and what, if anything, they should do about it. To Trichet, the problem was a banking panic, a one-off moment of market uncertainty. To King, it was a necessary corrective to a long period of banking excess. To Bernanke, it was a more deeply intertwined set of risks to the banking system and the overall economy. He came to this view partly because the United States was ground zero for the housing downturn and bad mortgage lending that spurred Europe's problems. But it was also a matter of Bernanke's academic training. A leading scholar of the Great Depression, the chairman had theorized that the era was so troubled economically because of what he called the "financial accelerator": Bank failures fueled economic weakness, which fueled even more bank failures, which in turn fueled further economic weakness. He was determined, if it became necessary, to use every tool at the Fed's disposal to halt this vicious cycle.

It was sheer luck that the Federal Reserve had a chairman so well prepared for the moment. Bernanke's academic training as a monetary economist, particularly as a scholar of the Depression, hadn't come up in his interview with President George W. Bush in the summer of 2005, when the native of tiny Dillon, South Carolina, was being considered to replace legendary Fed chair Alan Greenspan. But that background would influence his every action from that August Thursday on. Bernanke seemed almost haunted by the fear that he would make the same mistakes central bankers did in the 1920s and '30s, which left mass human misery in their wake.

Whatever their perceptions or prejudices, central bankers all have an awesome power: the ability to create and destroy money. Why is a piece of paper with Andrew Jackson's face on it worth twenty dollars? Why can that piece of paper be exchanged for a hot meal or a couple of tickets to a movie? It's only a slight exaggeration to answer, "Because Ben Bernanke says so." The bill may have the U.S. treasury secretary's signature on it, but at the top it reads, "Federal Reserve Note." Central bankers uphold one end of a grand bargain that has evolved over the past 350 years. Democracies grant these secretive technocrats control over their nations' economies; in exchange, they ask only for a stable currency and sustained prosperity (something that is easier said than achieved). Central bankers determine whether people can get jobs, whether their savings are secure, and, ultimately, whether their nation prospers or fails.

Over two continents, five years, thousands of conference calls, and trillions of dollars, euros, and pounds deployed to rescue the world financial system, central bankers would take the primary role in grappling with the global panic that began in earnest on August 9, 2007. They would act with a speed and on a scale that presidents and parliaments could never seem to muster. Over the next half decade, Jean-Claude Trichet, Ben Bernanke, and Mervyn King would create the world to come.

E ver since the first central banker set up shop in seventeenth-century Sweden, offering paper notes as a more convenient alternative to the forty-pound copper plates that had been the currency of what was then a great empire, money has been an abstract idea as much as a physical object. The alchemists of medieval times never did figure out a way to create gold from tin, but as it turned out, it didn't matter. A central bank, imbued with power from the state and a printing press, had the same power. With that power, it creates the very underpinnings of modernity. As surely as electric utilities and sewer systems make modern cities possible, the flow of money enabled by the central banks makes a modern economy possible. By standing in the way of financial collapse, they've enabled the gigantic, long-term investments that permit us to light our homes, fly in jumbo jets, and place a phone call to nearly anyone on earth from nearly anywhere on earth.

In modern times, when the amount of money exchanged electronically dwarfs the volume of commerce that takes place with paper money, even the physical work of printing paper dollars and euros is something of a sideline for the central banks. The actual work of creating or destroying money in modern times is as banal as it is powerful: A handful of midlevel workers sit at computers on the ninth floor of the New York Fed building in lower Manhattan, or on Threadneedle Street in the City of London, or at the German Bundesbank in Frankfurt, and buy or sell securities with a stroke of their keyboards. They are carrying out orders of policy-setting committees led by their central bankers. When they buy bonds, it is with money that previously did not exist; when they sell, those dollars or pounds or euros cease to exist.

Frequently, words alone are enough. To the layperson, the phrase "additional policy accommodation may be warranted" might seem either insignificant or unintelligible. But it's likely to inspire convulsive joy on the trading floors of Wall Street, London, and Hong Kong when spoken by the Bank of England governor or the ECB president or the Fed chairman: It's the central banker's way of saying he'll soon be flooding the world with pounds or euros or dollars.

Within an instant of the phrase's hitting financial newswires, the stock market will typically rally, making a retiree in Liverpool wealthier. The price of oil will usually bounce upward, making it more expensive for a truck driver in Stuttgart to ply his trade. And the cost of borrowing money will probably fall, making it cheaper for a young couple in St. Louis to buy a house. Sometimes it doesn't even take a full sentence, but a single word. When in 2006 a CNBC journalist at a weekend social event asked Bernanke whether markets had interpreted him correctly a couple of days before, he replied, "No," believing he was off the record. After she reported the conversation on Monday, the Dow Jones Industrial Average fell eighty-five points within minutes.

To a degree that's rare among high public officials, central bankers feel connected to the long thread of history. The successes of their predecessors made the world as we know it. The Bank of England played a crucial, if often overlooked, role in creating the stable financial system that allowed Britain to rule vast swaths of the world in the nineteenth century. The creation of the Federal Reserve enabled New York to supplant London as the world's financial capital in the years after World War I, enabling the rise of the United States as global superpower and setting the stage for a generation of prosperity that followed the Second World War. The (belated) achievement of the Fed and other world central banks in defeating the inflation of the 1970s laid the groundwork for a quarter century of stable prices and global prosperity—one that started crashing down on August 9, 2007.

They are also, of course, keenly aware of central banking's past failures, of which the Great Depression is only one. The actions of Bernanke and Trichet and King on that day in 2007—and on many days that would follow—were shaped by their knowledge of, for example, the collapse of Overend & Gurney in 1866. The mighty British bank's failure sparked a panic so great that the streets of the City of London were mobbed with depositors scrambling to take their money out of other financial institutions. Thanks to the recent invention of the electric telegraph, the panic soon spread to the countryside, and even to the far corners of the empire. Facing a freeze-up in the money markets, the Bank of England, as the writer and public intellectual Walter Bagehot famously wrote at the time, lent "to merchants, to minor bankers, to 'this man and that man,'" and thus stopped the run—though not the destructive economic downturn of its aftermath. What the ECB did on August 9, 2007, was an updated, electronic version of that same strategy, and Trichet, Bernanke, and King often invoked Bagehot's words as a model for their own crisis response almost 150 years later.

Bernanke and other Fed officials understood all too well the United States' aversion to the type of centralized political control embodied by a central bank. The lack of a central bank in the nineteenth century had meant that banking panics were an almost constant feature of the American economy. Even farmers' predictable need for cash each harvest season routinely brought the nation to the brink of financial shutdown. Yet the battle to establish the institution that Bernanke would one day lead was exceedingly bitter. The compromises needed to gain Congress's support resulted in an unwieldy structure that would be a challenge to lead, especially as those old arguments against centralized power reemerged a century later.

The men who led the global economy in the crisis that began in 2007 had come of age in the 1970s, when central bankers were so fearful of an economic downturn—and the political authorities—that they allowed prices to escalate out of control. "I knew that I would be accepted in the future only if I suppressed my will and yielded completely—even though it was wrong at law and morally—to his authority," wrote Fed chief Arthur Burns in his diary in 1971. "He" in this case was Richard Nixon, who insisted that Burns keep interest rates low and the U.S. economy humming in the run-up to the 1972 election. Prices rose so fast that steakhouses had to use stickers to update their menus according to that week's cost for beef. Central bankers have been vigilant about inflation ever since—for better and, especially in the 2000s, for worse, when some saw inflationary ghosts where there were none.

But no specters of the past loomed larger for Trichet, Bernanke, and King than the missteps taken by the central bankers of 1920s and '30s. It was then that the Reichsbank of Germany printed money on a massive scale to fund the nation's government, so much so that people needed wheelbarrows to carry cash to the grocery store and would buy bicycles or pianos to hold value that reichsmarks couldn't. That hyperinflation led to the desperate circumstances that allowed the Nazis to gain support. What came next would enable their rise to power.

The Great Depression was at its core a failure of central banking. Just a few blocks away from the building in Basel, Switzerland, where the central bankers of the early twenty-first century drank good wine and plotted their response to the contemporary crisis, the central bankers of the early 1930s met in a hotel and found far less to agree upon. Blinkered by nationalistic distrust, a misguided commitment to keep their currencies tied to gold, and the lack of a common understanding of how economies work, they concluded that the global economic crisis of 1931 was beyond their ability to combat. Even the technological limits of communication in that era—transatlantic phone calls were accomplished with great difficulty, and jet travel wasn't yet an option—stood in the way of men like the Reichsbank's Hjalmar Schacht and the Bank of England's Montagu Norman. Their shortcomings led millions of people into dire poverty and created a fertile environment for World War II.

The European currency union that Trichet led—and which in a later phase of the crisis he would take extraordinary steps to try to preserve—was itself a direct result of that conflict. Born in Lyon in 1942, during the German occupation of his homeland, the ECB president grew up in a country rebuilding after the devastations of occupation and war. Like other postwar leaders, he was so intent on creating a continent where armed conflict might never break out again that he made a unified Europe the mission of his lifetime. The euro was their crown jewel, the physical embodiment of that effort—and an accomplishment that the great global crisis of the twenty-first century would eventually threaten to destroy.

The partnership between Trichet, Bernanke, and King was one between men of different backgrounds, temperaments, and intellectual proclivities— differences that would loom large in the events yet to unfold. Beginning that Thursday, the three men atop the central banks of the major Western powers could only look to each other to find ways to see beyond those differences.

When they took their respective jobs—in 2003 for Trichet and King, in 2006 for Bernanke—they joined a brotherhood of uncommon intimacy. The world's top central bankers meet in person frequently—at an economic conference each summer in Jackson Hole, Wyoming, on the sidelines of countless global summits, and, most significantly, six times a year in Basel, where they take brief refuge from the politics, personal attacks, and hard choices that come with doing a job most people don't quite seem to understand and more than a few regard as sinister.

They speak the same language, literally and figuratively: All speak good English and are deeply versed in the discourse of economics. Foreign ministers, finance ministers, and defense ministers may have cordial relations with their counterparts from other nations. Some may even become friends. But none of those leaders have the same sustained, intimate exposure as the central bankers to the personalities and thinking, idiosyncrasies and blind spots of their international colleagues. Central bankers understand more deeply than perhaps anyone else where other countries are coming from. They share a closeness unheard of elsewhere in international relations, knowing with great confidence that what is said at the table in Basel will stay there.

There were some older connections between the leaders of the ECB, the Fed, and the Bank of England, too: King and Bernanke had shared an office suite as young faculty members at MIT; Trichet and King had met when King was a student at Cambridge and Trichet, a young civil servant, had gone abroad to study the British tax system. But the panic that began that August day in 2007 would test their bonds as well as their ability to come together to guide the global economy toward prosperity.

Mankind had given them incredible power. Now was the time to show that they had learned history's lessons. As the consequences of a generation of bad lending and rising debt started to unfold, this committee of three knew better than anyone just how high the price of failure could be.

To understand fully how these three men came to wield such incredible power, one first must know where central banks came from to begin with. That story starts, of all places, in Sweden, a very long time ago.

# Part I

—∞∞∞—

## RISE OF
## THE ALCHEMISTS,
## 1656–2006

# ONE

# Johan Palmstruch and the Birth of Central Banking

He was a broken and desperate man, at the end. Johan Palmstruch, a Latvian-born, Dutch-raised, Swedish-residing banker defended himself against a prosecution that likely seemed more like an inquisition. A nation wanted to know where its money had gone, and the best answer Palmstruch could muster was to describe the chaos of those final days of the world's first central bank, when depositors and government investigators lined up outside the bank's doors, *"snork, pork,* scolding and swearing." Who, he asked, "in the midst of such daily tumult, threatening, swearing, scolding and parleying, in danger of life and limb . . . could note and thereby keep a book?"

The investigation into Palmstruch's Stockholms Banco had discovered not only that tens of thousands of daler were missing from its vault, but also that the near failure of the bank had cost the Swedish crown a vast sum. Palmstruch was ordered to repay what the bank had lost. When he couldn't, he was to be executed. This was, after all, 1668, not 2008, and Palmstruch's actions as a man with the power to print money at will had decimated Swedes' personal savings, wrecked their national economy, and forced the government to intervene to prevent complete catastrophe.

Palmstruch's sentence was commuted in 1669, and he was released from prison in 1670. When history's first central banker died a year later, he was known not as a monetary wizard, but as a criminal who'd taken the economy of one of Europe's great powers on a wild ride. During the course of half a decade, there had been a credit boom and an accompanying rise in the standard of living, then a surge of inflation, followed by a credit bust and a recession.

In other words, over just a few short years, Sweden had experienced both the best and the worst of central banking. But Johan Palmstruch and everyone else involved in Stockholms Banco had also done something more: They had begun the modern era of global finance, and all that is great and awful that would emerge from it. To properly understand how the Boys in Basel responded to the financial conflagration of 2007 to 2012, it helps to understand how they came to wield such power to begin with. And that is a story that begins with Johan Palmstruch.

The country may now be better known for minimalist furniture and pop music than for imperial designs, but for much of the seventeenth century Sweden was one of Europe's great powers. It commanded an empire that stretched across Scandinavia and into what are now the Baltic nations and parts of present-day Germany, Poland, and Russia.

The nation attained its prominence on the global stage despite lacking some of the advantages of its rivals in continental Europe. With one million or so citizens, Sweden was only one sixth as populous as Britain and one twentieth the size of France. Its agricultural sector wasn't terribly productive either—after all, the country is dark and cold eight months a year. Food was so scarce that peasants mixed tree bark into their bread dough to make it go farther. But the Swedish economy wasn't without strengths: Without the productive farming of France or Britain, it relied heavily on fishing and iron and copper mining. But for a truly vibrant commercial sector to exist, of course, there needs to be a medium of exchange, a method of trade more flexible than mere barter: salt, perhaps, or seashells or metal coins. In 1534, with Sweden newly established as an autonomous state, it minted its first daler. The similarity in pronunciation to the present-day U.S. currency is no coincidence.

Well into the seventeenth century, however, the Swedes were having a hard time getting their daler into the hands of people who wanted them. They needed a system of institutions to store, distribute, and lend money. In Amsterdam, Hamburg, and London there had emerged companies that did just that, and in parts of Italy variations on the idea had been around for centuries. But the Swedish language had no word for it in the early 1600s. So in 1619 the king and members of the merchant class got together, borrowed the Italian term *banca*, and turned it into the Swedish word *bank*. They couldn't agree on who would provide the start-up financing for these new institutions. King Gustavus Adolphus and his powerful chancellor, Axel Oxenstierna, wanted the towns of Sweden to fund the banks. The merchants in those towns wanted the king to take on the expense—and the risk. During the stalemate, three decades would go by in which Sweden lost ground in commerce because there wasn't enough money circulating. The Swedes had a word for a banking system, but not the system itself.

An outsider would change that.

Hans Witmacker was born in 1611 in what is now the Latvian capital of Riga, the son of a successful Dutch merchant. As a young man, he went to work as an entrepreneur in Amsterdam, which had the world's most highly developed banking system at the time. At the age of twenty-eight, Witmacker was jailed for failing to pay his debts. Once released, he made his way to Stockholm, then a bustling world capital of forty-five thousand people, to remake himself. He even took on a new name: Johan Palmstruch.

No portraits of Palmstruch or descriptions of his personal manner have survived. But it seems fair to assume that he was a smooth talker. He must have conveyed seriousness, probity, and wisdom and been able to make people trust him without a second of doubt. Those abilities were surely coupled with enough charm and charisma to endear him to the wealthy and powerful. If that wasn't the case, none of what happened next makes any sense.

King Karl X Gustav was hoping to realize Gustavus Adolphus's dream of establishing a bank that would finally modernize Swedish commerce. He trusted a forty-five-year-old foreigner who presumably talked a good game about his knowledge of the Dutch banking system. By royal decree, the king authorized the creation of Stockholms Banco on November 30, 1656, to be run by Johan Palmstruch. It is unclear whether he knew anything of Palmstruch's checkered past.

Palmstruch certainly knew how to cover all his political bases. Half of the bank's profits were to be given over to the king. And Palmstruch gave more than a dozen powerful Swedes, the chancellor of the realm and the president of the board of trade among them, a share of the bank's profits without requiring them to put up any capital. One of those shareholders was later named by the king as "chief inspector of the banking system"—which, it is safe to say, isn't currently considered a best practice in the field of bank regulation.

Palmstruch, not unlike the investment bankers who were inventing new mortgage securities in the 2000s, was a master of what is now called financial innovation. There were numerous problems attached to using copper as the nation's official currency standard, as Sweden had done since 1624. For one thing, when copper is stored in bank vaults, it can't be used for all the other practical uses that it's good for. And as later governments that tied the value of their money to a precious metal have learned, having a copper-based currency created wild swings in the value of money due to factors beyond any one country's control. When the German economy was devastated following the Thirty Years' War, for example, it dramatically drove down the price of copper and thus caused a collapse in the value of Sweden's currency.

Then there was a more practical problem, one specific to a country that had recently begun to issue coinage as not so pocket-sized metal plates: Copper is really heavy. A ten-daler plate, the most common unit of currency, measured about twelve by twenty-four inches and weighed more than forty-three pounds. It was enough to buy sixty-six pounds of butter or thirty-three days of work from an unskilled laborer. The copper plates still turn up now and again in the waters around Stockholm, because when one was dropped while being loaded or unloaded onto a ship, there was no retrieving it. Daler plates were, presumably, hell on bank tellers' backs.

Palmstruch's first innovation was to hold the giant plates in Stockholms Banco's vault, while offering a paper note as a receipt. This idea was compelling to King Karl X Gustav. In the bank's charter, he mentioned the "good convenience" Swedish subjects would receive in the form of relief from "hauling and dragging and other trouble that the copper coin entails in its handling."

The success of this innovation led to a great inflow of deposits into the bank—400,000 copper daler by 1660, just three years after its opening, the equivalent of $76 million in today's dollars. And even sooner, the leaders of the bank came up with another financial innovation. As Palmstruch would later testify, Gustaf Bonde—the shareholder in the bank who was also its chief government inspector—"came to the exchange bank towards spring 1659 in the morning, stood there looking around, and exclaimed with these words: 'I see here in the exchange bank good stores of money and it seems to me to be best now to make a beginning with the loan bank.'" That is: Hey, guys, we have all this money just sitting around. Why don't we lend it out and actually make a return on it!

Stockholms Banco began lending money to companies to finance their inventories of tar, salt, and sugar. And to noblemen and -women and holders of high government office, it began guaranteeing the loans with all manner of collateral. Land was the most common, but less conventional lending occurred as well: One woman borrowed 2,700 daler against a silver candelabrum. And some loans weren't collateralized at all, but were given only on the personal guarantee of one noble or another.

The system worked great for a while. The country's nobility enjoyed cheap access to credit and was able to live more comfortably than it might have otherwise. Merchants were able to borrow money to invest in the future. No longer reliant on their own savings to fund expansion, they could use somebody else's savings for that purpose, with Stockholms Banco as the intermediary. Commerce flourished.

That is, until King Karl X Gustav died in 1660, and the council that replaced him to lead the country—the new ruler was a small child at the time—decided to devalue the daler. The new currency had less copper in it than the old currency did, so the old plates were worth more than their official value would suggest. It would be as if the value of paper suddenly skyrocketed so that a dollar bill contained $1.10 worth of paper. The people of Sweden had a logical response: They all showed up at Stockholms Banco en masse to withdraw their old daler.

Palmstruch, of course, had lent out much of the money; it was no longer sitting in the vault waiting for depositors to show up. He dealt with this by trying to call in loans. This caused further problems: His clients, of course, had become accustomed to living in part off of borrowed money, and they either wouldn't or couldn't readily pay the bank back. Palmstruch wrote that people were showing up "every day in large numbers not only while the Bank is open but even extraordinarily at my home to assail me morning, afternoon, and evening, presenting their pledges and entreating me to be allowed to borrow money, which so moves me to Christian compassion and troubles my heart that also the burden of my office feels almost too great and unbearable."

One can almost imagine a distressed Palmstruch standing at the doors of his bank on the winding, narrow streets of central Stockholm, buffeted by the cold Scandinavian wind, crying like George Bailey in *It's a Wonderful Life:* "You're thinking of this place all wrong, as if I had the money back in a safe. The money's not here. Why, your money's in the Petersson estate! And in Mr. Nilsson's inventory of pickled herring! And in Mrs. Kristensson's silver candelabrum!"

Then, in 1661, Palmstruch found a solution that changed the course of finance forever.

He might not always have had enough copper in the vaults to meet the demands of his depositors, but he could always print paper. He would issue paper notes that the holder could redeem for daler at will. He got the idea from paper receipts that copper mines issued to their workers and traded in their communities like modern currency. China had used paper money centuries earlier, but this was the first time something so closely resembling modern money was used in Europe. Unlike earlier notes issued by European banks over the centuries, these weren't tied to a specific account or deposit but could be freely traded from person to person. The government went along with the plan, agreeing that the banknotes could be used to pay tax bills. Modern money—backed not by some precious metal, but by the credibility of a single financial institution and its leader, Palmstruch—had arrived in Europe.

With that, one understanding of money—as a physical object, its value rising and falling depending on supply and demand for the metal it's made of—was replaced by another. Money was instead an idea, something unrelated to the actual value of the material on which it is printed. Instead, its value is set by the institution—specifically, the central bank—that issues it. Like Palmstruch's printed paper, modern currency holds its value ultimately because of public confidence in the authority that stands behind it. A government can say that one dollar or pound or krona is equal to a certain amount of gold or silver or copper—but it is always within the power of that government to change that ratio, or abandon the relationship entirely. (Western nations would use gold and other metallic standards for their money for centuries to come; not until 1971 would most major industrial nations' currencies fully decouple from gold.)

In Sweden in the 1660s, paper money was wildly popular. Palmstruch literally couldn't print it fast enough; it started to be traded in all the great financial centers, Amsterdam and London and Paris and Venice. No longer held back by the need to have backing for loans in the form of copper holdings, the bank increased its lending dramatically and opened new branches. The royal family alone borrowed 500,000 daler.

Before long, there was vastly more paper money floating around than there was copper daler in the vault. By 1663, the bank was down to a piddling 4,000 copper daler in its vault—and a depositor had notified it that he wished to withdraw 10,000.

As word started to spread that the bank was paying back depositors slowly and irregularly, closing on some days, and generally behaving as if it had something to hide, the loss of public confidence fed on itself. Stockholms Banco notes were traded at a 6 to 10 percent discount to what they theoretically represented—which just made people all the more eager to withdraw their money. Suddenly those paper notes were worth less than they had been, each one buying less herring or tin or lumber than it had before—the phenomenon now called inflation. As Palmstruch single-handedly increased the supply of money, the price of most everything rose.

The government was getting rather concerned, and it ordered Palmstruch to call in loans so that the bank could pay depositors. This wasn't a move taken lightly: The chancellor was strongly opposed, surely in no small part because he was the bank's single largest borrower. After considerable debate, the parliament decided not to dissolve the bank, despite some evidence of "irregularities and inconveniences." As it turns out, the decision to cut back on loans and vastly reduce the paper money in circulation had a negative rather than a positive effect: Businesses that had become accustomed to operating using borrowed funds couldn't do so. Money, which had been all too readily available just two years earlier, became very hard to get, and a deep economic downturn followed. It was the first recession (or possibly depression—economic statistics hadn't been invented yet) caused by a contraction of the money supply.

By 1667, the Swedish government had taken over and then liquidated Stockholms Banco. Palmstruch was tried for fraud and lost his privilege of running a bank. But Sweden's experiment with a central financial authority wasn't over. For all the tumult Stockholms Banco had caused, the problems it was created to solve still remained. The Swedish parliament realized it needed to re-place the bank with *something*—ideally, something that would be under tighter government control and more stable.

The Swedish government was, for its era, uncommonly democratic. There were four estates represented in parliament—the nobility, the merchant class, the clergy, and the peasantry. It was the nobility and the merchants who were most eager to rebuild a central bank. After all, such an institution would benefit them most, allowing more availability of cash and the smoother flow of commerce. But after the Palmstruch debacle, they believed it needed the explicit financial and legal backing of the government. These bank supporters eventually persuaded the clergy, the intellectuals of the day, to their side. The peasants represented in the Riksdag were a tougher sell. They didn't want to give the government's financial backing to an entity that would primarily benefit the upper classes. More important, the peasantry also submitted to the government that it had "no understanding of the matter" and that "the other good gentlemen of the other Estates may do what seems best to them in the case and what for them could be beneficial, but allow the peasant to be free from such things as he does not comprehend."

So they did. The wealthy, the business interests, and the intellectuals combined to create the world's first true central bank, without the participation of the working class. The Bank of the Estates of the Realm set up shop in a palace in central Stockholm in 1668. It would later become the Sveriges Riksbank, which remains the central bank of Sweden to this day.

It wouldn't be the last time that a central bank would be established with something less than enthusiastic endorsement from the working class.

While Sweden was at work setting up a modern financial institution, modern science was quickly overtaking the ancient study of alchemy. For centuries, across Europe and in the Islamic world, mankind had sought ways to turn mundane materials into far more precious gold and silver. In the medieval world, alchemists included everyone from garden-variety con artists to skilled technicians of metallurgy to some of the most brilliant scientists of the day. Sir Isaac Newton, it was once said, was not in fact the first modern scientist, but the last of the alchemists. (This was said, as it happens, by an economist of wide-ranging intellectual interests named John Maynard Keynes.) Alchemists were an insular group, speaking a language that outsiders couldn't grasp and disdainful of the uninitiated. Those outside the club viewed it as a shadowy cabal.

As it turns out, though, mankind didn't need a magic potion to create gold from thin air. As Johan Palmstruch and the Swedes had discovered, all it took to create wealth where there had been none was some paper, a printing press, and a central bank, imbued with the power from the state, to put it to work.

# TWO

# Lombard Street,
# Rule Britannia, and
# Bagehot's Dictum

On Thursday, May 10, 1866, at 3:30 p.m., customers of banking giant Overend, Gurney & Co. came upon something very disconcerting indeed. Pinned to the door of the firm's headquarters on London's Lombard Street, where the financiers of that great imperial capital did their work, was a note. "Sir," it said. "We regret to announce that a severe run on our deposits and resources has compelled us to suspend payment, the course being considered under advice the best calculated to protect the interest of all parties. . . . I remain your faithful servant, William Bois, Secretary."

The firm was among the great powers of not only British, but also global finance—which in the 1860s were more or less the same thing. It was formed when the Gurneys, a Quaker family from Norwich that ran the leading bank in the rural areas of East Anglia, sought to expand its reach into the fast-paced, big-money world of dealing bills—corporate debt, essentially—in the City of London. It wasn't dissimilar to the successful regional American banks, like Bank of America and Wachovia, that in the 2000s dove into the sea of Wall Street.

Samuel Gurney and his partner, John Overend, may have never heard of a subprime mortgage or a collateralized debt obligation, but that didn't stop the company they created in 1809 from finding some exotic and unwise ways to lend money. There was the plantation in Dominica, a tiny island in the West Indies, for example, and the railroad line that connected the two bustling Irish metropolises of Portadown and Omagh. Repeatedly, there was the habit of chasing a loan gone bad with even more money on the distant hope that things would turn around. There was greed. There was avarice. There were simple analytical failures. And maybe there was even a bit of fraud.

The result: In the spring of 1866, Overend & Gurney was in big trouble. Depositors came in in droves to withdraw their funds as rumors of losses spread. A railroad contractor, they'd heard, had defaulted on a £1.5 million loan. A group of merchants that traded with Spain and relied on Overend & Gurney for capital had collapsed. The bank's partners were selling their country estates to free up cash. Wrote one correspondent in London, "One unlucky man, I am told, presented a cheque at Overend Gurney's for sixty thousand pounds, and was told to call again in half an hour; on his return the shutters were up."

The day after the note went up on the door of 65 Lombard Street, all hell broke loose. If the great Overend & Gurney could go under, after all, then seemingly any other bank could do the same. Who could trust that money kept in some ledger in some grand building would be there come morning? On what became known as Black Friday, crowds gathered to see the letter on the door of Overend, then turned on the other banks. "The doors of the most respectable banking houses were besieged, more perhaps by a mob actuated by the strange sympathy which makes and keeps a mob together than by creditors of the Banks," wrote the *Times*, "and throngs heaving and tumbling about Lombard Street made that narrow thoroughfare impassable." Added *Bunker's Magazine*, "It is impossible to describe the terror and anxiety that took possession of men's minds for the remainder of that and the whole of the succeeding day." With the help of a recent invention, the electric telegraph, word of the panic rapidly made its way to even the rural corners of England, which experienced runs of their own.

Sweden had long since faded from global preeminence, but the innovation of Johan Palmstruch had been copied in Britain, with the creation of the Bank of England in 1694, aiding the nation's rise to great power status. But now its entire financial system was on the verge of collapse. What would the Bank of England do about it? The answers the central bankers of that era came up with would serve as a model of sorts for Ben Bernanke, Mervyn King, and Jean-Claude Trichet a century and a half later. The work of the men on Threadneedle Street after the Overend & Gurney collapse show how the Bank of England was a surprisingly important piece of Britain's Victorian-era dominion over the globe.

By the late 1860s, the United Kingdom, with a population of around thirty million, just over 2 percent of the humans on earth, ruled an empire that stretched from New Delhi to Toronto, Hong Kong to Johannesburg. There are many reasons for its economic might. Among them: the coal fields of the North that provided the raw fuel for industrialization, a culture that encouraged entrepreneurship and innovation, and a political system that was able to adapt to democracy without the revolutions and bouts of Napoleonic aggression that characterized certain neighbors across the Channel.

But even all that wouldn't have been enough to maintain an empire on which the sun never set without the great financial power concentrated on Lombard Street.

The most authoritative chronicler of this era in finance is an Englishman named Walter Bagehot. He was born in 1826 to a banking family in the South West town of Langport and died young, in 1877. With a lively intellect and cutting literary style, he wrote essays on Milton and Shakespeare before becoming the editor of the *Economist,* which was owned by his uncle, in 1860. His efforts to run for Parliament failed miserably, but he was nonetheless such an important commentator on and explicator of the politics and economics of Victorian Britain that he was known as the "Spare Chancellor"—that's to say, nearly as influential in matters of money as the finance minister.

Bagehot wasn't one of history's great practicing economists, like John Maynard Keynes or Milton Friedman. He wasn't one of the great philosophers of political economy, like Adam Smith or Karl Marx. Indeed, most historians know him best for his work more or less inventing the concept of the English constitution as an accumulation of ideas rather than a written document. Yet among central bankers he has achieved iconic status for his 1873 book *Lombard Street: A Description of the Money Market,* an analysis of the demise of Overend & Gurney and the Bank of England's response. To this day it remains something of a bible for central bankers dealing with a financial panic. At the 2009 Federal Reserve Bank of Kansas City conference in Jackson Hole, where contemporary central bankers gather every August, Bagehot's name was mentioned forty-eight times. Keynes and Friedman and Smith and Marx combined for zero.

· · ·

B akers make bread. Watchmakers make watches. What is it, precisely, that bankers make? The answer goes a long way to understanding how important British banking was to that nation's great empire—and why crises, whether in 1866 or 2008, have always been a fact of modern finance.

The idea of giving one's money to a bank doesn't come naturally. When people save money, they generally like to be able to *see* it rather than have it exist as a paper record of a deposit at an institution in the center of town. For centuries, banks in Europe were more a logistical necessity for businesses that wanted to trade with each other over long distances than places for savers to keep their money. That had changed in Britain and a few other countries by the nineteenth century, thanks in part to the paper banknote that Johan Palmstruch invented in Sweden 150 years earlier.

As Bagehot wrote:

> When a private person begins to possess a great heap of bank-notes,
> it will soon strike him that he is trusting the banker very much, and
> that in return he is getting nothing. He runs the risk of loss and rob-
> bery just as if he were hoarding coin. He would no more run the risk
> by the failure of the bank if he made a deposit there, and he would be
> free from the risk of keeping the cash. . . . So strong is the wish of
> most people to see their money that they for some time continue to
> hoard bank-notes. . . . But in the end common sense conquers.

As an increasingly affluent merchant class came to that commonsense conclusion, banks in Britain became something more than grease for the wheels of commerce. But that didn't happen in the other major European powers, the potential rivals to the British in global supremacy. In 1873, total deposits at the banks of London amounted to £91 million, compared to £15 million in France and £8 million in Germany. Why? Banknotes—and the bank deposits that result from their existence—are possible "only in a country exempt from invasion, and free from revolution," Bagehot explained. That's because "in such great and close civil dangers a nation is always demoralized; everyone looks to himself, and everyone likes to possess himself of the precious metals. These are

sure to be valuable, invasion or no invasion, revolution or no revolution." The
Netherlands and Germany were at the time in perpetual danger of invasion,
and France, of course, was destabilized for decades after its 1789 revolution.

"This therefore is the reason why Lombard Street exists," Bagehot wrote.
"That is, why England is a very great Money Market, and other European countries but small ones in comparison. In England and Scotland a diffused system
of note issues started banks all over the country; in those banks the savings of
the country have been lodged, and by these they have been sent to London. No
similar system arose elsewhere, and in consequence London is full of money,
and all continental cities are empty as compared with it."

What Overend & Gurney and its competitors did, in other words, was take
the savings of millions of merchants and farmers from across Britain and
gather them into great stockpiles of capital in London. This matters a great
deal. Money saved under a mattress is useful only to its owner—and only on the
day that he needs to spend it. But a dollar saved in a checking account is simultaneously available to the account holder at a moment's notice—in the modern
world, it can be withdrawn from any of millions of automated terminals in any
city on earth—and available to fund enormous long-term investments by others. Economists call this "liquidity transformation."

One individual can't easily amass enough capital to build a rail line from
New Delhi to Mumbai or a giant textile factory capable of producing hundreds
of bolts of cloth each day. But if you put together the savings of thousands of
people and have a smart banker choosing which projects are promising enough
to deserve loans, suddenly you have the savings of the masses going to fund the
large, complex, and risky endeavors that are essential to an industrial economy.
"A million in the hands of a single banker is a great power; he can at once lend
it where he will," Bagehot wrote. "Concentration of money in banks, though not
the sole cause, is the principal cause which has made the Money Market of England so exceedingly rich, so much beyond that of other countries."

The place where all that wealth was concentrated was the Square Mile—
1.1 square miles, to be precise—known as the City of London, a warren of winding medieval streets that is a mere speck in the great metropolis of London. In
the mid-nineteenth century, the most important intersection in global finance was at what is now the Bank tube stop. Toward the northeast is Threadneedle Street, home of the Bank of England. Across the street from the bank is

the Royal Exchange, which for centuries was where stocks and bonds were traded. (Now it's a luxury shopping mall.) And off to the southeast goes Lombard Street, where the bill dealers did their work.

Bills of exchange were the lifeblood of nineteenth-century British finance, the method by which the savings of millions of Britons were channeled into productive use. A shipbuilder constructing oceangoing steamships would issue these paper bills, essentially IOUs, to buy the iron and lumber he needed. The seller of the iron could hold on to the bill and wait for payment, if he wanted, or he could take it to his banker, who could buy the bill at a "discount"—say, £970 for a £1,000 bill. That £30 gap represents interest earnings for the bank, compensation for getting the iron dealer his money there and then rather than in three or six months. (The closest present-day equivalent is commercial paper.) When money was tight—when there were more borrowers looking for cash than bankers ready to extend credit—the discount increased. And vice versa.

Typically, the market for these bills was, to use modern terminology, deep and liquid. Merchants could always get easy access to cash by selling their bills to bankers, who could in turn manage their own balance sheets by going to Lombard Street, where the bill brokers could find a ready buyer at a reasonable price. It was a machine that ran as smoothly as any great new invention of the Industrial Revolution.

Until, at least, Mr. William Bois, Secretary of Overend Gurney & Co., posted that note on the door of 65 Lombard Street.

After the Overend collapse, savers all over Britain didn't know which institutions they could trust. Would their bank be next? They had no idea, so they thought it safest to withdraw their money and wait out the storm. But this very act makes the failure of more banks that much more likely. No bank has the cash on hand to pay off withdrawals if everybody wants to pull their deposits out at the same time. The institution must try to sell off whatever it can to come up with the money—in Overend & Gurney's case, bills of exchange. As more bills were dumped onto the market, their price fell, meaning that even sound banks ended up incurring a loss—which made their depositors all the more eager to withdraw their funds.

The details may vary, but this type of vicious cycle is at the core of any financial panic, whether in 1866 or 1929 or 2008. If not stopped, it can shutter businesses on a mass scale and wipe out the savings of a nation. In any case, it has a psychological effect. As Bagehot described it, "The peculiar essence of our banking system is an unprecedented trust between man and man. And when that trust is much weakened by hidden causes, a small accident may greatly hurt it, and a great accident for a moment may almost destroy it."

On Threadneedle Street, the leaders of the Bank of England viewed it as their job to stop that cycle cold. Their goal in such situations wasn't to act like private bankers, hoarding cash for themselves, but to prevent the banking system as a whole from shutting down. On the morning of Black Friday, May 11, 1866, the bankers of London lined up at the Bank of England's Discount Office. "The bankers accustomed to pledge their securities with Overend and Gurney went wild with fright," according to one contemporary account, "besieged the Bank of England and the Chancellor of the Exchequer, and communicated their apprehensions to the public . . . for four or five hours it was believed that half the banks in London would fail." Bank governor Henry Lancelot Holland had to decide whether to fulfill the demands for liquidity—which would mean exposing his institution to far greater risk than it had taken in the past.

His decision was, in effect, to extend credit as far as the eye could see, and damn the naysayers—and there were naysayers, including on the Court of the Bank of England, the equivalent of its board of directors. The strategy was, at its core, simple: If a banker or broker or trader had a bill or other security that would be valuable in a time the markets were functioning normally, it could be pledged at the Bank of England for short-term cash—but with a "haircut," or a discount on what it was thought to be truly worth. "Every gentleman who came here with adequate security was liberally dealt with," Holland said later.

It was essentially using the ability of the Bank of England to issue pounds as a barrier against the further spread of the crisis. Holland had to receive special permission from the chancellor of the exchequer, William Gladstone, to surpass legal caps on the Bank of England's lending. The first day, it extended £4 million in credit. Over the ensuing three months, £45 million was extended, "by every possible means . . . and in modes which we had never adopted." Recall that this was a time when all the bank deposits in Britain totaled around £90 million. Relative to the size of the British economy at the time, it would have been the equivalent of the Federal Reserve extending about $3.5 trillion in the aftermath of the 2008 Lehman Brothers crisis.

The panic gradually subsided, preventing the economic ruin of an empire. Months later, Holland described the Bank of England's actions this way: "Banking is a very peculiar business, and it depends so much upon credit that the very least blast of suspicion is sufficient to sweep away, as it were, the harvest of a whole year. . . . This house exerted itself to the utmost—and exerted itself most successfully—to meet the crisis. We did not flinch from our post."

From these events, Bagehot drew a series of lessons now known as Bagehot's dictum. In a panic, he wrote, a central bank must take its resources and "advance it most freely for the liabilities of others. They must lend to merchants, to minor bankers, to 'this man and that man,' whenever the security is good."

The shorthand version, familiar to all present-day central bankers, is this: Lend freely, on good collateral, and, as Bagehot also specified, charge a penalty interest rate, "that no one may borrow out of idle precaution without paying well for it." It's a simple guideline, but a powerful one. The central bank should open its doors, and its vaults, using its vast stores of the one thing in demand—cash—to stop that vicious cycle. And it should lend only on good collateral, which is to say, against securities whose values have been depressed only by the atmosphere of panic, not by fundamentals. However, the bank should charge a high enough interest rate on these loans that borrowers don't take unjustified advantage of them.

But there are a couple of other lessons from the collapse of Overend & Gurney that don't fit neatly into Bagehot's dictum. First, even if a central bank moves aggressively to stop a financial panic, it still may not be enough to prevent a nasty economic downturn. Because the Bank of England's lending during the panic was directed only at firms that were illiquid—and thus was little good for those that were insolvent—plenty of banks failed besides Overend: the Bank of London, Consolidated Bank, the British Bank of California. And whenever banks fail and credit tightens, businesses of all types are forced to pull back on their activity. The London, Chatham and Dover Railway was building major rail lines in Canada and the Crimea financed by bills of exchange when Overend & Gurney went under. The projects collapsed following the tightening of credit. The funding for a rail line under the Thames evaporated as well.

With no lending available, ironworkers and coal miners and shipbuilders and others who depended on business expansion to make a living found themselves out of work on a mass scale. Economic statistics for this era are unreliable, but estimates by a trade union put the UK unemployment rate at 2.6 percent in 1866, and at 6.3 percent in 1867 after the credit freeze.

A second lesson of the Overend & Gurney crisis is that when a central bank intervenes on massive scale to stop a panic, it does so at its political peril. In the aftermath, the ire of a nation was directed at the Bank of England. An institution with public backing had, after all, done a great favor to wealthy bankers whose bets had gone sour. And the economy—the conditions faced by the masses of workers and merchants—were terrible anyway. The *Times* editorialized that the bank had saved firms that were unworthy, that it had "mulcted for the unthrifty," and, invoking the biblical parable of the ten virgins, that "the foolish virgins made so much clamour they compelled the wise virgins to share their carefully collected oil."

Some of the hand-wringing came from Threadneedle Street itself: Many of the Bank of England's directors were aghast at what Governor Holland had done in the crisis. Thomson Hankey, a director on the Court of the Bank of England, wrote that the idea of the central bank acting as a lender of last resort was "the most mischievous doctrine ever broached in the monetary or banking world in this country; viz, that it is the proper function of the Bank of England to keep money at all times to supply the demands of bankers who have rendered their own assets unavailable." Although the bank had secured the blessing of the chancellor of the exchequer, its actions during the crisis were undertaken without formal legal authority. Legislation to empower the bank to play such a role in the future went nowhere in Parliament.

A century and a half later, Ben Bernanke & Co. would discover once again that lending freely to "this man and that man" may be the best course of action in a financial panic—but that not all men will approve.

# THREE

# The First Name Club

The mustachioed man in the silk top hat strode to his private railcar parked at a New Jersey train station, a mahogany-paneled affair with velvet drapes and well-polished brass accents. Five more men—and a legion of porters and servants—soon joined him. They referred to each other by their first names only, an uncommon informality in 1910, intended to give the staff no hints as to who the men actually were, lest rumors make their way to the newspapers and then to the trading floors of New York and London. One of the men, a German immigrant named Paul Warburg, carried a borrowed shotgun in order to look like a duck hunter, despite having never drawn a bead on a waterfowl in his life.

Two days later, the car deposited the men at the small Georgia port town of Brunswick, where they boarded a boat for the final leg of their journey. Jekyll Island, their destination, was a private resort owned by the powerful banker J. P. Morgan and some of his friends, a refuge on the Atlantic where they could get away from the cold New York winter. Their host—the man in the silk top hat—was Nelson Aldrich, one of the most powerful senators of the day, a lawmaker who lorded over financial matters in the burgeoning nation.

For nine days, working all day and into the night, the six men debated how to reform the banking and monetary systems of the United States, trying to find a way to make this nation just finding its footing on the global stage less subject to the kinds of financial collapses that had seemingly been conquered in

Western Europe. Secrecy was paramount. "Discovery," wrote one attendee later, "simply must not happen, or else all our time and effort would have been wasted. If it were to be exposed publicly that our particular group had got together and written a banking bill, that bill would have no chance whatever of passage by Congress."

For decades afterward, the most powerful men in American finance referred to each other as part of the First Name Club. Paul, Harry, Frank, and the others were part of a small group that, in those nine days, invented the Federal Reserve System. Their task was more than administrative. After all, some of the same motivations that had driven the American Revolution—distrust of central authority, of big money, of out-of-touch elites—had ensured that the United States wouldn't have a successful central bank for the first 130 years of its history.

The men at Jekyll Island weren't just trying to solve an economic problem—they were trying to solve a political problem as old as their republic.

The U.S. financial system needed remaking. The United States had a long but less than illustrious history with central banking. When the republic was formed, the states were burdened with debts they had racked up to finance the revolution; fighting off British control hadn't come cheap. Alexander Hamilton, the first treasury secretary, believed a national bank would stabilize the government's shaky credit and support a stronger economy—and was an absolute necessity to exercise the new republic's constitutional powers. The century-old Bank of England had shown the usefulness of a central authority to guide national finances. It could issue debt on behalf of the government and thus ensure that the nation could always fund itself. It could issue paper money so a single currency could be used wherever the national flag flew. And it could guide the use of the nation's savings, making sure they funded investment instead of sitting around as gold in a vault, waiting for a rainy day.

But Hamilton's proposal faced opposition, particularly in the agricultural South, where lawmakers believed a central bank would primarily benefit the mercantile North, with its large commercial centers of Boston, New York, and Philadelphia. "What was it drove our forefathers to this country?" asked James "Left Eye" Jackson, a fiery little congressman from Georgia with a proclivity for getting into duels. "Was it not the ecclesiastical corporations and perpetual monopolies of England and Scotland? Shall we suffer the same evils to exist in this country? . . . What is the general welfare? Is it the welfare of Philadelphia, New York and Boston?" Some founding fathers, including Thomas Jefferson and James Madison, believed that the bank was unconstitutional.

Hamilton won the battle after persuading President George Washington that although the Constitution didn't explicitly permit the creation of a national bank by the federal government, it also didn't explicitly prohibit it. Washington signed Hamilton's bank bill into law in February 1791. By the end of the year, the Bank of the United States was open for business in Philadelphia. By 1805, it had an additional seven branches along the East Coast and in New Orleans. But by the time the bank's charter expired six years later, Hamilton had died in a duel of his own, Madison was in the White House, and private banking interests had begun to view the national bank as competition. The Bank of the United States closed down.

In 1812, though, that came to seem like a mistake. The United States found itself at war with Britain—Madison's time in the White House would even be interrupted by the British burning it down. If there is one thing central banks have proved themselves very good at over their three and a half centuries of history, it is financing wars. And without a central bank to issue government debt, the United States faced financial challenges that would have been unimaginable for its Bank of England–backed opponent. Madison, who had a few years earlier judged a central bank to be unconstitutional, reluctantly supported starting up the Bank of the United States all over again.

The Second Bank of the United States was founded in 1816 and run most prominently by Nicholas Biddle, a brilliant young man of a literary bent who had finished first in his class at Princeton at age fifteen and helped negotiate the Louisiana Purchase. He did a lot of things that a modern central banker would applaud. He worked to eliminate the tendency for the dollar to have different values in different parts of the country, with western-issued banknotes generally being viewed as less valuable than eastern ones. He figured out that he could either tighten or loosen credit conditions—thus either fighting inflation or boosting economic growth—by buying and selling banknotes to influence the availability of credit across the nation. And at first, Biddle tried to keep himself away from partisan politics. Referring to Jonathan Swift's assertion that "Money is neither Whig nor Tory," he told a correspondent that "the Bank is neither a Jackson man nor an Adams man, it is only a Bank."

But once the continued existence of the national bank came into question, Biddle became not just political, but positively Machiavellian.

When rural southerner Andrew Jackson was elected president in 1828, it was on the strength of a vigorously populist campaign. Jackson was anti-urban, anti-intellectual, anti–big business—and very much anti–Bank of the United States. "Both the constitutionality and the expediency of the law creating this bank are well questioned by a large portion of our fellow citizens, and it must be admitted by all that it has failed in the great end of establishing a uniform and sound currency," Jackson said in his first message to Congress. He would, he said, veto any extension of the bank's charter, which was set to expire in 1836.

With the help of powerful pro-bank senator Henry Clay, Biddle in 1832 pushed for an early renewal of the charter. The advice was more than a little self-serving: Clay hoped to be elected president himself, and he knew the bank issue was divisive enough to build a campaign around. The debate in Congress was furious. The existence of a national bank, Missouri senator Thomas Hart Benton argued, would lay the groundwork for "the titles and estates of our future nobility—Duke of Cincinnati! Earl of Lexington! Marquis of Nashville! Count of St. Louis! Prince of New Orleans! . . . When the renewed charter is brought in for us to vote upon, I shall consider myself as voting upon a bill for the establishment of lords and commons in this America, and for the eventual establishment of a king!"

"Czar Nicholas," as Biddle became known among his opponents, resorted to dirty tricks to try to save the bank. He put politicians on the bank's payroll. He offered newspaper editors the then vast sum of $1,000 to publish his own articles in favor of the institution—and to keep their authorship secret. He even contracted credit in the West, where antibank fervor was strongest, a thuggish use of the power of the national bank to punish his enemies.

The rechartering of the Second Bank of the United States squeaked through Congress, but Jackson made good on his promise to veto it. With the bank's end in sight, Biddle took to an aggressive campaign of tightening credit, causing a deep economic downturn. His thinking was that this would show the country what it would be like not to have a central bank. But the tactic backfired: Biddle and the bank took the blame for the recession, making Jackson's decision seem like a wise one.

From the end of the Second Bank in 1836 until 1863, during the so-called Free Banking Era, there was no effective national currency in the United States. Money was issued and backed by individual private banks chartered by their respective states. A $10 note might have been worth $10 if issued by a financially healthy local bank, but only $7 if the bank that issued it was viewed as less healthy or was farther away from where the money was spent. That meant paper money couldn't serve as a reliable store of value. And there was no lender of last resort, which meant that banking panics like the ones Walter Bagehot wrote about in Britain could be devastating for the national economy. There were severe panics—and accompanying recessions—in 1837, 1839, and 1857, as well as many smaller ones.

Even more problematic, when the Civil War broke out in 1861, the federal government lacked a central bank to finance it. Privately owned U.S. banks bought government bonds only reluctantly, and foreign financiers refused to buy the debt of a country whose very existence was in question. The dilemma prompted an overhaul midway through the war. With the National Banking Act of 1863, the federal government began chartering banks—institutions that were the predecessors of modern-day behemoths like Citibank and J.P. Morgan Chase—and put them under tighter regulation than their state-licensed counterparts.

But some problems remained unsolved. For example, the supply of dollars was tied to banks' holdings of government bonds. That would have been fine if the need for dollars was consistent over time. But one overarching lesson of financial history is that that's not the case. In times of panic, for example, everybody wants cash at the same time. The U.S. banking system wasn't elastic, meaning there was no way for its supply of money to adjust with demand. That meant a panic could rapidly ripple across the country, with every bank seeing more demand for cash than it could fulfill, resulting in a wave of bank failures and an economic depression. It happened in 1873, when Philadelphia investment bank Jay Cooke & Co. failed after losing money on railroad securities. The downturn was so severe that until the 1930s, the 1870s were the decade known as the "Great Depression."

It didn't take much to trigger a panic in those days of inelastic currency. Just the routine passing of the agricultural seasons caused problems. Every fall, farmers across the nation needed money to pay workers to harvest their crops and bring them to market; the money could be repaid a few months later, once the farmers had sold their goods. Until then, though, there was more demand for dollars than banks could easily match—after all, new gold and Treasury bonds didn't suddenly appear just because the grain harvest was ready. To deal with this problem, banks created private clearinghouses to transfer funds among themselves, so that money made its way from big-city banks to more-rural places each fall.

In typical years, the seasonal shortage of dollars wasn't catastrophic. But if it coincided with other economic problems, it could be disastrous. Thus, besides the 1873 crisis, there were lesser panics in 1884, 1890, and 1893.

Then came the Panic of 1907, the one that finally convinced American lawmakers to deal with their country's backward financial system. It started with a devastating earthquake in San Francisco in 1906. Suddenly, insurers the world over needed access to dollars at the same time. They dumped bonds and other assets to come up with the cash they needed to pay claims.

In what was then still an agricultural economy, it was also a bumper year for crops, and an economic boom was under way—so companies nationwide wanted more cash than usual to invest in new ventures. In San Francisco itself, deposits were unavailable for weeks following the quake: Cash was locked in vaults so hot from fires caused by broken gas lines that it would have burst into flames had they been opened.

All of that meant the demand for dollars was uncommonly high, at a time when the supply of dollars couldn't increase much. This manifested itself in the form of rising interest rates and withdrawals. In the pattern that should look familiar—Johan Palmstruch experienced it in the 1660s—withdrawals begat more withdrawals, and before long, banks around the country were on the brink of failure.

Then, in October 1907, the copper miner turned banker F. Augustus Heinze and his stockbroker brother Otto tried to corner the market of his own United Copper company by buying up its shares. Money gushed out of the banks and brokerages with which Otto did business. But the corner failed, and the price of United Copper stock tumbled. Investors rushed to pull their deposits out of any bank even remotely related to the disgraced F. Augustus.

First a Heinze-owned bank in Butte, Montana, failed. Next came the huge Knickerbocker Trust Co. in New York, whose president was a Heinze business associate. Depositors lined up by the hundreds in its ornate Fifth Avenue headquarters, holding satchels with which to remove their cash. Bank officials standing in the middle of the room and yelling about the bank's alleged solvency did nothing to dissuade them. The failure of the trust led every bank in the country to hoard its cash for itself, unwilling to lend it even to other banks for fear that the borrower could be the next Knickerbocker.

It is true that the United States, in that fearful fall of 1907, didn't have a central bank. That doesn't mean it didn't have a central banker. John Pierpont Morgan was at the time the unquestioned king of Wall Street, the man the other bankers turned to to decide what ought to be done when trouble arose. He was not the wealthiest of the turn-of-the-century business titans, but the bank that bore his name was among the nation's largest and most important, and his power extended farther than the (vast) number of dollars under his command.

Morgan had bailed out the U.S. Treasury in 1895 during an earlier wave of panic by organizing other Wall Street titans to back federal debt. It was inevitable that when the 1907 crisis rolled around, Morgan held court at his bank's offices at 23 Wall Street while a series of bankers came to make their requests for help.

Morgan asked the treasury secretary to come to New York—note who summoned whom—and ordered a capable young banker named Benjamin Strong to analyze the books of the next big financial institution under attack, the Trust Company of America, to determine whether it was truly broke or merely had a short-term problem of cash flow—the old question of insolvent versus illiquid. Merely illiquid was Morgan's conclusion. The bankers bailed it out.

It wouldn't last—with depositors unsure which banks, trusts, and brokerages were truly solvent, withdrawals continued apace all over New York and around the country. At nine o'clock on the night of Saturday, November 2, 1907, Morgan gathered forty or fifty bankers in his library—executives of the biggest banks huddled in its east wing, those from the troubled trust companies in the west. Morgan and his closest advisers assembled in a private chamber. "A more incongruous meeting place for anxious bankers could hardly be imagined," wrote banker Thomas W. Lamont. "In one room—lofty, magnificent—tapestries hanging on the walls, rare Bibles and illuminated manuscripts of the Middle Ages filling the cases; in another, that collection of the Early Renaissance masters—Castagno, Ghirlandaio, Perugino, to mention only a few—the huge open fire, the door just ajar to the holy of holies where the original manuscripts were safeguarded."

The bankers awaited, as Lamont put it, the "the momentous decisions of the modern Medici." In the end, Morgan engineered an arrangement in which the trusts would guarantee the deposits of their weaker members—something they finally agreed to at 4:45 a.m. Medici comparisons aside, what is remarkable is how similar Morgan's role was to that of Timothy Geithner, the New York Fed president, a century later. Both knocked heads to encourage the stronger banks and brokerages to buy up the weaker ones, bailing out some and allowing others to fail, working through the night so action could be taken before financial markets opened.

With a big difference, of course: Geithner was working for an institution that, however less than democratic its governance, was created by the U.S. Congress and acted on the authority of the government. His major decisions were approved by the Fed's board of governors, its members appointed by the president and confirmed by the Senate. His capacity to address the 2007–2008 crisis was backed by an ability to create dollars from thin air.

Morgan, by contrast, was simply a powerful man with a reasonably public-spirited approach and an impressive ability to persuade other bankers to do as he wished. The economic future of one of the world's emerging powers was determined simply by his wealth and temperament.

Enough was enough. The Panic of 1907 sparked one of the worst recessions in U.S. history, as well as similar crises across much of the world. Members of Congress finally saw that having a central bank wasn't such a bad idea after all. "It is evident," said Senator Aldrich, he of the silk top hat and the trip to Jekyll Island, "that while our country has natural advantages greater than those of any other, its normal growth and development have been greatly retarded by this periodical destruction of credit and confidence."

The legislation Congress enacted immediately after the panic, the Aldrich-Vreeland Act, dealt with some of the financial system's most pressing needs, but it put off the day of reckoning with the bigger question of what sort of central bank might make sense in a country with a long history of rejecting central banks. It instead created the National Monetary Commission, a group of members of Congress who traveled to the great capitals of Europe to see how their banking systems worked. But the commission was tied in knots.

Agricultural interests were fearful that any new central bank would simply be a tool of Wall Street. They insisted that something be done to make agricultural credit available more consistently, without seasonal swings. The big banks, meanwhile, wanted a lender of last resort to stop crises—but they wanted to be in charge of it themselves, rather than allow politicians to be in charge.

The task for the First Name Club gathered in Jekyll Island in that fall of 1910 was to come up with some sort of approach to balance these concerns while still importing the best features of the European central banks.

The solution they dreamed up in those long sessions on Morgan's sea-island retreat was to create, instead of a single central bank, a network of them around the country. Those multiple central banks would accept any "real bills"—essentially promises businesses had received from their customers for payment—as collateral in exchange for cash. A bank facing a shortage of dollars during harvest season could go to its regional central bank and offer a loan to a farmer as collateral in exchange for cash. A national board of directors would set the interest rate on those loans, thus exercising some control over how loose or tight credit would be in the nation as a whole. The men at Jekyll drafted legislation to create this National Reserve Association, which Aldrich, the most influential senator of his day on financial matters, introduced in Congress three months later.

It landed with a thud. Even though the First Name Club managed to keep its involvement secret for years to come, in a country experiencing a populist resurgence—in no small part due to the anger at the trusts generated by the Panic of 1907 and the subsequent recession—the idea of a set of powerful new institutions controlled by the banks was a nonstarter, particularly after Democrats took control of Congress following the 1912 elections. Yet the central problems that Aldrich and the First Name Club were trying to solve were still very much there.

Aldrich's initial proposal failed, but he had set the terms of the debate. There would be some form of centralized power, but also branches around the country. And what soon became clear was that the basic plan he'd laid out— power simultaneously centralized and distributed across the country and shared among bankers, elected officials, and business and agricultural interests—was the only viable political solution. The debate over a central bank came down to how to balance power among regional banks and a central authority and among those different constituencies.

Carter Glass, a Virginia newspaper publisher and future treasury secretary, took the lead on crafting a bill in the House, one that emphasized the power and primacy of the branches away from Washington and New York. He wanted up to twenty reserve banks around the country, each making decisions autonomously, with no centralized board. The country was just too big, with too many diverse economic conditions, to warrant putting a group of appointees in Washington in charge of the whole thing, Glass argued. President Woodrow Wilson, by contrast, wanted clearer political control and more centralization—he figured the institution would have democratic legitimacy only if political appointees in Washington were put in charge. The Senate, meanwhile, dabbled with approaches that would put the Federal Reserve even more directly under the thumb of political authorities, with the regional banks run by political appointees as well.

But for all the apparent disagreement in 1913, there were some basic things that most lawmakers seemed to be in harmony about: There needed to be a central bank to backstop the banking system. It would consist of decentralized regional banks. And its governance would be shared—among politicians, bankers, and agricultural and commercial interests. The task was to hammer out the details.

Who would govern the reserve banks? A board of directors comprising local bankers, businesspeople chosen by those bankers, and a third group chosen to represent the public. The Board of Governors in Washington would include both the treasury secretary and Federal Reserve governors appointed by the president and confirmed by the Senate.

How many reserve banks would there be, and where? Eight to twelve, the compromise legislation said, not the twenty that Glass had envisioned. An elaborate committee process was designed to determine where those should be located. Some sites were obvious—New York, Chicago. But in the end, many of the decisions came down to politics. Glass was from Virginia, and not so mysteriously, its capital of Richmond—neither one of the country's largest cities nor one of its biggest banking centers—was chosen.

The vote over the Federal Reserve Act in a Senate committee came down to a single tiebreaking vote, that of James A. Reed, a senator from Missouri. Also not so mysteriously, Missouri became the only state with two Federal Reserve banks, in St. Louis and Kansas City. The locations of Federal Reserve districts have been frozen in place ever since, rather than evolving with the U.S. population—by 2000, the San Francisco district contained 20 percent of the U.S. population, compared with 3 percent for the Minneapolis district.

And in a concession to those leery of creating a central bank, the Federal Reserve System, like the First and Second Banks of the United States, was set to dissolve at a fixed date in the future: 1928. One can easily imagine what might have happened had its charter come up for renewal just a couple of years later, after the Depression had set in.

The debate over the Federal Reserve Act was ugly. In September 1913, Minnesota representative George Ross Smith carried onto the floor of the House a seven-by-four-foot wooden tombstone—a prop meant to "mourn" the deaths of industry, labor, agriculture, and commerce that would result from having political appointees in charge of the new national bank. "The great political power which President Jackson saw in the First and Second National banks of his day was the power of mere pygmies when compared to the gigantic power imposed upon [this] Federal Reserve board and which by the proposed bill is made the prize of each national election," he argued.

It wasn't just the fiery populists who opposed the bank. Aldrich, the favored senator of the Wall Street elite, complained that the Wilson administration's insistence on political control of the institution made the bill "radical and revolutionary . . . and at variance with all the accepted canons of economic law."

For all the noise, the juggling of interests was effective enough—and the memory of 1907 powerful enough—for Congress to pass the bill in December 1913. Wilson signed it two days before Christmas, giving the United States, at long last, its central bank. "If, as most experts agree, the new measure will prevent future 'money panics' in this country, the new law will prove to be the best Christmas gift in a century," wrote the *Baltimore Sun*.

The government, of course, hadn't solved the problem of panics—though it had gained a better tool with which to deal with them. And opposition to a central bank, rooted as deeply as it was in the American psyche, didn't go away. Instead, it evolved. Whenever the economic tide turned—during the Great Depression, during the deep recession of the early 1980s, during the downturn that followed the Panic of 2008—the frustration of the people was channeled toward the institution they'd granted an uncomfortable degree of power to try to prevent such things from happening.

But after more than a century of trying, the United States had its central bank. New York was poised to compete on a more level playing field with London as a capital of world finance. And as the years passed, the series of compromises that the First Name Club dreamed up a century earlier in Jekyll Island, and the unwieldy and complex organization it created, would turn out to have some surprising advantages—even in a country that had previously been better at creating central banks than keeping them.

# FOUR

# Madness, Nightmare, Desperation, Chaos: When Central Banking Goes Wrong, in Two Acts

Rudolf von Havenstein was a civil servant of the highest order: a kind and generous man of unquestioned integrity who had trained as a lawyer, served as a judge, and made a distinguished career for himself in the Prussian Finance Ministry.

He was also very likely the worst central banker in history.

Created in 1876, the German Reichsbank was crucial to the newly unified nation's emergence as a global industrial and financial power. By the time Havenstein became its president, in 1908, the bank was well along the way to establishing a modern financial system, phasing out gold, silver, and copper coins in favor of paper banknotes. Over the last few years of the nineteenth century and the first few of the twentieth, careful monetary policy and near-miraculous economic expansion made the German economy and its financial industry an emerging rival to Britain's. Germany became a leading exporter of iron, steel, and chemicals. But soon enough there were ominous rumblings of armed conflict on the continent as this new economic and industrial power bumped up against the existing powers of Britain and France. Havenstein viewed it as crucial that the Reichsbank be well positioned to enable the government to finance such a war.

On June 18, 1914, ten days before two bullets fired in Sarajevo killed Archduke Franz Ferdinand and his wife and ignited a global conflagration, Havenstein summoned the leading commercial bankers of Germany. It's ambiguous whether what he told them was a request, an order, or a threat: They would need to double the liquidity in the banking system over the next three years, he said, ensuring that marks were circulating in the economy instead of sitting around in banks. Ostensibly, this was to try to guide Germany through a bit of an economic rough patch. The true goal was to ensure that the nation would have the financial wherewithal to wage war.

Havenstein viewed the war as a clash of economies as much as a clash of armies. He wrote that England's "jealousy and ill-will toward our economic flowering, our growing world trade and growing power at sea is in the final analysis the basic cause of the world war." He had no apparent reluctance to putting the Reichsbank to work financing the conflict, which in the early days was expected to be a fleeting affair. His primary objective was to keep German commerce going despite the disruption. "The precondition for this continuation of economic activity was the most extensive use of the old source of credit, the Reichsbank," Havenstein said in September 1914.

Ordinary Germans were encouraged to give up their stores of gold coins and jewelry in exchange for paper money issued by the Reichsbank, which gave the government greater ability to finance the war effort through the central bank. Historian Gerald D. Feldman wrote that the encouragement of paper money "took on a patriotic and fetishistic quality of previously unimaginable proportions." Havenstein spoke warmly of individuals—the wife of a wealthy industrialist, his own brother-in-law—who moved their savings into paper money and persuaded others to do the same. A Reichsbank propaganda poster shouted, "Gold for the Fatherland! I gave gold for our defense and received iron as honorable recompense. Increase our gold stock! Bring your gold jewelry to the gold-purchasing bureaus."

That this mass issuance of paper money was steadily driving down the value of the mark was held back from public discussion by censorship, even as it was obvious to anyone going to the market to buy groceries. Havenstein and other Reichsbank leaders attributed the general rise in prices to hoarding. Inflation was high—but not yet catastrophically high. At the start of the war, the exchange rate was 4.2 marks to the U.S. dollar. On Armistice Day in November 1918, the rate was 7.4, which suggests an annual depreciation against the dollar of about 13 percent. That isn't much higher than the inflation rate the United States experienced in the early 1980s.

But a precedent had been set, and three conditions were in place that set the stage for everything that was to come: Germany was now a nation in which money was a piece of paper, not a gold coin; that piece of paper was understood to buy less with every year that passed; and Rudolf von Havenstein had made it his mission to use his ability to print money to fund the needs of his government, whatever they might be.

The German government's strategy of funding itself with Herr Havenstein's printing presses—taking on extraordinary debt in the meantime—was premised on winning the war. Transitioning to a peacetime economy would have been a challenge even if that had happened. (Managing Britain's debt-laden economy in the 1920s was certainly no picnic.) But at peace talks in France, the victorious Allies were determined to exact vengeance—a nicer word would be "compensation"—for the war. The resulting Treaty of Versailles wasn't so much the product of a negotiation as a list of demands made by the Allies: that Germany would give up colonies in Africa, as well as land comprising an eighth of its area, a tenth of its population, and 38 percent of its capacity for steel production.

Most devastating of all, this now smaller, poorer country was to pay vast reparations—a total of 132 billion gold marks, equivalent to more than three years of national income. The three billion gold marks it was to owe each year represented 26 percent of the value of its exports. That debt was lowered in subsequent years, but until finally closing out the debts in 2010, Germany still owed money to foreign investors who had purchased reparations-related bonds.

Economist John Maynard Keynes, who had left Cambridge to aid the war effort at the British Treasury, was disgusted by what he saw at the Versailles conference. So hungry were the Allies for vengeance, so lacking in magnanimity, that they'd put an impossible set of burdens on the defeated Germany. He was so distressed at the potential legacy of the treaty that he became physically ill. He resigned from the Treasury before the agreement was signed and quickly wrote *The Economic Consequences of the Peace,* which presented the reparation demands put upon Germany as a great risk to the world, and the prewar peace a rarer and more delicate phenomenon than most people realized.

"Very few of us realize with conviction the intensely unusual, unstable, complicated, unreliable, temporary nature of the economic organization by which Western Europe has lived for the last half century," Keynes suggested at the beginning of *Consequences*. "If the European civil war is to end with France and Italy abusing their momentary victorious power to destroy Germany and Austria-Hungry now prostrate, they invite their own destruction also, being so deeply and inextricably intertwined with their victims by hidden psychic and economic bonds."

On June 28, 1919, the Treaty of Versailles was signed by two relatively obscure German officials—one "thin and pink-eyelidded," the other "moon-faced and suffering," and both "deathly pale," according to a British eyewitness. They had good reason to be: Their nation's economy was wrecked, and its political environment was a fragile coalition of centrists facing ongoing threats from left-wing Bolsheviks and right-wing nationalists alike. Germany had incurred so much debt during the war that coming up with the cash for even the first reparations payment would be tremendously difficult.

Printing money was the only option. The war debts were denominated in gold, not paper currency. But so long as the currency held *some* value, it was a quick way to raise funds that could then be converted into gold to pay off the Allies. Havenstein, however, was soon to discover the brutal math of using the printing press to fund a government. As new marks circulated out into the economy, there was more money chasing the same number of goods, so prices rose a little. Each mark was now worth less. To adjust for inflation, the Reichsbank had to print even more marks to fund the same amount of government spending, which created an even steeper rate of inflation.

Year-to-year price increases weren't just high; they were exponential. At the end of 1920, a dollar would have bought you 73 marks. At the end of 1921, 192 marks. At the end of 1922, 7,589. In November 1923, that same dollar would have bought you 4.2 trillion marks.

The catalog of strange anecdotes from the time is extensive. There are the restaurant meals that cost more when the bill came than when they were ordered, the thieves who stole baskets full of money—keeping the baskets and leaving the money behind. The simple act of spending money became burdensome; photographs from the time show people hauling giant suitcases of cash for routine purchases. Communities developed ersatz barter systems. A shoe factory, for example, might pay its workers in bonds for shoes, which they could use to buy food at the bakery or butcher shop. Physical goods—shoes, bread, meat—would, after all, hold their value in a way that paper money wouldn't. In an effort to offer a stable savings vehicle, the city of Oldenburg offered "rye bills," bonds whose value matched that of 125 kilograms of rye bread.

For longer-term savings, people turned to other physical goods, even when they had no need for them. A 1923 report from Augsburg shows individual Germans buying six bicycles, seven or eight sewing machines, two motorcycles, all as means of savings. Pianos were also popular, Bavarian authorities reported, even among those who didn't play. Workers rushed to spend their paychecks the moment they received them. Bankers became accustomed to doing business in trillion-mark notes; one clerk wrote that inscribing all those zeros "made work much slower and I lost any feeling of relationship to the money I was handling so much of. It had no reality at all, it was just paper."

German hyperinflation wiped out the savings of an entire generation of what had been an increasingly prosperous merchant class. A waiter interviewed by Ernest Hemingway said that a year earlier he had saved up enough money to buy a tavern; by that time, in 1923, "that money wouldn't buy four bottles of champagne." A British social worker in 1922 wrote that "in well-furnished houses there are chairs devoid of leather which has been used for shoes, curtains without linings which have been turned into garments for the children. This sort of thing is not the exception but the rule." Strict rent-control laws meant that rents couldn't keep up with soaring prices, so by the third quarter of 1923 the typical German household paid only 0.2 percent of its income for housing; landlords were essentially bankrupted. But whatever workers saved on rent, they spent on food as farmers hoarded harvests and drove prices up further still—92 percent of their income, up from 30 percent before the war.

"You could see mail carriers in the streets with sacks on their backs or pushing baby carriages before them, loaded with paper money that would be devalued the next day," said Erna von Pustau, a German woman who was interviewed by Pearl S. Buck. "Life was madness, nightmare, desperation, chaos."

So what on earth was Rudolf von Havenstein thinking? He understood what the fragile German government would face if he cut off its cash: massively higher costs to borrow money, which would force it to slash spending, likely bringing on an economic depression. That, in turn, might bring political revolution. But even if he did have some grand strategy—albeit an unsuccessful one—this accomplished, honorable man stubbornly persisted in viewing the inflation problem as everyone's fault but his own. It was the fault of the government for running huge budget deficits, he argued—which was true enough, but the inflation only resulted when the Reichsbank printed money to fund those deficits. It was also the fault of currency speculators, who sold marks in hopes of profiting from their decline. And there were plenty of those—but it was the Reichsbank's policies that proved their bets correct.

A speech Havenstein gave on August 17, 1923, at the zenith of the hyperinflation, shows the extent of his myopia. "The Reichsbank," he said, "today issues 20,000 milliard [billion] marks of new money daily. In the next week the bank will have increased this to 46,000 milliards daily. . . . The total issue at present amounts to 63,000 milliards. In a few days we shall therefore be able to issue in one day two-thirds of the total circulation."

In a single day, Havenstein would increase the money supply by two thirds—and this, he seemed convinced, was a good thing. He took an almost perverse pride in the Reichsbank's ability to conquer the technical problem of producing and distributing such vast sums. "The running of the Reichsbank's note-printing organization, which has become absolutely enormous, is making the most extreme demands on our personnel," he said in that August speech. "Numerous shipments leave Berlin every day for the provinces. The deliveries to several banks can be made . . . only by aeroplanes."

The streets of Berlin, Munich, and Düsseldorf were thick with discontent, their populations having weathered a decade of misery and ruin and looking for answers wherever they might find them. Communists and fascists competed with each other as beneficiaries of this mass anger. "People just didn't understand what was happening," wrote the publisher Leopold Ullstein. "All the economic theory they had been taught didn't provide for the phenomenon. There was a feeling of utter dependence on anonymous powers—almost as a primitive people believed in magic—that somebody must be in the know, and that this small group of 'somebodies' must be a conspiracy."

On November 8, 1923, a group of nationalists stormed a beer hall in Munich where high Bavarian officials were gathered. A charismatic young veteran named Adolf Hitler took the stage. "A new national government will be named this very day in Munich!" he said to roars from the crowd. "A new German National Army will be formed immediately. . . . The task of the provisional

German National Government is to organize the march on that sinful Babel, Berlin, and save the German people! Tomorrow will find either a National Government in Germany or us dead!" Neither of those things happened after the Beer Hall Putsch. But forces had been unleashed that would shape Europe, and the world, for generations to come.

Four days later, Finance Minister Hans Luther had had enough of hyperinflation. He summoned Hjalmar Horace Greeley Schacht, a brash and ambitious banker whose father had admired the American abolitionist. Schacht was to become currency commissioner, charged with introducing a new German currency that would, it was hoped, be the reliable store of value that the papiermark was not. From a small, dark former broom closet in the finance ministry, with a single secretary, he worked the phones day and night, hoping to introduce a new currency backed by the nation's land. Though working just down the street from each other in Berlin, Schacht and Havenstein didn't speak, and the latter, though physically weak and deluded about his role in the disaster that had befallen the country, refused entreaties to resign.

It wasn't an issue for long. On November 20, eight days after Schacht began his work, the currency commissioner set an exchange rate: Each newly issued rentenmark would be worth a trillion papiermarks. The new currency would be worth the same against the dollar and the pound and the franc that the old one had been before the war. That very evening, Havenstein collapsed in a meeting, of a heart attack. In a single day, both German hyperinflation and its creator had died.

W all Street, the writer H. L. Mencken famously said, is a thoroughfare that begins in a graveyard and ends in a river. The symbolic center of the U.S. financial industry may have always connected the Trinity Church cemetery and the East River, but the line never seemed more apt than on October 24, 1929, the day known to history as Black Thursday. Thousands of people descended on the narrow, winding streets of lower Manhattan to gawk; six hundred police officers were dispatched just to contain them. They had showed up to witness the chaos of a mass selloff in a stock market that had seen nothing but buoyant optimism for the decade preceding. Their common expression, one observer wrote, was "not so much suffering as a sort of horrified incredulity."

But here's the thing about Black Thursday: Although it's remembered as the start of what became the Great Depression, it wasn't, in the end, all that dark a day. The Dow Jones Industrial Average fell a whopping 20 percent in the initial hours of trading, but as the day progressed, the grandees of American finance gathered at J.P. Morgan & Co.'s headquarters at 23 Wall St. and agreed to intervene. The Dow ended the day down a mere 2 percent. The headline of the next day's *Wall Street Journal* read, "Bankers Halt Stock Debacle."

But interventions by bankers can only delay a market correction, not stop it. Black Thursday was followed by Black Monday and then Black Tuesday, on which the Dow dropped 13 percent and 12 percent, respectively. Altogether, it was enough to push stocks 40 percent below their all-time highs the previous month, an abrupt reversal for what had become the great American wealth machine.

The crash of the U.S. stock market was a big deal, of course, and made headlines worldwide. But by all rights it should have been containable. There's no reason why it should have caused a decline of economic activity in the industrial heartland of Germany or the mass unemployment of coal miners in Britain or a collapse of the global monetary system. The stock crash in New York wasn't enough to have caused all those things.

It required the help of a series of analytical misunderstandings and outright failures by the world's central bankers.

Six years after Hjalmar Schacht fixed the mark, Germany was once again an industrial power on the rise. With a stable currency, factories had started churning again and the stock market had boomed. Berlin in the mid-1920s became a place of prosperity, urbanity, and artistic innovation. With its booming economy and investment opportunities, Germany was among the great destinations for foreign capital. By 1927, in fact, Schacht was getting worried that the economy was overheating, fueled by money flowing in from abroad.

The central bankers of France and Britain, meanwhile, were grappling with tensions that had emerged between their nations due to the gold standard—as well as a bit of personal animosity. In the 1920s, most of the world's major economic powers had returned to backing their currencies with gold, a practice they had abandoned to fund World War I. Roughly speaking, the supply of money in a national economy must match the pace of economic growth if prices are to remain stable. A growing economy, then, means an ever-growing need for gold.

But as growth returned to each of the major industrial nations, miners didn't suddenly become more productive. London, the prewar capital of world finance, had the gold. The surging economies of France, Germany, and the United States needed it. Those nations bought gold in London to fill their vaults—or more commonly, to make a paper notation that would reassign the ownership of gold permanently stored in the vaults of the Bank of England.

By 1927, this had created a dilemma for Montagu Norman, the brilliant and eccentric governor of the Bank of England. He faced an unpleasant choice: He could either raise interest rates in a British economy that was failing to recover from its wartime doldrums, tightening the national money supply and thereby slowing growth and encouraging unrest. Or he could risk a crisis of the pound, if people lost confidence that Britain could keep its currency pegged to gold.

The dilemma was compounded by Norman's miserable relationship with his counterpart in Paris, Banque de France governor Émile Moreau, who had made life difficult for the British by hoarding huge quantities of gold. The divide between Norman and Moreau was deeper than mere policy disputes. Moreau spoke no English and Norman spoke fluent French, yet Norman insisted that their discussions occur in his native tongue. At their very first meeting, in 1926, Moreau concluded that Norman was "an imperialist seeking the domination of the world for his country which he loves passionately" and "not a friend to us French." Norman left with the impression that Moreau was "stupid, obstinate, devoid of imagination and generally of understanding but a magnificent fighter for narrow and greedy ends." They were even physical opposites. As author Liaquat Ahamed put it, the tall, distinguished, even dandyish Norman contrasted sharply with the Frenchman, who was "short, squat, and bald, looking like a provincial notary out of a novel by Flaubert."

At the Federal Reserve, the conflict wasn't with one of the other central banks, but within the Fed system itself. Today, the powers and responsibilities of the various parts of the Fed—its presidentially appointed Board of Governors in Washington, its powerful New York branch, the eleven other reserve banks scattered around the country—are well understood, and Washington is clearly in charge. In the 1920s, however, the lines were fuzzier. Benjamin Strong, the president of the New York Fed, led a secret meeting with Schacht, Norman, and Moreau's deputy on a Long Island estate in 1927—but he pointedly didn't invite anyone from the Board of Governors. He believed that managing international economic relationships was his sole concern. The position of chairman of the Board of Governors, later to be held by the likes of Alan Greenspan and Ben Bernanke, was viewed as so weak that Roy Young left the job in 1930 to become president of the Boston Fed.

Strong died in 1928 and was replaced by George L. Harrison, a young, patrician lawyer. Harrison engineered a series of interventions during the October 1929 stock market crash, only to be overruled by his colleagues in Washington. The next week, he and the New York Fed made an overnight decision to inject $50 million into the financial markets without even seeking permission from Washington—which earned a rebuke from Young. With the U.S. financial system in crisis, the Federal Reserve, created to deal with just such an event, was paralyzed by internal power struggles.

The global financial system constructed by Benjamin Strong, Émile Moreau, Montagu Norman, and Hjalmar Schacht had brought the world years of prosperity. But both the economic conception on which it was based, the gold standard, and the institutions and individuals charged with managing it were more feeble and fragile than anyone had imagined.

As news of the Wall Street crash traveled around the world, investors pulled their money out of both New York's banks and other stock markets. In the United States, the impact was surprisingly large, with industrial production falling 11 percent in just two months. But the path to global depression was a winding one. Things actually seemed to be on the mend by early 1930, as the Federal Reserve responded to the market crash by easing credit, cutting the discount rate from 6 percent to 2.5 percent. Harrison argued for deeper, faster rate cuts, but the New York Fed president was held back by his colleagues in Washington and, even more so, at several of the other reserve banks around the country.

Those officials viewed the crash in moralistic terms, as the inevitable consequence of the boom that had preceded it—a hangover, in essence, that was punishment for a nation that had overindulged. It would be "inexpedient to exhaust at the present time any part of our ammunition in an attempt to stimulate business when it is perhaps on a downward curve . . . in a vain attempt to stem an inevitable recession," said the Fed's Open Market Committee in its official statement of January 1930. After all, it would be over soon enough, and the worst was already in the past. "Undoubtedly for a time we were in a serious condition," said Fed governor Charles S. Hamlin in a speech in May 1930. "Fear," however, "was at once dispelled and calm judgment and intelligent effort came to the front. I can see the dawn of normal activity, and believe the sun will soon rise."

At first, the impact of the crash in Europe seemed small—stock prices in London and Paris fell, but far less than they had in New York. But failures of policy turned that small shock into something much larger. The German economy had been fueled by investment from the United States, so the collapse on Wall Street had an outsized impact on growth in Germany, leading to an economic contraction in late 1929 and early 1930. The country had an unemployment insurance program that was budgeted to assist 800,000 jobless people at any given time. But the slumping global economy had put 1.9 million Germans out of work by early 1930.

The government was inclined to pay for the extra obligations by running a budget deficit. Schacht would have none of it, though, viewing deficit spending as the route back to the hyperinflation of the early 1920s. He publicly accused the government of bungling its finances, and the government listened. Germany balanced its budget by raising a wide variety of taxes—not just on income, but also on warehouses, mineral water, and beer. Instead of counteracting the negative effects of the U.S. crash, the German government's policies slowed the economy further.

The old pattern between Britain and France, meanwhile, was becoming even more destructive. With the United States and Germany entering a severe recession and Britain avoiding one thanks only to the aggressive interest rate cutting of the Bank of England, comparatively prosperous France was enjoying massive inflows of gold. With more and more of the metal in French hands, central banks in other nations had less and less ability to increase the supply of money if things got worse.

Then things got worse.

The U.S. stock market crash set in motion what Ben Bernanke would later call the financial accelerator. Banks suffered losses from the crash and thus pulled back on lending. Less lending meant weaker economic growth. A weaker economy meant further bank losses—and so on. The distinguished gentlemen of the Federal Reserve, meanwhile, looked at an economy getting steadily worse—unemployment was about 9 percent in 1930, up from 3 percent in 1929—and drew exactly the wrong conclusion. Their interventions in late 1929 to try to encourage growth had failed. To redouble those efforts, they concluded, would be foolhardy. Federal Reserve banks "have ample reserves and stand ready to finance a growing volume of business as soon as signs of recovery express themselves in an increasing demand for credit," said Charles Hamlin, a Fed governor who had been the first chairman of the central bank, in November 1930. In other words, the Fed is ready to pump money into the banking system—but only once conditions improve.

Hamlin said this in a month in which 256 U.S. banks failed, unable to repay their depositors. In December, it was 352 more, including the gigantic Bank of the United States. As the banking system collapsed, millions of Americans lost their savings and the supply of money in the economy shrank. The Fed and President Herbert Hoover stood by and watched and hoped. In 1931, the unemployment rate climbed to 16 percent. In 1933, it reached 25 percent.

The banking crisis spread to Europe when Credit-Anstalt, one of Vienna's largest and most important banks, failed spectacularly in May 1931, as years of lending for questionable projects caught up with it. The Austrian government guaranteed the bank's deposits—and suddenly found its own creditworthiness in question. The global bank run was on. If Credit-Anstalt could collapse, what about similarly overextended banks in Amsterdam and Warsaw? Or in Frankfurt and Munich?

When large-scale withdrawals began at the major German banks, the Reichsbank was in an impossible position. A collapse of the German banking system would be a catastrophe for the economy. Yet for the central bank to backstop the system would mean expanding the money supply at a time when its gold reserves were already dwindling. That would require abandoning the gold standard in a nation with fresh memories of the bad things that can happen when a currency is backed only by the credibility of the government.

The only option open for Hans Luther, Schacht's successor as head of the

Reichsbank, was to go to his neighbors and ask for help, hat in hand. On July 9, 1931, Luther boarded a private plane from Berlin. He met with Dutch officials in Amsterdam, then with Montagu Norman and other British officials at the Croydon Aerodrome, London's main airport in the days before Heathrow. But there was only one country with the resources to backstop the German banking system, only one that had experienced massive inflows of gold over the previous five years: France, the nation that Germany had supplanted as the great European power leading up to the war, and the one most eager to punish Germany at Versailles.

Luther went to Paris and pleaded his case. But years—centuries, really—of resentment and fear stood in the way. The French would make the sorts of massive loans that Germany needed to avert economic collapse only if it could extract its pound of flesh: a ban on nationalistic political activity, abandonment of plans to build battleships, a closer union with Austria. It was a deal that Germany couldn't accept.

Luther's last, desperate attempt at a deal was to travel to Basel to plead his case to the Bank for International Settlements (BIS), which had been created only a year before. Then, as now, central bankers' weekends in Basel were filled with delicious food and wine and a rare opportunity for brotherhood. Norman had played a crucial role in creating the organization, and had "made the central banker into a kind of archpriest of monetary religion," as a BIS executive once said, with other central bankers flocking to his room to meet. It was for Norman, as biographer Andrew Boyle wrote, "a spiritual home away from home." But efforts to craft a coherent international policy among the central banks were hobbled.

There was no common framework for understanding what was happening in the global economy, so the bankers all had different understandings of the causes of the disaster. Reliable economic data was sparse in most countries. The absence of jet travel made regular participation by U.S. and Japanese officials all but impossible, so Basel was overwhelmingly a European club. And the Americans weren't even allowed to participate initially: The U.S. government, always skeptical of international entanglements, forbade the Federal Reserve from becoming a member of the BIS. The crisis facing Germany in the summer of 1931 was, Norman concluded, just "too big for the central banks."

The seeds of World War II were planted on the day Hans Luther finally ran out of potential saviors, July 13, 1931. Had the Germans and French been able to work out a deal, it might well have prevented all-out economic collapse and steered Germany away from nationalism and militarism. Instead, the Reichsbank hiked interest rates to try to maintain the gold standard. A two-day "bank holiday" was declared and foreign exchange controls put in place to reduce outflows. Unemployment soared to 34 percent. So did hostility to the French and to most other non-Germans. The Nazis went from fringe party to ruling power. Even clever, urbane Hjalmar Schacht became an ally of Hitler, serving as a top economic official throughout the 1930s. (He would turn away from the Nazis as their anti-Semitism became more pronounced, and he collaborated with the anti-Hitler resistance during World War II.) The vision of a peaceful, democratic Germany crashed against the rocks of a monetary system with no give, no flexibility.

In Britain, the squeeze created by the gold standard similarly became too much to bear. The collapse of the German banking system only heightened fears that the London banks would be next, and withdrawals began on a vast scale. The British government itself had to turn to J.P. Morgan and other American banks for an emergency loan. Like the Reichsbank, the Bank of England would have to hike interest rates to try to maintain the value of the pound relative to gold and stop outflows—which would further slow the economy at a time when unemployment already topped 20 percent. As Keynes told a group of parliamentarians privately, "I declare to you, and I will stake on it any reputation I have, that we have been making in the last few weeks as dreadful errors of policy as deluded statesmen have ever been guilty of."

Montagu Norman's deputies—Norman himself was suffering from one of his periodic bouts of illness and was on a ship in the middle of the North Atlantic—concluded that they had no choice but to abandon the gold standard. Norman, the great central banker of his age, received a cable on his ship back from Canada that read, "Sorry we have to go off tomorrow and cannot wait to see you before doing so." Norman interpreted this to mean that his deputy, Sir Ernest Harvey, wouldn't be greeting him on his return. In fact, it meant that the Bank of England was going to go off the gold standard. Keynes, a friend remembered, was "chuckling like a boy who has just exploded a firework under someone he doesn't like."

It took the United States two more years, when Franklin Delano Roosevelt became president, to abandon a dollar pegged to gold. By that point, a quarter of the U.S. population was unemployed. In each of the major industrial countries, however, the abandonment of gold signaled the end of a great economic contraction and the beginning of the long slog back from depression.

I n 1933, the United States and the major powers of Western Europe all had more or less the same productive capacity that they'd had in 1929: the same factories, the same farmland, the same people with knowledge and ability and eagerness to toil. But when prices are falling and credit is collapsing—the sort of deflationary cycle that the central bankers allowed to take hold in the early 1930s—the whole system shuts down. Goods become less valuable; debts become more onerous. Despair sets in. Studs Terkel interviewed an Iowa farmer named Oscar Heline: "Grain was being burned. It was cheaper than coal. Corn was being burned. A county just east of here, they burned corn in their courthouse all winter, '32, '33. In South Dakota, the county elevators listed corn as minus three cents. *Minus* three cents a bushel. If you wanted to sell 'em a bushel of corn, you had to bring in three cents." This when there was mass hunger in the cities.

Too much money and rapidly rising prices can be profoundly damaging, as Germany in the early 1920s showed. And too little money and falling prices can be too, as all the Western powers in the 1930s demonstrated. As the damage bounced from financial markets to the economy to banks to government finances and back again, it also bounced back and forth across the Atlantic from the United States to the financial capitals of Europe. And the world's central bankers were essentially helpless to stop it, limited by their rigid adherence to the gold standard and an inability—or unwillingness—to cooperate with one another.

But both German hyperinflation and the Great Depression also teach a more basic lesson: When central bankers fail, so do societies.

# FIVE

# The Anguish of
# Arthur Burns

All the president's men would require two helicopters that Friday—and for the sake of the world economy, they had best leave from separate locations. If the members of the press who watched Marine One take off from the South Lawn of the White House had known the full list of officials who were joining Richard Nixon at his country retreat in Camp David that August weekend in 1971, they would have been tipped off that some major shift in the nation's currency policy was in the offing, which could have ruined the whole thing.

The second helicopter had to depart instead from Bolling Air Force Base, away from public view. On the car ride over, Nixon economic adviser Herbert Stein told speechwriter William Safire, "This could be the most important weekend in the history of economics since March 4, 1933," when Franklin Delano Roosevelt declared a bank holiday to stop runs on stricken American financial institutions.

After the twenty-eight-minute flight, Nixon gathered the men in the living room of the Aspen Lodge, overlooking Maryland's Catoctin Mountain. There was Treasury Secretary John Connally, who had been seated in the car with John F. Kennedy when the president was shot, and who was also wounded. There was White House aide Pete Peterson, who would later become a pioneer of the private equity industry. There were, among others, budget director George Shultz and his deputy Caspar Weinberger, who in the 1980s would guide the end of the Cold War as secretary of state and secretary of defense respectively. The tall, quiet treasury undersecretary who was present, Paul Volcker, would have as large an imprint on history as any of them.

The men were there to brainstorm about the dollar. The currency had been pegged to gold at $35 an ounce for decades, but that peg was coming under attack: Other nations had become convinced the dollar's true value was less, so they were taking advantage of its "convertibility" to swap dollars for gold. Rumors that the value of the dollar would be reset at a lower level only fueled more redemptions—better to get gold while the getting was good. If the officials assembled at Camp David couldn't find an answer, the United States would eventually run out of gold. In the interest of total secrecy, Nixon explained, there were to be no outgoing phone calls. Volcker mused at one point that given a billion dollars and a free hand, he could have made enough in trading profits from his knowledge of what was about to happen to cover the nation's entire $23 billion deficit.

One answer would have been for the Federal Reserve to raise interest rates, to try to bring the value of the dollar up to be more in line with its gold peg. But with unemployment already at 6 percent and the president running for reelection the next year, that was a nonstarter as far as Nixon and his aides were concerned. He already blamed his loss of the presidency in 1960 on monetary tightening by the Fed in the run-up to the election. So Nixon instructed his team to find ways to deal with the crisis that wouldn't blow a hole in the U.S. economy. Arthur Burns, chairman of the nominally independent Fed, pledged his full support, despite his opposition to what seemed would be the summit's inevitable result: the abandonment of the gold standard. "Mr. President," he said, "I'll help in any way I can."

At the end of the weekend, each member of the fifteen-man team received a spiffy Camp David windbreaker embroidered with his name, and Nixon interrupted *Bonanza* to give an address from the Oval Office. The United States was putting in place wage and price controls, attempting to reduce inflation by legal fiat. And the nation was closing down the "gold window," ending convertibility of the dollar to gold. The financial architecture that the world leaders had created in 1944 in Bretton Woods, New Hampshire, to prevent a recurrence of catastrophe that was the Great Depression was over. And what followed was the twentieth century's *other* great failure by the world's central bankers.

The windbreaker bunch hoped that they had finally found a way to halt inflation that wouldn't spark a recession. As it turned out, however, the Great Inflation had only begun. Although this failure would have less ghastly consequences than the central bankers' mistakes of the 1920s and '30s, Burns was convinced that it would lead to no good.

"My efforts to prevent closing of the gold window . . . do not seem to have succeeded," the Fed chairman wrote in his diary on the eve of the meeting. "The gold window may have to be closed tomorrow because we now have a government that seems incapable, not only of constructive leadership, but of any action at all. What a tragedy for mankind!"

Arthur F. Burns was the consummate professor, with white hair parted down the middle, thick glasses, and a pipe perpetually in his hands. He was "invariably courteous, with an old-world flair," one profiler wrote. Having been born in 1904, he had a deep-seated fear of letting the economy again lurch toward the mass unemployment he witnessed as a young man. "He is a creature of the Great Depression," a former student said of him in 1969. "That was a period when he was growing to professional maturity, and he saw the whole economic system disintegrate before him. The lesson he learned was that the avoidance of catastrophic change is the first objective of economic policy."

Nixon made clear that he expected Burns to ensure that the American postwar economic boom didn't falter on his watch—particularly in the run-up to the 1972 election. "I respect his independence," Nixon said at Burns's swearing-in in the East Room of the White House in January 1970. "However, I hope that independently he will conclude that my views are the ones that should be followed." Lest there be any confusion about what sort of views those were, Nixon continued, "That's a vote of confidence for lower interest rates and more money."

Senior Fed staffer Stephen Axilrod recalled being summoned to the White House to give a briefing on the finer points of monetary policy. Toward the end, John Ehrlichman, one of the president's closest aides, stopped by in a surprise visit. "When you gentlemen get up in the morning and look in the mirror while you are shaving," Axilrod recalled Ehrlichman saying, "I want you to think carefully about one thing. Ask yourselves, 'What can I do today to get the money supply up?'" Of Nixon, Burns wrote in his diary, "I knew that I would be accepted in the future only if I suppressed my will and yielded completely—even though it was wrong at law and morally—to his authority."

When Burns showed flashes of independence, the Nixon administration found nasty ways to apply pressure. Charles Colson, a presidential adviser who would later be implicated in the Watergate break-in, spread the story that Burns had asked for a 50 percent pay raise at a time when he was urging policies to rein in pay hikes nationally. Another rumor spread by the White House held that the administration was contemplating changing the governance of the Fed, putting it under the authority of the executive branch and doubling its board of governors to fourteen members, diluting the chairman's authority. Burns compared it to FDR's ill-fated plan to pack the Supreme Court forty years earlier.

Still, the Fed chief responded just as Nixon and his aides had hoped. When meeting with the president, Burns even adopted the language of a political operative. "Time is getting short," he told the president on December 10, 1971, less than a year before the election, according to Oval Office tapes. "We want to get this economy going."

Apart from political pressure, Burns's actions were influenced by some fundamental economic misunderstandings. It was an era of supreme confidence in the ability of wise policymakers to fine-tune the economy, as well as a time that any amount of unemployment seemed unacceptable, even when the trade-off was higher inflation. Two of the greatest economists of their generation, Paul Samuelson and Robert Solow, argued that even 3 percent unemployment—stunningly low by any historical standard—was a "nonperfectionist's goal." Inflation had averaged only 2 percent from 1950 to 1968, but in pursuit of exceptionally low unemployment, the Federal Reserve began tolerating prices rising at a faster pace—first 4.7 percent inflation in 1968, then 5.9 percent in 1969. By the end of 1970, *Time* had published a cover featuring a massively enlarged dollar bill, with a single tear running down George Washington's cheek and "Worth 73 cents" scrawled in red.

In just a few short years, inflation had lodged deep in the postwar American psyche. Businesses and consumers began to accept ever-rising prices as the new status quo. In a contract negotiated in 1970, the Teamsters union won 15 percent annual pay increases, railway workers got 13.5 percent, and construction workers averaged 17.5 percent. It's fair to assume that the economic output of truck drivers, railway workers, and construction tradesmen wasn't in fact rising at double-digit rates during that period. Instead, the higher pay was the result of higher prices. It, in turn, led to even higher prices—for bread and milk and everything else.

This vicious cycle was taking hold in the early 1970s, and Burns did little to stop it. The Fed even cut its interest rate target at the start of 1971, when annual inflation was over 4 percent, then eased policy again in the fall in the aftermath of the abandonment of the gold standard.

The Fed chief also had some bad luck. The weather was lousy for agriculture in the United States in 1972, driving up prices for all manner of food products in 1973. The price of meat, poultry, and fish rose more than 40 percent in the twelve months ending in August 1973—so fast, noted author David Frum, "that steakhouse menus arrived with stacks of little white handwritten stickers over their printed prices."

And in October 1973, Egypt launched a surprise attack on Israel on the Jewish holiday of Yom Kippur. The United States soon came to Israel's aid. In retaliation, on October 16, the Organization of Petroleum Exporting Countries hiked the price of oil 70 percent. The action shook confidence in the future availability of oil so much that companies began hoarding it. The price of gasoline in the United States soared from 42 cents a gallon to 55 cents a gallon over the course of only six months, and the psychological toll on Americans may have been even worse than the economic: With rules in place that made it hard to shift supplies away from areas with plenty of fuel to those with shortages, parts of the country simply ran out of gasoline. The iconic image of the era became that of dozens of heavy, inefficient cars lined up at one of the few stations without a SORRY, NO GAS sign out front.

Just as they would three decades later, spikes in commodity prices created a difficult dilemma for central bankers. Higher prices for food and gasoline are normally viewed as one-time jumps beyond the control of central bankers, who don't generally respond by raising interest rates. But if higher prices feed into self-fulfilling expectations of high inflation, there's more of a case to raise rates (though the importance of inflation expectations was not widely accepted then, at least among leading policymakers like Burns). For Burns and the Fed, the oil price shock came at the worst possible time, when those self-fulfilling expectations were already getting out of control. Consumer prices rose 8.9 percent in 1973, then 12.1 percent in 1974.

Even after Nixon had resigned in disgrace and the less thuggish Gerald Ford took over in August 1974, Burns and the Fed had no answers. To raise interest rates enough to bring inflation down to a more manageable level, they thought, would cause an unacceptably deep economic downturn. Haunted by the Depression of their youth, it seemed a trade-off they could not abide. In 1978, Burns's final year in office, the consumer price index rose 9 percent.

To succeed Burns, President Jimmy Carter appointed the hapless G. William Miller Fed chairman. Miller was a corporate chief executive from Oklahoma, a lawyer by training, and had no real background in economics. He placed an egg timer on the table at board meetings to limit the verbose intellectuals to three minutes of talking each. He also put out a THANK YOU FOR NOT SMOKING sign, which his colleagues ignored as they lit up. He viewed the Federal Reserve, a staffer once said, "as a diversified conglomerate of which he was chairman of the board."

Most significantly, Miller, fearful of a recession, refused to tighten the money supply to fight inflation. By the summer of 1979, with inflation at 10 percent, Carter had had enough. He "promoted" Miller to treasury secretary as part of a cabinet shake-up, a job with less concrete authority. That left him with a vacancy in the Fed chairmanship. He turned to the nation's most accomplished shaper of economic policy, a man who'd been a civil servant under four presidents and played a crucial role in remaking the international financial system earlier in the decade, including at Nixon's Camp David retreat during the summer of 1971. It was a personnel decision that would shape the world economy for decades to come—and help ensure Carter's loss to Ronald Reagan in his 1980 reelection campaign.

Paul Adolph Volcker was a six-foot-seven giant of a man, hired for a giant job. Carter picked him to be Fed chair because, at a time when world financial markets were fast losing confidence in the U.S. economic system, Volcker, then president of the New York Fed, offered something no other candidate could: instant credibility. In his meeting with the president before the appointment, Volcker told Carter he was inclined to tighten the money supply to fight inflation. That's what Carter was looking for—but he almost certainly didn't understand just what he was getting.

Volcker, a jowly man with a tendency to mumble, had done brief stints in banking but never spent enough time in the private sector to acquire much wealth. The son of a town manager in Teaneck, New Jersey, he smoked cheap Antonio y Cleopatra cigars, lived in a tiny, cluttered apartment in Washington, and ate dinner in a dingy Chinese restaurant rather than the grand salons of Georgetown. In a quirk of the Federal Reserve System, he had to take an approximately 50 percent pay cut to accept his promotion. (Heads of regional Fed banks, viewed as similar to private-sector employees, are paid more than members of the Board of Governors, who are considered more purely public servants.) The second most powerful man in America made about $60,000 a year.

Consumer prices rose 13 percent the year Volcker took over. One Fed governor, Henry Wallich, had been a boy in Germany during the German hyperinflation of the early 1920s. "I used to say that I never, never thought this could happen in the United States," Wallich once said. "But now I only say one 'never.'" By September, Volcker had concluded that the entire Fed playbook needed to be scrapped. Instead of just raising interest rates here and there to try to target the price of money a different approach would be needed—one that would almost certainly drive up the cost of borrowing to unprecedented levels.

On an air force jet en route to an International Monetary Fund conference in Belgrade, Volcker explained his plans to Carter's economic advisers. They didn't like them one bit. Sure, Carter wanted lower inflation. But higher interest rates affect the economy with a lag of many months. There was barely a year to go until the president would be running for reelection, which meant that just as their boss was asking voters for another term, unemployment would be skyrocketing due to the new Volcker policy.

As it happens, the retired Arthur Burns was also headed to Belgrade, where he gave a lecture. He described how central bankers, no matter how much they may wish to fight inflation, can't really do so without the support of political authorities. The speech, full of self-justification and excuse making, had the melodramatic title "The Anguish of Central Banking."

October 6, 1979, was a historic day in Washington. John Paul II was in town for the first papal visit to the White House. And Paul Volcker had summoned the Federal Open Market Committee to a grand boardroom overlooking the National Mall to try to finally end the Great Inflation. The meeting began a few minutes after 10 a.m., three and a half hours before Carter greeted His Holiness at the North Portico. "Scylla and Charybdis have now come together," Volcker said, meaning that there were simultaneous great risks of economic contraction and continued rapid inflation. "The idea that we can absolutely thread the needle between the risks is probably a nice hope, but it may be an illusion. At this stage you've got to place your bets one way or the other and move."

After six hours of skilled bureaucratic gamesmanship by Volcker, his committee agreed to the course the chairman wanted to pursue: The Fed would begin targeting not the price of money, as it had previously, but the quantity of money in the banking system. Normally, the Fed would have set a price for money—the interest rate—and the quantity of dollars in the economy would depend on how banks, businesses, and consumers reacted to that price. It's the equivalent of a restaurant setting the price of a hamburger at $10 and then selling however many hamburgers its customers are willing to buy at that price.

But now, to address the fact that too many dollars were floating around in the economy, the Fed was taking a different approach. Instead, it would announce the quantity of money it wanted, and adjust interest rates as necessary to get there. It would be the equivalent of a restaurant announcing that it plans to sell one hundred hamburgers, and then tweaking the price to achieve that goal, whether that meant $10 or $8 or $12. In effect, the Fed was pledging to slow down the growth of the money supply, no matter how high it would need to push interest rates to do so. After years of astronomical inflation, getting the money supply down to the bank's new target wouldn't be easy. Hamburgers were about to cost a whole lot.

Volcker's press aide, Joe Coyne, began calling reporters to notify them that there would be a news conference that evening. Journalists who write about central banking don't routinely get phone calls on a Saturday afternoon to announce a surprise press conference, and many arrived in their weekend clothes. After Coyne phoned CBS News, the Washington bureau chief called back to say he had only one camera crew working that day—and it was covering the pope's visit. "I said he would remember the press conference long after the pope had left town," Coyne later recalled.

With more than fifty reporters packed into the boardroom, Volcker walked in at 6 p.m., flanked by two aides, each a foot shorter than the chairman. He started by correcting two pieces of misinformation that had been floating around financial markets the week before. "I will tell you that the major purpose of this press conference," he said, "is to show that I have not resigned, the way early rumor had it yesterday, and I'm still alive, contrary to the latest rumor."

Then he got to the heart of the matter: The Fed's policy committee had decided to start targeting the money supply and had raised the bank lending rate by a full percentage point. The press focused primarily on the latter move, which was more easily understandable. It wasn't just the seemingly technical nature of the change in the Fed's policy change that made the reports that day deemphasize it; Volcker actively tried to play down the importance. When asked whether the action would cause an economic downturn, he said, "Well, you get varying opinions about that." As Yale economist James Tobin put it later, "Burns smoked a pipe. Volcker smoked a cigar. Both produced smokescreens."

Volcker would soon become one of the most unpopular people in the country as the Fed raised rates to try to get the money supply in line with its new target. "The Credit Crunch Is On," blared *Newsweek* in March 1980, noting that Sears Roebuck was demanding higher payments from its credit customers and that Chase Manhattan Bank had stopped making unsecured personal loans. With interest rates topping 20 percent, few could afford a home mortgage. Construction activity practically came to a halt.

Homebuilders began mailing two-by-fours to Volcker in protest. (Decades later, he gave one to Ben Bernanke; it still sits on a shelf in the chairman's office.) Automakers were similarly livid: High interest rates meant that consumers couldn't afford to buy cars either. Not to be outdone by the construction workers, they mailed Volcker the keys to unsold vehicles. But farmers may have had it worst of all. During the late 1970s, many had taken out loans to buy more land on the assumption that crop prices would keep rising at an extraordinary clip. When food prices fell and interest rates rose, people across Middle America lost their farms. They protested by driving their tractors to Washington and circling the Federal Reserve's grand marble headquarters.

Other protests weren't as peaceful. In 1981, one man who said he was upset about high interest rates plowed past guards at the Fed's headquarters carrying a sawed-off shotgun, a pistol, a knife, and a fake bomb. He was tackled by a guard just short of the main boardroom, and Volcker was assigned a full-time security detail for the first time.

The big man went before Congress repeatedly, smoking his cigars and trying to explain the Fed's strategy as lawmakers channeled the rage of their constituents toward the schlumpy man who'd made it harder for them to borrow and buy. "We're destroying the American Dream," said Republican representative George Hansen of Idaho. A building-trades magazine accused Volcker of "premeditated and cold-blooded murder of millions of small businesses."

When Volcker concluded that the vicious cycle of high inflation had been broken, in 1982, he finally began cutting interest rates. That year, prices rose only 3.8 percent, the lowest in any twelve-month period in a decade. The cost of getting inflation expectations back down to reasonable levels had been the worst economic downturn since World War II, with millions of Americans out of work.

But the Volker recession set the stage for great things. Americans would no longer endure the discomfort of ever-rising prices. Businesses could begin investing with greater confidence that those investments would pay off. Lenders could be more comfortable about extending loans, confident that the money they were paid back would be worth something. And the Fed had gained credibility as a fighter of inflation, breaking the cycle in which it had become a self-fulfilling prophecy. Volcker's achievement even made it easier for Alan Greenspan to maintain low and steady inflation; once people trusted that the Fed would do whatever it took to keep prices from spiraling out of control, it often took only a small interest rate move—or even mere words from the chairman—to rein in rising prices.

The central bankers, having seen what can happen when they create too little money or too much, had seemed to learn their lessons, and a Goldilocks economy took hold in much of the world, a period of sustained prosperity and low inflation. The Great Inflation had ended, and the Great Moderation had begun.

# SIX

# Spinning the Roulette Wheel in Maastricht

Behind the thick walls of the Bank of England, the traders were fighting a battle. And they were losing.

They were buying pounds, with furious speed and on a vast scale. First £300 million, then another £300 million. By 8:40 a.m. that morning of Wednesday, September 16, 1992, they were up to £1 billion. They were trying to prop up the value of their currency on global markets, but no matter how many pounds they bought, the numbers on their screens barely budged. What they didn't know was that the night before and an ocean away in New York, financier George Soros had given his chief portfolio manager, Stan Druckenmiller, a remarkable order: Sell sterling, as much as you can. And don't stop.

Druckenmiller had concluded that the British government was no longer going to be able to hold its currency at the level it had pledged to two years earlier under the European Exchange Rate Mechanism. The idea was that the nations of Europe could boost their economies if their different currencies maintained a steady value relative to the others'. It would be much easier for a company to do business across Europe, for example, if it could be confident that the deutschmark and the franc and the lira wouldn't constantly fluctuate against each other. When, in one of Margaret Thatcher's final acts as prime minister, Britain joined the exchange rate mechanism, it committed to keeping the value of a pound sterling at 2.95 deutschmarks, plus or minus 6 percent.

But Druckenmiller and Soros were convinced that the underlying value of the pound was in fact below that, amid inflation and weak growth in the UK. They were betting that the currency would inevitably fall to levels that more closely matched its fundamentals, and that the government couldn't afford to keep its value artificially high by entering the market to buy sterling. Finland and Italy had already dropped out of the exchange rate mechanism under just such pressures, sending their currencies plummeting and making vast sums for anyone who had bet accordingly. Mervyn King, then the Bank of England's chief economist, had gone to Frankfurt two days earlier, arriving at the Bundesbank amid Wagnerian bursts of thunder and lightning to plead with it for help maintaining the peg, a trip he later called "probably one of the world's most unsuccessful diplomatic missions." The endgame was coming for Britain.

The two investors decided to sell sterling "short"—that is, to sell borrowed pounds, which they would repay later, after the pound dropped. "Go for the jugular," Soros told Druckenmiller that Tuesday night.

The Quantum Fund, which they ran, sold pounds to anyone who could buy—the Bank of England when the London markets were open, investors around the world the rest of the time. Soon others started to dump sterling too. The Bank of England could keep buying, but the more it bought, the more British taxpayers stood to lose if the nation eventually did abandon its currency peg.

That Wednesday, Prime Minister John Major's government made an emergency decision to hike interest rates a stunning 2 full percentage points, then hiked them by another 3 percentage points on Thursday. It hoped to reverse the sell-off and leave the speculators with egg on their face, even at the risk of devastating British economic growth. But Soros and other global investors showed no hesitation. The selling continued unabated.

At 7:40 p.m. London time the evening of September 17, Chancellor of the Exchequer Norman Lamont stood before the British Treasury. "Massive speculative flows have continued to disrupt the functioning of the exchange-rate mechanism," he told the assembled cameras. He had called a meeting of European finance ministers to discuss what to do next. "In the meantime the Government has decided that Britain's best interests would be best secured by suspending our membership of the ERM with immediate effect."

The pound immediately plummeted. George Soros and Stan Druckenmiller had broken the Bank of England, made a billion dollars for themselves and their investors, and become legends in the world of finance. But the exit of Britain, Italy, and Finland from the exchange rate mechanism meant that if the very different nations of Europe were to create a single unified financial system, in which money could flow as freely between nations as it does among U.S. states, it would take something more binding than a mere promise.

It would take the euro.

I n the first century AD, a merchant from Rome could travel to Londinium via Colonia Claudia Ara Agrippinensium and Lutetia Parisorum and use the same denarii to pay for goods at each stop on his way, the German economist Otmar Issing noted. That is, he could travel from Rome to London via Cologne and Paris and use the same currency. The twenty centuries since then, however, have been less kind to those who might benefit from a Europe under a single political and financial authority, the best efforts of Charlemagne and Napoleon notwithstanding.

In the years after World War II, the leaders of Western Europe looked for a way to leave the strife of the first half of the twentieth century behind by creating a new economic union. Countries that are deeply intertwined economically tend not to go to war with one another, and the United States had become the most powerful nation on earth thanks to having a large, populous area in which people could trade freely with each other. The challenge for the postwar Europeans was to create economic unity in a way that would respect both national identity and democracy. They started with Germany and France, and with steel and coal—the two countries whose conflict had been at the core of the twentieth-century wars, and the two materials most needed to fight one.

"The solidarity in production thus established will make it plain that any war between France and Germany becomes not merely unthinkable, but materially impossible," said French foreign minister Robert Schuman in a proclamation on May 9, 1950. "By pooling basic production and by instituting a new High Authority, whose decisions will bind France, Germany and other member countries, this proposal will lead to the realization of the first concrete foundation of a European federation indispensable to the preservation of peace."

When the treaty for a steel and coal collective was signed less than a year later, it included not just France and West Germany, but also Italy and the Benelux countries. The "High Authority" would be the European Economic Community, which would eventually become the European Union, which now includes twenty-seven nations and half a billion people. It oversees markets through the Brussels-based, twenty-four-thousand-employee regulatory colossus known as the European Commission. It has expanded its turf a bit since the 1950s and now besides steel and coal oversees the acceptable curvature of bananas and whether prunes can be marketed as a laxative.

But the economic genius of the United States comes not just from the free flow of goods across borders and standardized regulation of commerce. The nation also benefits from having a single currency in use from Maine to California. By 1970, European leaders were searching for ways to bring the same benefits to their own continent. Their first answer was the "snake in the tunnel" of 1972. The idea was that the value of the franc, the lira, and the rest (the "snake") would be allowed to fluctuate within a narrow range relative to the U.S. dollar (the "tunnel"). It fell apart in two years. The exchange rate mechanism began in 1979; it lasted rather longer, ending with Soros's bold bet in 1992.

What did them in was that each European currency was managed by a different central bank with a different culture and objective. The German Bundesbank was hard-nosed and independent and had the primary goal of keeping inflation low, while the Banca d'Italia was more under the thumb of politicians and set monetary policy more indiscriminately. In the 1980s, inflation averaged 2.9 percent a year in Germany, 7.4 percent in France—and 11.2 percent in Italy.

The idea of a monetary union had been an explicit goal of the continent's leaders since 1969, but political realities stood in the way. Higher-inflation countries like Italy, France, and Spain envied the stable prices of Germany and were eager to attach themselves to the credibility of the Bundesbank. Germany, however, was unwilling to turn over partial control of its money supply to people who had a looser view of acceptable levels of inflation. "Not all Germans believe in God, but they all believe in the Bundesbank," European Commissioner Jacques Delors once said. If there were to be a single currency for Europe, something would have to change the Germans' political calculus.

. . .

A t 6 p.m. Berlin time on November 9, 1989, Günter Schabowski, an East German functionary who served as his government's spokesman, stood before the media in East Berlin. Across central Europe, at the frontiers between the Soviet Bloc and the West, the law preventing border crossings was starting to break down—first in Hungary, then in Czechoslovakia. Just before Schabowski's press conference, he was handed a document with the latest travel rules between East Berlin and West Berlin, divided since 1961 by a wall that was a fitting symbol of the Cold War.

Schabowski didn't have time to read the document carefully, and in the final minutes of an hourlong conference he seemed confused in describing the rules. "Today, as far as I know, a decision has been made," said Schabowski. "It is a recommendation of the Politburo that has been taken up, that one should from the draft of a travel law take out a passage." When would this take effect? "Immediately, right away," said Schabowski. "The question of travel, of the permeability therefore of the wall from our side, does not yet answer, exclusively, the question of the meaning of this, let me say it this way, fortified border."

It seemed, as far as anyone could tell, that Schabowski had announced that the Berlin Wall was open. Masses of East Germans, long prevented from entering West Berlin, began gathering around the wall's checkpoints. The guards on duty didn't know what to do. The high officials who could have explained that Schabowski had blundered—or ordered the guards to use force to disperse the crowds—were stuck in meetings. At 10:30 p.m., the guards at the Bornholmer Street border crossing, having seen the press conference and facing hordes of people chanting, "Open the gate! Open the gate!" did just that. Herr Schabowski had, quite inadvertently, ended the era of a divided Germany.

In the months that followed, West German leaders seized on the moment to reunite their nation, divided since the waning days of World War II. For France and other European powers, barely four decades removed from the horrors of war with a united Germany, the idea was anathema. French president François Mitterrand, in a series of subtle diplomatic moves in the days and weeks after the Wall fell, made clear that Europe would support a reunified Germany only if Germany supported Europe.

Germans from Chancellor Helmut Kohl down might not have liked the pressure from the French. But it was also understood as the price still being paid for the horrors of Nazism. It was something that had been clear even before the Holocaust; as German philosopher Karl Jaspers wrote in 1933, his nation's "destiny today is that Germany can only exist in a united Europe, that the revival in her old glory can come about only through the unification of Europe, that the devil with whom we will inevitably have to make our pact is the egoistic, bourgeois society of the French."

European finance ministers and central bankers set to work on arduous negotiations to figure out how the monetary union would work. On December 3, 1991, in one of the many rounds of diplomacy that occurred in Brussels, French finance minister Pierre Bérégovoy and Jean-Claude Trichet, head of the French treasury, met with their German counterparts. They had a message from President Mitterrand. The French demanded that the monetary union they were negotiating be irreversible, that it forever bind their nations, and that it begin on a fixed date before the dawn of the twenty-first century. The French won their demand to have a new European currency by January 1, 1999—but in return they conceded to the Germans that the European central bank would be modeled after the Bundesbank, with the strong safeguards to independence that kept German inflation low.

Hundreds of negotiators and officials gathered in the Dutch town of Maastricht on February 7, 1992, to complete the treaty. As the Limburg Symphony Orchestra played Mozart, the finance and foreign ministers of Europe one by one signed the leather-bound books containing the 189-page agreement. It called for monetary unification of all the nations of the newly named European Union, with special exceptions for Britain and Denmark, both more eager than the rest to keep their options open. Besides a monetary union, it created a European Parliament, called for coordination on defense policy, and allowed the free movement of citizens across borders within the EU.

Ruud Lubbers, the Dutch prime minister and thus the host of the gathering, celebrated the moment with a glass of champagne. "It's done now," Lubbers said. "There is nothing left but to drink a toast. *Les jeux sont faits, rien ne va plus.*"

It's a gambling reference, what a croupier at a roulette table says when betting has closed: The wheel has been spun; no more wagers. Now we can only wait to see the results.

. . .

After Maastricht, MIT economist Rudiger Dornbusch suggested, many British and even more American economists could be divided into three camps: "It can't happen," "It's a bad idea," and "It can't last."

It takes more than a single currency to have a viable economic union, the Euroskeptics said. It also takes political union—joint policies on everything from bank regulation to taxes—and a population that's comfortable moving around. More fundamentally, it requires that people in different parts of the currency area feel that they have common obligations to each other, that they are truly one nation. In an economy as large as Europe's, there will inevitably come times when some parts have different economic situations—one place might experience a bust in the local housing market at the same time another is experiencing a boom in its local industries. When those two places are served by the same central bank, then one powerful tool to deal with a weakening economy isn't there.

The United States is a big country that has had its own challenges achieving a unified political system. But consider some of the ways "asymmetric shocks" are handled in a place where the Federal Reserve has to set a single monetary policy for a nation of 300 million people.

When unemployment and poverty are high in one place, the U.S. government funnels money there from more prosperous places. And it's not just in times of unique economic distress. Some states persistently receive more money from the government than they pay in taxes—particularly those with higher concentrations of people who receive food stamps or unemployment benefits. In 2005, Alabama paid, on average, $5,434 in taxes per resident to Washington. But Washington sent back to Alabama $9,263 per person. Much richer New Jersey paid $9,902 per person to the federal government but received only $6,740 in return. Yet American political unity is such that one never sees politicians or newspapers in New Jersey complaining about lazy Alabamans taking New Jerseyans' money.

The same applies with the United States' banking system. The agencies that guarantee the nation's banks—most prominently the Federal Deposit Insurance Corporation—are arms of the U.S. government, not of any given state. So if banks start to fail in one geographical area, the entire country stands behind them. The bailout of savings and loans nationwide cost U.S. taxpayers an estimated $123.8 billion between 1986 and 1995 and the private sector another $29.1 billion. Losses in Texas—where in the late 1980s savings and loans failed in massive numbers amid a real estate bust and falling oil prices—accounted for about 62 percent of that, according to one estimate. Imagine what would have happened if the federal government hadn't been in place to rescue the state's banks. The Texas government would have faced a dire choice: Either let the banks fail, in which case its citizens would lose their savings and the economy would collapse, or bail them out, in which case the state would have been thrown into a fiscal crisis. Texas's total state tax collections in 1986 were only $10.2 billion. With only those funds available, it would have taken more than nine years for the state to pay for its bank bailout, even if it stopped paying for anything else—schools, roads, public safety. But again, when the rest of the country bailed out Texas banks in the late 1980s, there wasn't much grumbling among residents of, say, Connecticut.

And when the economy is terrible in one part of the United States, Americans are able to pick up and move to where conditions are better. In 2007, for example, 787,000 more Americans relocated from the Northeast to the South than the other way around. That reflects the brighter economic prospects in Sun Belt metropolises like Houston and Atlanta than in fading northern industrial centers like Buffalo and Providence. The Maastricht Treaty ensured that Europeans would have the legal right to relocate in a similar fashion. But moving within the United States is a different thing entirely from, say, emigrating from Portugal to Germany, as much as one might joke about how New Yorkers and Texans speak a different language.

It all boils down to this: Economic unity isn't just about having the same currency. It's about having unified political institutions and, more broadly, a sense of cultural togetherness. Europe, argued the Brits and Americans, lacked this. It wasn't, to use the technical term, an "optimal currency area." Barry Eichengreen of the University of California at Berkeley showed how the economies of different parts of Europe have more variances in their growth patterns than those in different parts of the United States—implying the need for more integration of fiscal policy, not less. In a much-cited 1997 essay, Martin Feldstein of Harvard raised the idea that being yoked to the same currency would actually increase the likelihood of conflict between European nations. "In the beginning there would be important disagreements among the EMU member countries about the goals and methods of monetary policy," wrote Feldstein in *Foreign Affairs.* "These would be exacerbated whenever the business cycle raised unemployment in a particular country or group of countries. These economic disagreements could contribute to a more general distrust among the European nations." Summing up the conventional wisdom of the Euroskeptics was Paul Krugman, then of MIT, writing in *Fortune:*

> Here's how the story has been told: a year or two or three after the introduction of the euro, a recession develops in part—but only part—of Europe. This creates a conflict of interest between countries with weak economies and populist governments—read Italy, or Spain, or anyway someone from Europe's slovenly south—and those with strong economies and a steely-eyed commitment to disciplined economic policy—read Germany. The weak economies want low interest rates, and wouldn't mind a bit of inflation; but Germany is dead set on maintaining price stability at all cost. Nor can Europe deal with "asymmetric shocks" the way the United States does, by transferring workers from depressed areas to prosperous ones. . . . The result is a ferocious political argument, and perhaps a financial crisis, as markets start to discount the bonds of weaker European governments.

European economists were well aware of this sort of commentary. What the Americans didn't understand, they said, was that the common currency was only part of the story. Europe might not be an optimal currency area *yet.* But the monetary union was one of the steps necessary to make it one; once the euro was in place, all the other forms of integration would follow. As for those European economists who had their own doubts—well, political leaders had a strategy for dealing with them. As Belgian economist Paul De Grauwe explained to the *New York Times* years later, "The European Commission did invite economists to present their views. It was a Darwinian process. I was invited, but when I expressed my doubts I wasn't invited anymore. In the end only the enthusiasts were left."

With euro enthusiasts in charge, monetary union was on an irreversible course. There were things to negotiate, of course. The new central bank would, at German insistence, be located in Frankfurt rather than in Brussels, where most pan-European institutions are headquartered. It would have a single mandate, to maintain stable prices. (The Fed, by contrast, is charged with maintaining both stable prices and maximum employment.) It would be strictly forbidden from using its ability to print money to fund governments; any hint of Weimar Republic–style monetizing of government debt was *verboten*.

But as that crucial deadline of January 1, 1999, approached, there remained the question of who would run such an institution. And the battle over that answer was characterized by the sorts of nationalistic outbursts, hardball negotiations, and ugly compromises that would haunt the euro many years later. In 1997, the consensus had been that Wim Duisenberg, the head of the Dutch central bank, would become the first president of the European Central Bank. Duisenberg had the particular advantage of being viewed by Germany as sufficiently committed to hard money and monetary independence while also being regarded by the rest of Europe as being sufficiently non-German to be someone it could support. Germany had, after all, gotten most of what it wanted in the structure and location of the ECB. If the first president of the bank had been a German as well, it might as well be called the Neue Bundesbank.

On November 3, 1997, French president Jacques Chirac made a phone call that threw Duisenberg's candidacy into doubt. He had decided to nominate Jean-Claude Trichet, Chirac told the prime minister of Luxembourg. With Germany getting a central bank of its own design on its own soil, Chirac demanded that the French get the first presidency, for a single eight-year term. Trichet was hardly ideal from a domestic perspective; his German-style emphasis on low inflation had alienated French politicians on both the left and right. But Chirac was determined to put him forward, for a variety of reasons, ranging from the symbolic (his desire to have a Frenchman in charge) to the cynical (his desire to put his domestic political opponents in an uncomfortable position) to the seemingly irrelevant (his annoyance at liberal Dutch drug laws).

At the start of May 1998, European leaders gathered in Brussels for a crucial final round of negotiations in advance of the launch of the common currency eight months later. Ironically, the man chairing the weekend discussion was one whose government had elected not to take on the euro at all. British prime minister Tony Blair was an enthusiast of forging closer connections with

Europe, but his own chancellor of the exchequer, Gordon Brown, had repeatedly found reasons to forestall any commitment.

The compromise that started to emerge seemed promising: Duisenberg would take the ECB presidency for some short length of time before handing it off to Trichet for a full eight-year term. Chirac suggested that Duisenberg retire on his sixty-fifth birthday, in June 2000. But the Dutch were angered at the idea of having their man forced out after a short period. So were the Germans, who saw it as an affront to the idea of central bank independence—after all, the whole purpose of giving the ECB president an eight-year nonrenewable term was so that politicians like Chirac couldn't micromanage when a new leader takes over.

"Who is this man who says we must waste all this time talking about a few weeks longer he stays in the job?" Chirac reportedly said at one tense point in the talks.

"You say, 'Who is this man?' He is not someone who just turned up off the street, you know," retorted Dutch prime minister Wim Kok.

"*Bof!*" snorted Chirac, adding a moment later, "We have already accepted the bank would be in Frankfurt."

With the French threatening to veto Duisenberg, and the Dutch and Germans threatening to veto Trichet, Blair proposed a compromise: Duisenberg would make a personal and voluntary announcement that he would retire before his full term was out. (As it turned out, he stepped down and was replaced by Trichet in 2003.) The French would get their president within a reasonable time frame, and the Dutch and Germans would get at least the appearance of a central bank independent from politics. As he left the negotiations in Brussels that weekend, Helmut Kohl, among the great statesmen of the postwar period, looked bedraggled, and described the concluded talks as "the most difficult hours I have experienced in Europe."

On January 1, 1999, the euro launched, first for electronic transactions, and three years later as a paper currency. Its value was fixed in stone that day: 1.95583 German deutschmarks, or 2.20371 Dutch guilders, or 1,936.27 Italian lira. To make it easier to refer to the new currency, the European Commission ordered up a new symbol, similar to those for the dollar or the pound. Designers settled on a sign that has origins as old as European civilization's: €, an adaptation of the Greek letter epsilon.

The new currency worked surprisingly well in its first several years, with no major economic downturns and low and steady inflation. But how many years of success had to pass before the "it can't last"–ers seemed just as wrong as the "it can't happen"–ers? Choosing a president had been contentious enough—what about fighting the aftereffects of a megacrisis?

*Les jeux sont faits, rien ne va plus.*

# SEVEN

# Masaru Hayami, Tomato Ketchup, and the Agony of ZIRP

Woodstock, Vermont, is a ridiculously charming New England town of three thousand people, and the Woodstock Inn a particularly quaint destination at its center. On two days in October 1999, however, the group that gathered there was interested in something other than antiques stores and fall foliage. Some of the world's highest-profile economists and central bankers descended on Woodstock that month to discuss "Monetary Policy in a Low Inflation Environment," a conference organized by the Federal Reserve Bank of Boston. Among them were a number of the top economic policymakers of Japan—and where they went, so did a surprisingly large contingent of the hypercompetitive Japanese press corps, buzzing around with television cameras and tape recorders.

Most industrialized nations were booming in the late 1990s. But Japan was the big exception. The world's second largest economy was experiencing the aftermath of a giant property bubble, mired in a cycle of zero growth and falling prices. In Woodstock, the message from American and British economists to the representatives of the Bank of Japan was: This is your fault. You can solve it. But to beat back deflation, you will need to be a lot bolder than you've been in the past. One of the speakers, Princeton professor Ben Bernanke, saw a particularly bewildering failure of policy.

"Extreme policy mistakes were the primary cause of the Great Depression," Bernanke said from the lectern at the Woodstock Inn. "And today in Japan one hears statements from policymakers that are eerily reminiscent of the 1930s. . . . There are strong reasons to believe that aggressive monetary expansion . . . could raise prices and stimulate recovery in Japan. But the downside of central bank independence is that, if for whatever reason the central bank seems determined not to take necessary policy measures, there is little that can be done, at least in the short run."

"Does the technical feasibility of preventing deflation imply that protracted deflation will never occur?" Bernanke asked, before giving his own answer. "No, because we cannot legislate against timidity or incompetence."

It is hard to overstate the extent to which, in the late 1980s, the economic juggernaut of Japan seemed to be taking over the world. Four decades removed from the end of World War II, the nation was growing faster than the United States or Europe. It was exporting the most advanced electronics and most reliable automobiles in the world. And it was buying land—lots and lots of land.

The things that got people's attention in the United States—and inspired some jingoistic outrage—were the high-profile acquisitions by Japanese investors on U.S. soil: Rockefeller Center in 1989, Pebble Beach golf course in 1990. But big deals abroad were nothing compared to what was happening in Japan's domestic real estate market, where the prices of office and apartment buildings in Tokyo and the other major cities were being bid up to unfathomable levels. It was calculated that the garden around the Imperial Palace in Tokyo, all 1.3 square miles of it, was worth as much as the entire state of California. The market value of the land in Chiyoda, a Tokyo district with thirty-nine thousand residents in 1990, was equal to that of all the land in Canada, home to twenty-eight million. Rents for residential space in Tokyo were four times higher than in New York City—and the price of residential land was a hundred times higher.

The run-up in prices was a classic case of credit-fueled mania, facilitated by some financial engineering, or *zaitech,* as its Japanese variant came to be called. The savings of an increasingly prosperous nation, one running trade surpluses with the rest of the world, was channeled into Japanese banks. Those banks, in turn, lent to anyone who planned to buy land, which served as collateral. After all, land prices had always gone up in modern Japan. It seemed reasonable to believe they would continue to do so. Loan officers would even show up unannounced at companies with which they had no prior business relationship and offer them money for real estate purchases premised on future appreciation.

People dreamed up theories of how the high land prices and extraordinary amount of bank lending made sense: Japan is an island, so its land is finite—yet its capacity for growth is apparently infinite. That analysis overlooked the fact that the appreciation was concentrated in six major cities, and that there remained huge undeveloped expanses of rural Japan that could accommodate further growth.

The Bank of Japan played an important, if poorly understood, role in the economic boom. In the years just after World War II, the Japanese central bank was remarkably powerful, not merely managing the supply of yen in the economy, but also actively making decisions on what major industrial companies could and couldn't invest in. Governor Hisato Ichimada, first appointed with the approval of U.S. occupiers in 1946, was so powerful that, a colleague once explained, "He was called Pope, because under him the central bank's power was stronger than that of the government." When Kawasaki asked for permission to build a steel plant, Ichimada answered, "Japan does not need any more steel," adding that "I can show you how to grow [the wild herb] shepherd's purse there."

In the years that followed, the BOJ became a more conventional central bank. In the late 1980s, as the speculative bubble was inflating, all that money the banks were pumping out was going to bid up the prices of assets like office buildings and shares of stock—not driving up the prices of rice or gasoline. With inflation well under control, the BOJ saw no need to tighten the money supply, and the boom continued unabated. By 1989, when things were getting truly out of control, the bank finally hiked interest rates, trying to prick the bubble. In hindsight, the action succeeded all too well.

The end of the Japanese bubble wasn't so much a pop as a fizzle. Soon, the very cycle that had led to ever-rising asset prices and bank lending was working in reverse: Prices for real estate and other assets fell, banks faced losses so they cut back on new lending, and economic growth ground to a halt. In the early 1990s, the Bank of Japan did what a central bank is supposed to do when the economy weakens: It cut interest rates, giving businesses more incentive to invest for the future and consumers more incentive to spend their money instead of save it. But it did so slowly, failing to understand the degree to which the national economy was in peril. It lowered its rate from 6 percent in 1991 to 0.5 percent in 1995. The Japanese economy seemed to improve a bit in 1996 before resuming its fall in 1997.

In a milder version of the deflation that paralyzed the world economy in the early 1930s, prices were stagnant to falling. That made the overhang of debt incurred in the boom years even more onerous, as the yen being used to repay loans were more valuable than those that had been originally lent out. Steady deflation even made the BOJ's low-interest-rate policies less effective at boosting growth, because it meant that "real," or inflation-adjusted, interest rates were higher than they would have been during a time of inflation.

On March 20, 1998, Masaru Hayami, a longtime corporate executive who had worked at the BOJ many years earlier, became the central bank's twenty-eighth governor. It was four days before his seventy-third birthday. He inherited a once booming economy that was mired in nearly a decade of economic stagnation and falling prices. The usual tool a central bank uses to guide the economy was already proving ineffective. What could Hayami-san do to try to fix the Japanese economy? And, more importantly, what *would* he do?

E conomists call it ZIRP: zero-interest-rate policy. The challenge that Hayami inherited—and which seemed at the time to be a uniquely Japanese phenomenon—was that the Bank of Japan had already cut rates to zero and the economy was still lousy. Cutting interest rates further isn't very plausible. A negative rate would mean, in effect, charging bank customers to keep their money in savings accounts, and would lead to people taking their money out of banks to avoid that charge.

As Japan started grappling with this problem in the late 1990s, some of the biggest minds in academic economics, both Eastern and Western, started coming up with possible solutions, arguing that the BOJ still had plenty of ability to boost economic activity—if it was courageous enough to act. They pointed out that because the institution had the unique and unlimited ability to create Japanese currency, there was no reason it had to allow the yen to become too dear. The BOJ, for example, could pledge to keep its low interest rates in place for many years to come, or until inflation finally returned to normal levels. If people viewed the promise as credible, the economy would pick up as businesses started charging higher prices in anticipation of higher inflation.

But talk is cheap, and the BOJ could, these economists argued, move more directly to increase the supply of money in the economy. The bank could create yen from thin air and use them to buy things—government bonds, shares of stock, office buildings. The existence of all those extra yen in the economy would create enough inflation to break the cycle of falling prices. In one story that made its way around the Bank of Japan and was repeated by economist Richard Koo, but which may be apocryphal, Bernanke visited Tokyo in the early 2000s as a Fed governor and argued that the BOJ could pump yen into the economy by buying *anything*—even tomato ketchup. Bernanke doesn't remember saying it, and John Taylor, who served as a top U.S. treasury official at the time and also visited the Bank of Japan, had used exactly that metaphor for years. In all likelihood, Taylor was the one who used it, and the BOJ rumor mill conflated the two American academics-turned-policymakers.

Even if Bernanke never used it, the ketchup line gets at one of the basic problems facing a central bank in a zero-interest-rate world: Although the bank has the unlimited ability to create money, getting that money circulating around in the economy isn't necessarily easy. When a bank raises or lowers interest rates, it changes the price of money in the economy, but it doesn't determine who gets money and who doesn't. It doesn't, in other words, favor the makers of ketchup over those who make mustard—or, for that matter, houses or clothing or automobiles. In theory, choosing winners and losers in the economy is a job for democratically elected officials—for fiscal policy, not monetary policy. Modern societies have generally accepted that it's a good idea to have unelected economists turning the dials of the money supply. If they start deciding not just the amount of money created but also what it's used to buy, however, they've gone an undemocratic step too far.

In a time of ZIRP, a central bank needs some help from fiscal authorities to spread its newly created money through the economy. Getting it can mean violating the independence from politics that modern central banks hold dear. Bernanke acknowledged this reality in a 2002 speech about Japan's troubles: A central bank, he said, could buy government bonds, and fiscal authorities could then use that money to temporarily cut taxes. It would be a "helicopter drop" of money on an ailing economy.

Later, when critics nicknamed him "Helicopter Ben," Bernanke surely regretted invoking that particular metaphor.

Masaru Hayami spent his adult life witnessing a Japan ascendant. Born in 1925, he spent the middle decades of the twentieth century rising through the ranks of the Bank of Japan. Although he held only an undergraduate degree, he worked on the international staff, representing the bank in Basel and in other overseas forums. He was a devout Christian, unusual in a predominantly Shinto and Buddhist nation, and peppered his public comments with references to Bible verses. He also had, people who knew him said, a deeply felt sense that a strong currency was equivalent to a strong nation. "In the first half of the postwar period, he attended many negotiations with Western countries when the yen was very weak," said Kazuo Ueda, a BOJ policymaker from 1998 to 2005 and now a University of Tokyo professor. "Probably he thought the weakness of currencies is painful. . . . Over time the economy developed, the yen became stronger, and maybe he saw some causal relationship between the two." That made him reluctant, as governor of the Bank of Japan, to do anything that would push the value of the yen down sharply—even if that's exactly what economic theory suggests the nation needed to get its economy back on track.

Besides, he saw many other problems that needed repair before the country could return to long-term prosperity: a banking system that was slow to write down bad loans and recapitalize, networks of industrial companies that protected each other from the brutality of global competition, a political system that wasn't capable of making hard decisions. He seemed skeptical of the theories that academics, both inside the BOJ and from the West, offered as answers to the nation's problems. According to some who were in policy meetings with him, he didn't always understand other economists' technical arguments.

In late 1998, the interest rate that investors demanded to lend the government money rose sharply, from 0.7 percent to 2 percent for ten-year Japanese government bonds. Politicians pressured the BOJ to intervene in the bond market by buying securities in order to push rates downward. But Hayami viewed such an action as a grave threat to independence, comparing it to when the bank printed money to fund the government's military buildup in the 1930s and '40s, resulting in a period of high inflation. "Purchasing Japanese government bonds can't be an option," Hayami told the parliament. "It would be detrimental to fiscal discipline and generate vicious inflation."

Hayami, however, was willing to make more conventional interest rate cuts and use the power of communication. In February 1999, the Bank of Japan went all in on ZIRP, cutting its target short-term interest rate from 0.25 percent to 0.15 percent. (It had been 0.5 percent when Hayami took office the previous year.) The governor pledged that ultralow rates would stay in place "until there are prospects for an end to deflationary fears," which would seem to imply a fairly long time. Yet the cut held for little over a year.

"To this outsider," Bernanke said in January 2000, "Japanese monetary policy seems paralyzed, with a paralysis that is largely self-induced. Most striking is the unwillingness of the monetary authorities to experiment, to try anything that isn't absolutely guaranteed to work."

Indeed, Hayami was eager for any excuse to get away from a low-interest-rate policy—and began backing away from the policy in the early months of 2000, when the Japanese economy did seem to be gaining some ground. "We are getting closer to the stage where we can say deflationary concerns have been wiped away," Hayami said in a May 2000 news conference that essentially reneged the earlier promise of a long period of low rates. The policy was formally abandoned in August as the bank hiked rates back up to 0.25 percent and then to 0.5 percent.

When the Japanese economy slumped again, Hayami's BOJ took a different step: quantitative easing. "The BOJ had to do something to ease, but the governor did not want to do exactly the same thing, because it would be clear that he had made a mistake," said Ueda. So in addition to cutting rates back to zero, the bank began buying bonds to increase the amount of money in the economy, aiming for the Japanese banking system to increase the number of yen on its books from four to five trillion, a rise then equivalent to about $8 billion.

"The decision to end the zero-interest-rate policy was not wrong," Hayami said in a press conference announcing the change in March 2001. Driven by the governor's desire to save face, the action was something that no modern independent central bank had undertaken before. Almost against his will, Masaru Hayami had pioneered a very unusual type of monetary policy—one that Helicopter Ben and the Federal Reserve would adopt a decade later to fight the megacrisis.

"It was a very difficult decision to make," Hayami told reporters in 2003. "It was the first time that this had been done. I was very unsure and even felt fear. At times like those, I would remember . . . that God is always with me, that Jesus loves me and that He sees and knows all."

Central bankers are a conservative bunch. The awesome responsibility that society grants them comes with a demand for certain traits: seriousness, sobriety, caution. No head of state would entrust control over an entire economy to someone inclined toward frivolity and risk-taking. Most of the time, that's just fine. We want central banks to be led by people who are boring. The idea of "first, do no harm" is a powerful one, and a central banker who was too quick to experiment could do a great deal of harm to his economy.

But it is precisely when an economy needs the most help from a central bank that the job demands what seem like radical departures from orthodoxy. The very qualities that lead to a person's being selected to help lead a central bank make him reluctant to engage in the bold experimentation that might help get an economy out of a deep rut.

For all its excessive caution, the Bank of Japan did eventually cut rates to zero, pledge to keep them there, and purchase a variety of assets with newly created yen—and even those efforts weren't enough to "fix" the economy. A generation of Japanese has seen diminished prospects; if economic output per person had risen at the same pace from 1991 to 2011 in Japan as it did in the United States, the average Japanese person would have an extra $9,500 a year in income.

Monetary policy is indeed powerful—but it's not all-powerful. As Princeton economist Alan Blinder put it in the closing session on that fall day in 1999 at the Woodstock Inn, "Does an economy with a zero nominal interest rate follow more or less the same economic laws as it does in normal times—except that one variable is stuck at zero? Or is the situation more akin to physics at zero gravity, or near absolute zero temperature, where behavior is fundamentally different, even strange? I think the conclusion we seem to be reaching here at Woodstock is that it may indeed be a new world."

Ueda, representing the Bank of Japan, closed the event with a pledge—and a warning that would prove all too prescient once the Federal Reserve, the Bank of England, and the European Central Bank had joined their Asian counterpart in the strange new world of ZIRP.

"I promise," he said, "to bring all the interesting ideas I have heard in this conference to the attention of my colleagues in Tokyo. Meanwhile, I must say that one of the most important messages of the conference has been: Do not put yourself into the position of zero rates. I tell you it will be a lot more painful than you can possibly imagine."

EIGHT

# The Jackson Hole Consensus
# and the Great Moderation

For the world's central bankers, the gathering at Wyoming's Jackson Lake Lodge in August 2005 was a moment of triumph. After centuries in which their predecessors had frequently failed to guide the nations of the world through boom and bust, inflation and deflation, they had finally, it seemed, learned all the important lessons of how to manage an economy. The 110 central bankers and other economists convened in the Explorers Room seemed to have all the answers, and they had created a more stable and prosperous world than any known before.

One scholar after another took to the lectern in that Friday morning, standing beneath elk-antler chandeliers to pay tribute to the great man. Alan Greenspan, slightly hunched and with big glasses, a hangdog face, and a smile as enigmatic as that of the *Mona Lisa,* was soon to step down as the chairman of the Federal Reserve, the central bank that decided the fate of the then $12.6 trillion U.S. economy, the largest in the world. Colleagues from nations large and small in every corner of the globe had come together to see Greenspan off into retirement properly and consider his legacy. The official name of the event was the Federal Reserve Bank of Kansas City Economic Policy Symposium. But it's known across the world of finance simply as Jackson Hole, for the ancient glacial basin where the gathering takes place each summer. If Basel is where central bankers come together to discuss the latest economic developments among themselves, Jackson Hole is where they address bigger, longer-range issues, surrounded by both the broader community of economic thinkers and spectacular scenery.

Taking the stage, Allan Meltzer, the leading historian of the Federal Reserve, asserted without reservation that Greenspan held "the top rank" among the many men who'd run the central bank in its ninety-two-year history. Bank of England governor Mervyn King said that Greenspan's "departure from the central-banking scene will deprive us of a source of wisdom, inspiration, and leadership." Two other colleagues, while acknowledging "some negatives" in Greenspan's record, wrote that "when the score is toted up, we think he has a legitimate claim to being the greatest central banker who ever lived"—praise that seems all the more generous when one considers that the lead author of that paper was Princeton's Alan Blinder, who had resigned as Greenspan's vice chairman after a brief and unhappy experience a decade earlier.

If anything, people outside that room had been even more effusive in their praise. Bob Woodward titled his 2000 book about Greenspan *Maestro*. The year before, *Time* magazine had put Greenspan on its cover as a member, with Bob Rubin and Larry Summers of Bill Clinton's Treasury Department, of "the Committee to Save the World." He was named a commander of the French Legion of Honor and granted an honorary British knighthood. ("It's a very unusual day for an economist," Greenspan said after Queen Elizabeth II knighted him at her Balmoral estate in Scotland.)

It was the high point of what had already been dubbed the Great Moderation—a moderation, that is, of the various forces that had whipsawed national economies in centuries past: boom and bust, inflation and deflation, financial panic and its attendant destruction of wealth. The U.S. economy had been expanding for a quarter century, interrupted by only two brief and shallow recessions. The unemployment rate averaged 5.5 percent during Greenspan's nineteen years in office, compared with 6.4 percent in the preceding two decades, and inflation was held in check. The great powers of continental Europe, after a century in which they regularly met each other on the battlefield, had become so intertwined economically that they were sharing a currency. The British economy was in a veritable boom, with London prospering as a global banking hub and threatening to reclaim from New York the title of world financial capital. China and other developing nations were growing rapidly, pulling hundreds of millions of people out of dire poverty into the global middle class, in no small part by absorbing the lessons of free markets and their sound management taught by the West's leading economic thinkers.

The men and women in the Explorers Room had a sense of common purpose, believing that they were guiding the entire world toward an ever more prosperous future—and doing quite a good job of it, thank you very much. They had learned from the mistakes of their predecessors and had the knowledge, the tools, and the will to keep even the nastiest of economic events from leading to widespread human misery. During Greenspan's time as Fed chair, there had been two recessions, and the Great Moderation also included two stock market crashes in the United States, a long economic stagnation in Japan, and financial crises in Mexico, Russia, and Argentina. But none of these became a global calamity.

In Jackson Hole in 2005, it seemed as if the world's economic problems had been more or less solved.

The Federal Reserve Bank in Kansas City, Missouri, one of the twelve regional outposts of the U.S. central bank, in 1978 began hosting an annual conference for scholars to gather and present their research. It was a low-profile affair at first, rotating among various cities and focusing on matters close to the hearts of those living in the Rocky Mountain region the bank served. "Western Water Resources: Coming Problems and the Policy Alternatives" and "Future Sources of Loanable Funds for Agricultural Banks" were two early topics. No one attending the first few conferences would have confused them with events of global significance.

Roger Guffey, the Kansas City Fed president, and Tom Davis, its head of research, wanted to change that, to make the conference something special among economic policymakers. The first step was to shift the discussion from local concerns such as water and agriculture to broad issues of monetary policy. The next was to attract a top-tier crowd—which meant securing the attendance of Federal Reserve chairman Paul Volcker. Volcker was known to be a devotee of fly fishing, and Guffey and Davis surmised that if they could hold the event at a time and place with good opportunities to fish for trout, Volcker would come— and where Volcker went, the great economists and policymakers of the day would follow.

Davis called up a contact in Colorado, where the event had been held in the recent past.

We need a place for our symposium where people can fish for trout, he said.

"What time of year are you going to hold it?" the contact asked, Davis later recalled. August was the answer.

"Well, if you're going to hold it in August, you can't fish for trout in Colorado because it's too warm . . . Can you go to Wyoming?"

As we've seen, Volcker was under intense criticism for his high-interest-rate policies back in the muggy former swampland of Washington; the neighborhood where the Fed's offices are located is called Foggy Bottom for a reason. Debt-loaded farmers surrounded Federal Reserve headquarters with tractors. Texas representative Henry B. Gonzalez even called for the chairman's impeachment. Guffey and Davis's 1982 invitation to fish and talk shop somewhere far away from the office couldn't have been better timed.

Volcker quickly became a regular in the crisp mountain air of Jackson Hole, one year staying out so long fishing that he showed up for the formal opening dinner still wearing his angling gear. Soon many of the world's other central bankers started making the voyage to the tiny airstrip hard by the Rockies every August as well. Today, most tourists roaming the Jackson Lake Lodge's RV-studded parking lot seem unaware that the people milling around near the lobby's stuffed grizzly bear are among the world's top economists and most powerful policymakers. They are invariably more impressed by the CNBC camera crew set up outside and the intense-looking, earpiece-wearing security guards than the central bankers themselves.

The 110 attendees, including a handful of journalists, are chosen by the Kansas City Fed president, with the guest list constrained by the size of the Jackson Lake Lodge's fur-trapper-modernist ballroom. This is surely the only conference of its type to which a Nobel laureate such as Berkeley economist George Akerlof would find himself invited only as the spouse of San Francisco Fed president Janet Yellen, not on his own account. Inevitably, small talk at the kickoff dinner devolves to analyzing who is and isn't in attendance that year. *New York Times* columnist Paul Krugman, himself a Nobel laureate and once a regular attendee, concluded that he was blackballed from the conference for criticizing Greenspan too harshly.

By 2005, Jackson Hole had its own traditions and even folklore. Don Kohn, who was a Greenspan adviser and vice chairman of the Fed until 2010, leads a Friday afternoon hike known as the Don Kohn Death March for its strenuousness; economists who are happy to chatter about monetary policy transmission mechanisms during the first mile tend to be too winded to do so by the last. The European attendees grumble about the American-style coffee, and one year—no one can quite remember which—European Central Bank president Jean-Claude Trichet gave from the podium a politically incorrect explanation of why the French trappers who first came across the nearby mountains called them "les Grand Tetons." Then there's the old saw, repeated with many permutations, about the central banker who entered the lodge's gift shop and asked for a copy of the *New York Times*. "Do you want today's or yesterday's?" the possibly apocryphal clerk is said to have asked. "Today's," replied the perplexed banker. "Then come back tomorrow."

In the formal sessions, a series of economists stand and present academic papers on which the rest of the participants then comment, sometimes scathingly. The major economic journals may be considered more desirable venues for works of high-grade macroeconomic theory, but Jackson Hole is where papers on the practical questions of how to manage a modern economy are delivered and discussed. Here the focus is on the concrete decisions facing policymakers. Were interest rates kept too low in major industrial economies in the early years of the 2000s? At Jackson Hole, two top academic economists, John Taylor of Stanford and Alan Blinder of Princeton, might offer contrasting views, both in response to a paper by Charles Bean, the number two official at the Bank of England charged with actually making interest rate decisions for a nation of sixty-two million people.

But the informal sessions might be a greater attraction for many central bankers, some of whom travel from the other side of the earth to attend. Besides fishing trips and hikes, there are between-session coffee breaks, western-style buffet meals on Friday and Saturday nights, and, for a persistent few, late-night talks at the Blue Heron Lounge over a bottle of Snake River Pale Ale or glasses of whiskey. A few smoke cigars.

It was over these cigars and meals and coffees and hikes that the "Jackson Hole Consensus" was formed. Harvard economist Martin Feldstein coined the term, and Bean had a go at codifying the concept in a paper presented at the conference in 2010, referring to the mutually agreed-upon "ingredients of a successful policy framework" for central banking. But the Jackson Hole Consensus was more than just the collective wisdom of the world's leading central bankers; it was viewed as almost a recipe for how to keep the Great Moderation going. Among the ingredients:

- Monetary policy is the best means of economic stabilization. The messy realities of politics mean that fiscal policy—taxing and spending— isn't a very good tool for dealing with the routine ups and downs of the economy. Let central bankers handle those by adjusting how much money to push into or suck out of the banking system.

- Central bankers are at their best when insulated from politics. Let us make our own decisions about what is best in the long term, without you politicians hassling us.

- Stable prices are the goal. The best thing we central bankers can do for an economy is make sure that prices change gradually and predictably over time.

- Markets work. The prices of assets—tech stocks, say, or houses in Florida—are determined in markets that are pretty darn efficient. Sure, there might be the occasional bout of irrational exuberance, but it's better for us to clean up the mess afterward than to try to deal with those bubbles proactively.

- Financial crises are history. An advanced nation, with skilled central bankers and modern financial markets, could never have the kind of catastrophic financial crisis that drags down an entire economy for a generation. We know too much about how to prevent it.

These ideas weren't outlandish given what the world was experiencing. Consider the events in the United States just a few years before. The stock market had ascended to too-good-to-be-true heights throughout the late 1990s, rising more than 20 percent each year from 1995 to 1999. Investors had convinced themselves of the emergence of a "New Economy" promising both perpetual prosperity and astonishing returns on even the most ill-planned ventures that happened to have ".com" in their names. Just as that bubble was bursting and reality was setting in, in September 2001 the United States suffered a devastat-

ing terrorist attack that created a wave of fear and panic across the land, insti-
gated years of war, and even destroyed some of the physical infrastructure of
the U.S. financial system by rendering much of lower Manhattan inaccessible.

And amid all that, what happened? The Federal Reserve began lowering
its target for short-term interest rates in January 2001, just as the stock market
decline began to pinch the broader economy, and it cut rates eleven times that
year—once just six days after the September 11 attacks—so the tumbling stock
market was counteracted by cheaper money, which created greater financial incentive for consumers to buy cars and houses and for businesses to borrow
money to buy new equipment. The morning of the attacks, the Fed—Greenspan
was in transit back from Basel, so Vice Chairman Roger Ferguson was in
charge—issued a statement: "The Federal Reserve System is open and operating. The discount window is available to meet liquidity needs." Translation: The
Fed is ready and willing to flood the banking system with dollars to avoid a situation in which Americans show up at their ATMs to withdraw cash but can't
because their bank is out of money. Within a few days, the Fed was swapping
dollars with the European Central Bank, the Bank of England, and the Bank of
Canada to try to prevent the global banking system from shutting down.

There was a postboom recession in 2001, all right. But the interventions
by the Greenspan Fed were so successful at arresting the economy's decline that
it was the mildest recession of the modern era. By the time the world's central
bankers gathered to honor Greenspan in Jackson Hole, the unemployment rate
was back down to 4.9 percent, lower than it had been during even a single
month in the 1980s.

Yet for all the global prosperity that the Jackson Hole Consensus had
brought by that August, there were already hints that something was off. In the
United States, home prices were reaching untold new highs. By 2006, the average U.S. home cost 5.2 times as much as the median American income. From
1985 to 2000, it'd cost only about three times as much. The increase was even
more dramatic in certain parts of the nation, particularly Sun Belt cities like
Miami, Phoenix, and Las Vegas, where the real estate market bore more than a
few resemblances to the Internet stock boom of a few years earlier. "South Florida is working off a totally new economic model than any of us have ever experienced in the past," a Miami real estate broker told the *New York Times* in 2005.

Lenders made their terms easier, competing for business by offering a proliferation of home loans that bankers never would have considered in a different era: zero-money-down loans, in which a person could buy a house without putting up any cash; stated-income loans—or, as they quickly became known, "liar loans"—in which people declared how much money they made rather than proving it; negative-amortization loans, in which the payments the consumer made each month weren't even enough to cover the interest due, meaning the amount they owed rose over time rather than fell. It was a new era in which speculation in real estate seemed like a riskless path to fantastic wealth.

The United States wasn't the only place where housing prices were climbing to heretofore unknown levels. On the sunny Mediterranean coast of Spain, retirees from Britain and Germany were buying up houses so fiercely that prices rose 145 percent from 1997 to 2005. In Britain, a nation in the midst of the best fifteen years of economic growth in a century, home prices increased 154 percent during the same period. In Ireland, thanks to a favorable business climate and rapid job creation, prices rose 192 percent. Across the planet, people were rapidly concluding that four walls and a roof were more valuable relative to earnings than they had ever been before. The *Economist* tallied the value of all housing in the developed world as having risen to $70 trillion in 2005, from $30 trillion just five years earlier.

But the run-up in home prices was an effect, rather than a cause, of some fundamental problems in the world economy. And indeed, the nations where home prices soared were the same ones where household debt levels also rose to previously unknown levels. In 1980, total American household debt—mortgages, credit cards, auto loans, and everything else—amounted to 52 percent of economic output. By 2005, Americans had run up enough debt to put that number at 97 percent, meaning it would take just about one year of the nation's entire economic production to pay it off.

Over that quarter century, and particularly from 2000 to 2005, the ability to borrow money easily became a salve for all manner of economic hurts. Jobs may have been scarce at times—both the 1991 and 2001 recessions were followed by slow, "jobless" recoveries—but consumers were able to keep buying things because they could always put them on a credit card or take out a second mortgage when times were tough. The result: Americans in 2005 had $41,000 in household debt for every man, woman, and child in the country, up from

$6,400 in 1980. If debt levels had grown only as fast as the overall economy, consumers would have owed less than half as much.

The details were different in other countries where home prices rose, but the basic trend wasn't: In Spain, for example, mortgage debt rose at an average rate of 20 percent a year from 2000 to 2004, a period in which home prices rose 16 percent a year. It's almost impossible for real estate prices to go through that kind of rapid price increase without borrowed money making it possible, which raises a question: Just who was doing all that lending—and *why*? To answer that, you have to go back a little bit.

I n the late 1990s, a string of emerging nations experienced deep financial crises. Investors lost confidence in what had been rapidly growing economies in, among other nations, Thailand, Indonesia, and South Korea and pulled their money out. The countries' currencies and stock markets collapsed, and millions found themselves newly unemployed. Governments around the world—not just the ones directly affected by that crisis—took a lesson away from the experience: What global investors give—an influx of investment dollars—they can also take away. And they'll probably take it away at the worst possible time.

If you're a head of state in a fast-growing economy, that tells you one big thing: You'd better have a lot of savings in the bank. You need reserves large enough to allow your country to weather a withdrawal by speculators. So you'd better buy some of the safest investments on earth. If you're an extremely wealthy individual in the developing world—a manufacturing company owner in China, say, or an oil potentate in the Middle East or a well-connected businessman in a former Soviet republic—your thinking is much the same. Why worry about the risk that your government could fall, or that you could lose favor or otherwise lose the great privilege to which you've become accustomed?

The best way to protect against those hazards would be to own a bunch of ultrasafe investments in a country that's politically stable. For various other idiosyncratic reasons, some cultural, some legal, even people in many advanced countries were similarly eager for safe investments during the early 2000s. Germany, with its saving-oriented populace, had so much money filling its banks that they had to find other places to put their money. With the baby boomers in the world's advanced economies in their peak earning years, pension funds were desperate for places to park cash, too.

In 2005, Ben Bernanke, then a Federal Reserve governor, called all of this extra cash the "global savings glut." Because there was so much of it, there were more people looking for safe, secure places to put money than there were safe, secure places to put it. Capitalism is a powerful force for creating that which is in demand—even something as intangible and elusive as a safe investment. To try to meet the demand for reliable places to park cash—and to make a great deal of money for itself along the way—the finance industry more or less conjured them out of thin air.

Any one mortgage can be quite risky as an investment. The borrower might lose his or her job and be unable to repay it, or prices in the home's neighborhood might go down instead of up. But if you put a whole bunch of mortgages together into a single pool that people can buy or sell in financial markets, you get rid of some of that risk. And to turn all those risky mortgages into an ultrasafe investment, you can create tiers: Instead of just one bundled-mortgage bond, there can be several.

At the bottom is a security for people who want to take on some risk and get a greater return. The first time somebody doesn't pay back his or her mortgage, those investors lose money—that's the price they pay for getting a higher return on their investment. At the top is a security for more cautious investors, people who don't give up a dime until the losses hit, say, 40 percent of what was loaned out. Those investors get paid a much lower return for their investment. But they also have almost no risk of losing their money. After all, what are the odds that so many people will be unable to repay their mortgages? Or that housing prices will have fallen so far that 40 percent of what was loaned out is lost? Low, indeed—or at least it seemed so.

As if by magic, the financial industry transformed all those risky loans to individual borrowers into that which global investors most coveted—a supersafe investment the firms that rate the safety of bonds would call AAA. The basic idea had been around since the 1980s, but it took off in a previously unseen way in the 2000s. In the United States alone, $901 billion of these privately issued mortgage-backed securities were issued in 2005, up from $36 billion a decade earlier.

And the trick wasn't just applied to mortgages; the big financial firms did the same thing with almost any type of loan you could imagine: credit cards, student loans, corporate loans. In the United States, there were $8.1 trillion worth of such securities in existence in 2005, up from $2.6 trillion in 2000. When that number peaked, in 2007, it had reached almost $11 trillion. Each one of those eleven trillion dollars was simultaneously an asset to one party (perhaps a German bank, or South Korea's government investment fund, or a wealthy Indian) and a debt of someone else (perhaps a family in Florida who bought the three-bedroom house with a pool that they'd long dreamed of using borrowed money, or a family in Kansas who paid for a trip to Disneyland with their credit card, or a real estate developer in New York who bought an office tower at an unprecedentedly high price).

The idea that one man's debt is another's savings is nothing new. Banks have been the intermediary in that exchange for centuries. But in the old days, a banker could look a borrower up and down, study his financial standing, and make the loan knowing that if the borrower didn't repay, it was the banker's problem. In this new era, the people with direct contact with borrowers were separated from the lenders by a chasm. The mortgage brokers who proliferated in storefronts all over the country were mere suppliers for the Wall Street bundlers. The brokers knew that some of these were terrible loans, but the big Wall Street firms had such a hunger for the fees they could earn by assembling packages and creating new securities to sell all over the world that they had little interest in knowing too much about what they were getting. The global investors buying the securities did so without necessarily understanding all the gory details of who the borrowers were and what their capacity to repay might be. The gold seal of an AAA rating was enough.

The giant banks were the great intermediaries that made possible an apparent explosion of wealth. There were, by 2007, $202 trillion in financial assets on earth, 3.6 times the annual economic output of everyone on the planet; in 1990, the ratio was 2.6. That represents an extra $42 trillion in paper wealth over what would have existed had the ratio stayed constant. Global megabanks, hedge funds, insurance companies, and countless other financial firms were links in the chain that connected borrowers taking on ever larger amounts of debt with the global savings glut. And in Jackson Hole in 2005, almost no one seemed to understand just how weak that link was.

But what *did* they understand? What did central bankers know about what was out of whack in the world economy? And when did they know it?

On both sides of the Atlantic, central bankers had been fretting about the run-up in housing prices, even if they weren't quite sure what to do about it. Without solid answers, they resorted to just trying to describe, with gentle euphemism, what was occurring in the property markets. There were "elements of buoyancy" in Spanish and Irish housing markets, as Jean-Claude Trichet put it in May 2007. Greenspan had conceded two years earlier not that a bubble was building, but that there was "froth"—a number of small bubbles in certain markets. "It's pretty clear there is an unsustainable underlying pattern," he told the Economic Club of New York. Three weeks before the 2005 Jackson Hole conference, Mervyn King was sufficiently worried about a British housing bubble that he tried to raise interest rates in order to slow down the housing market. Unusually for a central-bank governor, he was outvoted by Britain's interest-rate-setting committee. The joke that went around London financial circles was that as a fan of the perpetually mediocre Aston Villa football club, King felt comfortable losing.

The debate that went on behind closed doors at the Federal Reserve in 2005 reveals how challenging it was for the central bankers to convert their sense that something was wrong in housing into concrete policy. When the Fed's Federal Open Market Committee met privately around the grand mahogany table overlooking Constitution Avenue in Washington to set interest rate policy for the United States, those concerns were sometimes aired—but rarely with a sense of urgency about finding policies that might alleviate them.

"Hardly a day goes by without another anecdote-laden article in the press claiming that the U.S. is experiencing a housing bubble that will soon burst, with disastrous consequences for the economy," said a dismissive Richard Peach, an economist at the Federal Reserve Bank of New York, in a confidential presentation to the FOMC on June 29, 2005. The rapid gains in the housing market, he said, "could be the result of solid fundamentals underlying the housing market": low interest rates, strong productivity, peak earning of the baby boom generation, and rising incomes, particularly among the affluent.

The same day, the committee heard a presentation on how a housing decline might affect the financial system. "Neither borrowers nor lenders appear particularly shaky," economist Andreas Lehnert told Fed leaders as he gave an analysis of exposure to risky mortgage lending by U.S. banks and other institutions. "Perhaps it would be best simply to venture the judgment that the national mortgage system might bend, but will likely not break, in the face of a large drop in house prices."

Fed policymakers were attuned to the possibility that housing prices could decline, perhaps sharply. But they failed to understand just how deeply intertwined housing had become with the financial system, or how vulnerable the system was to a shock. "In the event of a sharp drop in housing prices, the odds of a spillover to financial institutions seem limited," said Michael Moskow, the president of the Chicago Fed.

In the hundreds of pages of transcripts from Fed policy meetings in 2005—not made public until years later—there are occasional glimpses of officials understanding the problems that were emerging. They almost seemed onto something when Mark Olson, a Fed governor, said he had heard that lending was being funded more by the private pools of mortgages being ginned up by Wall Street than by the more traditional mortgages backed by the government-sponsored Fannie Mae and Freddie Mac.

"Not in the United States. I don't know what country or planet," said Lehnert.

Olson cut him off.

"The planet was Earth. The country was the United States," he retorted. "And the person making the observation was talking about . . . what they see as a growing and undisciplined secondary market."

They quickly figured out that Olson was talking about the flow of new debt being issued, while Lehnert was thinking of the total amount outstanding. That miscommunication cleared up, the subject was immediately dropped.

What the Fed lacked in this and other discussions about risks to the economy wasn't technical expertise. It had that in spades. It wasn't attention or discipline either. The discussions were exhaustive, involving a group of very smart people trying earnestly to come to the right answer. What the Fed lacked was creativity, the ability to see how housing and finance could interact with one another and cause greater damage than either could independently—particularly how the rapid increase in housing prices could threaten the financial system worldwide. In eight closed-door meetings over the course of that year— the transcripts take up nearly eleven hundred pages—there wasn't a single mention of some of the developments in the financial system that could allow the popping of the housing bubble to turn into a global crisis: the excessive use of borrowed money by investment banks, for example, and the deep insinuation of mortgage-related securities of questionable safety into the machinery of modern finance.

In the Fed's 2005 meetings, the moment of most brutal clarity about the situation the U.S. economy faced wasn't in any of the technical discussions of home price indices or the evolution of securitization markets. It was in a wry aside, made by Director of Research David Stockton. Stockton noted that a number of indicators suggested the housing boom could be ending. He continued:

> I offer one more piece of evidence that I think almost surely suggests that the end is near in this sector. While channel surfing the other night, to the annoyance of my otherwise very patient wife, I came across a new television series on the Discovery Channel entitled "Flip That House." As far as I could tell, the gist of the show was that with some spackling, a few strategically placed azaleas, and access to a bank, you too could tap into the great real estate wealth machine. It was enough to put even the most ardent believer in market efficiency into existential crisis.

In other words, the underlying causes of the global financial crisis were hiding in plain sight. Plenty of central bankers fretted about a global housing bubble. A smaller number worried about a global debt bubble—not just in mortgages, but also in consumer and corporate debt. A smaller number still saw a vast and rapid expansion of the financial sector as something that could threaten worldwide financial stability. And you had fundamental imbalances in the global economy that were at the root of it all—which central bankers were well aware of but undecided about how to correct. They just didn't see how all these pieces fit together.

Ironically, part of the problem was the very success of central bankers. Investors had learned a lesson from the Great Moderation: that central bankers had mastered the economy. Inflation, in all the advanced nations and a growing number of emerging ones, had been conquered. Central banks could contain the impact of any adverse event that might come along, whether a financial crisis in fast-growing Asian economies or a popped stock market bubble in the United States, and prevent any widespread losses. In a seemingly riskless world, investors were willing to take all the more risk.

Greenspan, who held more power over the financial future than any other individual on the planet, understood these interconnections, if not the degree to which the world economy was in peril. Lower risk premia—the compensation investors demand for taking on extra risk—that were "the apparent consequence of a long period of economic stability" had helped to push asset prices higher, he said from the lectern at Jackson Hole. The rising prices of stocks, bonds, and homes had led to much greater wealth and purchasing power, and the vast increase in the value of those assets was, Greenspan said, "in part the indirect result of investors accepting lower compensation for risk."

"History," he noted, "has not dealt kindly with the aftermath of protracted periods of low-risk premiums."

B ut one of the other economists at Jackson Hole that year was more prescient than even Greenspan—or, indeed, anyone else who speculated about what the world had to fear at that moment of economic triumphalism.

In hindsight, many have pointed to a paper that International Monetary Fund chief economist Raghuram Rajan presented as a rare moment of clarity at the 2005 conference. Rajan indeed had an astute understanding of the ways in which the financial industry, with misguided compensation policies that encouraged risk-taking, was making the world a more dangerous place: Bankers were paid big bonuses for making money in the short run even if they were betting poorly in the long run. But he identified only one portion of what could go horribly wrong.

It was Hyun Song Shin, then a professor at the London School of Economics, who in a response to Rajan's paper most accurately portrayed the state of the global economy.

"I'd like to tell you about the Millennium Bridge in London," he began. In order to celebrate the advent of the year 2000, the British built a stunning new pedestrian bridge across the Thames. Its lateral-suspension design precluded the need for clunky-looking columns, making it a study in engineering elegance.

"The bridge was opened by the queen on a sunny day in June," Shin continued. "The press was there in force, and many thousands of people turned up to savor the occasion. However, within moments of the bridge's opening, it began to shake violently." The day it opened, the Millennium Bridge was closed. The engineers were initially mystified about what had gone wrong. Of course it would be a problem if a platoon of soldiers marched in lockstep across the bridge, creating sufficiently powerful vertical vibration to produce a swaying effect. The nearby Albert Bridge, built more than a century earlier, even features a sign directing marching soldiers to break step rather than stay together when crossing. But that's not what happened at the Millennium Bridge. "What is the probability that a thousand people walking at random will end up walking exactly in step, and remain in lockstep thereafter?" Shin asked. "It is tempting to say, 'Close to zero.'"

But that's exactly what happened. The bridge's designers had failed to account for how people react to their environment. When the bridge moved slightly under the feet of those opening-day pedestrians, each individual naturally adjusted his or her stance for balance, just a little bit—but at the same time and in the same direction as every other individual. That created enough lateral force to turn a slight movement into a significant one. "In other words," said Shin, "the wobble of the bridge feeds on itself. The wobble will continue and get stronger even though the initial shock—say, a small gust of wind—had long passed. . . . Stress testing on the computer that looks only at storms, earthquakes, and heavy loads on the bridge would regard the events on the opening day as a 'perfect storm.' But this is a perfect storm that is guaranteed to come every day."

In financial markets, as on the Millennium Bridge, each individual player—every bank and hedge fund and individual investor—reacts to what is happening around him or her in concert with other individuals. When the ground shifts under the world's investors, they all shift their stance. And when they all shift their stance in the same direction at the same time, it just reinforces the initial movement. Suddenly, the whole system is wobbling violently.

Ben Bernanke, Mervyn King, Jean-Claude Trichet, and the other men and women at Jackson Hole listened politely and then went to their coffee break. It would be two more years before the bridge started to wobble, and three more before it came falling down.

# Part II

PANIC,
2007–2008

NINE

# The Committee of Three

T

wo years after Alan Greenspan's grand send-off in Jackson Hole, the question for the conference was whether his successor could make the trip at all. Markets were in chaos in August 2007, and the symposium was to take place just three weeks after the European Central Bank's surprising intervention during the BNP Paribas crisis. Ben Bernanke's closest advisers debated whether they could jet off to the wilds of Wyoming with the markets so on edge. Cell phone coverage had arrived at the Jackson Lake Lodge only a few years earlier, and Internet connectivity was still iffy. If another wave of panic broke out, would they be able to gather the information they needed and act decisively?

But if they canceled their usual appearances, markets could become even more jittery: *If they can't even go to Jackson Hole, this thing must be even worse than we thought.* So Fed information-technology and -security staffers from Washington were dispatched to Jackson. Across the hall from Bernanke's second-floor room at the lodge, away from the main event spaces, they set up a conference room with secure phone lines, Internet connections, and Bloomberg financial-data terminals so Fed officials—and their international counterparts, if it came to that—could do their jobs from a distance.

Bernanke and his inner circle—New York Fed president Tim Geithner, Board of Governors vice chairman Donald Kohn and member Kevin Warsh, Fed monetary affairs director Brian Madigan—spent much of the two days of proceedings in their secure conference room on the second floor, plotting their response to the emerging panic.

It was too bad: The topic of that year's conference was housing finance, and some of the presentations were quite prescient. Robert Shiller of Yale, for example, warned that the long housing boom was soon likely to go bust, with severe economic consequences. "It does not appear possible to explain the boom in terms of fundamentals such as rents or construction costs," he argued. "A psychological theory, that represents the boom as taking place because of a feedback mechanism or social epidemic that encourages a view of housing as an important investment opportunity, fits the evidence better."

Still, the discussion was overwhelmingly focused on the United States, with no real recognition of just how deeply all those bad U.S. home loans had become embedded in the world's financial infrastructure, from European banks to giant insurer AIG. There was little sense that the problem went beyond subprime mortgage securities. The Millennium Bridge was wobbling, and everyone was uneasy—but not uneasy enough. And that was as true of the three leading Western central bankers as anyone.

Jean-Claude Trichet and the ECB were injecting money into the European banking system, a practice they'd begun with no real warning to their counterparts in Washington and London. Bernanke and the Federal Reserve were acting as lender of last resort to banks too, as well as weighing whether to start trying to protect the overall economy by cutting interest rates. Mervyn King and the Bank of England were standing by, content for the moment to let the banks suffer the consequences of years of risky lending.

The three men didn't know it yet, but they were in the early stages of what would become perhaps the world's most important partnership—one in which their varied backgrounds, different personalities, and unique pathways to power would shape the course of all that was to come.

J ean-Claude Anne Marie Louis Trichet was a career bureaucrat with decades of crisis-fighting experience—and also a reader of poetry, philosophy, and literature who saw his profession as a central banker as being about something much bigger than economics. "I am convinced that economic and cultural affairs, that money and literature and poetry, are much more closely linked than many people believe," he said in 2009. "Poems, like gold coins, are meant to last, to keep their integrity, sustained by their rhythm, rhymes, and metaphors. In that sense, they are like money—they are a 'store of value' over the long term. They are both aspiring to inalterability, whilst they are both destined to circulate from hand to hand and mind to mind."

To Trichet, the ECB was the most concrete symbol of European unity, an answer to the discord that had roiled his continent for hundreds—even thousands—of years. "Economic and monetary union is a magnificent undertaking that forms the basis of Europe's prosperity and shared stability," he said in the same speech, citing the words of Derrida, Dante, Proust, and Goethe as representing the philosophical underpinnings of a united European continent.

Trichet was part of a generation of leaders determined—and newly able—to learn from the mistakes of their parents and build a different order for Europe. He was the consummate European, which for elites of his generation meant being devoted to an identity beyond one's status as a Frenchman or German or Italian. As a child, that meant traveling to Germany, Austria, and Italy with a favorite uncle and having a pen pal in Britain. As an adult, it meant quite a bit more. As Trichet told French news magazine *L'Express*, "It was . . . a very emotional moment" when on June 17, 2004, he held his first telephonic meeting of the ECB's General Council, a sprawling group that includes even central bankers from European countries that don't use the euro. "I went round asking if everyone was there. The governor of Estonia? 'Yes, I'm here.' Lithuania? Malta? Cyprus? They were all there. That's what Europe is all about, and it is impressive."

The son of a professor of Greek and Latin, Trichet displayed an early enthusiasm for literature and philosophy. After parental encouragement to study mathematics and the sciences, he served an engineering traineeship deep underground in a coal mine. But he was drawn to politics and soon left mining to study at the École Nationale d'Administration, the finishing school for the French civil service. It was a time of tumult, coming just after clashes between radical students and police in 1968. Like many, Trichet was involved with left-wing student activism. For his dedication to workers' rights, his fellow members of the Unified Socialist Party nicknamed him "Justix," a punning reference to the indefatigable Gallic hero of the *Asterix* cartoon series. Trichet finished near the top of the Administration class of 1971—fifth out of one hundred—

began a long career at the French treasury, and married Aline Rybalka, a Ukrainian-born translator for the French foreign ministry.

Trichet came of age as a policymaker during the arduous negotiations toward European unity, in which sheer stamina—the ability to stick to a position into the wee hours of the night—could be as important as anything else. He led the ECB governing council, a sprawling group of twenty-three central bankers, using all that experience, using control over the agenda and the clock to almost always guide interest rate decisions in his preferred direction. He was a master of using whatever advantages his role as chairman offered: He once led negotiations with representatives from twenty-seven nations on bank capital rules in 2011. The meeting started first thing in the morning, but as the lunch hour passed and staffers put out sandwiches in the hallway, Trichet didn't call for a break. By late afternoon, the increasingly hungry negotiators were more willing to yield, if only so they could get something to eat.

Depending on the situation, Trichet could deploy not only persistence, but also arm-twisting, head-knocking, logrolling, or whatever he might need to close the deal. These were the skills that enabled him to rise to head of the treasury sixteen years after graduation and to governor of the French central bank six years after that. "If I had to choose any of us to represent me in a complicated transaction, to negotiate on my behalf, it would be Trichet, without hesitation," said one of his fellow central bankers. He was among those representing France in the negotiations over the Maastricht Treaty, which would create the euro. From 1985 to 1993, he was chairman of the Paris Club, a group of global financial officials that negotiates debt restructuring for troubled Latin American and other developing nations.

From that experience, Trichet was as prepared as anyone on earth for the kinds of difficult talks between banks and governments that arise when a nation's finances get out of control and its economy hovers on the brink. "Crisis is part of his DNA," Finnish Central Bank governor Erkki Liikanen once said of him. More diplomat than economist, by 2007, he was as experienced a manager of financial crises as anyone on earth.

With his mellifluous accent and stylish attire, Trichet could be a charmer as well. "With slightly condescending flattery and a touch of the well-appointed courtier, Trichet greets interlocutors with unfailing respect," noted longtime ECB watcher David Marsh. "He kisses ladies' hands with old-fashioned gallantry—whether they be [German] Chancellor Angela Merkel or the wives of Frankfurt-based journalists—and flamboyantly addresses former British Chancellors of the Exchequer as '*Monsieur le Chancelier.*'" Yet even people who've spent hundreds or thousands of hours in his company professionally have said they felt little sense of a strong personal bond. Trichet remained, whatever the situation, formal and proper, relentlessly on message, reluctant to show even a hint of self-doubt. He was easy to respect but hard to know.

As head of the Banque de France, Trichet oversaw the logistical details of preparing for his nation's incorporation into the eurozone, frequently clashing with politicians who viewed his *franc fort* ("strong franc") policy as damaging to French exports and hence jobs. It was said that Trichet "spoke French with a German accent," meaning that despite being a Frenchman by birth, he had the same hard-money philosophy as a German—which made him a perfect choice to be one of the initial leaders of the ECB when it was established in 1998.

After being exonerated in a scandal over disclosures of information by the large commercial bank Crédit Lyonnais while he was at the treasury, Trichet was appointed to his eight-year term as ECB president in 2003. An exceptionally hard worker, he was attuned to every detail of managing the central bank, personally reviewing department budgets and tweaking language in press releases in an institution with sixteen hundred employees.

"My life compass has been the deepening of European unity based upon reconciliation and a profound friendship to the service of prosperity and pace," Trichet once said. The crisis that began with a phone call to Saint-Malo on August 9, 2007, would scramble that compass, as the currency he'd helped create to unify a continent would instead threaten to pull it apart.


Unlike Trichet, whose career was one long ascent through the ranks of European leadership, Ben Shalom Bernanke was in many ways an unlikely titan of the global economy. Born in Georgia in 1953 and raised in tiny Dillon, South Carolina, he showed uncommon intelligence at an early age, skipping the first grade, representing South Carolina in the 1965 National Spelling Bee, and getting the highest SAT score in the state, a near-perfect 1590. His achievements were enough to win him admission to Harvard, but his mother was reluctant to let him go to college so far away. She relented only after being assured by Kenneth Manning, a young African American from Dillon who had himself attended the school and encouraged Bernanke to apply, that "there were Jews up in Boston."

Bernanke excelled at Harvard, winning an award for best undergraduate economics thesis. He went to graduate school at MIT in a time when the institution was turning out a slew of PhDs who would go on to be significant shapers of economic policy. In 1977 alone, the program produced Mario Draghi, Trichet's successor as ECB president; Olivier Blanchard, the International Monetary Fund's chief economist; and Paul Krugman, the Nobel laureate and influential *New York Times* columnist. Bernanke finished two years after them, studying under Stanley Fischer, later an IMF chief economist and head of the Bank of Israel and something of an intellectual godfather to a generation of central bankers.

"If you had known Ben Bernanke as a student you would have never picked him as a future central banker," Robert Solow, a Nobel laureate economist at MIT, later told Bloomberg News. Bernanke didn't even look the part, Solow added: "He had a lot of hair, and when I say a lot of hair, I mean a lot of hair."

Indeed, in the early years of his career, Bernanke showed little inclination to be anything other than a first-rate academic. He married Anna Friedmann, a Wellesley grad who would go on to be a seventh-grade Spanish teacher, and they moved first to California and then to New Jersey, where he became a star economist at Princeton. He wrote important papers on the intersection of finance, economics, and monetary policy, exploring the policy failures that created the Great Depression and emerging as an advocate of "inflation targeting," or establishing a goal for how much prices should rise and adjusting monetary policy accordingly.

But even as he produced outstanding academic work, Bernanke began to discover his talent for guiding groups of people to a decision. A skilled listener and persuader, he became economics department chair at Princeton in 1996. It is a thankless job, with all the responsibilities of leadership but little explicit power—high-powered academics, after all, don't like being told what they should teach or research. Bernanke often joked that his biggest responsibility was deciding whether to bring bagels or doughnuts to faculty meetings, though that undersells the scope of his duties. He navigated the faculty through decisions on, for example, whether to increase course offerings in finance, in such a way that everyone could feel like part of the process, even if he or she disagreed with the ultimate decision.

Bernanke also served on the Montgomery Township, New Jersey, school board at a time when it was deeply divided over whether to raise taxes to build more schools. The issue was so hard-fought that a fistfight broke out outside one meeting. Bernanke's instincts were to side with the low-tax group, former colleague Dwight Jaffee told the *Washington Post*, but "he would look at the numbers and make computations about whether it made sense to build new schools. . . . He really has faith in doing the numbers right and then living with them." His was ultimately the tie-breaking vote for a bond issue that raised local property taxes.

It took a couple of accidents of timing to turn the number-crunching professor into one of the most powerful men in the world. First, in 2001, Bernanke was a finalist to become Princeton's provost, the school's chief academic officer and number two administrator. Had he gotten the job, he would surely have had a different answer when Glenn Hubbard, President George W. Bush's chief White House economist, called in 2002 about a potential appointment to the Federal Reserve Board of Governors. Bernanke hadn't seriously considered entering government before, but the idea was appealing, not least because of a new sense of public spirit inspired by the September 11, 2001, terrorist attacks. He was soon confirmed to serve in Alan Greenspan's Fed, and he displayed a particular gift for explaining the policy board's thinking to the world. His official photo from 2002 showed him looking the part of the disheveled professor, hair sticking out in all directions, his beard untrimmed and extending all the way down to his collar.

A mere three years later, the seventy-nine-year-old Greenspan decided to retire. It was a time of political weakness for the Bush administration: The government's response to Hurricane Katrina had been mishandled, the war in Iraq was a still-unfolding disaster, and Bush's previous high-profile appointment, of White House Counsel Harriet Miers to the Supreme Court, had gone down in flames amid doubts about her stature. The Senate was in no mood to confirm more controversial—and ideologically conservative—possible Fed chairmen like Hubbard or Reagan administration economic adviser Martin Feldstein. As a relative newcomer to Washington, Bernanke became the safe choice for a president with an approval rating of 40 percent and falling.

As one of the most powerful men in the United States, he still preferred quiet evenings at home with his wife to the Georgetown social scene favored by Greenspan. Bernanke wore suits off the rack from the midlevel clothier JoS. A. Bank and took no apparent joy in the little luxuries that came with the office, such as a security detail and a car and driver. He came into the office most Saturdays and Sundays, wearing jeans, in order to think through decisions in a solitude that was impossible to obtain during the week.

There was, of course, also a downside to being a Beltway neophyte. Greenspan had advised presidents on economic policy for nearly twenty years before being named to the Fed chairmanship; Bernanke had to learn the political side of his job on the fly. He seemed genuinely perplexed, aides said, when senators with whom he had warm relations in private would pillory him in televised hearings; it took time for him to learn that this sort of thing was simply the routine hypocrisy of politics.

He may not have looked the part at first; Bernanke is likely the only high official to have been mocked for his socks by both the president of the United States and the *Washington Post*, on separate occasions. (He wore tan instead of navy.) But Bernanke worked to shape a different image on ascending to the Fed chairmanship, to assure the powerful that he was a steady hand at the tiller of the global economy. He attended private events with the giants of finance and politics to better understand their world—going to dinner at the Jackson Hole home of James Wolfensohn, the überconnected former World Bank chief, for example, or traveling to the Bilderberg conference, a subject of great fascination to conspiracy theorists that in practice is just a bunch of rich, influential people getting together to bat around ideas for a couple of days. Bernanke enlisted a speaking coach and worked to stop a quaver that crept into his voice when he was nervous, and he even started looking sharper, getting more frequent haircuts and grooming his beard more carefully. (He talks baseball with Lenny Gilleo, the in-house barber at the Federal Reserve's Washington headquarters, during his trim every three weeks or so.)

But there was one thing Bernanke didn't need to change: his approach to leadership. At its eight annual meetings, the mighty Federal Open Market Committee—the Fed's Board of Governors in Washington plus the presidents of its twelve regional banks—can be a fractious group of nineteen (with twelve having a vote at any given time). Although the chairman is always the first among equals, in a formal sense his is only one vote. He isn't, in a technical sense, the "boss" of any of the other committee members and must lead instead through persuasion and force of intellect. As Bernanke took command of the committee, he turned to the same management techniques he used as an academic department chair and school board member. "It's not Ben's personality to pound the table and scream and say you're going to agree with me or else," said Alan Blinder, a colleague of Bernanke's at Princeton, in 2009. "It's not his way. I've known him for twenty-five years. He succeeds at persuading people by respecting their points of view and through the force of his own intellect. He doesn't say you're a jerk for disagreeing."

After presentations from staff, the meetings begin with an initial go-round in which every official presents his or her view of the economy, followed by a coffee break. While his colleagues caffeinate, Bernanke goes into his office next door to the boardroom and types out a few notes about what he's just heard. When the committee reconvenes, the chairman, speaking from his notes, says something to the effect of "Here's what I think I heard," then runs through the range of views. Some of the policymakers who'd frequently found themselves at odds with Greenspan and felt shut out of debates ended up having warmer relationships with Bernanke as a result. "The chair of any committee can respond to comments that challenge his view in ways that inform the committee that the issue isn't worth discussing," said Richmond Fed president Jeff Lacker. "This chairman doesn't do that. He takes other views seriously."

Bernanke's academic research hadn't been discussed when President Bush was weighing his appointment to the Fed chairmanship. But as the crisis emerged in 2007 and deepened in 2008, Bernanke's work would become all too relevant. He had documented how problems in the financial sector tend not to stay in the financial sector, but to spread to other areas of the economy, slowing down overall growth. This, he argued, was a major cause of the deep downturn of the 1930s, a large part of what made the Great Depression great. When banks and other lenders suffer major losses, as they did with mortgage debt in 2007, they pare back lending of all kinds. That weakens the economy, which causes banks' losses to mount further, setting up a vicious cycle—the "financial accelerator," as Bernanke and frequent coauthor Mark Gertler called it. From the earliest days of the crisis, the Fed chief was concerned that the problems in the U.S. housing market could spiral into something very dangerous indeed.

Bernanke's academic background had prepared him intellectually for what was to come. The question was whether his quiet style of leadership could guide the Federal Reserve through the storm.

M ervyn Allister King—just "Governor King" at the time, but "Sir Mervyn King" from 2011 on, when he was knighted—may have seemed far removed from his international counterparts in those early days of the crisis, but it wasn't due to a lack of familiarity. He actually had long-standing connections to both Trichet and Bernanke. King was a student at Cambridge in the 1960s when Trichet visited to study the British tax system and became acquainted with the future governor, and he and Bernanke in the 1980s shared adjoining offices at MIT. Instead, King's independence in August 2007 was of a piece with the supremely self-confident man who ran the Bank of England.

An armchair psychologist might see his self-assured style as typical of someone whose place among the elite was earned not by birth, but through keen intelligence, hard work, and sheer cussedness. The son of a railway clerk, King was born in 1948 and raised in Wolverhampton, a small city in the West Midlands. At grammar school he displayed a precocious intelligence, and he eventually found his way to King's College, Cambridge, to graduate study at Harvard, and then to a professorship at the London School of Economics, where he was viewed as among the most promising young British economists of his generation. After joining the Bank of England as chief economist in the early 1990s, he remade the bank in his image: rigorous in its analysis, theoretical in its approach, unsparing in its dismissiveness toward employees or departments that didn't come into line with his own predispositions and high standards.

He was a great lover of sports, peppering his speeches with references to Aston Villa, and periodically (and with sometimes unfortunate timing) skipping an afternoon of work to take in a tennis, cricket, or soccer match. He'd been an energetic sportsman in his student days, playing intramural cricket and soccer with great competitive fervor, if not necessarily great ability. An apparently inexhaustible source of energy, King played tennis with Alan Greenspan and other leading officials, and often walked the five miles from his Notting Hill flat to the Bank of England's headquarters on Threadneedle Street instead of taking his bank-provided car service.

His love of competition extended to his work at the bank, and his adversaries there and in the government found clashing with him a very unpleasant business. To his friends in the international economics club or on the London social scene, King was a charmer, with a sharp wit and lively eyes. To his colleagues at the bank, he could be an intellectual bully, sure of his correctness and willing to use every method available to get his way, including isolating and undermining those who disagreed with him. Chancellor of the Exchequer Alistair Darling described him as "incredibly stubborn" and "exasperating" and wrote that the core problem of the Bank of England was that King ran it "as an autocratic fiefdom of the Governor"—this from a man who had twice given King that position.

King had become the bank's chief economist in 1991, a low point for the Old Lady of Threadneedle Street. Inflation had been high for decades, and George Soros was just about to "break" the bank by forcing the pound out of the currency bond.

As the bank's top economist, King set about rebuilding the institution's credibility as a maker of monetary policy. He hired some of the brightest young PhDs in Britain and shoved out many from the bank's old guard, who had become better at backslapping than economic analysis. His success at that job helped convince Tony Blair's Labour government, in 1997, to grant the bank the independence from political influence it had long sought. Thanks in no small part to King's work, no more would interest rate policy be driven by what elected officials wanted. "He made independence credible by raising the bar on the intellectual caliber of economics at the bank," said Rachel Lomax, who served on the Monetary Policy Committee from 2003 to 2008. King was rewarded with the newly created job of deputy governor for monetary policy in 1998, and then with the governorship in 2003.

Although his days as a professor were long behind him, he hadn't abandoned his academic mind-set. As governor, he focused on theories of how the British economy works, debating, developing, and refining economic models. When dealing with some of the more mundane decisions the bank needed to make, he sought to return to "first principles": What's the purpose of central banks? How does monetary policy work? And King often urged colleagues to seek advice from academic theorists rather than from those with more practical experience. One recalled when there was a discussion over how the bank should handle the logistics of auctions for newly issued British government bonds. King recommended calling several top researchers in "auction theory," as opposed to people with actual experience in the market for UK government bonds.

According to colleagues, the governor was privately disdainful of the economic views of commercial bankers and businesspeople without training in academic economics. He was a warm and ebullient presence and a clever wit to the groups of artists, intellectuals, and government leaders for whom he threw intimate dinner parties, but when he was to speak at some big event for financial grandees, he tended to skip the cocktail hour and show up just in time to fulfill his obligation.

In contrast to monetary policy, with its elegant theoretical underpinnings, the regulation of banks is a messy business—one the BOE had largely ceded to the new Financial Services Authority as part of the 1997 deal to gain political independence. "Financial stability became a downplayed part of the institution," said Kate Barker, a member of the Monetary Policy Committee from 2001 to 2010. Former Bank of England economist Richard Barwell told the *Financial Times,* "Before the crisis, working in financial stability was an absolute career graveyard."

Those who prospered were the economists whose interest in creating theoretical models of how the economy works mirrored King's own. Employees with other approaches saw their careers stall out and frequently left. "His grip on the intellectual approach of the bank had become very tight," said Barker. King's attention to detail and desire for total control extended to the smallest things: At an annual summer gathering for staffers and their families to enjoy barbecue and sports, one former employee told the *Financial Times,* King "fusse[d] . . . about who has turned up, who will win the toss, all the little stuff."

King, judged tone deaf as a child, was viewed as insufficiently musical to join his school orchestra. But as an adult he discovered classical music and took to it with great passion, even serving on the advisory council of the London Symphony Orchestra. He viewed his stewardship of the Bank of England and the British economy as something like directing a great musical performance.

"I think the role of conductor combines the ability to be a free spirit, to use imagination, as well as to be an intellectual study, which is what I did for most of my life," King told radio host Gilbert Kaplan in a 2004 interview about his love of music. "The ability to do that and also to lead a team, just to get a team of people playing for you. That's what I've tried to do at the Bank of England and what I think I would have much enjoyed doing as a conductor."

King's players tuned up in the lengthy Friday afternoon gatherings leading up to a Monetary Policy Committee meeting the following Thursday— although some were clearly more favored by their conductor than others. With many of the hundred or so bank staffers in attendance presenting their latest economic data and analyses, the "bank agents," who are scattered around Britain and charged with staying in contact with commercial banks and businesses, were consigned to a minor role. "The meeting would go on for three hours," according to David "Danny" Blanchflower, a member of the Monetary Policy Committee whose private disagreements with King eventually turned into a very public feud. "And it would all be theory, and in the last ten minutes, the agents would report—and they said something that was completely different than what the theory said."

At the much smaller meetings of the MPC itself, the discussion was focused on applying the bank's various models—models that assumed a functioning financial system—to current economic circumstances. Even when King was dealing with deepening problems in the banking system in the summer of 2008, he kept the conversation theoretical, sharing little of what he knew with his fellow committee members. "The Monetary Policy Committee was kept out of the loop," said one person who was on the committee in that era. "Mervyn was holed up in his office reading and thinking. There wasn't a sense of urgency or a lot of meetings. The rest of us were like, 'My God, what are we doing?'"

As the crisis expanded, financial markets were enveloped by uncertainty. But there could be certainty of one thing, at least: At the Bank of England, the King of Threadneedle Street reigned supreme.

A t the end of August 2007, the three men were in different places, figuratively and literally. Bernanke was at the Jackson Lake Lodge, plotting crisis response from the secret crisis center set up one floor up from the ballroom. Trichet canceled his voyage there at the last minute, citing personal reasons. King, who usually dispatched deputy Charles Bean to the gathering, did so once again.

On the evening of Friday, August 31, 2007, buses lined up at the lodge to take conference attendees and their spouses to the evening's entertainment. Economists and bankers don't necessarily wear jeans and cowboy hats well, but on this occasion they wore them nonetheless. While they nursed light beers, a local rancher tried to demonstrate the techniques of horse whispering. The bucking mare ignored the rancher's reassuring body language and quiet words and refused, no matter how delicate the rancher's approach, to submit to a saddle. The parallels with the financial crisis then just starting to unfold were so obvious that a murmur went through the crowd: Central bankers were whispering to the financial markets, trying to calm them. But just as in the show, soothing words might not be enough.

The rancher suggested that his guests might want to go ahead and get their buffet dinner of beef brisket and baked beans while he kept working on the horse. Sure enough, by the time dinner was done, the animal had calmed down enough to allow the rancher to ride her. The financial markets would be harder to tame.

# TEN

# Over by Christmas

The morning of Friday, September 14, 2007, Mervyn King and Alistair Darling flew to Porto, Portugal, for a scheduled meeting of European Union central bankers and finance ministers. The timing of their trip to the riverside city best known for its sweet fortified wine was terrible.

For the past several weeks, Northern Rock PLC, a bank based in the North East of England with £100 billion in assets, had been in crisis. Its business was to issue mortgages, which would then be packaged and sold on financial markets—and since August, mortgage securities had been toxic to global investors. Northern Rock faced a cash crunch, as depositors discovered just how bad its situation was, a classic bank run. Television news programs showed ominously long lines of Northern Rock customers waiting to pull their deposits. "You don't want to be the ones in the end of the queue that the money's run out," an uncertain customer said to the cameras outside a branch in Reading.

In a palatial Moorish hall, the governor of the Bank of England and the chancellor of the exchequer watched from afar—on TV, just like many of those Northern Rock customers determined not to be in the end of the queue when the money ran out. "They're behaving perfectly rationally, you know," King told Darling, the chancellor later recalled.

It was an accurate statement—but hardly what Darling wanted to hear. Britain had seen a number of bank failures over the years. But the two men had overseen the first run on a British bank since Overend & Gurney's in 1866.

Known before 1997 as the Northern Rock Building Society, Northern Rock had established itself as a very modern variety of bank. Much of its deposit base came from the Internet, with people all over the country parking their savings there electronically to take advantage of high interest rates. Its home mortgage loans—many made to buyers in the gritty shipbuilding and coal-mining towns of the North East—weren't held on its own books the way lending banks had done for centuries. Instead, Northern Rock sold them as securities—as quickly as it could, to investors around the world. It had expanded at a breakneck pace, growing around 20 percent a year for seventeen years straight. By 2007, it was a large bank, with shopping-center branches around the UK, but hardly enormous—it was about one twentieth the size of Barclays, for example.

When the financial system started to shudder in August 2007, what had previously seemed like Northern Rock's strengths turned out to be terrible weaknesses. Investors, newly fearful that mortgage securities could turn out to be worthless, had little interest in buying more of them. They also didn't want to lend money to a bank that was built almost entirely on home lending.

In continental Europe or the United States, this wouldn't have been much of an issue, because the European Central Bank and the Federal Reserve had relaxed their emergency lending programs so banks like Northern Rock could get money on favorable terms. But King's concerns about moral hazard meant that the Bank of England would offer no such accommodation until it was too late. When Northern Rock needed cash, it explored using its one branch in Ireland—part of the eurozone—to access money through the ECB. It concluded that getting the legal details in order would have taken two or three months— far too long to wait.

As the weeks passed, Northern Rock's cash crunch became increasingly self-perpetuating. With its future in doubt, the bank was less likely to get any money from lenders on private markets; their reluctance made its cash shortage all the more acute.

The weekend of September 9, King was meeting with the other central bankers in Basel when Darling and chief British bank regulator Callum McCarthy reached him by phone. They argued that the Bank of England needed to follow the lead of the ECB and the Fed by supporting the banking system more actively. King was typically stubborn.

"During the conference call, I became increasingly frustrated at Mervyn's insistence that normal judgments could still apply in what were obviously deeply abnormal circumstances," Darling wrote later.

King may have been insistent on making banks pay for their previous mistakes, but the Bank of England's job for three hundred years had been to prevent a bank collapse and the broader public panic that might ensue if British subjects no longer believed their deposits were safe. His strategy was to step in as lender of last resort to Northern Rock, if necessary—but he insisted on ensuring that the Bank of England truly was the bank's last resort, and on charging a "penalty" interest rate for emergency loans, making them an undesirable option for any other banks that might wish to go to Threadneedle Street for help.

King argued that an emergency loan to Northern Rock would be most effective if it was covert. After all, if the public knew that Northern Rock had had to turn to the Bank of England for funds, it could increase the sense of panic. But lawyers for both banks fretted that a failure to disclose the loan immediately might be illegal, giving Northern Rock shareholders an inaccurate impression of the bank's health. A subsequent investigation questioned that interpretation of the law but acknowledged that it would have been hard to keep any large-scale loan to Northern Rock secret for long in the "febrile and fevered atmosphere of that period."

Indeed. On Thursday, September 13, the Bank of England was pulling together a funding deal for Northern Rock that was to be announced the following Monday, in a carefully plotted rollout meant to reassure depositors and investors that their money was safe. At 8:30 that evening, however, BBC business editor Robert Peston went live on the air to break the news that a bailout was imminent. There'd been a leak, and the careful rollout wouldn't be an option.

Depositors suddenly knew not only that Northern Rock was desperate enough to go to the Bank of England for funds, but also that there was no guarantee from the government that their deposits were safe. The bank's tiny storefront branches filled up with even two or three people lined up inside; new arrivals had to wait outside. Once queues started forming and TV news cameras started broadcasting them, the "Run on the Rock" was well under way. People who had made deposits online began withdrawing at such a pace that the bank's servers couldn't handle the load. When word got around that Web customers were unable to withdraw, the panic worsened still.

The run ended Monday, September 17, when Darling announced that the government would stand behind all deposits to Northern Rock—despite the fact that there was no clear-cut legal authority allowing it to do so. "It was pretty shambolic," said one British official involved. But it was enough. The lines abated; the run stopped. The government had bought time to nationalize the bank and shut it down in an orderly way, with depositors' money protected.

That same day, Darling had a previously scheduled meeting with Hank Paulson, the U.S. treasury secretary. "Your guy Mervyn has a high pain threshold," Paulson told him. "I hope you have, too."

During the summer and fall of 2007, the major central banks all had different interpretations of the emerging crisis. King and the Bank of England saw a necessary and even healthy market correction after years of excessive risk-taking by the banks. They were disinclined to step in and rescue the banks from their bad decisions, lest they reward dangerous behavior. Jean-Claude Trichet and the ECB saw a banking panic. Their banks were more exposed to shaky U.S. mortgage securities than anybody had realized, but the ECB and bank regulators across Europe pumped euros into the system to keep their banks awash in liquidity. It would be enough, they hoped, to prevent the European economy from facing any real peril.

Ben Bernanke and the Fed saw a dual threat of a banking panic and recession: The crisis endangered both the financial system and the U.S. economy as a whole. They would use their tools to keep banks afloat, just as the ECB had. But Bernanke's study of how the financial system interacts with the rest of the economy made him fearful that lending would dry up and slow the U.S. economy to a crawl—or worse. To combat that risk, in mid-September the Fed started cutting the federal funds rate, and by extension lowering the cost of money across the economy, to try to encourage overall economic growth.

Meanwhile, many of the other leading central banks, including the Bank of Japan and those in the emerging nations of Asia and Latin America, took an isolationist stance: The difficulties in the American and European financial markets are someone else's problems. They probably won't affect us here, and we have our own domestic issues to worry about. King was the first to discover how severe those domestic issues could be—and just how connected to the rest of the world's problems they really were.

After the big interventions by the ECB and the Federal Reserve, and the more halting efforts of the Bank of England, the sense of crisis ebbed in October. The U.S. stock market even reached new highs that month. But that reversed at the end of the year, as the patchwork of measures the world's central bankers had put in place started to reach the limits of their effectiveness.

It was time for the bankers to stop working individually, at different speeds and with different tactics, and begin addressing the crisis together. In the run-up to the crisis, what few policymakers or private economists fully understood was just how important European banks had become to the U.S. financial system.

As economist Hyun Song Shin—he of the prophetic Millennium Bridge metaphor—explained in a 2011 paper, European banks, more than any others, had the ability to buy the allegedly risk-free mortgage and other assets being created by Wall Street with little or no capital to protect against losses. That helps explain why, by early 2008, non-U.S. banks—most of them European— had more than $10 trillion in exposure to the United States, equivalent to about 70 percent of U.S. economic output. They had roughly that much in both assets (bonds that they owned) and liabilities (money they owed someone else), particularly money market funds. It seemed like a system in balance: A German bank might have lots of dollar assets and lots of dollar liabilities, but they were more or less equal.

But when mortgage securities backed by home loans in Florida began to tumble, the assets side of that ledger fell in value—and what that German bank really needed to ride out the losses was dollars, not the euros that the ECB was able to offer. Typically, it could have easily borrowed euros from the ECB and temporarily swapped them for dollars on international currency markets. The very nature of this crisis, however, was that trust had evaporated among the banks that would normally help each other out in just that way.

At dinners in Basel, at a late September conference honoring the fiftieth anniversary of the German central bank, and in countless phone calls, the world's central bankers brainstormed how they might overcome this problem. The conversations were so open-ended and wide-ranging that different participants have different recollections of how particular ideas originated. Bernanke, Trichet, and King discussed things in one-on-one conversations, then brought in representatives of the smaller central banks. They all dispatched staff, mainly their market operations chiefs, to hammer out the details, including how and when to put out an announcement and what it would say.

On December 12, 2007, they released a statement: "Today, the Bank of Canada, the Bank of England, the European Central Bank, the Federal Reserve, and the Swiss National Bank are announcing measures designed to address elevated pressures in short-term funding markets." That they were all moving together, the central bankers hoped, would send a signal to the world that would have its own benefits to confidence.

The five banks announced that they would be reemploying a measure they had used in the aftermath of the September 11, 2001, terrorist attacks: They would swap currencies with each other to ensure the free flow of funds around the globe. For example, the Fed could give $10 billion to the ECB in exchange for an equivalent value of euros. The ECB could then lend those dollars out to banks in the eurozone that were suffering a dollar shortage. After some fixed period—say, ninety days—the two central banks would return each other's money. The Fed was, indirectly, funneling dollars to the eurozone and Swiss banks that desperately needed them.

The second arm of the strategy was for the major central banks to force money out the door in sufficient volume, and on sufficiently relaxed terms, that commercial banks would see the wisdom of taking advantage of it. It was an attempt to overcome the stigma that had kept commercial banks from taking central-bank money—basically, an offer they couldn't refuse. For the Bank of England, that meant increasing the amount of cash it would lend out for a three-month span almost fourfold, to £11 billion, and accepting even AA-rated bonds as collateral, not just the higher-rated varieties it usually required. Both international bankers and some Bank of England insiders believed that the global nature of the effort allowed King some face-saving: It seemed less like a flagrant reversal of policy than it would have had the Bank of England acted on its own.

The Fed, meanwhile, introduced a new program that would essentially force money into the banking system. Instead of waiting for banks to come to the discount window, the central bank announced that it would reverse the process: It would distribute $40 billion by the end of the year in two auctions, guaranteeing that money would go out the door to *someone*—that someone being whatever bank would pay the highest interest rate. It was called the Term Auction Facility, or TAF. What the American public didn't know at the time— and Fed officials were in no rush to enlighten it—was that the someone in question was, overwhelmingly, the U.S. affiliates of European banks.

Out of the first $20 billion lent out under the program, only trivial amounts went to American banks—$10 million to Citibank, for example, and $25 million to Wachovia. Taking out $2 billion each, meanwhile, were the New York–based arms of WestLB, Dresdner, DZ Bank, and Landesbank Baden-Württemberg, all German, and Dexia, headquartered in Belgium and France. The list of those borrowing substantial amounts from the Fed in that auction also included banks from Britain, Japan, Canada, Spain, and Finland, all of which took out far more than U.S. banks.

"The TAF laundered the crisis," one Fed official said years later. "It made it look like we were solving a U.S. problem, when the real problem was the exposure of European banks to the dollar."

When the extent of lending to foreign banks was publicly disclosed—three years later, after it was forced by congressional order—Fed officials pointed to the role that those institutions played in supporting U.S. credit markets. The foreign banks, after all, were one of the key ways that Europeans' savings were funding Americans' credit cards and home mortgages. Moreover, the Fed was legally prohibited from discriminating against foreign-owned banks in its lending at the discount window, which is what TAF effectively was. But it's hard to imagine that the Fed could have thrown its resources so readily to foreign banks had the American public—and its legislative representatives—understood what it was doing.

For their part, Trichet and the ECB were worried that announcing an exotic new program to channel dollars to European banks could create deeper fears for their solvency, forcing investors to conclude that things were even worse than they'd thought. So they publicly spun participation almost as a favor European banks could do for the Fed to help its efforts to unfreeze lending markets in the United States. "We think it is a right way to cooperate in the month of January," Trichet said in a 2008 press conference. The connections between the swap lines and the TAF may have been little understood by the

American public and policymakers, but they were well understood at the ECB as being two ways to address the same problem: European banks running short of dollars. Internally, they even referred to their own dollar lending as "Euro-TAF."

The joint action helped ease the sense of panic in the money markets at the end of 2007, but the relief was short-lived. A dangerous pattern was setting in: Bernanke's dreaded financial accelerator. When credit tightens and banks become more cautious, they cut back on lending out money and injecting it into the economy. Less lending means slower economic growth—fewer houses built or goods consumed. A weaker economy causes banks' losses to mount, making them pull back on lending all the more. It was just this vicious cycle, Bernanke argued, that made the Great Depression great.

Early in 2008, the financial accelerator was revving up in the United States. While the economy had weathered the earlier phase of financial panic, by December 2007 the nation was officially in recession. With every piece of economic data, it became more evident that the U.S. economy was sinking into a downturn, while most economies in Europe were merely slowing down—and the developing world was growing gangbusters.

The problems that had been most severe among European banks had, by March 2008, pivoted across the Atlantic to the U.S. investment banks. Whereas more traditional U.S. banks like Bank of America or J.P. Morgan fund themselves in large part with deposits from individuals and businesses—money that tends to stay put—investment banks like Bear Stearns rely on faster money. They fund their operations to a large degree in the "triparty repo market"— effectively depending, every single evening, on lenders being willing to extend them credit against solid collateral. It was usually a steady source of funds. After all, Bear Stearns had been around since 1923, surviving eighty-five years' worth of crises without its lenders having lost any money. Even on March 13, 2008, long after the firm's business of packaging mortgages into securities had begun falling apart, shares of its stock were worth a combined $8 billion.

But investors were paralyzed by the potential for future losses, as well as skeptical that the assets Bear had on its books were worth what it claimed they were. And the firm had left itself little room for maneuver: It had $398 billion in total assets on its books, but also owed $387 billion in debts. That meant it wouldn't take much of a dip in the value of mortgage securities for Bear

Stearns to become insolvent. On the evening of Thursday, March 13, the lenders didn't show up: They refused to give the firm the overnight money that was its lifeblood.

Bear Stearns was functionally bankrupt, and Bernanke had a predicament. The Fed had long acted as lender of last resort—but only to traditional banks. Bear Stearns may have acted like a traditional bank in many ways, but it was a different sort of animal. It wasn't regulated by the Fed. It didn't obey capital rules set by the Fed. It had no access to emergency lending by the Fed. Bernanke had no obligation to do anything but watch Bear Stearns go bankrupt and try to clean up any damage to the economy afterward.

Among the key lessons of Bernanke's academic work on the Great Depression, however, was that when financial institutions are allowed to fail, they can bring an entire economy down with them. In terms of size, Bear Stearns was less than three times as large as Northern Rock. But in terms of importance— how deeply intertwined it was with the rest of the financial system—it was far more consequential. Bernanke and his inner circle were convinced that the impact of Bear's bankruptcy on world financial markets would be devastating.

There was no time to do any careful number crunching, but their best guess, in discussions that went all night, was that Bear Stearns' collapse would instantly cause funding to dry up for the next-largest investment bank, Lehman Brothers, and possibly more beyond that. It could lead to a collapse in money market mutual funds, the savings vehicles where millions of individuals and businesses parked their cash and which had invested in the short-term debt of firms like Bear. And it would precipitate perhaps a 25 percent drop in the overall stock market, devastating Americans' wealth. None of this was based on rigorous analysis. Rather, a decision involving billions of taxpayer dollars would have to rely on the gut instincts of a handful of crisis fighters: Geithner, career Fed official Don Kohn, former investment banker and Bernanke inner circle member Kevin Warsh, and New York Fed markets chief Bill Dudley.

If they could do anything to stop all that from happening, they decided in predawn discussions that Friday morning, they must. The option they came up with was to invoke a provision in the Federal Reserve Act, known as 13(3), that allowed the Fed to lend money to any "individual, partnership, or corporation" in "unusual and exigent circumstances." In a single morning, they'd thrown out ninety-five years of precedent and placed the resources of the Fed behind not a bank but a securities firm. Over the ensuing weekend, Geithner and the Fed hammered out a deal to resolve the Bear Stearns crisis: The Fed would take on $30 billion worth of Bear assets, and J.P. Morgan would buy what was left over. At the same time, the Fed, using that same emergency 13(3) authority, opened its discount window to all the investment banks—Lehman Brothers, Goldman Sachs, Morgan Stanley—aiming to head off a cash crunch at those firms.

For nearly a century, the Fed had been lender of last resort to American banks. In the space of three months, it expanded that role to encompass both banks headquartered across Europe and the masters of the investment universe on Wall Street. No less a figure of authority than Paul Volcker, the former Fed chair and conquerer of inflation who had a unique moral authority, noted the historic change.

"What appears to be in substance a direct transfer of mortgage and mortgage-backed securities of questionable pedigree from an investment bank to the Federal Reserve seems to test the time-honored central-bank mantra in time of crisis: Lend freely at high rates against good collateral," Volcker told the Economic Club of New York less than a month after the Bear bailout. "Test it to the point of no return."

The summer of 2008 was another of the intermittent lulls in the storm, a time when the financial crisis seemed to be fading and other concerns rose to the fore. That led both Trichet and King to make costly mistakes.

That summer, an epic run-up in the cost of oil and almost every other global commodity was driving overall prices higher. Corn, copper, concrete— the price of anything that comes from the ground—was going up as booming demand in China and other developing countries outpaced supply. Such a jump in prices has the effect of making the economy too hot and too cold at the same time: Consumers have to spend more on fuel, which means they have less to spend on everything else, worsening economic conditions overall. Normally, central bankers don't adjust monetary policy to counteract short-term changes in commodity prices. After all, just because oil soars one month doesn't mean it will the next. The hike is a one-time thing.

But that logic breaks down when rises take place so often that consumers start to believe they're not one-time things but a permanent state of affairs. Businesses pencil in steady price increases. Unions demand higher raises. Lenders levy higher interest rates to make up for the fact that the euros they are repaid in the future will be worth less than those they loan out now. Once those things happen, inflation is self-perpetuating. And in that summer of soaring fuel prices, Trichet saw exactly that starting to happen: Airlines were adding surcharges to their ticket prices. Labor unions were demanding pay hikes of 4 or 5 percent, not the 2 or 3 percent with which the ECB would be more comfortable.

To this point in the crisis, Trichet had been determined to keep the ECB's attempts to prop up the European banking system separate from its monetary policies. In September 2007—just as the Federal Reserve was starting to cut interest rates as part of an all-out assault on the crisis and its possible economic effects—he drew a telling analogy. "Television dramas tend to be made about medical-rescue teams, hospital emergency rooms, and heart surgeons, not about the internists who regularly take your blood pressure and check your cholesterol," Trichet said in a speech in Frankfurt. "A central bank has one emergency room, which—sporadically—tackles casualties of car accidents and applies angioplasty and bypass surgery. But these activities—critical as they are to the functioning of the system—make up a small fraction of their duties. Central banks are for the most part made up of legions of internists who stare at your X-rays and engage in sober consultations."

And in their sober consultations in the summer of 2008, Dr. Trichet and his team of *médecins* saw rising inflation as the greatest risk on the horizon.

The ECB's monetary policy group is large and diverse, with members drawn from across the eurozone. In the Eurotower, a modern skyscraper near the train station in downtown Frankfurt, they gather every month around a circular table in the thirty-sixth-floor boardroom to debate monetary policy (with a second monthly meeting occurring for administrative matters). The president and five other executive board members are appointed by the heads of state of Europe in a secretive process rife with backroom dealing. In practice, four of the six slots are usually filled with people from the four biggest eurozone economies: Germany, France, Italy, and Spain. In total, the meetings include the heads of each national bank in the eurozone—from the mighty Bundesbank, responsible for the financial well-being of eighty-two million people, to the minuscule Central Bank of Malta, which safeguards the wealth of only 418,000.

Ireland is the only eurozone nation in which English is the native language of a majority of the population. The selection of English as the language in which ECB business is conducted represents a compromise: The Germans couldn't stomach their central bank deliberating in French, and the French couldn't stomach it using German. In theory, the people gathered around the table for the Governing Council are there to argue, with varying degrees of English proficiency, for what's best for the eurozone as a whole, not their own nations. In practice, of course, it doesn't always work that way. But to try to forestall any nationalistic temptations, the ECB keeps minutes and voting records secret for thirty years. It's easier for the head of the Bank of Italy to vote for a policy that isn't helpful to Italy, goes the logic, if nobody knows about it for a generation. (The Fed and the Bank of England, by contrast, release the information within weeks.)

This sprawling committee of twenty-three people of different nationalities actually made it easier for Trichet to practice his delicate art of managing a group toward consensus. On the first Thursday of the month, the same day the Bank of England makes its decision, the group would gather at 9 a.m. The bank's chief economist would spend the first hour walking through his staff's analysis. Then Trichet would give his own view of what the committee ought to do. That ensured that those without strong opinions would gravitate to what the president had argued. Then, in summarizing the discussion and counting votes, Trichet would interpret anyone who didn't specifically say how he or she was voting as being on his side in the debate.

The sheer size of the committee, and the need to make a decision in time for the announcement to be made at noon, meant that each member could be granted only five minutes or so to state his or her view, which worked in Trichet's favor: Long debates that might lead somewhere he didn't want couldn't really break out, because there just wasn't time. And the fact that open dissent was, officially at least, to remain secret meant that Trichet didn't have to worry if a few of his committee members weren't happy with a decision. It would be breaking the rules of the game for them to blab about their objections to the press.

A statement announcing the outcome of the meeting would be released within hours, at 1:45 p.m. At 2:30, Trichet would take the stage for a press briefing to explain the decision, where by 2008 he was a master at sending the subtle signal he intended the markets to receive, no more and no less. He had come to use code words to signal to the world what the ECB had up its sleeve. For example, if he said that the council would be monitoring inflation with "strong vigilance," it was a signal that an interest rate hike would almost certainly be coming the next month.

At the June 8, 2008, meeting of the Governing Council, the group was divided. As Trichet put it that day, "We exchanged many opinions and views around the table, as always, with a very candid exposition of our analysis. A number of us thought that . . . we had a case for increasing rates. A number of us considered that there was a case for increasing rates, but at a later date, and some amongst us considered that there was not necessarily a case for doing so." The compromise: This time, Trichet wouldn't pledge "strong vigilance" and a near-certain rate hike but rather "heightened alertness," which raised the possibility of a hike without committing to it; often, central bank communications is the art of managing such fine distinctions.

The Governing Council met again on July 3—just when, it turned out, many commodities were at all-time highs. The price of light sweet crude oil had reached $145 per barrel. It had been $100 per barrel as recently as April, and only about $73 a year earlier. The inflation rate in the eurozone was 4 percent. Trichet that morning steered the council toward an interest rate hike, using his tools of persuasion to guide a still-divided committee.

As the Frenchman announced a 0.25-percentage-point rise in the ECB's target for interest rates, he delivered a stern message to anyone who might have thought that the ECB wasn't serious about stopping inflation: "We are solemnly telling all economic agents, corporate businesses, price setters in the economy, and social partners that the worst decision they could take would be precisely to believe that what we are observing today, namely this protracted period of high inflation, will last in the medium term."

But as it turned out, eurozone inflation wasn't really the problem.

The Bank of England, meanwhile, couldn't decide whether inflation or recession was the greater threat to the economy. So the bank elected for patience. Even after its governor's noninterventionist approach had facilitated the first British bank failure in 141 years, the institution was biding its time, neither raising nor lowering interest rates, waiting to see what might happen next.

Among the nine members of its Monetary Policy Committee, expat Dartmouth professor "Danny" Blanchflower was the only one convinced that the British economy was in grave peril and immediate action was necessary.

Blanchflower envisioned the rapidly spreading financial crisis driving up joblessness and crushing consumer spending. He wasn't the most persuasive spokesman for that argument internally; even some MPC members who were sympathetic to Blanchflower's views thought that he'd offered more vague warnings rather than hard evidence—and in the King of Threadneedle Street's domain, hard evidence was everything. It was common knowledge among bank staff that the surest path to career advancement was working on what mattered most to Mervyn: the Monetary Analysis and Statistics Division, which he'd created. The "MA Way," full of theoretical rigor, ruled the land. Blanchflower, by contrast, practiced what he called "the economics of walking about," making decisions based on the messy realities of the world as he found it.

By late August, Blanchflower was fed up with trying to persuade his fellow committee members that he was right. So he called a reporter at Reuters and told him what he really thought. "We are going to see much more dramatic drops in output," he told the news service, predicting that two million Britons would be unemployed by Christmas. "I feel that things I have been fearful about have come to pass, and I have actually been pretty accurate in what's coming and I have failed to convince the others of what is appropriate."

"Sitting by doing nothing is not going to get us out of this," Blanchflower warned. At the MPC's monthly meeting the next week, he said, he would be pushing for a rate cut of more than 25 basis points.

Furious, King called Blanchflower into his office.

"How dare you do that?!" Blanchflower recalled him raging.

"What's it got to do with you?" asked Blanchflower.

King complained that Blanchflower had violated central banking's unwritten rules, which call for secrecy, tact, and, above all, collegiality.

"I don't care what you think," Blanchflower later recalled saying (a spokesman for King denied the exchange happened as Blanchflower described it). "How dare you speak to me like that. It has nothing to do with you. Piss off. Just piss off. I'm an independent member of the committee, and I think you're all completely mad. I represent the British people. I don't represent you, and I think you're wrong."

With that, Blanchflower walked out, his already poor relationship with King now fully off the rails.

Two weeks later, on September 11, 2008, Blanchflower and King sat with a row of colleagues in Portcullis House, a striking modern building on the bank of the Thames that contains offices of members of Parliament. They were addressing the House of Commons' Treasury Committee, and although Blanchflower was more diplomatic than he'd been in King's office, he left little doubt of what he really thought.

"I do have a somewhat more doom-laden view," he began in response to a question from MP John McFall. "I think we are going to see a deeper decline than others think."

What did the chairman of the MPC make of that prediction? "I do not think we really know what will happen to unemployment," King said during the hearing. "At least, the Almighty has not vouchsafed to me the path of unemployment data over the next year. He may have done to Danny, but he has not done to me."

Blanchflower was visibly upset just recalling the episode three years later. "Well, I just read the data, shithead!" he said. "Literally, I could've punched him. He was only sitting two seats down from me."

The world's central bankers admired the ingenuity and even the elegance with which Bernanke and Geithner engineered the rescue of Bear Stearns—a "masterful" rescue, as one European central banker said later. They assumed that the Americans would be up to the task the next time a major financial institution teetered on the brink. In fact, in that outwardly calm summer of 2008, Bernanke and Geithner were coming to grips with just how limited their power might be.

Bernanke pushed his staff to think broadly about the Fed's options to try to bolster the financial system; he famously sent e-mails with the subject line "Blue Sky," instructing staff to brainstorm ideas. But as the same forces that brought down Bear Stearns started to endanger Lehman Brothers, they found there was little under the clear blue sky that they could do.

Like Bear Stearns and many other Wall Street firms, Lehman was heavily involved in the creation of mortgage-backed securities. It also relied to a great extent on borrowed money, with $700 billion in total assets against only $25 billion in capital. In July, Lehman came to the New York Fed with a proposal: that it convert itself into a bank holding company, the sort of institution that would come under explicit oversight by the Fed, and in exchange gain access to the full range of central-bank programs that insure steady funding. To Geithner, the proposal seemed "gimmicky." This securities firm didn't look like a bank or smell like a bank. Why should the Fed pretend it was a bank?

At the same time, Fed officials in New York and Washington were game-planning what to do if Lehman encountered trouble similar to Bear's. On the evening of July 14, in a conference call with Geithner, Donald Kohn, and others, New York Fed markets desk chief Bill Dudley laid out a proposal for how the central bank might deal with a Lehman failure. His idea, described in detail in an e-mail exchange the next day, was to divide Lehman in two: a "bad bank," consisting of $60 billion of complex mortgage and other securities that were hard to value in a time of crisis, of which $55 billion would be funded by the Fed, and a "clean Lehman" consisting of everything else, which would be a more liquid, less leveraged investment bank stripped of ugly assets. In exchange for providing billions for the bad bank, the Fed would be given stock in the good bank.

The concept had theoretical elegance, but Fed lawyers in Washington were appalled. The emergency lending authority they'd used with Bear allowed them to lend against safe collateral, not to invest in the stock of an investment bank. There was, in this plan, no other buyer that could come in and take over like J.P. Morgan had done with Bear. Kohn hadn't pushed back much against the proposal in the evening conference call, according to an e-mail, but a Fed lawyer, Kieran Fallon, told general counsel Scott Alvarez that he would "raise significant concerns" over the proposal. Nothing similar to what Dudley had outlined ever materialized.

Less than a week later, Bernanke sent an e-mail to his closest advisers: "Our Options in the Event of a Run on LB." Patrick Parkinson started his reply this way: "The short answer is the one that Tim [Geithner] gave to the FOMC on Wednesday: There are no good options." He went on to give the long answer, explaining that even if the Fed were to take the dramatic step of extending $200 billion in credit to Lehman Brothers—at a time when the central bank's total balance sheet was $930 billion, essentially putting more than 20 percent of its resources to work for a single firm—it wouldn't necessarily fix the problem. "Absent an acquirer our action would not ensure LB's survival," Parkinson wrote on July 20.

The Fed injection might be enough for Lehman to satisfy its overnight lenders, but because of the stigma effect, the firm would likely face demands of cash from other entities it did business with. Or, if investors started to question the Fed's ability to fulfill mounting demands for cash in overnight-lending markets, it might not be enough. "That's not to imply that it would not be worth the gamble, but it would be a gamble," Parkinson concluded.

As Lehman's finances became ever more fragile in the summer of 2008, the consensus at the Fed was that there were no good options to save it unless a buyer came forward. "If we think that the run had progressed too far and that it wouldn't be sold," said New York Fed economist Jamie McAndrews in a July e-mail, "then any lending we did to it would be a permanent addition to the government's balance sheet—like Northern Rock, again."

The reckoning for Lehman came much as it did for Bear: slowly, then all at once. After months of a low murmur of worry, the actual collapse in confidence happened over just a few days, on the heels of the U.S. government's putting Fannie Mae and Freddie Mac into conservatorship, a form of bankruptcy. After a summer of relative calm, the crisis was back, and as the Fed had long feared, the markets were zeroing in on Lehman.

On the morning of Thursday, September 11, New York Fed officials sent colleagues in Washington a five-page plan for the weekend titled "Liquidation Consortium." The plan was to bring together the heads of the financial firms that had the most to lose if Lehman went down, "to provide a forum where these firms can explore possibilities of joint funding mechanisms that avert Lehman's insolvency" as well as more widespread financial devastation. The Fed wanted to invite only institutions that would stay at the negotiating table. If one left, the document noted, "many more may follow."

To minimize the possibility of leaks, the Fed gave less than two hours' notice to the invited executives, but when the executives showed up on Friday afternoon, news photographers were already arrayed around the New York Fed's headquarters in lower Manhattan.

The next two days were the most consequential for global capitalism in modern times. The guiding principle of the weekend was that Wall Street, not the Fed, would be the one to bail out Lehman Brothers. Geithner and Hank Paulson scurried between rooms, looking desperately for a buyer, or at least for a consortium of stronger firms that might, as Geithner phrased it, put "foam on the runway" for Lehman's crash.

As officials in the United States braced for impact, the central bankers and finance ministers of Europe gathered at one of the grandest villas in the south of France, nestled between Nice and Monaco in the village of Beaulieu-sur-Mer. They clinked champagne glasses in hundred-year-old gardens overlooking the Mediterranean, in a house that was built at the start of the twentieth century for, appropriately enough, a banking heiress, Béatrice Ephrussi de Rothschild. An opera singer's tenor carried through the late summer air. Apart from the absence of ball gowns on the women and white ties and tails on the men, one attendee observed, the scene looked as if it were taking place before World War I.

The opulent setting wasn't the only thing that called to mind the Great War. As Bank of England deputy governor for monetary policy Charles Bean had said in a parliamentary hearing that very morning, the same one in which Blanchflower wanted to punch King, "We thought a year ago, when this crisis first emerged, that it 'might be over by Christmas,' a bit like World War I, but as it has gone on we have realized that there are far deeper and more well-seated problems that will take longer to unfold." That the global crisis would, in different forms, go on for years more and profoundly endanger European unity made the comparison only more apt.

But the central bankers in Europe had little grasp of the peril their countries were facing. On that moonlit evening on the French Riviera, and the next day in more businesslike meetings in Nice, the mood was one of confidence that the Americans would take care of their mess. They had in the past, and Bank of America seemed poised to scoop up Lehman. The Europeans were constantly stepping outside to send e-mails or place calls to their contacts in the United States—and constantly heard very little in response. No one knew for sure how the details of the talks at the New York Fed were proceeding, in no small part because Geithner and Paulson were far too busy to loop in their counterparts overseas. Thus the discussion in Nice focused on longer-term reforms to financial regulation. Trichet even gave a speech in which he offered his thoughts on the current "financial-market correction," carefully avoiding the word "crisis."

As the Europeans left Nice on the evening of Saturday, September 13, the Americans were watching everything fall apart. Bank of America had elected to acquire Merrill Lynch, not Lehman Brothers. And British bank regulators were uncomfortable with Barclays buying Lehman, which could turn the American government's problem into the British government's problem. On Sunday, the Americans got to the end of the line: They had no buyer for Lehman.

The idea of a consortium had collapsed, in no small part due to the fragile finances of the very banks that it would have comprised. The Fed is allowed to lend money only against sound collateral. Whatever the arguments against the Bear Stearns bailout, the Fed had a plausible case that it would get its money back. Lehman was insolvent—a loan wouldn't solve its problem, and there was no legal way for Bernanke or Paulson to hand money over to a private firm. It's not clear that U.S. politicians, from President George W. Bush to congressional Democrats who were tiring of Wall Street bailouts, would have stood for it anyway.

That's why, Bernanke explained to Trichet in a phone call that Sunday, Lehman Brothers would have no choice but to file for bankruptcy protection first thing Monday morning.

Bernanke, not sounding terribly persuasive, said that he was hopeful that in the six months since Bear Stearns' failure, banks worldwide had girded themselves for the possibility of another large institution going down. Under no circumstances should you allow this firm to fail, Trichet argued, angry that the Americans would act so recklessly with a company that had deep financial interconnections with major banks all over the earth.

"We have no other options," Bernanke told Trichet.

"I think," the Frenchman replied, "that the result of this will be very grave indeed."

## ELEVEN

# A Wall of Money

The decision to let Lehman Brothers go bankrupt, in the end, wasn't really a decision at all. Never were Ben Bernanke and Tim Geithner and Hank Paulson equipped with a workable plan for preventing the firm from going bankrupt. By the time Lehman was on the brink, the crisis fighters were running up against the legal and political limits of their ability to stop it from going over.

That, however, wasn't what they told the outside world at the time. They wanted to project confidence and calm, to give the impression that the Lehman bankruptcy was a deliberate decision they'd made out of their conviction that the financial markets were sufficiently prepared for the possibility of such a failure—which had seemed imminent ever since the near collapse of Bear Stearns six months earlier. That was the message Fed officials voiced to reporters, their contacts in the markets, and even other central bankers.

"It was a bit crazy how calm they seemed," said one European central banker. "They were taking a big risk, and it seemed like a political choice that Paulson had made, but they framed it in terms of 'the markets are well prepared for this.'"

Privately, other central bankers blamed Paulson and the Bush administration more than they did Bernanke and Geithner. But even those sympathetic colleagues didn't understand the dilemma that the Fed had faced. "For central banks with different traditions and governments with the ability to guarantee their banks, they found it inconceivable that we would be constrained the way we were," said one American official. In any case, the result was plain: By allowing a financial institution of such great international economic reach to go bankrupt, the Fed had failed the global community of central bankers.

There was no time for remorse, however. On Monday, September 15, 2008, after a sleepless weekend dealing with Lehman, Geithner and his colleagues at the New York Fed faced a whole new crisis: American International Group, an insurance company with a $1 trillion balance sheet and 116,000 employees, was on the brink of collapse.

AIG had operations in almost every corner of the world economy: writing insurance policies against fire for homeowners, guaranteeing pension plans for municipalities, leasing 747s to airlines. But what had accounted for a surprising portion of its earnings in the previous few years—and the part of the company that now threatened to bring the whole thing down—was its financial products division. It had developed a wildly lucrative business of guaranteeing those seemingly high-quality mortgage bonds created by Wall Street. With AIG standing behind such securities, investors considered them virtually riskless. The insurer, meanwhile, viewed the odds of losing money on insuring these supersafe bonds as so low that it didn't reserve any money for payouts.

As the mortgage securities AIG guaranteed lost value, its clients—global banks including the French Société Generale, Germany's Deutsche Bank, and the United States' Goldman Sachs—demanded that AIG put up billions of dollars to ensure it would make good on the potential losses. But the firm's insurance arms were heavily regulated and couldn't just shift cash over to its financial products division.

Typically, AIG could have easily borrowed money in order to buy itself time to sell off some of its profitable businesses. But the banks were hardly in the mood to extend $75 billion in loans to a troubled company. They had their own problems—becoming the next Lehman chief among them. Raising the money on the stock market wasn't an option either. After Lehman Brothers filed for bankruptcy protection that Monday morning, the Dow Jones Industrial Average fell 504 points, one of the largest single-day drops in its history, and many of the overseas investors who had made large-scale investments in big U.S. financial companies in the earlier phase of the crisis had seen their money all but wiped out. The appetite of investors for new shares of a troubled insurer was nonexistent.

Geithner became convinced that the collapse of AIG would be catastrophic for the financial system—even though, as late as Lehman Brothers weekend, essentially no one within the Federal Reserve understood the risks the company had been taking or what might happen if it were to go under. The Office of Thrift Supervision was nominally in charge of overseeing AIG, due to the firm's long-ago acquisition of a savings and loan, but this most hapless of U.S. financial regulators was hardly up to the task of regulating a company that large and complex.

Fed leaders had to do some very quick, very scary guesstimation. "The failure of AIG, in our estimation, would have been basically the end," Bernanke said in a lecture years later. "It was interacting with so many different firms. . . . We were quite concerned that if AIG went bankrupt, we would not be able to control the crisis any further." There was, at least, a plausible option for the Fed—unlike with Lehman, for which there had been no good legal options for a bailout. This time, Washington wouldn't let down the world. Under the same "unusual and exigent" emergency lending authority it had used with Bear Stearns, the central bank could make the multibillion-dollar loan to AIG that private banks were at that moment unable or unwilling to make. The loan would, in a sense, be "secured" by AIG's insurance businesses, which the firm would have to sell in order to raise repayment funds. But there was no way to know for sure if taxpayers would ever get their money back.

When Bernanke and Paulson went to Capitol Hill the evening of Tuesday, September 16, to explain their plan for a Fed bailout of AIG, the reaction was one of incredulity. Senate majority leader Harry Reid clutched his head in his hands. "I want you to understand that you have not received the official blessing of Congress," he said.

"Do you have $80 billion?" asked Representative Barney Frank, to which Bernanke replied, "I have $800 billion," referring to the size of the Fed's balance sheet at the time. If anything, that understated the resources at Bernanke's disposal: For an institution that can print money, there are no real limits.

Bernanke and Geithner, in their own minds, applied a rigorous and ruthless logic when making their decisions about which institutions they would bail out and which they wouldn't. They depended on the exact financial circumstance of the company in question and the legal options available. To the outside world, though, their actions looked simply like flailing around.

A metaphor in wide circulation in the fall of 2008 was of dominoes: One investment bank falls, knocking over an insurance company, knocking over a commercial bank, and so on. But, as Bush adviser Edward P. Lazear would argue later, a more apt comparison was with popcorn. Rather than one failure predictably following another, they happened nonsequentially, as if the financial firms were all kernels of popcorn in a pan. There was one common source of heat: the realization that losses on a wide range of securities—mortgages at first, but ultimately lots of other kinds of lending—were going to be far greater than anyone had imagined possible. The kernels don't pop at the same time; some don't pop at all. But they were all exposed to heat. The great struggle for the world's central bankers in the days after AIG was to find a way to turn off the stove.

On September 16, as Bernanke and Geithner focused on what to do about AIG, another kernel looked ready to explode. Reserve Management Co. was one of the earliest innovators of a product that had transformed the way many people around the world save, as well as how many companies fund themselves. Introduced in 1971, the Reserve Primary Fund, like all money market mutual funds, performed many of the functions of a bank, both for savers and for borrowers, but without all the costly regulation and overhead of a bank. What does a bank do? It takes money from people who wish to save and lends it out to others who wish to invest. A money market mutual fund does the same thing: Savers deposit money, and the managers of the fund invest that money in safe, short-term investments—commercial paper issued by General Electric to manage its cash flow, for example, or Treasury bills issued by the U.S. government. Or the repurchase agreements that investment banks use to fund themselves.

Unlike a bank, though, a money market fund doesn't have to maintain a large cushion of capital—it invests nearly all of its investors' money in securities. It doesn't have the costly overhead of bank branches and tellers, so it can generally pay a higher rate of interest to savers and demand lower interest rates from borrowers. But it also lacks the range of government guarantees that the banking system has—federal deposit insurance, as well as access to emergency Fed lending. Indeed, the funds exploded in popularity in the 1970s and '80s in no small part to get around regulations, specifically caps on bank interest rates. Nonetheless, the investments seemed so safe that Americans parked their cash in them in remarkable quantities: $3.8 trillion by August 2008, or $12,000 for each American man, woman, and child, more than half the total amount of money on deposit at U.S. banks.

The Reserve Primary Fund accounted for only $62 billion of that total. And of its $62 billion in assets, only a bit more than 1 percent—$785 million— was invested in securities from Lehman Brothers. Yet when Lehman went under, the entire fund came close to collapse. From its public disclosures, investors were well aware that the Reserve Primary Fund had significant investments in Lehman. The evening of Sunday, September 14, as the investment bank appeared headed for bankruptcy, Reserve Fund managers fretted that they could see people withdrawing money from the fund as a result—up to $1.5 billion, they figured, according to e-mails that became public in subsequent litigation. At 8:37 a.m. on Monday, they had already received $5 billion in redemption requests.

When people demanded their money back, it meant that the fund's managers needed to sell other assets to get the necessary cash. And the week of September 14, 2008, was one of the worst weeks in the history of finance to try to sell commercial paper and other short-term investments. The Reserve Primary Fund may not have been a bank, but it was experiencing a run on the bank nonetheless. It announced Tuesday evening that it would have to "break the buck," meaning that shares in the fund normally worth $1 would in fact be worth only 97 cents.

In response, investors started pulling their money out of other money market funds, making $169 billion in withdrawals the very next day. A vicious cycle was setting in: As investors yanked their money from the funds, the funds were forced to dump commercial paper into the market to free up cash, causing their value to fall further, creating more losses. At the same time, the withdrawals threw into doubt the funding that many U.S. corporations use to pay for everyday operations.

As the New York Fed's market monitoring staffers made their daily calls to sources on the trading desks of Wall Street and beyond, and more senior Fed officials sounded out old contacts of their own, they were told of a situation that seemed on the verge of spinning out of control: More funds would break the buck, putting $3.8 trillion of Americans' savings at risk. And all that money being pulled out of mutual funds meant less cash available for banks, as well as companies that fund their operations with commercial paper. If the money market funds went, so would the solvency of banks that had weathered the collapse of Lehman and the near collapse of AIG, along with the ability of much of corporate America to make its payroll.

"We came very, very close to a depression," Bernanke told *Time* magazine in 2009. "The markets were in anaphylactic shock."

M odern economies can be astonishingly resilient to shocks. Pop a giant stock bubble, as occurred during the dot-com crash of the early 2000s, and the downturn might be mild as investors lick their wounds, capital is diverted to other uses, Webvan employees get new jobs, and everybody goes about their business. But mess with the very core of the financial system—people's confidence that their savings are secure—and the consequences are far more dire.

The idea that money itself may be unsafe triggers an almost primal fear in even the most levelheaded of investors. The problem in the Panic of 2008 wasn't that some investments lost value. It's that many of the investments that lost value—money market mutual funds being a prime example—had been viewed as absolutely safe. The basic reality of modern monetary systems had been laid bare: Money is simply an idea, a concept—a giant confidence game, even. People wanted out.

That was the feeling in the air that week in September 2008. The question was, what would the world's central bankers do about it? Could Walter Bagehot's time-honored approach to stopping a panic—lending freely to illiquid, not insolvent, firms at a penalty interest rate—be made to work when the panic was happening almost everywhere on earth at the same time, and in markets where traditional rules didn't apply?

The Fed's strategy for dealing with the panic was emblematic of its overall approach to the crisis. Bernanke, the Great Depression scholar, had particular admiration for Franklin Delano Roosevelt's strategy during the 1930s. Not every program his administration undertook did much good, but there was a spirit of experimentation, of throwing everything the government had against the wall to see what would stick. As the money market funds trembled, Bernanke directed his troops to adopt the same approach: Try everything.

First, just three days after the Reserve Fund broke the buck, came the Asset Backed Commercial Paper Money Market Mutual Fund Liquidity Facility, or AMLF. With Fed staffers in New York and Washington already stretched thin with crisis fighting, the program was administered by the Federal Reserve Bank of Boston, which had particular expertise in money market funds: The city is home to a number of the major mutual fund groups, as well as State Street, a bank that carries out transactions for many of the funds. The idea was to use infrastructure that had long been in place to channel money to banks to back up the money market funds instead. The Fed would lend money to banks, which could then buy the securities the money market funds were selling off and pledge them to the Fed, with the banks themselves taking no financial risk for their role as intermediary.

The program lent out $24 billion on its first day of operation, September 22, 2008, and $217 billion before the panic wound down, routing money through banks like State Street and J.P. Morgan Chase to mutual funds run by household-name companies such as Janus and Oppenheimer. To satisfy the Fed's lawyers, the program could accept commercial paper backed only by specific assets, such as credit card loans due. But with a buyer in the market for even just a subset of the securities they owned, the money market funds could raise enough money to avoid breaking the buck.

It took a little longer to come up with the next mode of attack. The Commercial Paper Funding Facility, announced on October 7, focused on the other side of the same problem, the difficulty companies were having selling their commercial paper, due in large part to the money market funds not being available as a buyer. With the CPFF, the Fed used its 13(3) authority to lend money in "unusual and exigent circumstances" to fund a "special purpose vehicle" (SPV) that purchased commercial paper from eligible issuers. Participants in the program could sell to the SPV only after paying a fee of 0.1 percent of their total commercial paper balance—a requirement designed to provide the Fed some measure of protection. If some of the borrowers defaulted, the theory went, any losses would be covered by those fees—in other words, by the companies that took part in the program, not taxpayers.

Before it was all over, in early 2010, some $738 billion in commercial paper had been purchased from affiliates of eighty-two different companies. Big banks, both domestic and foreign, were on the list. So were some of the mainstays of the U.S. corporate sector. Verizon used the program on two successive days in late October 2008, borrowing a combined $1.5 billion. The finance arm of Harley-Davidson turned to the CPFF thirty-three times for a combined $2.3 billion, helping ensure it could continue making loans to potential buyers of its motorcycles. The major American auto firms' finance arms—Ford Credit, GMAC, Chrysler Financial Services—all took part in the program. So did General Electric. Golden Funding Corp., which lends to McDonald's franchisees so they can build or renovate their restaurants, turned to the CPFF eight times for a total of $203 million, helping ensure the continued availability of Big Macs across the land.

In the Rooseveltian spirit of experimentation, the Fed created so many emergency lending facilities that a document just listing and summarizing them required a legal-sized piece of paper covered in small type. There was even a complex program called the Money Market Investor Funding Facility, announced on October 21, that never lent a single dime. The MMIFF aimed to create another place where the money market funds could dump their holdings—but Fed staff couldn't figure out how to make the program attractive to participants while also protecting taxpayers against losses, an ongoing problem in emergency lending.

At the time, commentators often asked: Where's the money going? Exactly who's borrowing from the Fed? The answers, revealed by information made available only much later, turned out to be everywhere—and everyone. Wrote *Time* magazine, in naming him its "Person of the Year," Bernanke "conjured up trillions of new dollars and blasted them into the economy; . . . lent to mutual funds, hedge funds, foreign banks, investment banks, manufacturers, insurers and other borrowers who had never dreamed of receiving Fed cash; jump-started stalled credit markets in everything from car loans to corporate paper; . . . and generally transformed the staid arena of central banking into a stage for desperate improvisation."

No wonder his eyes look tired.

The shock of the Lehman failure quickly spread across the Atlantic. The thing that European banks had feared since August 2007—that another major bank might have such grave losses on its books that lending money to it would be dangerous—had happened. If Lehman Brothers could go belly up, couldn't any big bank? And that being the case, why would a banker willingly lend dollars to one of his competitors for interest rates of only a couple percent? As had been the case in late 2007, dollars were in particularly short supply, a problem for banks that might be headquartered in Frankfurt or Zurich or Paris but had vast quantities of dollar loans on their balance sheets.

The lending rate between banks, which typically wouldn't have been higher than the 2 percent target the Fed then had in place, soared to over 5 percent in the weeks after the Lehman bankruptcy. That's a misleading number, though: It really reflects a market that had shut down, with lots of entities out there hoping to borrow dollars but no one willing to lend. Interbank lending just wasn't happening. As a result, even banks that could easily weather direct losses from money they were owed by Lehman found themselves unable to get the cash they needed to meet their daily obligations. Due to the unusual status of the dollar as the closest thing there is to a global currency, there was a worldwide shortage of dollars that threatened to bring down the entire global economy.

"This is clearly outside the textbook case of a financial crisis," said Stefan Ingves, governor of Sweden's central bank, the Riksbank. "We couldn't just create our own currency to lend to the banks. We can't produce dollars, and we can't produce euros."

The panic quickly trickled down to the retail level, particularly in countries that had unreliable systems for the government insurance of deposits. Ordinary depositors, seeing a major global institution go down and the financial markets gyrate, started pulling their money out of banks far from Lehman's Manhattan headquarters. Officials were reduced to public pleas to their citizens: "Irish bank deposits are not in any danger," announced Brian Lenihan, the Irish finance minister, on September 19. "People should not be going to their banks and making withdrawals on the basis of unfounded suggestions voiced on radio programs."

Conference calls among the world's central banks picked up as they worked through ways they might collectively address the burgeoning crisis. The banks' markets chiefs—Bill Dudley of the New York Fed, Francesco Papadia at the ECB, and a half dozen counterparts around the globe—worked together to expand the strategy they had first deployed nine months earlier to address the milder form of panic spreading at that time. The calls usually happened early in the morning New York time, when it wasn't the middle of the night in London, Frankfurt, or Tokyo. They were usually led by Dudley. After all, the central problem was a shortage of dollars—so the one institution in the world with the capability of creating dollars was in the driver's seat.

The bankers were looking for ways not merely to deal with the panic roiling the financial system, but also to handle, in Geithner's terminology, the "theater" correctly. Apart from the substance of what they might do, they reasoned, the simple fact that all the world's central banks were acting in concert might help boost confidence. A German bank would be more inclined to lend dollars to a Swiss bank if it could be confident the Swiss bank wasn't going to find itself short of cash when it was time to pay the money back. "Making it known that we were getting the fire engines rolling was almost as important as what the engines would do once they arrived at the scene," said one American official.

Unlike the earlier phase of the crisis, when Mervyn King and the Bank of England were reluctant partners in the crisis-fighting efforts, this time everyone was on the same page. At 3 a.m. New York time on September 18, four days after the Lehman failure, the fire engines cranked up their sirens. At the end of 2007, the Fed had announced a combined $24 billion in swap lines with the ECB, Bank of England, Bank of Canada, and Swiss National Bank. Now, according to an announcement made in time to beat the opening of European markets, that amount would be enlarged by $180 billion. Six days later, again with a middle-of-the-night announcement, the Fed added to the program another $30 billion and another four central banks—those of Australia, Denmark, Norway, and Sweden.

It was the basic strategy of late 2007 blown out: More dollars were pumped into the banking system, in more different countries, on easier terms. There were legal guarantees to make sure American taxpayers wouldn't lose money on the deal, but the real assurance came not from anything written on paper but from the bonds of trust established in years of talks in Basel and elsewhere. It was unfathomable, Bernanke and his colleagues believed, that their counterparts across national borders would ever try to renege.

When members of Congress asked about the swaps, Bernanke emphasized that the European banks benefiting from the program also made loans in the United States, so the action could be seen as benefiting the U.S. economy directly. But more fundamentally, he was convinced that the world financial system was so deeply interconnected that Europe's fortunes were the United States' fortunes too. "In a way," a European central banker said later, "we became the thirteenth Federal Reserve district."

By December 10, foreign central banks had borrowed $580 billion of Fed money—a quarter of the U.S. central bank's total assets. The Fed also pumped dollars into individual foreign banks that had U.S. subsidiaries: at peak levels, $85 billion for the Royal Bank of Scotland, $77 billion for Switzerland's UBS, $66 billion for Deutsche Bank, $65 billion for the UK's Barclays, $59 billion for Belgium's Dexia, and $22 billion for Japan's Norinchukin. The scale of lending to foreign banks, revealed more than two years later only after congressional legislation and a Freedom of Information Act lawsuit that the banking industry appealed to the Supreme Court, was a closely guarded secret even by the standards of the always secretive Fed. Normally, dozens of people within the Federal Reserve System would have been privy to data about which banks were borrowing money. During the panic, this information was so closely held—and, had it been known publicly, so potentially explosive—that only two people at each of the dozen reserve banks were allowed access to it.

Beginning in October, a new round of supplicants came calling. In formal letters to Bernanke, in whispered asides to his deputies in the hallways in Basel, several of the world's developing nations made a request: Help us out. As late as March 2009, when Fed governor Kevin Warsh was representing the central bank at a meeting of the finance ministers of the Group of 20 economic powers in Horsham, England, emissaries from one after another of the world's emerging nations tried to buttonhole him in the hallway to make their pleas for help.

Banks in these economies were facing the same shortage of dollars as their counterparts in wealthier neighbors. Behind closed doors, this became the subject of a thorny new debate. The Fed didn't have the same intimate, longstanding relationships with the Central Bank of Brazil or the Bank of Mexico that it did with the Bank of England or the Bank of Canada. And there had already been rumblings of concern among some of the reserve bank presidents that the lending of dollars across international borders amounts to fiscal, not monetary, policy. The Richmond Fed in particular had a long tradition of dissenting from any type of swap arrangement for that very reason; its president,

Jeffrey Lacker, often clashed with the New York Fed's Tim Geithner on that and many other issues.

But most important, sending money to poorer countries with less stable political systems would be a greater risk. So Bernanke and his colleagues came up with criteria for safely expanding Fed swap lines: The country had to want access to them. (China and India weren't particularly interested.) The country had to be a significant player in the world economy or a significant financial center, so that Bernanke could justify the assistance to Congress as being in the interest of the U.S. economy. (Brazil, Mexico, South Korea, and Singapore qualified; Peru didn't.) The country had to have a central bank that was viewed as politically independent and trustworthy. (Russia, for example, would have been ruled out.) On October 29, 2008, came an announcement: "Today, the Federal Reserve, the Banco Central do Brasil, the Banco de Mexico, the Bank of Korea, and the Monetary Authority of Singapore are announcing the establishment of temporary reciprocal currency arrangements."

Since its founding, the Federal Reserve had been the lender of last resort for the United States. In late 2008, Ben Bernanke's Fed became the lender of last resort to much of the world.

On the evening of Wednesday, September 17, just a day after making the decision to bail out AIG, Bernanke and his staff gathered in his office overlooking the National Mall. The Fed chief had decided it was time to make clear to Paulson that the central bank could no longer bail out individual insolvent firms. It was one thing for the Fed to support illiquid firms or markets, where disruptions were caused by fear rather than balance-sheet facts. It was another for it to support insolvent institutions, a job for Congress and the administration. Bernanke told Paulson in a phone call that he thought they needed to go to Congress to ask for a rescue package. The next morning, Bernanke was prepared to make the same point more emphatically in another call, but Paulson cut him off: The treasury secretary had reached the same conclusion.

That afternoon, the two men met with President George W. Bush at the White House. With his blessing, they then traveled to Capitol Hill to speak with the leaders of Congress. In an ominous meeting in House Speaker Nancy Pelosi's conference room, they warned congressional leaders that the entire financial system was on the verge of implosion, and that the consequences for the U.S. economy—not yet obvious at that early date—could be disastrous. "It is a matter of days," Bernanke told the lawmakers, "before there is a meltdown in the global financial system." Congress needed to enact massive legislation to allow the Treasury the latitude to address the problem—and fast.

That day, and in a series of difficult congressional hearings that followed, Bernanke stood by Paulson's side, explaining and advocating what would become the $700 billion Troubled Asset Relief Program. His vigorous support was essential. Paulson, a former Goldman Sachs executive, had plenty of intensity, but he also had trouble explaining complex economic concepts to nonspecialists. Reporters covering his hearings often joked about the difficulty of quoting him because of the way his sentences circled back on themselves in an unintelligible mess. ("What we are seeking to address with this," Paulson said in a September 23 Senate Banking Committee hearing, "is we are seeking to address—first of all, we're dealing with complicated securities, mortgage and mortgage-related, and we've got various asset classes here, and we need different approaches for different asset classes. But when we use the market mechanisms, we want—we're looking at thousands, you know, of institutions, because to make this run properly, we need to deal with big banks, small banks, S&Ls, credit unions, because what we're trying to do here, and I think we'll be successful, is to develop mechanisms where we—where we get values out there, where there's some value that the market can look at.")

Bernanke's experience as a scholar of the Great Depression gave him credibility, and his clear, methodical speaking style made him persuasive. He viewed his role as not to advocate for a specific law, but to explain the economics of the situation and the necessity for immediate, bold action. Although Bernanke wasn't involved in the detailed negotiations over the TARP—he figured out that an initial vote on the proposal had failed in the House when he glanced at the Bloomberg data terminal on his desk and saw a giant dive in the stock market—he would be forever associated with the unpopular legislation by both lawmakers and the public.

Congress finally passed the TARP on October 3. Ten days later, Paulson summoned the heads of nine of the biggest and most important banks in the United States into the Treasury building. He lined them up, each with a name-plate, on one side of a twenty-four-foot mahogany conference table. They had been told the night before to be there at 3 p.m. without being told why; a few resisted the last-minute request, though by 2:59 all were lined up in their as-signed spots. Paulson, Bernanke, Geithner, and FDIC chair Sheila Bair entered and took the seats across from the bank executives. Paulson ran the meeting: The banks would each be taking billions of new capital from the new govern-ment bailout program, he said. Any who refused would surely be hearing from their regulators on the matter—here the presence of Bernanke and Bair strengthened the implicit threat. Geithner read off how much capital each bank would be taking: $25 billion for Citigroup, $10 billion for Morgan Stanley, and so on. Some of the executives, worried about diluting existing shareholders and the new restraints that might come on their own salaries, raised various objec-tions. Bernanke, ever the conciliator, said, "I don't really understand why there needs to be so much tension about this."

The TARP was among the most unpopular programs the U.S. government has ever undertaken; when Paulson and Bernanke had their meetings with the bankers, CBS and the *New York Times* were conducting a poll that would show only 28 percent support of the newly passed bailout plan, and even two years later senators who voted for it were pummeled by their opponents for doing so. The whole point of the program was to shift the burden of rescuing the banks away from Bernanke and the Fed and into a program that had more democratic legitimacy. But by standing by Paulson's side at every step of the way—on Capi-tol Hill, and in telling the bankers about the money they would be taking—Bernanke would be haunted by the TARP and its political taint for many years to come.

I n Europe, Trichet was also being forced into the political arena.

In the early morning hours of Tuesday, September 30, the leaders of Ireland, a nation of four million people and the world's fifty-seventh largest economy, with a GDP smaller than Louisiana's, made a decision that set in mo-tion events that altered the history of Europe. The country's banks were overburdened with bad loans for Irish and British real estate, and the people who funded the banks—both ordinary Irish savers and the global investors who bought the banks' debt—were fast losing confidence.

Trichet had called Irish finance minister Brian Lenihan to deliver a stern message. "You must save your banks at all costs," Trichet said, Lenihan recalled later. Trichet warned Lenihan and Bank of Ireland governor John Hurley that the panic that had started with Lehman was rapidly spreading to the banks of Europe. Plenty of institutions were in trouble—in Germany, the Netherlands, and France. But on that Monday, Ireland was hit particularly hard. Anglo Irish Bank shares declined a whopping 46 percent to lead a national stock market crash of nearly 13 percent—the worst one-day drop in the country's history.

Lenihan called a meeting of the heads of the biggest Irish banks that evening to figure out what to do. The government decided, at about 4 a.m., and without consultation with anyone outside the borders of this small country, to guarantee the liabilities of six major Irish banks—to guarantee that all the bondholders and depositors owed money by these private concerns would be made whole, at the government's expense.

Hurley called Trichet at 6 a.m. to tell him of the plan. British chancellor of the exchequer Alistair Darling found out about it on the BBC morning news. The reaction across Europe was of shock—and, as time passed, anger. For one thing, Trichet and his colleagues thought that the extensive steps they had taken to funnel euros (and dollars, through the swap lines) to banks would be enough to keep them from experiencing runs. For another, Ireland had just taken a step that would expose its government to huge expense if the banks' losses turned out to be worse than it appeared. And Ireland had created a situation in which its banks had stronger state guarantees than other European banks.

It would take more than a year for investors to ask the important question: Could the Irish government even *afford* to guarantee its banks? At the time, money gushed into Irish banks—and out of banks in the rest of Europe, particularly Britain. Darling called Lenihan at about nine that morning, telling him that the actions had placed Britain in an "an impossible position," inasmuch as the British government had no desire—or, it feared, resources—to create a similar guarantee for its own massive banking system. European nations were grappling with the sudden realization that not only were their banks more exposed to the United States than they would have imagined—"What were they doing screwing around in the United States?" French president Nicolas Sarkozy was said to have asked his staff after a $9.2 billion bailout of the Franco-Belgian bank Dexia)—but also that the crisis could soon turn into an every-man-for-himself situation in which money flitted from nation to nation depending on which was offering the best guarantees.

In private conversations with European finance ministers and heads of state, Trichet argued for consistency. It simply wouldn't do, he told them, for every European nation to have a different set of policies for guaranteeing the obligations of its banks. National leaders agreed with that idea in principle; they just couldn't agree on the details of how to abide by it. Sarkozy called leaders of Germany, Britain, and Italy to the magnificent Élysée Palace in Paris the following weekend to try to hammer out a coordinated plan. The French were floating the strategy of creating a pan-European backstop for the banks, a single authority backed by the whole of the union that would make it unnecessary for Ireland and Belgium and every other country to take action independently.

There were huge technical and political challenges to enacting such a sweeping plan with the kind of speed needed. But most significantly, Germany, the largest economy in Europe, wasn't on board. It preferred to keep bank rescues a strictly national affair. It's no coincidence that under such a scheme, Germany would likely end up covering the costs of a bank bailout in a smaller, less economically powerful country like Ireland. "To put it mildly, Germany is highly cautious about such grand designs for Europe," said German finance minister Peer Steinbrück just before the summit in Paris. "Other countries are free to think about it. I just don't see any German interest in it."

Sarkozy reportedly turned to his aides after meeting with German chancellor Angela Merkel and whispered, "If we cannot cobble together a European solution then it will be a debacle. But it will not be my debacle; it will be Angela's. You know what she said to me? *'Chacun sa merde.'*" To each his own shit.

Like Bernanke during the TARP debate, Trichet played the role of influencer, not decider. At the summit, he emphasized the importance of making new financial backing for banks consistent among nations. But he wasn't a vigorous advocate for socializing the cost of bank bailouts across the EU, as the French government preferred. Whatever his true preference at the time, he was the consummate dealmaker, and he saw no deal to be made given the vehemence of the opposition from Germany. Said one European official who observed Trichet at work, "He is very adaptable. He has a skill for adjusting his position according to what is possible at the time."

Publicly, Trichet was dismissive of the idea that Europe's lack of a central government hampered its response to the banking crisis. "Who can say we've done worse than the other side of the Atlantic?" he told reporters on October 6. "There is no lack of coordination—there is a European spirit. We have different governments, and they have different means of intervention."

The meeting in Paris closed with agreement on a strategy so vague as to be meaningless. Sunday night, Angela Merkel rushed back to Berlin, where adviser Jens Weidmann warned her that people were withdrawing 500-euro notes at a remarkable pace; the beginnings of a German bank run were under way. Merkel went on television to reassure her public. "I'm telling all citizens with savings that their deposits are safe," she said. "The federal government will guarantee that." A spokesman later explained that she wasn't announcing a specific legal guarantee of German banks, but merely stating a broad principle. That didn't matter much, though: It sounded to the rest of the world like she'd just announced that Germany would be doing exactly what she'd spent the previous six days attacking Ireland for doing.

Over the ensuing days, European leaders would reach a broader agreement on how deposit guarantees should work. But it had no hint of common financial resources. That is to say, Germany would back German banks, Spain Spanish banks, and so on. This was particularly problematic for countries that had banking systems that were huge relative to their economies: Ireland's bank guarantees meant putting the government on the hook for bank liabilities that added up to four years' economic output!

Bernanke would spend the three years that followed dealing with fallout from his successful lobbying of Congress on bailing out the banks. Trichet would spend his time dealing with the results of European political leaders' failure to act in concert for the same purpose.

I n the run-up to the Lehman bankruptcy, the differences in monetary policy on the two sides of the Atlantic had become stark, with the ECB having raised interest rates in July 2008 to tighten the money supply, the Bank of England having left them unchanged for six months, and the Fed having lowered them in early 2008 to loosen the money supply. But in the frantic days of September and October 2008, signs were everywhere that the economic damage from the crisis could become severe—though how severe no one knew yet. There were new reports of mass layoffs seemingly every day, both in the United States and Europe. Global trade was plummeting, according to data from shipping companies. And the inflationary pressures that so worried Trichet and King the previous summers quickly abated—oil, $145 a barrel in July, would drop to about $40 a barrel by the end of the year.

All signs were pointing to a global economy that was crashing on the rocks of recession or even depression. It was time for the central banks to stop worrying about high inflation and start pumping money into the economy. Bernanke and King, the old officemates at MIT, figured that if all the major central banks acted together, they would have a greater impact than if any one of them acted alone, or even if they all did the same thing separately. And by moving as one, they could eliminate any distortions that might result in currency markets if they moved separately—something Trichet was particularly concerned about. If the ECB cut interest rates, he worried, the euro could decline excessively. By early October, though, he was ready to stand with Bernanke and King. Just three months after raising rates, Trichet prepared to reverse his decision.

The triumvirate spoke with some of their colleagues at the smaller central banks—Bernanke with Mark Carney at the Bank of Canada, King with Philipp Hildebrand of the Swiss National Bank, and Trichet with Stefan Ingves of Sweden's Riksbank. Bernanke called a special meeting of the Fed policy committee, via a videoconference system that arrayed the policymakers' faces across the screen in squares like in the intro to *The Brady Bunch*.

The joint announcement released at 7 a.m. New York time on October 8, 2008, of the first globally coordinated monetary easing in history, left little doubt where the Boys of Basel had ended up, whatever their differences had been in the run-up to the crisis. "Throughout the current financial crisis, central banks have engaged in continuous close consultation and have cooperated in unprecedented joint actions such as the provision of liquidity to reduce strains in financial markets," it read. After noting that inflation pressures had diminished, it continued, "Some easing of global monetary conditions is therefore warranted. Accordingly, the Bank of Canada, the Bank of England, the

European Central Bank, the Federal Reserve, Sveriges Riksbank, and the Swiss National Bank are today announcing reductions in policy interest rates. The Bank of Japan expresses its strong support of these policy actions."

With the course of action established by that cooperative effort, the banks continued to lower rates individually over the coming weeks. As the Bank of England's monetary policymakers prepared to gather in November, analysts expected them to cut rates by another half a percentage point. But the economic numbers were even worse than in-house pessimist Danny Blanchflower had imagined. In advance of the meeting, he met with Tim Besley, a Monetary Policy Committee colleague who'd been on the opposite side of the interest rate argument just a few months earlier. Besley had pivoted—the economy had deteriorated farther and faster than he'd thought possible. "What are we going to do?" Besley asked, according to Blanchflower's recollection.

"We've got to cut 150," Blanchflower replied. They should, he was arguing, cut interest rates by a percent and a half, three times as much as markets were expecting. Besley went to speak to the more hawkish, inflation-focused members of the committee. Blanchflower went to speak to King. "This has gone completely mad," he told the governor. "Unless you cut by 150 the second after the decision, I will call a press conference and immediately lay out what you have done."

King was quickly coming to the same view; he had a stubborn streak, but was willing to change his views when the world around him offered persuasive evidence that he had been wrong. And the evidence was piling up that the British economy was in free fall due to the global crisis. The committee gathered the afternoon of Wednesday, November 5, to have its initial discussion of the decision it would make the next morning. King started the meeting. "'I realize where we are,'" Blanchflower recalled him saying. "'This is a very serious situation. And just to put this on the table, just so we don't get confused, I have a proposal on the table that we cut by 150 basis points.'"

After reaching a decision at about 11:30 a.m. on November 6, Blanchflower and his colleagues went to their offices, sworn to silence to ensure there were no leaks before the public announcement at noon. In the moments before the central bank shocked the market with its 150-point cut, Blanchflower was awed by the fact that after months of fighting an unsuccessful battle for the bank to cut rates, he had finally won—though it did take a global financial collapse to make it happen. "I'm shaking. I'm absolutely bloody shaking," he said. There was a countdown to the announcement, scheduled to happen at precisely noon Greenwich Mean Time, so that all news outlets would get the information at exactly the same time. The media, financial markets, and even other Bank of England staff were stunned by the aggressiveness of the move. Finally, the Bank of England, the most reluctant crisis fighter in the 2007 phase of things, was ready to pull out its big policy guns.

At the Federal Reserve, Bernanke wasn't content to quit at the October rate cut either. But given the slashing of rates the Fed had done earlier in the year, there wasn't much room for more cuts. After the joint rate cut and another by the Fed three weeks later, the federal funds rate on November 1 was only 1 percent, already a historically low level. In other words, the device three generations of Federal Reserve chairmen had used to prop up faltering economies was no longer working. The Fed could lower rates down close to zero, perhaps, but not below that. If interest rates were negative—meaning savers would actually lose instead of make money over time—people would just take their money out of the banks.

But a decade earlier as an academic, Bernanke had argued that even if *short-term* interest rates hit the so-called zero lower bound, a central bank wasn't out of options for fighting a slumping economy. It could always lower longer-term interest rates too. In late 2008, the economy was in free fall—but just how much so wasn't clear. (Gross domestic product was falling at a 9 percent annual rate, but the first data that became available that winter put the pace of contraction at only 3 percent.) On November 25, the Fed's Board of Governors announced a plan to buy up to $500 billion in mortgage-backed securities guaranteed by government-sponsored companies like Fannie Mae and Freddie Mac. But in their hurry to try to pump money into the financial system, the Fed's lawyers made a mistake: It wasn't within the power of the Board of Governors to have made that decision. This was a form of monetary policy, so it had to be decided by the full Federal Open Market Committee, which includes presidents of reserve banks around the country.

In the days before the December 16 meeting, Bernanke called his colleagues across the country. All of them agreed that the economy was in terrible shape. Some were angry that they hadn't been included in the decision on mortgage securities. Others were already antsy about the vast expansion in Fed lending. Bernanke wanted the next policy announcement to be a show of decisiveness and unity. And he wanted not merely to cut rates, but to cut them to zero and pledge to keep them there for some time, as well as to give a formal blessing to the plan to purchase mortgage-backed securities in order to pump money into the economy through alternate means.

Usually, Bernanke viewed the dissent of one or two policymakers from a decision as the sign of a healthy committee. ("If two people always agree," he's said, "one of them is redundant.") But for this move, he very much wanted unanimity. After all, if the Fed could take such action unanimously, it would create greater confidence that it was truly committed to keeping rates low for a long time. Dallas Fed president Richard Fisher was reluctant to go along with the move, however, viewing it as a risky proposition that wouldn't help the economy much. He initially voted against the action—then, while his colleagues ate lunch and staffers prepared the announcement, approached Bernanke privately and asked to change his vote. "I felt after going for a walk down the hall that I didn't want to pull the legs out from under Ben," Fisher later said. "I didn't want to be perceived as not being a team player."

Bernanke's years of respectful consensus building had paid off, just when he needed it most.

That fall and winter, the central bankers of the world worked nonstop, in constant touch with each other, the weight of history constantly on their minds. After Liaquat Ahamed's book *Lords of Finance: The Bankers Who Broke the World,* an account of how the central bankers of the 1920s and '30s bungled their way into the Great Depression, was released in January 2009, Geithner tried reading it in the evenings. Over and over, he had to put it down and stop, horrified that even highly intelligent, well-meaning policymakers could mishandle a situation badly enough to create mass human misery.

But what the world's most powerful central bankers did in that fall of 2008 was, piece by piece, build a wall of money, attempt to fight the panic on a scale commensurate with its severity. They did it by lending to banks and investment firms and even individual businesses. They did it by swapping dollars and euros and pounds with each other and their counterparts in emerging nations. They did it by trying to influence their governments to bail out insolvent banks. With people in almost every country on earth hoarding their money, the central bankers created more of it, flooding the financial system, substituting their own bottomless resources for those of newly fearful world investors.

They didn't prevent a steep decline in the world economy. From May 2008 to March 2009, the global stock market fell in value by almost $27 trillion, a 47 percent drop, wiping out wealth equivalent to the goods and services produced by every human on earth in half a year. If you look at a graph of the U.S. stock market, the period of 1929 to 1931 tracks very closely with that of 2007 to 2009. So do measures of the economy more broadly, such as industrial production. But in the 1930s, the declines continued for years. In the recent episode, they leveled off in the spring and summer of 2009.

There was far more work to do. But the wall of money built by the global central bankers had held.

# Part III

---·∞∞∞·---

## AFTERMATH,
## 2009–2010

# TWELVE

# The Battle for the Fed

T he hallway outside Room 2128 of the Rayburn House Office Building was crowded with dozens of people sitting on the floor. Dressed in lived-in sweats, skintight shorts, and tattered-looking winter coats, they hardly looked like a crowd waiting to view a hearing of the House Committee on Financial Services. They weren't. The various students, bike messengers, and even homeless people vying for one of the few dozen seats open to the public were members of an unlikely Washington profession: those who earn money by holding a place in line for well-heeled financial lobbyists. And on March 24, 2009, with the unemployment rate rising, economic output plummeting, and the stock market at 1997 levels, they had some even more unlikely competition: a group of middle-aged women in bright pink shirts and life jackets, holding signs that read WHERE'S MY JOB?, WHERE'S MY IRA?, and BAIL US OUT.

These representatives of Code Pink, a left-wing group that arose to protest the Iraq War and had broadened its interests to include economic issues, had gotten there first, thus claiming the seats right behind the witness table, which would soon be occupied by Fed chairman Ben Bernanke, Treasury Secretary Tim Geithner, and New York Fed president Bill Dudley. American International Group, the giant insurance company that the Fed had bailed out six months before, would be paying out $165 million in bonuses to its employees, honoring earlier contractual commitments made to retain the people responsible for winding down its cash-sapping financial products division. The wrath of an angry Congress was about to descend upon Bernanke and his two colleagues.

"This is a very important public hearing," said Massachusetts congressman and committee chair Barney Frank as the proceedings got under way. "It will not be disrupted. There will be no distraction. My own view is that critical conversation, indeed, whole sentences and even paragraphs, advance even a negative view more than bumper stickers, no matter what sort of bumper those stickers are worn on." The Code Pink protestors held up their signs.

The committee leaders from both parties started by giving long speeches. Then the three witnesses delivered their opening statements. As Geithner proceeded to talk about "a broad set of regulatory reform proposals, specifically related to systemic risk," Frank interrupted him.

"Will you please act your age back there?" said Frank to the demonstrators. "Stop playing with that sign. If you have no greater powers of concentration, then you leave the room."

It was Bernanke's turn. "AIG faced severe liquidity pressures that threatened to force it imminently into bankruptcy—" Frank interrupted again: "The next one that holds a sign will be ejected. I do not know how you think you advance any cause to which you might be attached by this kind of silliness."

Once the prepared statements were finally done, Frank told his sixty-some committee members how it would be: They would have five minutes each. No exceptions. "I wish we didn't have the five-minute rule, and I wish we didn't have so many members. And I wish I could lose weight without dieting," he said.

Michele Bachmann, the firebrand conservative congresswoman from Minnesota who two years later would have a brief turn as a front-runner for the Republican presidential nomination, wondered if the government was in the midst of "a historic shift, jettisoning the free-market capitalism in favor of centralized government economic planning." She proceeded to question the constitutionality of the Federal Reserve and ask whether there were plans to abandon the dollar and move to an international currency.

"How do the three of you operate in your own mind?" implored Ron Paul, the Texas congressman who made his own 2012 presidential run and authored the book *End the Fed*. "Do you operate with the idea that capitalism failed, and they need us more than ever before to solve these problems?"

Illinois representative Donald Manzullo confronted Bernanke and Geithner over why the government bailout of AIG helped people whose savings were insured by the company to avoid losing out at a time when Americans' stock portfolios were being hammered. "The American people have lost 40 to 50 percent of their retirement plans," he said.

"The purpose of the action we took with AIG," replied Bernanke, "was not to help any specific counterparty."

"But you did," interrupted Manzullo. "That's what happened."

Americans were paying $40 billion "so that other people don't lose any of their retirement plans," Manzullo said. "That's what happened, isn't it?"

"Congressman," Bernanke said, "those losses the American people would have been—"

"Give me a yes or no, please," said Manzullo.

". . . would have been far greater—" continued Bernanke.

"No, did the people who took out—"

". . . would have been far greater—" Bernanke tried again.

"I'm asking the question," snapped Manzullo. "Did the people who took out insurance with AIG . . . get reimbursed 100 percent so they suffered very little loss? Yes or no?"

"It depends on the nature of those specific contracts," said Bernanke.

Frank interrupted once more: "I would ask the people in that second row to stop the gesturing and the conversations . . . If there's any further disruption, I would ask the officers . . . to simply escort people out."

To call it a circus would be unfair to Barnum and Bailey.

In the spring of 2009, people of opposing parties and differing political ideologies could all agree on one thing: The government agency that most clearly deserved to have its wings clipped in response to the economic crisis was the mighty Federal Reserve.

It was both a convenient and a logical target. To those on the left, the Fed had been blinded by the free-market dogma of its previous chairman, Alan

Greenspan, and thus had been unwilling to regulate big banks and protect consumers from taking out irresponsible loans. To those on the right, it had med-
dled in the free market, pushing too much money into the economy earlier in
the decade and then rescuing the banks from their poor decisions when things
turned ugly. People in both camps viewed it as a secretive organization with
inadequate oversight. A Gallup poll in the summer of 2009 found that 30 percent of Americans approved of the Fed's performance, a lower rating than even
that of the Internal Revenue Service.

As Bernanke and the Fed made their big decisions during the crisis—the
bailouts of Bear Stearns and AIG, the alphabet soup of programs to pump
money into the financial system—politics was a second-order concern. Bernanke and his inner circle concluded that they simply had to do what they
thought would best support the economy and hope that the politics would work
itself out. "If we come out of this with a Hall of Fame batting average, then we'll
be fine," Bernanke, a baseball fan, told his advisers. Even most of the very best
hitters in the Major League Baseball history recorded a hit less than a third of
the time. In other words: We're not going to hit every ball, but we have to keep
swinging, doing what we think is best, and as long as the overall results are
good, our mistakes will be forgivable.

Many of the decisions were made quickly and in the middle of the night
and involved questions that are supposed to be independent of politics. Plus, it's
hard to brief legislators about anything without it soon leaking to the press,
making it problematic to talk about questions that were still undecided. Congress was usually an afterthought, briefed only after a decision had been made
and announced—despite the fact that it ultimately controls the existence and
authorities of the central bank.

Every major financial crisis spurs a rethinking of financial regulation, and
as the Panic of 2008 raged, there was little doubt that the pattern would hold.
After President Barack Obama was inaugurated in January 2009, he made
overhauling the financial system a priority. "You never want a serious crisis to
go to waste," Obama's first chief of staff, Rahm Emanuel, said in November
2008. Initially, the new administration was hoping Congress would pass some
form of financial reform in time to take to an international summit in April
2009. That proved unrealistic given the sluggishness of the legislative process,
but the White House was still eager to move. When Neal Wolin, the deputy

treasury secretary, told Emanuel that it could take weeks to draft a bill, given the hundreds of pages of complex details to work through, Emanuel, who wanted a bill written in days, pointed at Wolin's computer and said, "Sit down and start fucking typing."

Christopher J. Dodd, a veteran senator from Connecticut, was chairman of the Senate Committee on Banking, Housing, and Urban Affairs, and he would be the one to try to craft a financial reform bill that could make it through the procedural gauntlet that was the United States Senate in 2009. A single senator out of the one hundred could slow activity on the Senate floor to a crawl on nearly anything, from the confirmation of a midlevel bureaucrat to passing Obama's signature initiative of overhauling the health care system. In earlier times, there had been an unwritten agreement against using that power except in really important cases, but by 2009 minority parties routinely filibustered anything controversial, requiring a sixty-vote supermajority and days or weeks to overcome objections.

Dodd, the son of a senator and a three-decade veteran of the institution, envisioned financial reform being done the old-fashioned way: with the two parties contributing their best ideas and hammering out a deal across the negotiating table that eighty or ninety senators from both sides of the aisle could happily support. "I don't want to be sitting on the floor of the Senate begging for a sixtieth vote with sixty guns pointed at my head," Dodd told an aide in the spring of 2009. "This is different, and it shouldn't be ideological."

The key to his strategy was going after the Federal Reserve.

Dodd himself was irritated that the Fed, under Greenspan, had done little to use its regulatory powers to rein in bad mortgage lending during the housing bubble. He didn't have the deep-seated populist objections to the central bank that some of his colleagues did, but Dodd did see the extraordinary actions the Fed had taken during the crisis as evidence of an organization with too much concentrated power. In one hearing, he compared giving the Fed more power after its failings during the crisis to a parent "giving his son a bigger, faster car right after he crashed the family station wagon."

Dodd also believed that a fundamental reason for the crisis was that the United States had so many different bank regulators—five of them at the federal level alone, plus separate banking authorities in each state. Banks had the ability to choose what type of charter—and hence what regulator—they would

have. That in turn gave regulators some incentive to take a hands-off approach, lest banks switch to different charters and a regulator lose relevance
and funding.

Dodd viewed cutting back the power of the Fed as an important way to
build bipartisan consensus. The Republican leader on the Banking Committee
was Senator Richard Shelby of Alabama, a particularly vehement opponent of
the central bank. Shelby had refused to negotiate on behalf of Republicans on
the Wall Street bailout legislation because he was opposed to passing it in any
form, and he believed the Fed's low-interest-rate policies in the early 2000s
were the main cause of the housing bubble. Dodd's plan was to replace the complex system of overlapping bank regulators with a single, newly created one—
that is, to take away one of the core powers that the Fed had long held dear, the
ability to supervise banks all over the country. It was, in Dodd's view, reining in
an agency that had grown too powerful. Shelby's staff described the approach
more colorfully: "Fuck the Fed."

That was in the rarefied confines of the U.S. Senate. As Dodd and Shelby
moved in their own way to unmake the modern Federal Reserve, another political threat was emerging from different quarters.

Texas representative Ron Paul was officially a Republican in 2009, though
he disagreed with the party on nearly as much as he agreed. He opposed both
the Iraq War and high defense spending, for example, and he favored the legal-
ization of narcotics. Paul had previously run for president as the nominee of the
Libertarian Party; in 1988 he won 0.5 percent of the national vote, which was
good enough for third place. His presidential ambitions found more success in
2008 and, especially, 2012, when his strongly antigovernment stance resonated
among Republican primary voters more than party leaders would have liked.
So opposed was he to government action of all stripes that when there was a
vote in the House on some inoffensive measure such as naming a rural post office after a deceased local official or designating May as Mental Health Month,
Paul was very likely to be the one dissenter in a 434–1 vote.

Unsurprisingly, Paul hated the Fed. He was in favor of a strict gold standard and ending the government's monopoly on issuing money. The idea of
paper money issued and guaranteed by the government is, after all, anathema
to someone who deeply distrusts government. Paul also had a penchant for conspiracy theories, and he used his position as a member of the House Financial

Services Committee to ask questions of Bernanke (and Greenspan before him) that no one else in the Congress would think to pose. At one hearing in 2010, Paul suggested that the Fed had some involvement with the Watergate break-in and funding Saddam Hussein in the 1980s, which Bernanke described as "absolutely bizarre."

But in 2009 Paul's long-running crusade against the Fed became a cause that seemingly everyone wanted to join. One of his criticisms was that the Fed kept too much information secret from Congress and the public. His answer was legislation that would allow Congress a freer rein to look into the Fed's business. Under existing law, political authorities didn't have the ability to demand details of the inner workings of Fed decisions on monetary policy or its dealings with foreign central banks. Central bankers view secrecy as a key to their ability to operate—it gives them the freedom to deliberate away from the pressures of politicians or the public. But this merely magnified the impression held by Paul—and by more and more of his colleagues—that the Fed was up to something nefarious.

Paul's name for his legislation was particularly inspired: "Audit the Fed." After all, every corporation gets audited; any institution of the Fed's size should be held to such routine accountability. In fact, on financial matters the Fed was already audited, with an independent inspector general in house, oversight by Congress's investigative arm, and reserve bank audits carried out by the same major accounting companies that audit every major corporation in America.

Paul wanted something more than the prevention of fraud and theft, though: He wanted Congress to be able to stick its nose into the decisions the Fed made on interest rate policies, foreign currency swaps, and emergency lending to banks. To Fed officials, Paul was asking for a tool with which Congress could bring political influence to bear on monetary policy. It's one thing to make an unpopular move knowing you'll have to explain yourself in a congressional hearing a few months later, quite another to know that investigators will soon subpoena every document that was created in the course of reaching that decision. To Paul, Audit the Fed was just a way to add a bit more democracy to an antidemocratic body.

Three hundred twenty of 435 representatives—nearly three quarters of the House—eventually signed on as cosponsors of the Federal Reserve Transparency Act. Vermont's Bernie Sanders, the lone socialist in the U.S. Congress,

took up the cause in the Senate, and by the spring of 2009 the effort to audit the
Fed was picking up momentum.

W ith the Fed under attack, the man at its helm was called to become a
politician himself. It wasn't a natural fit.

Ben Bernanke wasn't born to be a Washington operator. He had little
inclination—or skill—for glad-handing and backslapping. Unlike Greenspan,
who frequented the Georgetown social circuit with his wife, NBC newscaster
Andrea Mitchell, Bernanke preferred a quiet evening at home with his Kindle
or a trip to the theater with his wife. Bernanke took the Fed chairmanship hoping to add greater anonymity to the role—to be less the all-powerful deity that
Greenspan sometimes seemed, more the quiet functionary.

The financial crisis ruled out that possibility. In a crisis, people want
someone to step up and be in charge, and Bernanke did exactly that. But his
newness to Washington and discomfort with the trappings of power were obvious, particularly early on. When dealing with members of Congress, Bernanke
simply acted like himself, addressing questions as forthrightly as the confines
of his office would allow, explaining economics and the Fed's decisions with the
same simple language he once used to teach Princeton undergraduates. Before
a congressional hearing, he would sit for "murder boards"—prehearing sessions
lasting hours during which advisers fired off questions on the full range of subjects he might encounter, occasionally imitating the style of one of the more
distinctive members of Congress. He developed a style of detached reserve that
was effective in sometimes hostile hearings, responding calmly and deliberately
even when his questioner was in a blind rage. Only on the rarest of occasions
did he become testy or combative himself. But for the legislative battle in the
offing, mere politeness wouldn't be enough.

The Fed wasn't set up for a legislative war. Its legislative affairs office
comprised only five people—compared with about three thousand lobbyists
employed by the financial industry as a whole—and the Fed did not play the
hardball game of using press leaks and veiled threats to get its way on Capitol
Hill. The Fed style was more to state its case as directly and repetitively as it
needed to and hope that its technical competence and straightforward arguments would win the day. In preparation for political combat, in the summer of

2009 Bernanke hired a new chief lobbyist, Clinton treasury department veteran Linda Robertson. He also paid particular attention to maintaining a personal touch with key lawmakers. When Tennessee senator Bob Corker wanted to personally review hundreds of pages of confidential documents about the Fed's bailout of AIG, Bernanke welcomed him to the Fed's headquarters, joined him for breakfast, and prepared a room in which Corker could comfortably spend hour upon hour going through pages.

Bernanke readily admitted that the Fed had made mistakes, in particular not using its regulatory powers to reduce bad mortgage lending and otherwise protect consumers in the years just before the crisis. He agreed that the bailout actions the Fed had taken during the crisis were unpalatable, even as he defended them as having been absolutely necessary to prevent an even worse economic situation. But he viewed the approaches being dreamed up by Dodd and Shelby as potentially disastrous. He'd seen how other bank regulators, in the run-up to the crisis and then during it, had suffered from tunnel vision, focusing on the individual banks they regulated rather than thinking about more important economic interconnections.

"Mr. Chairman, I understand your objectives here—but I do believe it's a very, very serious matter to take the Fed essentially out of financial-stability management," Bernanke told Dodd in one hearing. "I do think that taking the Federal Reserve out of active bank supervision would be a mistake for the country."

But with the politics of the moment what they were, Bernanke and the Fed seemed ready to lose big. "If the Fed were running for reelection," a congressional aide told the *Washington Post*, "it would go home to spend more time with its family."

Bernanke wasn't the only one opposed to Dodd's plan to use Fed bashing as a means to financial reform. Geithner viewed the Federal Reserve as key to making the financial system less prone to crises than it had been in the past. In his view, whatever the mistakes of the preceding years, the Fed had been nimble in addressing the crisis while other financial regulators had been sluggish. Its people were smarter, and its abilities to print money and serve as lender of last resort provided the ultimate backstops to economic disaster. He saw a stronger Fed as a fundamental goal of financial reform and brought in two Fed staffers as detailees to the Treasury Department to help make his case.

On May 19, 2009, the treasury secretary brought the Democratic senators from the Banking Committee, along with key staffers who would be drafting financial reform legislation, to breakfast in a dining room on the second floor of the Treasury Department. Over coffee and eggs, Geithner laid down his three nonnegotiable goals: First, the Federal Reserve must keep the authority to oversee any bank big enough to bring down the financial system if it failed—$50 billion in assets was the number he had in mind. "If that were not the case," Geithner told his fellow Democrats, pointing to the White House next door, "I would recommend that the president veto this bill." Second, the government must retain the power to offer an emergency backstop of the banking system, which had proved crucial during the crisis. Third, the treasury secretary, rather than the appointee to a newly created job, must be put in charge of a new council of regulators meant to identify risks in the financial system and designate which firms needed an extra measure of oversight from the Fed.

Of course, the banks themselves had a few ideas about who ought to regulate them. From giants like J.P. Morgan and Citigroup to tiny, state-chartered institutions with a single branch, the banks wanted to stay under the purview of the Fed. "The Fed examiners always came in as bankers and understood the banker's experience of risk," said Camden R. Fine, president of the Independent Community Bankers of America. "Each regulator has its own cultural bias, and the Fed's bias is, 'We're a bank, too.'" Dodd's idea of some unknown new über-regulator alarmed the banks.

The giant banks were politically toxic in the wake of the Wall Street bailout, so they had to approach Congress carefully. If they advertised their position too loudly, it could be counterproductive. But they had Geithner making their case forcefully—even threatening a presidential veto. The thousands of smaller banks were on their own, with Geithner willing to take them out from under the Fed umbrella, if that's what was needed for a deal. But that didn't mean they were powerless. One of the best tools for gaining influence in Washington is simple geography: The more members of Congress view you as representing their hometown interests, the more they'll fight for you. There's an old joke about the perfect military aircraft having parts made in all 435 congressional districts, to ensure it will never be defunded.

America's small banks are the closest real thing to that mythical aircraft. In every town across the country there are community banks. Their executives and boards of directors tend to be pillar-of-the-community types—the ones who fund local charities and, especially, give money to congressional campaigns. That made the Independent Community Bankers of America—with its five thousand members operating twenty-three thousand bank branches and controlling $1 trillion in assets—a formidable lobbying power in Washington.

In meetings with Barney Frank and Dodd's senior staffers, Fine made an offer: The community bankers could never actively support legislation that would increase bank regulation. But so long as Congress left his members alone—and left the Fed in place as their regulator—they wouldn't try to fight the financial reform bill. "I told them we would come out swinging against Dodd's bill if it included a single regulator," said Fine. "They threatened to gut the Fed, and I told them they'd have a hell of a fight."

There was another group with plenty to lose if the responsibility for regulating banks across the United States was taken away from the Fed. For the far-flung reserve banks that comprise the Federal Reserve system, the approach that Dodd's staff was developing was something approaching an existential threat. Fed officials in cities like Kansas City and Dallas and Philadelphia had been out of the loop as officials in Washington and New York made their series of bailout decisions. The presidents of the other reserve banks had high regard for Bernanke personally; more so than Greenspan, they believed, he respected them, engaged with them, and listened to their thoughts and concerns. But many of them also felt that the Bernanke Fed had taken actions that endangered the credibility of the whole institution without informing many of its component parts.

Some of the crisis-era decisions had been made in such a hurry that, aside from New York, the reserve banks didn't even find out about them until they were announced publicly. At least one reserve bank president had been reduced to dialing in to one of the briefing calls that the Fed conducted for journalists to learn about the latest decision by his colleagues in Washington.

Perhaps the closest ally in the Federal Reserve System for the country's smaller banks was Thomas M. Hoenig, president of the Kansas City Fed since 1991. A veteran of supervising banks, he had been manning the discount-window desk when an Oklahoma bank called Penn Square failed in 1982, in turn causing the failure of Continental Illinois National Bank and Trust, the biggest in U.S. history until the 2008 crisis.

Hoenig loathed the too-big-to-fail banks, which he saw as benefiting from a public safety net that the smaller banks lacked. He also saw the ultra-low-interest-rate policies embraced by Bernanke as a major cause of the financial crisis. And from attending events around his Federal Reserve district, which encompasses parts of seven states in the center of the nation and contains no giant banks but hundreds of smaller ones, Hoenig had picked up early on the depth of public rage at the Fed. At one luncheon in Santa Fe, New Mexico, he gave a speech and then opened up the room for questions. "It was the most hostile crowd I've ever seen," he said later. "People were *angry.*"

Even though the regional reserve banks had nothing to do with the Wall Street bailouts, they had the most to lose if anti-Fed sentiment led to stripping the institution of its oversight power. Regulating banks was what Federal Reserve branches spent most of their days doing. Without that responsibility, they would have little to do besides the nuts-and-bolts work of providing cash to commercial banks in their districts. The reserve bank presidents always couched their arguments in terms of what was best for the financial system overall, but the politically savvy could see that the presidents had a great deal at risk.

The Fed's point man on bank regulation in Washington was Daniel Tarullo, an acerbic law professor appointed to the Fed Board of Governors by Obama. If Hoenig's world was one of small-town banks lending to their local farmers and factory owners, Tarullo's was one of trips to Basel to negotiate capital standards for the likes of Goldman Sachs. Hoenig feared that Tarullo and the Board of Governors would happily throw the smaller banks overboard if that was what it took to keep oversight of the giant banks. "I got the sense that they weren't going to interfere, but also that this wasn't their issue," said Hoenig, referring to his colleagues in Washington. "Everyone is influenced by their environment, and theirs is international and Wall Street, so that's where their focus is." Hoenig and a handful of the other reserve bank presidents were eager to make their way to Washington to make sure Bernanke, Geithner, and Tarullo didn't sell them down the river in order to strike a deal with Dodd.

The forces fighting on behalf of the Fed amounted to a powerful set of interests, though not all precisely aligned: Bernanke and his colleagues at the Fed Board of Governors; Geithner and the Obama administration; the private banks large and small; and the reserve banks around the country with their own business and political connections. The question, entering the financial reform debate in 2009, is whether that would be enough to conquer the deep-seated animosity to an institution that was so deeply unpopular on Capitol Hill.

When President Obama took office in early 2009, the conventional wisdom was that Bernanke would be a one-term Fed chair. Not only had he failed to prevent the worst recession in modern times, but he was a Republican working in a Democrat-led Washington. There was frustration among Democrats that Republican appointees had held the Fed chairmanship continuously since 1987, and there was even an obvious Democratic candidate for the job.

Larry Summers was notorious for bulldozing over his intellectual opponents, and he had been nudged out as president of Harvard University after making impolitic remarks about women in the sciences. But he was a first-rate economist, a former treasury secretary, and the obvious pick for Fed chair if Obama wanted to seek a change when Bernanke's four-year appointment ended in January 2010. In assembling his economic policy team at the start of his administration, Obama had asked Summers to join as his top economic aide in the White House. It was a way for Obama to put a seasoned hand in the West Wing at a time of economic crisis. And even though it was a demotion, really, for a former treasury secretary, it was a way for Summers to position himself as a loyal soldier deserving of the Fed appointment.

Through the early months of the Obama administration, Bernanke maintained polite relations with the new president. But theirs was no deep personal connection: They met privately only four times during those first six months. Meanwhile, Bernanke took a series of steps—both symbolic and substantive—to try to instill confidence in the nation's economy. In March 2009, he granted *60 Minutes* the first television interview with a Fed chairman in twenty-two years, and pronounced on the air that there were certain "green shoots" visible signaling an economic recovery. In July, he gave a town-hall-style meeting at the Kansas City Fed; it was broadcast on *PBS NewsHour* over three consecutive evenings. His aggressive monetary policy moves—zero interest rate policy and $1.75 trillion in bond purchases that had been announced to that point—

seemed to be having their desired impact of helping the U.S. economy pull out of its collapse. The recession, it would later be declared, officially bottomed out in June 2009.

Some in the Obama administration even viewed Bernanke's actions— particularly the public appearances—as part of a not terribly subtle campaign to position himself for reappointment.

Obama's decision on whom to appoint to the Fed chairmanship was a closely held one within the White House, confined to the president, his chief of staff Rahm Emanuel, and Geithner. This put Geithner in a difficult spot: Summers, as a Treasury official in the 1990s, had plucked Geithner from obscurity and promoted him into the department's highest-level job on international economic matters. Bernanke, meanwhile, was Geithner's partner from the dark days of the crisis, and they had remained friendly since.

But the reality was, by the time Geithner had to make a recommendation and Obama had to make a decision, eating breakfast weekly, there wasn't much of a decision to make. Bernanke had proved he would do whatever was necessary to keep the economy from collapsing. He'd won the confidence of Wall Street; in a survey of forty-seven bank economists by the *Wall Street Journal,* all but one said he should be reappointed. The senators who would have to vote to confirm him mostly respected him, even the ones who had objections to the Fed as an institution.

Summers could certainly do the job, but it wasn't clear that he could do it any better than Bernanke—and Summers's outsized personality risked making him less effective. After all, a Fed chairman doesn't make policy on his own, but by guiding a committee toward consensus, and Summers had never been much of a consensus builder. And Summers's service in the Obama White House, coupled with his difficult personality, meant that getting him confirmed in the Senate could be a challenge. Republicans would likely oppose him, worried he might be influenced by the White House once at the Fed. Even some Democrats would likely oppose him, bothered by his lifetime of controversial statements and role in deregulating the financial system in the 1990s.

With the economy fragile, Geithner and Obama went for the safe choice. At one of Bernanke's regular weekly meetings with Geithner in June, the treasury secretary posed a question: Would you like the president to consider appointing you to a second term? Yes, Bernanke said, he would. The Fed chief was exhausted, and on some level would have been content to go back to Princeton and a quiet academic career. But he wanted to complete what he'd started in addressing the crisis, and he wanted the implicit endorsement of his actions that reappointment would convey. The Wednesday evening before the 2009 Jackson Hole conference was to begin, Bernanke was summoned to the White House—after the "lid" had been put on, meaning there would be no new announcements that evening, so the White House press corps could go home. That helped make it less likely he would be seen entering the White House at a time when the world was on edge about whether he would be appointed. The meeting lasted less than ten minutes, with Obama, Bernanke, and Geithner in the room. The president praised his work and asked him to accept a nomination for another term—but to keep it secret until they could announce it at a time to their political advantage. Obama and Bernanke still had no special rapport, but competence and credibility were enough to win Bernanke reappointment.

At Jackson Hole that year, the question of whether Bernanke would be reappointed was a frequent topic of conversation over coffee breaks and meals. The Fed chair already knew the answer, but he didn't give any hints. The announcement took place the following week, when the president was on vacation in Martha's Vineyard. Unsure of how to dress when appearing with a vacationing president, Bernanke wore his usual dark suit; the president was without jacket and tie. When they both arrived at the high school gymnasium that was serving as a holding pen for the White House press corps, they each adjusted in order to have more or less the same look: Bernanke removed his tie; Obama put on a sport coat.

"As an expert on the causes of the Great Depression," Obama said, "I'm sure Ben never imagined that he would be part of a team responsible for preventing another. But because of his background, his temperament, his courage, and his creativity, that's exactly what he has helped to achieve. And that is why I am reappointing him to another term as chairman of the Federal Reserve."

Assuming, of course, that the Senate would confirm him. The Banking Committee met on December 17 to decide whether to advance Bernanke's confirmation to the full Senate—just six weeks before his term was to expire.

Chris Dodd, for all his complaints about the Fed's performance before the crisis, was full of praise for its chief. "I believe that Ben Bernanke deserves substantial credit as chairman of the Federal Reserve for helping us navigate those waters," he said, "not with perfection, but certainly, I think, stepping up at a critical time in our nation's history with some very wise leadership that benefited our nation."

Then it was Richard Shelby's turn. "Over the years we have enacted a number of laws which demonstrated our confidence in [the Fed]," he said. "We trusted the Fed to execute those laws when deemed prudent and necessary. I fear now, however, that our trust and confidence were misplaced . . . I strongly disapprove of some of the past deeds of the Federal Reserve while Ben Bernanke was a member and as chairman, and I lack confidence in what little planning for the future he has articulated."

As the remaining senators stated their views on Bernanke, one by one, a trend emerged. Almost to a person, and with varying degrees of politeness, the Republicans emphasized the negative. Jim Bunning of Kentucky, the only senator to have voted against Bernanke's confirmation four years earlier, noted that the day before *Time* magazine had named Bernanke its "Person of the Year." "Chairman Bernanke may wonder if he really wants to be honored by an organization that has previously named people like Joseph Stalin twice, Yasser Arafat, Adolf Hitler, the Ayatollah Khomeini, Vladimir Putin, Richard Nixon twice, as their person of the year," he said. "But I congratulate him and hope he at least turns out better than most of those people."

All but one Democrat on the Banking Committee voted in favor of the Fed chair—but only four of ten Republicans did. Although his confirmation had moved to the full Senate floor, Ben Bernanke had yet another fight on his hands.

Dodd's plan of targeting the Fed's powers was attracting some powerful opponents, but in late 2009 its political logic remained sound. Shelby was a wily negotiator, coming across as noncommittal even when consensus seemed possible and never revealing his bottom-line demands. Dodd's goal of a bipartisan financial reform bill at times seemed to be on the verge of coming together, at others on the verge of falling entirely apart. Whatever impulse Shelby had to collaborate with Dodd counted for little next to the Republican Party's overarching legislative strategy: to oppose all major initiatives of the Obama administration and, by blocking some of them, portray the president as ineffectual. Dodd was well aware of this, but he also knew that Republicans didn't want to be seen as defending Wall Street interests.

After months of negotiations that hadn't really gone anywhere, Dodd was ready to force the issue. On November 10, 2009, he introduced a 1,139-page bill to the Senate Banking Committee, figuring Shelby and the Republicans would have either to negotiate in earnest or vote against reform. The bill called for creating a new consumer protection agency to regulate financial products such as mortgages and credit cards. It also proposed stripping the Fed of the power to oversee banks and granting it to another new regulator. It even called for the selection of regional Fed presidents to be made by presidential appointees in Washington rather than commercial bankers and businesspeople in the reserve banks' districts. Dodd's was a different model of what the Federal Reserve should be: Instead of an institution that would oversee and serve as a backstop to the financial system, as it had in 2008, the Fed was to focus on monetary policy and not much else.

At the markup hearing to begin revising the bill in mid-November, Shelby, rarely looking up from a twenty-six-hundred-word statement, proceeded to attack almost every aspect of Dodd's bill. The bill's consumer protection agency would create "a massive new bureaucracy." Its consolidation of bank regulation, meant to entice Shelby and other Republicans, would "place all banks—state and federal—under a single, mammoth federal regulator." Dodd sat listening, his finger on his temple. Shelby didn't definitively rule out any cooperation on a bill. But he also didn't sound eager to hammer out an agreement. The dream of a bipartisan deal was fading with each new paragraph of Shelby's attack.

In the House, where parliamentary rules make it far easier for a majority to get its way, things were proceeding much faster. Barney Frank was working on a bill that would give the Fed more power over the banking system rather than less, in line with Bernanke and Geithner's preferred approach. But there was one component of the bill that reflected the House's populist wrath: Frank and North Carolina congressman Mel Watt put forward an alternative to Ron Paul's Audit the Fed proposal that would add new disclosure requirements for the central bank but would still prevent Congress from mucking about in monetary policy or the Fed's transactions with foreign central banks.

Paul was furious. "This is the bill that would allow the people to win over the special interests on Wall Street, as well as with the big banks," he argued in committee. The American people "are sick and tired of secret government and government out of control and Congress passing TARP funds and on and on, and nobody knowing what happened."

In his push to restore Audit the Fed, Paul joined with Alan Grayson, a first-term Florida Democrat and firebrand liberal populist who assailed the Fed with as much ferocity as the Texas Republican. But while support for Audit the Fed was bipartisan, House Democratic leaders were sympathetic to arguments from Bernanke and Geithner that what was being sold by Paul and Grayson as greater accountability and oversight was really just increased political control over monetary policy. That didn't mean they could contain the momentum in Congress, however, where anger at the power and secretiveness of the Fed was too powerful to overcome reservations. The Paul-Grayson amendment passed by forty-three votes to twenty-six in the Financial Services Committee on November 19 and was part of the over-arching Wall Street reform legislation the House passed three weeks later.

By the start of 2010, Dodd's strategy for reforming the financial system was in trouble. Shelby was as antagonistic to the Fed as ever, but negotiations with him over a broader bill weren't progressing, held back, Dodd's aides told him, by Shelby's ambition to rise within the Republican Party.

Dodd had to recalibrate his goals. He still wanted to cut back on the Fed's powers, but without the support of Shelby and the conservative Republicans he would need the vote of every single Democrat and a handful of centrist Republicans. And that was looking unlikely. Several members of his own party, including powerful New York senator Chuck Schumer, had already sided with Geithner and the Obama administration, which was dead set against taking the Fed out of the business of regulating Wall Street.

So Dodd started pushing the next best thing: keeping commercial banks with assets of $50 billion or more—the top thirty or so in a nation with eight thousand of them—under the supervision of the Federal Reserve while moving smaller institutions to a new regulator. Geithner and the administration seemed open to negotiating that approach. It would serve the treasury secretary's first-order goal of ensuring that the largest and most complex banks—not coincidentally, the same ones he had regulated as New York Fed president—would remain under the Fed's umbrella. Geithner had even mentioned $50 billion as a possible threshold in his first meeting with Dodd's staff. Bernanke was more opposed to the possibility. When discussing the oversight of big banks in private meetings with senators, he spoke in dire warnings: Without oversight of the largest financial firms, the Fed couldn't do its job as a central bank properly, and the entire U.S. economy would be at grave risk. In private meetings, law-makers said, he didn't speak of losing small bank oversight in quite the same dire terms. But he said repeatedly that he viewed the insight the Fed had into smaller banks across the country as essential to understanding the workings of an economy with 300 million people spread across the continent. A Federal Reserve system that didn't oversee smaller banks, Bernanke argued, would be at even greater risk of seeing the world only from the vantage point of Washington and Wall Street.

Some of the reserve banks were distrustful, fearful that their colleagues in Washington would too readily sell out the Fed's authority over small banks as a bargaining chip to ensure victory on other priorities. Kansas City Fed president Tom Hoenig and Richard Fisher, the politically connected president of the Dallas Fed, took it upon themselves to ring alarm bells among their fellow presidents in the Fed system.

In phone calls and at the Federal Reserve's Conference of Presidents—a meeting at which the twelve heads of the regional banks discuss operational matters—Hoenig and Fisher delivered a stark message to their less politically attuned colleagues: The threat to our institution is real. We cannot count on the Fed governors in Washington to protect us. So deploy every political connection you have to try to make our case to Congress. "We need to be involved in supervision, and if you think it's important, do something about it," Hoenig later recalled telling his colleagues.

Each reserve bank had a twelve-member board of directors made up of private bankers, businesspeople, and other community representatives. These tended to be well-off, politically connected people—and there was an army of 144 of them in every corner of the country. Many of the reserve bank presidents asked their board members to make calls to lawmakers with whom they were friendly to encourage them to protect the Fed. Some called local bankers' associations to ask them to lobby as well. (Others viewed this as an inappropriate cozying up to the industry they regulated.) The reserve bank presidents also began visiting Washington to meet with lawmakers to press their case. Some who were new to their jobs or had never been politically attuned met with legislators from their districts for the very first time, economists learning how to be lobbyists. By early 2010, Hoenig was a near-constant visitor to Washington, packing long days of meetings with members of Congress. He and his staff were sufficiently new to the art of lobbying that they often underestimated how long it would take to get from office to office among the complex of seven buildings where the legislators work.

The reserve bank presidents' argument was simple: Stripping small-bank regulation from the Fed would amount to cutting the regional bank system off at the knees, leaving all the power in Washington and New York. "I felt it was important in my own heart," said James Bullard, president of the St. Louis Fed. "This system is carefully designed to have a Washington component to the Fed and an important bank in New York, but also to get other representation around the country. It was part of the original compromise, and that seemed important to preserve."

D emocratic lawmakers were starting to feel assailed. Their landmark health care legislation had passed the Senate in December, but only after a long and ugly battle. They were being attacked as tools of Wall Street interests—an image not helped by Dodd's slow, consensus-driven approach to financial reform.

The recession may have technically ended, but the malaise had continued. At the end of 2009, the unemployment rate was a hair under 10 percent, still at its highest level since the 1980s. Against that backdrop, the unthinkable happened: In a special election held on Tuesday, January 19, 2010, a Republican was elected to the Senate in Massachusetts, the most liberal state in the nation, to fill the seat of the legendary Ted Kennedy, who had recently died of a brain tumor, thus costing the Democrats their sixty-seat supermajority.

There was a collective shock following the victory of Scott Brown against the hapless Massachusetts attorney general Martha Coakley, with Democrats scrambling to consider not only what might become of their entire legislative agenda, but also why their party had become so unpopular so quickly. The obvious answer was the economy, which had been wrecked by Wall Street. Which, the conventional wisdom went, had been aided and abetted by the Fed. Which was represented by Ben Bernanke. Coincidentally, it was less than two weeks before his term was set to expire on January 31—and while Obama had renominated him, he had yet to be confirmed by the Senate.

Two days after the election, Senate Democrats met for a weekly lunch to discuss their strategy. In a tense meeting, the more liberal members of the party, and even some of more middle-of-the-road temperament, were livid that at a time when voters were furious about the economy and Wall Street bailouts, legislators were being asked to confirm a guy who was responsible for both. "Massachusetts was kind of a wake-up call to many Democrats," said Bernie Sanders that week. "People are disgusted and furious with Wall Street and with the state of the economy, and a number of Democrats have been scratching their heads, saying, 'Why do we want to reappoint a guy who was a member of the Bush administration?'"

Byron Dorgan of North Dakota, no liberal bomb thrower, came out in opposition to Bernanke. He was followed by two farther-left senators, Barbara Boxer of California and Russell Feingold of Wisconsin. Most dangerous of all for the Fed chairman's prospects, Richard Durbin of Illinois, a close ally of Obama and the number-two-ranked Democrat in the Senate—the majority whip, whose job it is to round up votes—was on the fence.

Much was at stake in Bernanke's confirmation. Rejection would have left the Fed without a chairman at a time of nearly 10 percent unemployment and shaky confidence in the financial markets. In addition, having one of the president's highest-profile appointments rejected by a Senate controlled by his own party would have been a major loss for Obama. A fight began.

"The White House political guys didn't love Bernanke and weren't in it with their hearts, so it was a struggle to get them engaged," said one official involved with the effort. "But once they realized what a loss it would be for the president if the nomination went down, they got engaged."

In the White House, Rahm Emanuel and David Axelrod, the president's chief political adviser, began a campaign to lean on wavering senators. Emanuel, a man of manic intensity and with a deep Rolodex acquired from his days as a leader in the House of Representatives, worked the phones. So did the president himself, emphasizing the potentially disastrous impact to markets if Bernanke was rejected. Even Hillary Clinton, the popular secretary of state, mentioned the Bernanke confirmation in conversations with senators that were mainly about foreign policy matters.

Bernanke and his allies at the Fed were gearing up for battle in their own way. Like most of what came from the Fed, it was careful, methodical, and below the public radar. They set up a war room in Linda Robertson's office, tracking what was known about how each senator was leaning and influence they might bring to bear on him or her. Would they like a meeting with Bernanke? Forty-two senators took the chairman up on the offer, unprecedented in the experience of Robertson and others with experience in confirmations. Might a nudge from a sympathetic industry group help? The Fed had discreet contacts with some key business lobbies that were locked into battle with the White House.

The U.S. Chamber of Commerce was intensely opposed to the president's health care legislation, but the lobbying association's head, Tom Donohue, was willing to go to bat for Bernanke. He called Republican senators. The Financial Services Forum, a group that represents the CEOs of the twenty largest Wall Street firms, asked some of its members to make calls to senators with whom they had relationships. Jamie Dimon, the charismatic chief of J.P. Morgan, worked the phones. Even Lloyd Blankfein, the chief executive of Goldman Sachs—a firm that was a political pariah even as it remained a financial powerhouse—made at least one call, to Senator Bob Corker.

If Bernanke's job was going to be saved, it would be in part thanks to activism by executives of the country's most loathed companies, the major banks that helped cause the crisis.

The largest companies in America weren't the only Bernanke allies, however. On Thursday, January 22, Cam Fine of the Independent Community Bankers of America was out of town for a speech when he received an urgent text message: Durbin was thinking of coming out against the nomination. Fine returned to Washington and set up a war room in his office. His lobbying staff gathered intelligence about which senators were leaning for or against Bernanke; Fine called every one he thought might be willing to vote yes. The effort was driven by the belief that Bernanke, whatever his faults in the eyes of the small banks, would at least give them a fair shake.

"We didn't always agree with Bernanke, but I was convinced that if it wasn't him, we'd get some vice chair of Goldman Sachs running the Fed who didn't know what a community bank was, and that worried me," Fine said. "I'd much prefer an academic to a Wall Street trader."

The battle over Ben Bernanke was no longer about whether the balding former economics professor was the best person to lead the central bank for the next four years. It was about whether the U.S. government would allow itself to be guided by sheer populist rage.

The anger came from both the left and the right. Progressive advocacy group MoveOn.org told its members, "Fed chair Ben Bernanke spent trillions to bail out Wall Street, but he's turning a blind eye to regular Americans." Tea Party–affiliated South Carolina senator Jim DeMint released a statement opposing Bernanke's confirmation, maintaining that the Fed chair had "led the fight against bipartisan legislation in the House and the Senate to require a full audit of the Fed so Americans know what has taken place and what mistakes have been made." Calls and e-mails bombarded Senate offices—fewer than during the debate over the financial bailout in the fall of 2008, staffers said, but not by a lot.

On Friday, January 23, Dodd and Senator Judd Gregg, a New Hampshire Republican, issued a joint statement saying they expected Bernanke to be confirmed. And little by little, in the form of written announcements and television interviews, the tide started to turn.

"To blame one man for the financial implosion is simply wrong," said California Democrat Dianne Feinstein. Bernanke, "for reasons of stability and continuity, should be reconfirmed."

Durbin made his decision, if reluctantly: "I have some misgivings about Fed policy and economic policy," he said on *Face the Nation* on Sunday the twenty-fifth. "But I really do have to say, this man guided us through the worst economic crisis this nation has seen since the Great Depression."

Republican leaders played the vote cagily. On one hand, it was clear that they would like anyone else Obama might nominate less than Bernanke. On the other, Bernanke had become anathema to their conservative base. And they seemed to enjoy making the Democrats sweat and making the president expend time and political capital on the confirmation battle. By holding back Republican votes, they could force more Democrats to vote for Bernanke, saddling the opposition with an unpopular vote. That helps explain this appearance on *Meet the Press* by Senate Republican leader Mitch McConnell:

"He's going to have bipartisan support in the senate, and I would anticipate he'd be confirmed," McConnell said.

"Will you vote for him?" asked David Gregory, the program's host.

"He's going to have bipartisan support."

"But you won't say how you'll vote?" said Gregory.

"I'll let you know in the next day or so."

"You have concerns about his renomination?"

"I think he's going to be confirmed."

"But do you have concerns about his renomination?"

"Some of my members do, but I think he's going to be confirmed."

McConnell was right. On Thursday, January 28, barely a week after Bernanke's nomination seemed to be falling apart, the Senate voted 70–30 to confirm him. Eighteen Republicans and twelve Democrats voted against the reconfirmation, in the narrowest margin of any Fed chair in history.

But the center held, and Ben Bernanke got four more years.

There was no time to celebrate. The battle was already shifting back to financial reform. The regional Fed presidents were in full-on lobbying mode, trying to keep their role overseeing banks. Their basic pitch: We're the institutions that keep the Federal Reserve rooted in Main Street America. We're the counterweight to the big-bank-loving, bailout-giving guys in Washington and New York. Dodd's plan of putting only $50-billion-and-bigger banks under Fed oversight would create a system that was much more weighted toward big Wall Street interests.

"If you're a central bank in Washington or New York but without this other network, you're located in the nation's political or financial capital and preserving that independence is harder because there's no external ballast to balance those interests," said Charles Plosser, president of the Philadelphia Fed. "We have two failed banks down the street here—the First and Second Banks of the United States—which failed precisely because they had no balance. Their charters were revoked by Congress because of the perception that they were run for bankers and politicians and that the interests of people outside Washington, Philadelphia, and New York were being overlooked, so when the Fed was created the core tenet was to decentralize authority."

The reserve bank presidents pressed their case, calling and visiting lawmakers in Washington so aggressively that, according to one Senate aide, "Whenever I looked up, there seemed to be another of the regional Fed presidents in town." Many of them were more natural politicians than Bernanke, and they had much more experience in the kinds of interactions of which retail politics is made. Part of their job, for example, was giving speeches at the local chamber of commerce, trying to persuade businesspeople of the rightness of their policy ideas.

Much of their time was spent explaining to members of Congress just what these little-understood reserve banks around the country actually do. One congressman visited Richard Fisher at his office at the Dallas Fed, full of anger at the Federal Reserve for its work supporting big Wall Street banks and having signed on to Ron Paul's Audit the Fed bill. Fisher personally approved every discount-window loan the Fed made—even during the crisis, when the lending hit $9 billion a night—and as it happened, the day before, the discount window had extended credit to a bank in the congressman's district.

"I just lent $10,000 to a bank in your district last night," Fisher said. The congressman was startled—he had no idea that the Fed was so deeply involved in the routine operations of local banks.

"Would you have wanted to be involved in that decision?" Fisher asked. "Because effectively, if you are going to do what you signed on to do with the Ron Paul bill, you are going to be involved in that decision and making monetary policy."

It was an unusually snowy winter in Washington, a city consistently unable to deal with even a few inches of the stuff. When nearly three feet fell at Dulles International Airport on February 5 and 6, 2010, the federal government closed for days—"Snowmageddon" became the popular name for the storm.

The shutdown created a convenient opportunity for the newly confirmed Bernanke and his closest advisers to think through their strategy in the final push for financial reform legislation. With snow still on the ground and no one but a few security guards at work in the Eccles Building, Bernanke gathered together Don Kohn, the vice chair of the Fed Board of Governors; Kevin Warsh, a Fed governor who frequently acted as Bernanke's liaison to Republican politicians and Wall Street CEOs; Scott Alvarez, the Fed's chief lawyer; Michelle Smith, the Fed's communications chief; and Robertson.

The attendees started by discussing the core principles and goals of the Fed. They weighed the merits of being a more specialized agency focused on monetary policy and the financial plumbing of the big banks versus having a broader role overseeing nearly every bank in the country and protecting consumers. On one hand, a more targeted agency could be more effective. On the other, Bernanke and his advisers believed, the Fed was already better at doing its assigned tasks than most bureaucracies. It attracted high-quality staffers and was well run, which a new agency might not be.

What mattered, and what could be given up without much problem? The first priority, they concluded, was keeping political independence in their monetary policies. Audit the Fed needed to be fought at all costs.

The agency needed to keep oversight of the biggest banks in order to carry out monetary policy effectively and make sure the financial system was working. It was becoming clear that the financial reform being passed would place greater expectations on the Fed to guarantee financial stability, and it needed to regulate the likes of Citigroup and Goldman Sachs to be able to do that. The Fed also needed to keep the oversight of small banks for a few reasons, Bernanke's inner circle agreed: to have insight into a sector that was, in the aggregate, a major driver of U.S. economic activity, but also to maintain the ballast that comes from the Fed system having a vivid presence across the United States. Bernanke and his associates were more willing to give up its role as a regulator protecting consumers. That was never a core function of the Fed, and Bernanke's line to Congress became, in effect: If you choose to leave it with us, we'll carry out the responsibilities better than in the past, but if you want to take it away from us, that's your prerogative. The good news that snowy day in Washington was that, on the things that really mattered to the Fed, the tide seemed to be shifting in its favor.

For all the occasional distrust between Fed leaders in Washington and at the reserve banks, by this crucial period in the first months of 2010, the reserve bank presidents were becoming strong allies, each with something to offer the other. Bernanke and the Fed leaders in Washington had the inside game, with their relationships with Geithner and House and Senate leaders. But the reserve bank presidents had, in many cases, relationships with a wide range of members of Congress from across the United States—along with experience explaining financial concepts to people who aren't specialists.

As time passed, more lawmakers who weren't normally attuned to financial regulation started to focus on what would become the Dodd-Frank Act. And they often turned to their reserve bank presidents to help understand the issues. Robertson's staff even arranged events at the Fed's headquarters in Washington in which reserve bank presidents would invite congressional staff from their districts to come for hours of briefings.

Ironically, some of the sources of tension between the board and the reserve banks at times proved an asset.

Hoenig gave speeches assailing bailouts and the culture of too big to fail, implicitly criticizing the Fed's crisis-era decisions. As if trying to atone for his acquiescence to the low-interest-rate policies of the mid-2000s that may have helped stoke the crisis, he dissented from the Fed's monetary policy decisions at each meeting in 2010, objecting to the central bank's promise to keep interest rates low for an "extended period."

It may have irritated some of his Fed colleagues, but it also strengthened his credibility with many of the legislators who would decide the fate of the Fed. If you're annoyed by what the Fed has done over the past few years, so am I, his actions suggested to lawmakers. But the way you're responding is counterproductive.

Hoenig also went after a proposal meant to bring more democracy to the reserve banks by making the chairmen of their boards of directors subject to Senate confirmation. He and his reserve bank colleagues viewed this as an increase of political control over an institution that already had plenty– and as a consequence of decisions made in Washington and New York that had nothing to do with the regional banks.

The New York Fed, they thought, was particularly responsible. Stephen Friedman, a former Goldman Sachs chief executive, had been chairman of the New York Fed at the same time he was serving on Goldman's board. He was allowed to remain in both roles after Goldman elected to put itself under the Fed's regulatory umbrella in September 2008, and even received a waiver from New York Fed lawyers allowing him to buy more shares of Goldman at a time when the New York Fed's lending programs were helping to prop up the investment bank. Friedman resigned his chairmanship in May 2009, after his conflicts of interest came to light in the *Wall Street Journal*. But in the view of many reserve bank presidents, the damage to the reputation of the entire Federal Reserve System had already been done.

"That's what really drives me crazy," said Hoenig. "This exemption is made for a guy from Goldman Sachs, and suddenly the bankers in America all across the country are now villains. The bankers on our board from a little town in Nebraska and Denver, Colorado, are saying, 'What the heck happened?'"

As lobbying by the reserve bank presidents and Cam Fine's Independent Community Bankers of America began to make inroads, Dodd's staff was working toward a new compromise: The Fed would still regulate the more than five thousand "bank holding companies" nationwide, but it would no longer oversee the roughly nine hundred state-chartered banks.

Hoenig and Fisher pushed Kay Bailey Hutchison, a Republican senator from Texas, to take the lead on amending Dodd's legislation to make it more Fed-friendly. Fisher and Hutchison had run against each other for the Senate in 1994, an ill-fated venture into electoral politics for Fisher that predated his career as a central banker. In the incestuous world of Texas politics, they'd been friends before the race, and they remained friends after. But there was more than common history behind Hutchison's decision to become the standard-bearer for small-bank regulation by the Fed, according to Fine.

"We have a lot of community banks in Texas," he said. "And she was running for governor."

Hutchison's staff drafted an amendment that would undo the bill's last major remnants of the Fuck the Fed strategy. Banks with less than $50 billion in assets, instead of being shunted over to the FDIC and state regulators, would remain under the umbrella of the reserve banks in Dallas and Kansas City and beyond. Hutchison had a reputation as one of the quieter members of the Senate, neither the creator of grand bargains nor a practitioner of overheated rhetoric. But on this issue, whatever mix of political ambition and personal loyalties drove Hutchison to take up the cause, she pursued it with abandon, making her case with language very similar to that of Fisher, Hoenig, and the IBCA: We must prevent the Fed from becoming a creature only of the biggest banks.

On May 5, Hoenig, Jeffrey Lacker of the Richmond Fed, Charles Plosser of the Philadelphia Fed, and Narayana Kocherlakota of the Minneapolis Fed took seats in a hearing room in the Russell Senate Office Building. This would be a closed event, with only members of Congress and their staffs allowed in. With no cameras rolling, the usual bloviation was unnecessary; this session was meant for legislators to ask questions to which they actually wanted to know the answers. Around two dozen lawmakers from both parties and both houses of Congress came to the event, which was put on by the Joint Economic Committee and scheduled over the reservations of the Fed Board of Governors in Washington.

Over nearly ninety minutes, with the Capitol Hill press corps huddled just outside the door, members of Congress asked one question after another, apparently genuinely curious about what the reserve banks do and why it matters. Their tone was warm and friendly, free of the vicious anger that had characterized discussions of the Fed over the past year.

The message, the reserve bank presidents concluded, had finally gotten through.

A udit the Fed may have passed overwhelmingly in the House, but in the Senate finance reform bill that Chris Dodd put forward, it was nowhere to be found. Bernie Sanders wanted to change that, drafting an amendment that largely tracked with Ron Paul's.

Bernanke and Geithner both saw dire consequences if it was enacted: There would be intense new political pressures on the Fed's monetary policy, which would inevitably make policymakers more reluctant to make hard but necessary decisions. And provisions that would require disclosure of emergency lending to banks through the discount window would make banks reluctant to use those programs, making a financial crisis that much more likely. If the Sanders amendment passed the Senate as written, it would almost certainly become law, given that nearly identical provisions had been passed in the House bill earlier. There would be a committee to reconcile differences between the two versions of the legislation, but it couldn't very well scrap something that was in both versions.

Dodd and Senate majority leader Harry Reid were clear with Sanders: If he wouldn't agree to changes to his amendment that would protect Fed independence, making it acceptable to them and the Obama administration, they would use the elaborate procedural hurdles of the Senate to try to block it, preventing it from ever coming up for a vote. If, however, Sanders could reach an agreement with Dodd that would achieve his main goal of transparency but compromise on areas that threatened Fed independence, they would put their full support behind his amendment and move quickly for a vote.

On May 11, Sanders took to the floor of the Senate to formally introduce his amendment. His staff advised him to keep talking for as long as he could; they needed the time to hammer out a compromise on increasing oversight of the Fed. "The time is now that we have got to end secrecy at the Fed," said the white-haired Vermonter. "This money does not belong to the Fed. It belongs to the American people, and the American people have a right to know where it's going."

While he spoke, in the majority leader's office a few steps from the Senate cloakroom, itself a few steps from the Senate floor, Sanders's and Dodd's staffs started going back and forth with Reid's advisers looking on. Sanders's people agreed that monetary policy wouldn't become subject to oversight by congressional investigators. Dodd's staff conceded to making the Fed's emergency lending public, against the wishes of the big banks as well as the Fed—but only after a two-year delay that would help prevent banks from turning down the loans out of fear of stigmatization. Dodd's aides also agreed to a Sanders demand that there be a top-to-bottom investigation and full public disclosure of the Fed's lending during the crisis.

The deal they struck had something for everyone—for Sanders the liberal populist and the anti-Fed crowd from the Tea Party right, it demanded that the Federal Reserve reveal more information than ever before about its operations. But it did so in ways that Bernanke, Geithner, and Dodd believed would leave the central bank with enough discretion to fight inflation or backstop the banking system when it needed to.

"I had to make a political decision," Sanders told reporters later that day. "What people were telling me—friends of mine were telling me, Democrats, some Republicans, were saying, you know, 'We like the idea of transparency. We like the idea of an audit. But we are afraid that this is going to get into the day-to-day monetary policy of the Fed. We don't want that.'"

Whereas Sanders's original amendment would have been a hard-fought vote, the compromise version passed the Senate 96–0.

A day later, on May 12, it was the Hutchison amendment's turn. After a full year of jockeying, lobbying, and arm-twisting, the debate on the Senate floor wasn't a debate at all. Hutchison and her cosponsor, Democrat Amy Klobuchar of Minnesota, each spoke for about thirty seconds.

"This amendment ensures that the nation's monetary policy has a connection to Main Street and not just Wall Street," said Klobuchar. Citing one of her constituents, the president of the Grand Rapids State Bank, she continued, "All senators should be reminded that the Federal Reserve System was created to serve all of America, not just Wall Street."

Making the case against—sort of—was Dodd, who'd become resigned to seeing his goal of cutting back the Fed's authority go down in flames as one senator after another had heard from his or her local bankers. "I'm going to oppose the amendment, but I'm not going to speak against it," he said. He looked at Hutchison and put his hands up, gesturing, "I surrender."

And that was it. The vote began. Hoenig and four of his colleagues watched it on a TV in the library just outside his office high above Kansas City. They started out writing down how each senator voted, but after a few minutes it became apparent that keeping a running tally was unnecessary. The final vote was 91–8, on legislation that reversed Dodd's approach and left the Fed as regulator of almost all of the nation's banks. Hoenig walked down to the ninth floor of the Kansas City Fed's office tower, to where the bank examiners worked—the very department where he'd begun his career four decades earlier—and offered praise to a group that had been demoralized by becoming a pawn in the post-crisis negotiations.

There were still a few more steps to go before what became known as the Dodd-Frank Act would become law, including a series of all-night conference committee votes at which the differences between the House and Senate bills were hammered out. In that process, one final provision that the Fed detested—for making the powerful president of the New York Fed a presidential appointee rather than a technocrat appointed by a private board of directors like at other Fed banks—was defeated. On every meaningful front—audits of its monetary policy, its role in regulating banks big and small, Bernanke's confirmation—the battle for the Fed was over, and it was the mighty Federal Reserve System that had won.

But why? What allowed this deeply unpopular agency to emerge from the crisis scratched and bruised but, if anything, more powerful than it had been before?

However much Congress may have wanted to punish the Fed for its actions during the crisis, the task of regulating trillion-dollar banks is too complex to hand over to just anyone. The Federal Reserve, lawmakers began to realize as they studied the details, really did have the expertise and the means to do so.

But there was some luck involved, too. Having a Fed man as treasury secretary and the president's closest adviser on financial reform ensured that the administration would help fight for the central bank. A different treasury secretary and different president might have had different priorities. Bernanke would never be confused with a master legislative strategist, but his approach to dealing with lawmakers proved a good match for the moment: He was earnest and straightforward at a time when the great knock on the Fed was that it was excessively secretive and obfuscatory.

The Fed also found a surprising source of strength in the very structure that made its governance a mess: those dozen reserve banks scattered around the country, with their private boards of directors and thousands of community banks under their regulatory umbrella. The community bankers lobbied not just on the issues of their own narrow concern—who would regulate them—but also on issues that mattered to the Fed as a whole, such as monetary policy independence and Bernanke's confirmation.

The series of compromises made to pass the Federal Reserve Act back in 1913 may have created something of a monster. But its tentacles turned out to be so tightly wrapped around American business and politics—large and small, national and local—that it was almost impossible to kill.

# THIRTEEN

# The New Greek Odyssey

A re you sure?" asked the younger man.

"Are you *sure*?" he repeated in disbelief.

The older man, George Provopoulos, the governor of the Bank of Greece, was sure. The younger, George Papaconstantinou, Greece's newly installed finance minister, was learning that the job he'd long coveted might be a lot more challenging than he'd imagined.

Papaconstantinou and his colleagues in the Panhellenic Socialist Movement party had initially made their spending plans assuming that their nation's budget deficit would be about 6 percent of its economic output. But in the months before the election, the previous government had ramped up spending while collecting taxes less aggressively. By the time voters went to the polls, on October 4, 2009, Papaconstantinou was looking at a deficit of 8 to 10 percent of gross domestic product.

The Greek government may have its budgets and projections, but the Bank of Greece does the actual work of accepting tax payments and clearing outgoing checks. It knows better than any other entity what shape the country's finances are really in. The startling message the central bank governor had for the new finance minister on the morning of October 7: You, sir, are looking at a deficit of 12.5 percent—or higher. (Years later, Greek politicians were still trading accusations about just how much the incoming government knew of the shortfall as it campaigned on a platform of maintaining social spending—an agenda that would prove impossible to enact.)

The new government began working through its budget, setting a dozen or so analysts to work around a giant conference table. Every day, they found new expenses that hadn't been properly accounted for—€600 million owed to hospitals, for example, with no accurate record of when the expenses had even been incurred. Every evening, Papaconstantinou would leave and say, "Okay, guys, is that it?" It never was. "Basically, we were discovering that the Greek government *had* no budget," said Papaconstantinou later.

When all the numbers were in, even Governor Provopoulos's grim estimate would prove overly optimistic: The 2009 Greek budget deficit would end up amounting to 15.7 percent of its economy, the highest in the world.

It would fall to three men named George to try to narrow this chasm—Papaconstantinou, Provopoulos, and Papandreou, the prime minister. The decisions they made in Athens—and the reactions to them by Jean-Claude Trichet and the leaders of Germany, France, and other Western powers—would remake Europe and the world.

S ome countries experience financial crises because their banks face collapse. Others experience them because their public finances are out of control. But history teaches one consistent lesson: Regardless of how the crisis starts, it will soon spread. When a banking system fails, the economy inevitably collapses, straining public finances at the same time that the government takes on the extra expense of bailing out the banks. When a government faces a debt panic, that nation's banks inevitably come under strain as well, as budget cutting leads to a weaker economy and banks suffer huge losses on the government bonds they own.

Banking crises and public debt crises, in other words, are two sides of the same coin. But the wave of panic that began with that realization of the true state of Greek public finance in October 2009 had an added layer of interconnection. Greece's decision to adopt the euro in 2001 had yoked the fortunes of all of Europe to that of this relatively small country—and left the three Georges and their eleven million fellow citizens without the usual tools needed to deal with a crisis.

Greece was, at first glance, an unusual choice to join the seventeen-nation eurozone. Its economic output per person, about $13,000 in 1999, was only about half that of France and Germany. Its business environment was dysfunctional, with rampant bribery, onerous regulations, and unpredictable enforcement of them. Its political system was fragile, its democratic institutions not well entrenched—the nation had been governed by a military dictatorship as late as 1973. But Greece had something that neighbors such as Bulgaria and Turkey did not: It was where democracy was invented, the birthplace of the European idea, the original European empire. In geopolitical terms, it was the traditional border between Europe and the Arab world. Greece, for all its problems, was special.

And the idea of joining the eurozone was particularly attractive to the Greeks themselves. Long after most industrialized Western nations had conquered inflation, prices in Greece rose at double-digit rates every single year from 1973 to 1994. That meant the drachma became steadily less valuable as the years passed, which was a boon to the nation's tourism sector but meant that ordinary Greeks' savings blew away with the wind. Inflation was so high that lenders would give money to the Greek government or its citizens only on onerous terms. After all, they had to take into account the fact that the drachmas they were repaid would be worth less than those they had loaned.

In 1992, when low-inflation Germany could borrow money for a decade at 8 percent, Greece had to pay 24 percent. Both the major Greek political parties, the center-left Panhellenic Socialist Movement and the center-right New Democracy, were enthusiasts for joining the eurozone, with only the communist left and neofascist right, together amounting to around 20 percent of the population, opposing. Greece's problems during the 1980s and 1990s were anemic growth, double-digit inflation and interest rates, and large deficits. "With the adoption of the euro, Greece gained the credibility of the European Central Bank, which itself was modeled after Germany's Bundesbank," said George Provopoulos, the Bank of Greece governor, who was an academic at the time. "Gaining credibility meant low interest rates and inflation rates, which is what happened."

With decisions on monetary policy handed over to Jean-Claude Trichet and his colleagues in Frankfurt, Greek inflation hovered around 3 percent through the first decade of the 2000s. The cost of borrowing plummeted. Without the perceived risk of inflation, investors were willing to hand money over to the Greek government for pretty much the same interest rate they received for giving it to the German or French governments. In 2007, on the eve of the crisis, German ten-year borrowing costs averaged 4.02 percent. Greek rates were 4.29 percent. Investors had become complacent, viewing Greek debt as an essentially risk-free substitute for bonds issued by better-run countries like Germany, France, or the Netherlands. Indeed, under the bank regulations in effect in Europe, banks from those strong countries could buy Greek debt and treat it as a risk-free asset against which they needed to hold no capital, giving them every incentive to load up on the stuff. Unfortunately for Greece, and eventually all of Europe, the nation didn't take advantage of that environment. "What Greece needed to do was take advantage of this low-inflation-rate and interest-rate environment to adjust its economy," said Provopoulos.

Instead of fixing the fundamentals of their economy, the Greeks were cooking their books. One widely covered instance was a series of currency swaps arranged with the assistance of Goldman Sachs in the early 2000s that essentially allowed the Greek government to borrow money without issuing debt that would show up in official statistics. Less widely known were such tricks as underreporting how much the nation was spending on its military (a particularly large expense given perennially tense relations with Turkey) and the failure to account for debts owed to hospitals that Papaconstantinou's budget analysts discovered. The government fudged its numbers by selling off long-term assets—the rights to future airport fees, for example—in order to fund immediate spending. "The gravest thing was the fact that they didn't know themselves that they were lying," said one eurozone central banker. "We discovered progressively that you had an immense problem of the state functioning—the cheating, the mistakes in the figures, things done orally and not written down."

There's an old saw that it's only when the tide goes out that one learns who was swimming naked. The financial crisis triggered by the Lehman Brothers failure in September 2008 brought out the tide—and exposed a beach full of naked Greeks.

In Frankfurt, Jean-Claude Trichet received the news of Greece's dire public finances with the same surprise that Papaconstantinou had. Up to this point, the European Central Bank had most of its staff devoted to monitoring conditions in the bigger economies in the eurozone. A single economist spent only part of his time tracking the Greek economy. That changed in late 2009, as the ECB became more alarmed at Greece's fiscal situation with every basis-point rise in the nation's borrowing costs. In the Eurotower, a team of econo-mists was assembled to delve more deeply into the nation's budget. By Christmas, it had been dispatched on a secret mission to Athens to gather in-formation on the ground, primarily from the Bank of Greece and the finance ministry.

In hindsight, financial markets responded to the disclosures of Greece's dire situation surprisingly slowly: When the new government took office in early October, the country's bonds were yielding 4.44 percent. By the end of the month, that had risen only to 4.65 percent, and to 5.77 percent by the end of the year. Ironically, it was only as Papandreou's government started announc-ing its plans to rein in spending and collect more in taxes—a plan that disap-pointed markets with its timidity—that rates started to rise dramatically, to 7 percent by the end of January 2010.

But even those modest rises in the cost of borrowed money had huge im-plications for the nation. It's called "debt dynamics": When a country has high levels of debt, even small increases in the interest rate it must pay mean big trouble. In 2009, Greece's total debt equaled 129 percent of its annual economic output, so even a single percentage-point increase in interest rates would make repayment vastly more difficult. Greece was on the verge of a dangerous situa-tion in which huge debts make interest rates rise, and those higher rates in turn make the debts unsustainable.

This is hardly novel. Countries throughout history have found themselves in just such a predicament. In 1944, an institution was created for the sole pur-pose of dealing with such a debt crisis: the International Monetary Fund, which can lend money to nations in financial trouble to help them get back on their feet. Over the six decades of its existences—making plenty of mistakes along the way—the fund has learned how to structure the financial rescues of debt-laden states. But it has also learned, in Asia in the late 1990s and Latin Amer-ica in the early 2000s, the dangers of forcing a country to slash its budget too rapidly—that the resulting depression can bring social unrest and political in-stability. In the early days of the Lehman crisis, it put together a so-called Crisis Veteran Team to ensure that the accumulated knowledge of its most seasoned staffers would be passed along to their younger colleagues.

At the helm of the IMF was Dominique Strauss-Kahn, a charismatic and politically connected former French finance minister who came from his nation's center-left socialist party. It was an open secret that he was a likely candidate to challenge Nicolas Sarkozy for the French presidency in 2012—assuming, of course, he could avoid any nasty scandals resulting from his well-known sexual appetites.

Strauss-Kahn's standing as the possible next president of France boosted his credibility among many European leaders, but for Trichet and some others, the idea of bringing in the IMF was anathema. Part of it was cultural arrogance: We are Europe, birthplace of civilization, not some tinpot nation in need of an international bailout. It would be a "humiliation," Trichet once said, for the IMF to step in. Trichet was similarly resolute that there could not, would not be any default. Greece would pay its bills.

Trichet embraced a view, especially common in Germany, that was rooted in a sort of moralism. Greece had spent too much and taken on too much debt. It must cut spending and reduce deficits. If it showed adequate courage and political resolve, markets would reward it with lower borrowing costs. He put a great deal of faith in the power of confidence: Resolute action by political authorities would put the Greek economy back on a path of growth by improving confidence among investors, businesses, and consumers. "It is very important," Trichet said in January 2010, for those nations "which have a special deterioration to redress the situation in taking the appropriate bold and courageous measures for their own prosperity and recovery. We trust that this is essential to improve confidence, and you know the extent to which we consider that confidence is key in the present economic situation in Europe as well as in the world."

So Trichet was, through the end of 2009 and start of 2010, convinced that Greece could solve its own problems, reforming its tax system and cutting government spending and so regaining the confidence of bond markets. No need for a bailout from the IMF—or anyone else. Said one IMF official, "The attitude from the ECB was, 'Get out of our face, we don't need you guys, we are the eurozone, we created this, and we can take care of our own.'" Added another IMF official, "Trichet was the leader of the pack insisting, 'No IMF!' And the reason was not because he was against the IMF, but because he wanted the European governments to shoulder their responsibilities."

Trichet was equally insistent that the ECB would not take any action to bail out Greece: "No government, no state can expect any special treatment from us," he said in a January 2010 Q&A session in Frankfurt. Already, however, some American and British commentators were warning that Greece's financial troubles could force it to drop out of the eurozone. What did Trichet think about that possibility?

"I do not comment myself on absurd hypotheses," the ECB president replied.

M ake your way to the French Canadian metropolis of Montreal. Then, if you have the proper connections, hop on a military jet and fly four hours due north. You'll find yourself in Iqaluit, a town of fewer than seven thousand people on the southeastern coast of Baffin Island, directly across the Davis Strait from Greenland. At one time it was a pit stop for American fighter planes being sent across the Atlantic to fight in World War II. Now it's the capital of Nunavut, the largest and newest territory in Canada, but one so remote it has no roadways connecting it to the rest of the country.

This is the voyage that the world's leading finance ministers and central bankers made in the dead of winter in 2010. Canada wasn't the first nation to choose a less than convenient location for an international summit, though the meeting place of the Group of Seven finance ministers that February is among the more extreme examples.

The choice could have been made for a variety of reasons: to isolate officials from any potential distractions, including any noisy protestors; to celebrate the area's native Inuit culture; to try to persuade the Europeans that they should lift their recent ban on the importation of commercially hunted seal products; to remind attendees of Canada's deep connections to the Arctic—and hence its rights to the region's oil reserves. Whatever the relative weights of these factors in the Canadians' thinking, the results of these talks at the top of the world would have far-reaching consequences across the planet.

With the temperature an unseasonably warm 0° Fahrenheit, the attendees were treated to demonstrations of igloo making and other examples of native culture. The British press had fun with a photograph of Mervyn King wearing a giant fur-lined coat and riding a dogsled. "For God's sake, just don't get photographed clubbing a baby seal," said one central banker's communications adviser on the banker's way out the door. Or, for that matter, get caught eating any: All the officials except the Canadians skipped the final meal, at which raw seal meat was served. The Americans tried to fly home early Saturday, but were waylaid in Boston for the night; ironically, after they had experienced relatively pleasant weather in the Arctic, their plane couldn't land because Washington was being buffeted by a snowstorm.

Wearing sweaters and sport coats rather than their usual dark suits, the finance ministers and central bankers assembled in a circular conference room at the Frobisher Inn ("the largest full-service business hotel in the Eastern Arctic") under a domed ceiling of exposed wooden beams evocative of an igloo. Trichet made an impassioned plea to his European colleagues, one that suggested he might be changing his mind about giving Greece "special treatment": The Greek situation wasn't sustainable, he said. The government's borrowing costs were rising even in the face of its deficit reduction plans. Major banks in France and Germany and Spain owned hundreds of billions of euros of Greek debt, so a worsening of conditions in Greece could endanger the entire continent's banking system. And in financial markets, it was already becoming clear that whenever investors became worried about Greece, they also began shedding the debt of other European countries that seemed to have precarious finances, particularly Portugal and Ireland but also Spain and Italy.

Making one of his characteristic appeals to grand principle, Trichet argued that the threat wasn't just to Greece, but to the European project as a whole. It must be taken seriously. European leaders left the Arctic with a greater understanding of what was at stake. As Trichet departed Iqaluit, the gathered reporters asked how he was feeling about Europe's outlook. "Confident," he replied.

And a second thing happened at the summit: In the isolation of the Canadian wilderness, the leaders of the world economy collectively agreed that their great challenge had shifted. The economy seemed to be healing; it was time for them to turn their attention away from boosting growth. No more stimulus. The Greek problem was seen as evidence that it was time for all the nations of the world to begin reducing budget deficits. No more ultra-easy-money policies. Even Ben Bernanke, more wary of tightening monetary policy than most of his counterparts, would explain in a presentation a few days later how the Fed planned to exit from easy money. "We have spent considerable effort in developing the tools we will need to remove policy accommodation, and we are fully confident that at the appropriate time we will be able to do so effectively," he assured the House Committee on Financial Services.

Iqaluit was the moment the world's central bankers and other financial leaders began a great pivot toward tighter money and austerity. "The global economic situation has, of course, improved and is improving," said Canadian finance minister Jim Flaherty, the host of the gathering, summing up the conclusions reached in a press conference on February 6, 2010. "We need to . . . begin to look ahead to exit strategies and move to a more sustainable fiscal track." In other words: We're out of the woods.

It would turn out to be a wildly premature—and costly—pronouncement.

Three weeks later, Jürgen Stark, a member of the ECB's Executive Board and the central bank's chief economist, traveled to Athens. He was officially there as an observer of talks between the Greek government and Olli Rehn, the European commissioner for economic and monetary affairs and the euro. But there was more to his trip than that. Eurozone officials, persuaded by Trichet's efforts in Iqaluit, were ready to offer some financial backstop to the Greek government in case it lost access to bond markets.

But they insisted that Greece enact a wide-ranging program of budget cuts, privatizations, and improved tax collection in exchange. Trichet's belief in confidence-inducing austerity had won the day. The German government, however, wanted to ensure that Rehn and the European Commission would be adequately tough in their negotiations. That's where Stark came in. The ECB, with its roots in the Bundesbank, could serve as a powerful counterbalance for any temptation to let the Greeks off the hook. Stark, himself German, was to join Rehn in Athens as a sort of enforcer.

When Stark walked into the room for the talks at the Greek finance ministry on the morning of March 1, Papaconstantinou visibly tensed. He initially ignored Stark, speaking only with Rehn. But Stark wasn't shy about speaking up, and unbeknownst to Papaconstantinou, he and Rehn had eaten breakfast together that morning to plot their strategy. Divide and conquer wouldn't work in this meeting.

The Greek finance minister presented a plan for his nation to cut its budget deficit by about a third in 2010—from around 13 percent of economic output in 2009 to 8.7 percent. That would imply around 4 percent less economic activity in Greece, which amounts to a very steep recession. (By comparison, the U.S. economy contracted 3.3 percent in 2008.) To avoid a painful contraction, the budget cuts would have to be offset by some other economic change: lower interest rates from the ECB, for example, or trade partnerships that could drive up exports, or the sort of international investments in the country that, Trichet presumed, would result from increased confidence. But the talks that day in Athens weren't focused on the risk of recession or any steps that might relieve the pain. They were focused on the how and when of austerity.

The good news for Papaconstantinou was that both of the men on the other side of the table liked what they heard. Stark and Rehn left persuaded by the finance minister that his nation had an aggressive plan for reforming its finances, as well as the political will to carry it out. The Greeks described plans to increase the nation's value-added tax and step up tax collection, to freeze public pensions, and to eliminate the "fourteenth month's salary" for government employees. Greek workers, in addition to monthly paychecks, received so-called thirteenth- and fourteenth-month's checks to cover their holiday spending and summer vacations. Cutting one of them would be effectively slashing pay for those workers by 7 percent.

"The effort is not easy, however the reduction of deficit and debt is necessary and will contribute significantly to the improvement of the economy," Rehn told reporters. "The commission will continue to support the Greek authorities and the Greek people so that the economy will regain its viable course." Stark, meanwhile, reported back to his colleagues in Frankfurt that Papaconstantinou was serious about budget cutting.

Even as the urbane Papaconstantinou, with his dapper suits, rimless eyeglasses, and PhD from the London School of Economics, negotiated with European authorities, there were early signs of the strain that austerity would put on Greek politics. Three days after meeting with Stark and Rehn, about two hundred members of a union group affiliated with the Greek Communist Party stormed the finance ministry, draping a banner from its roof calling on workers to rise up against the proposed budget cuts.

And the streets of Athens weren't the only place where there was discontent. As discussion of a Greek bailout heated up, anger swelled in Germany as well. If Greeks hated the idea of losing their fourteenth paycheck or seeing their pensions cut, Germans hated nearly as much the idea of coming to the financial rescue of a country with such free-spending ways. In the pages of the *Bild*, a lowbrow, high-circulation tabloid, populist outrage at Greece turned alarmist and xenophobic. Its front-page headlines in the winter of 2010 included, "Is Greece making the German banks bankrupt?" and "Greeks quarrel and strike, instead of saving"—even "Sell your islands, you rotten Greeks, and the Acropolis too."

Nonetheless, by March 2010, the pieces for a eurozone rescue of Greece were finally coming together. The morning of March 25, Trichet stepped before the European Parliament in Brussels to deliver his regular testimony about the state of the monetary union. "*Sehr geehrter Herr Präsident*," he began in German, before moving to a few lines in French, then, for the bulk of his testimony, English. Near the end of the twenty-two-hundred-word presentation, he inserted a single sentence that sounded so obscure that many in attendance didn't realize its significance: "It is the intention of the ECB's Governing Council to keep the minimum credit threshold in the collateral framework at investment grade level (BBB–) beyond the end of 2010."

Translation: Even as Standard & Poor's and Moody's are downgrading their assessments of the creditworthiness of Greece and other European nations, we'll allow banks to post Greek bonds as collateral at the ECB in exchange for ready access to cash. It was an explicit reversal from Trichet's stated position of barely two months earlier; the ECB was willing to risk losses in order to keep cash flowing into Greece and prevent a fire sale if European banks suddenly started unloading Greek debt.

It wasn't Trichet's only reversal. German chancellor Angela Merkel had by this point changed her mind on involving the IMF in a Greek bailout, having concluded that the fund could offer not only extra financial firepower and experience, but also credibility-enforcing "conditionality," or demands for reform. Quite a few domestic critics, as well as French president Nicolas Sarkozy, thought her new position was an embarrassment—and that IMF involvement would give the United States, the fund's largest shareholder, power over Europe.

"She is betraying the very concept of Europe," editorialized the *Frankfurter Rundschau*. "In calling on the IMF, Merkel calls on none other than the United States, which dominates the IMF with its blocking minority of 17 percent. What a wretched state of affairs. What a disgrace for the European Commission and the European Central Bank."

But Merkel had a crucial ally. As late as March 4, Trichet had said that while "the IMF's technical assistance is very important," he did "not believe that it would be appropriate to introduce the IMF as a supplier of help" financially. But as the political wind shifted, so did Trichet. In a typical Trichet touch, the Frenchman barely acknowledged that there'd been any change in his view at all. "I never said myself, and neither have my colleagues, that the IMF did not have very good expertise," he said on April 8, after endorsing the agreement that brought the IMF in to help support Greece.

The agreement that Trichet and the leaders of the sixteen nations then in the eurozone hashed out in Brussels that Thursday—the announcement came at just before midnight—was a classic product of the Rube Goldberg contraption that is the European decision-making process. Hours were consumed not only by meaty issues like IMF involvement, but also by the question of whether the joint announcement would refer to a "European economic government" being created to handle any Greek rescue, or a "European economic governance." The French very much wanted the former, while a number of countries more worried about ceding national sovereignty wanted the latter. The finished product ran to only a page and a half and was exceptionally vague, essentially amounting to a promise that the governments of Europe wouldn't let Greece go bankrupt. "Euro area member states reaffirm their willingness to take determined and coordinated action, if needed, to safeguard financial stability in the euro area as a whole," the statement said—as if this mere assurance would be enough to keep private markets lending money to the troubled nation. Trichet promised in a press conference that "the mechanism decided today will not normally need to be activated."

There were no numbers in the communiqué that might give a sense of the financial resources the eurozone governments were willing to deploy to help Greece. The amounts that sources were whispering to reporters were in the paltry €20 billion range, about a third of it coming from the IMF. Any such disbursements would require the assent of all sixteen of the nations then using the common currency; even a Slovenia or a Malta or a Cyprus could, in theory, block collective action.

It was the first time European leaders had acknowledged the reality that with the yoke of a single currency, they would need to stand behind each other. But it was also a lost opportunity. This was a time when Greece's crisis was a relatively inexpensive one for Europe to solve; the nation's economic output was only about 2 percent that of the eurozone as a whole. But instead of simply writing a check and guaranteeing Greek finances, the message sent from Brussels in the spring of 2010 was that while the nations of the eurozone would stand behind their weaker members, they would do so reluctantly, only when they had absolutely no other choice, with huge procedural obstacles, and on a scale inadequate to the size of the problem.

It didn't take long for financial markets to reach exactly that conclusion. The cost for the Greek government to borrow money for a decade, 6.46 percent a couple of days before the summit, fell only to 6.28 percent the following day, hardly the move to be expected if markets were convinced that Europe stood behind Greece unconditionally. More worrisome, as the weather warmed up that spring, there was contagion in the air.

With the value of Greek bonds plummeting along with the nation's credit rating, global investors were quick to ask, "Who's next?" The answer, to many in the financial sector and the media, was an acronym: "PIIGS," for Portugal, Ireland, Italy, Greece, and Spain. Within the ECB, officials favored a different ordering of the same places. Their preferred acronym both put the nations roughly in order from most to least financially troubled and was at least somewhat less offensive to people who were natives of the countries in question. So the ECB focused on the "GIPSI" nations: Greece, Ireland, Portugal, Spain, and Italy.

Greece's financial problems should have been inexpensive to solve. But by moving slowly and timidly in addressing the nation's deteriorating financial position, European leaders ensured that a different price would be paid. Over the month of April 2010, the cost for Greece to borrow money soared to nearly 10 percent. The other GIPSIs also faced increases. Irish ten-year rates rose from 4.48 percent at the start of the month to 5.12 percent at the end. Portuguese borrowing costs rose from 4.22 percent to 5.14 percent.

It was herd behavior by global investors. In fact the GIPSI nations were very different from each other. The list included one country that was running huge annual budget deficits before the crisis (Greece) and four that weren't. It included two countries that had very large amounts of total debt relative to GDP (Greece and Italy) and three that didn't. (At this point, Spain actually had less public debt than fiscally sound Germany.) It included one country with flexible labor markets and a pro-business environment (Ireland) and four that put many obstacles in place to firing workers, cutting pay, or otherwise allowing businesses to adjust to a changing economy. Two nations were weighed down by huge losses in their banks (Ireland and Spain), while the others weren't. Three countries are small enough that their financial rescue would have been easily affordable by Europe as a whole (Greece, Portugal, and Ireland); two are so large that a financial rescue could strain the continent's resources to the breaking point. Here's a by-the-numbers summation along with Germany's numbers for comparison:

| Country | 2010 GDP | 2010 Deficit to GDP | 2010 Debt to GDP | Business environment* |
|---------|----------|---------------------|------------------|-----------------------|
| Greece | $305 billion | 9.6% | 142% | #100 |
| Ireland | $204 billion | 32% | 96% | #10 |
| Portugal | $229 billion | 7.3% | 83% | #30 |
| Spain | $1.41 trillion | 9.2% | 60% | #44 |
| Italy | $2.06 trillion | 4.6% | 119% | #87 |
| Germany | $3.32 trillion | 3.3% | 80% | #19 |

*Rank in 2012 World Bank "Doing Business" study of regulatory environment in 183 nations.

Even though the five GIPSI countries faced very different challenges, the markets started to view them as all in the same situation. Perhaps more problematic, so did many in the stronger European governments, imagining that the crisis was simply the result of profligate Southern Europeans spending money they didn't have—and they tailored their solution accordingly.

As interest rates rose steeply for Greece that April, it was becoming clear that the March 25 strategy of merely pledging to back the nation wasn't working. Greece had €8.5 billion in bonds coming due in May, and it was looking increasingly impossible for the government to roll that debt over—to find buyers for newly issued bonds—at an affordable rate. On April 23, Prime Minister George Papandreou acknowledged what had become obvious to anyone who understood the perils of debt dynamics in a country that owed so much money.

Standing in front of a picturesque seaside scene on the Greek island of Kastelorizo, just off the Turkish coast, Papandreou invoked his country's ancient history: "It is a national and imperative need to officially ask our partners in the EU for the activation of the support mechanism," said the prime minister, saying the country would need €45 billion in emergency loans. "All of us—the present government and the Greek people—have inherited a ship that is about to sink. . . . We are on a difficult course, a new Odyssey for Hellenism. But we now know the way to Ithaca and have charted our route."

It's worth remembering that the original Odyssey lasted a decade and included run-ins with cannibals, a witch who turned the captain's men into swine, and a violent one-eyed giant. The voyage Greece was about to undertake wouldn't be that much more relaxing.

F our days after Papandreou's acknowledgment that Greece was out of options without an international bailout, the markets again turned against the nation, and hard. Standard & Poor's cut Greece's debt to junk status, judging the country no more creditworthy than the shakiest borrowers. The cost for the nation to borrow money for ten years rose to a new high of 9.7 percent on April 27. But that actually understates the challenge. It wasn't just a higher interest rate that Greece was facing, but a shutdown in the function of its markets; there was, in effect, no longer a workable market in which the nation could borrow money. European leaders and the IMF returned to their negotiations to transform their vague concept of a Greek rescue into something more tangible.

All involved hoped that the deal announced on May 2 would be the end of the affair. It called for €110 billion to be provided to Greece over three years— the latest in an ever-escalating amount of cash being deployed to the country. Some €80 billion would come from the nations of the eurozone, the rest from the IMF—and they came with strings attached. Signed by Papaconstantinou and Provopoulos, the eighty-one-page memorandum of understanding with the IMF laid out what the Greek government would do to slash its spending and step up tax collection. It pledged a "frontloaded multiyear adjustment effort" reducing the annual budget deficit from more than 15 percent of GDP in 2009 to less than 3 percent by 2014. To make that happen, the Greek government agreed to raise taxes on cigarettes and alcohol, to put in place "presumptive taxation of professionals" so that doctors and other high earners couldn't evade their taxes so easily, and to cut pay for public employees.

The ECB was neck deep in the negotiations; if the other eurozone governments were to come up with cash to bail out Greece, they wanted their central bank to be on board as well. "We were also asked by the Heads of State and Government, to make an independent judgment on whether or not it was appropriate for them to activate the bilateral loans that they envisaged," Trichet said a few days later. "Their own decision would be taken only on the basis of our independent judgment." To show its dedication to the cause, the ECB once again extended its willingness to help Greece by taking its downgraded debt as collateral from banks around Europe. This time, the central bank pledged to accept the nation's debt indefinitely, no matter what might happen to its credit rating.

All this came at a price, however. If Trichet were to offer such extraordinary help to Greece and put its own balance sheet at risk, he would require that his staff have firsthand information about how Greece was faring in its austerity measures and reforms. Under the Greek memorandum of understanding, four times each year, a team of staffers from the IMF, the European Commission, and the ECB would travel to Athens to check on Greece's progress in fulfilling its end of the agreement—with a passing grade needed to receive the next disbursement of bailout funds. Greek officials started calling this group the "troika."

Suddenly, three organizations run by unelected officials—one of them the central bank—would effectively gain power over the taxing and spending policies of a democracy of eleven million people. The ECB was supposed to be insulated from politicians who might influence its decisions. But now the ECB would be doing quite a bit more than influencing the decisions of Greek politicians—it would, along with the IMF and the European Commission, be dictating them.

In the financial markets, there was a sense of relief. The Monday after the announcement, borrowing costs for the GIPSI nations fell and stock markets rallied. But, in an emerging pattern, the relief would be startlingly short-lived. As the week progressed, two things became clear: While Europe and the IMF might have come to Greece's rescue, they had no broader plan to deploy financial force in other nations that might get into trouble. And within Greece, there were signs that the agreement the government had struck would have a hard time sticking. The streets of Athens erupted in protests, as tens of thousands of people assembled in Syntagma Square in front of parliament, many carrying bats or hammers, throwing rocks, or heckling the ceremonial guards at the Tomb of the Unknown Soldier. On May 5, the demonstrations turned deadly when suspected anarchists threw a firebomb into Marfin Egnatia Bank. Three people inside perished.

On financial markets, developments were also ominous. Greek ten-year borrowing costs, 8.5 percent at the start of the week in the warm afterglow of the IMF deal, soared to nearly 11.3 percent by Thursday and 12.4 percent Friday. And the contagion was spreading rapidly to the other GIPSIs. Ireland, for example, saw its rate rise from 5.1 percent to 5.9 percent. These blips on traders' screens could cost the affected governments billions of euros a year in extra interest payments, making their already dire fiscal situations all the worse. If the trend were to continue, five countries with more than 130 million residents could very soon become insolvent. At that point, their only financial option might be to withdraw from the supposedly eternal eurozone and reintroduce their own currencies, which they could promptly devalue to lower their debt burdens. The result would surely be economic chaos across Europe and beyond.

Investors began to wonder just what the ECB might do to stop the panic from spiraling out of control. The core of the problem was that private buyers were selling off bonds. Could the ECB use its bottomless supply of euros to buy those bonds, thus pushing their interest rates down to more manageable levels? It would violate the spirit of the Maastricht Treaty, which specifies no money printing to fund governments. But by buying bonds on the open market instead of directly from governments, the ECB could get around that technicality. As analysts from the Royal Bank of Scotland wrote in a May 5 research note advocating such an action, "Better breaking the rule-book than breaking up the euro area!"

On May 6, the ECB's Governing Council held its regularly scheduled meeting to decide on whether to raise or lower interest rates. Twice a year, the bank holds the meeting not at its headquarters in Frankfurt, but in one of the capitals of the eurozone. This was one such occasion—the council had gathered in Lisbon. Trichet led a session that Thursday morning that was utterly routine, with officials from across Europe all offering their five minutes' assessment of

the state of the economy. By Trichet's design, they left unmentioned the burgeoning debt crisis, instead looking at data on inflation and concluding that
interest rates should remain unchanged. The first question asked of Trichet at
his press conference that afternoon was the obvious one: "Is the purchase of
government bonds an option to fight the consequences of Greece's fiscal crisis
on financial markets? Did you discuss this option today?"

"On your first question, we did not discuss this option," Trichet said, leaving the matter at that. When another reporter followed up a few minutes later,
he replied, "I will simply repeat that we did not discuss the matter, and I have
nothing further to say."

Stock markets worldwide sold off on the sense that Trichet had no bond-
buying plans up his sleeve. It wasn't so different from the runs the likes of
Northern Rock and Lehman Brothers had experienced two years earlier. Except now the entities losing their access to cash were the nations of Europe.

At 2:32 p.m. New York time—the ECB officials in Lisbon had already
gathered for dinner, though their work for the day was hardly done—a large
mutual fund company placed an order to sell $4.1 billion worth of contracts
tied to the overall value of the Standard & Poor's 500. Trading had already been
choppy, with more dramatic ups and downs than usual as investors reacted to
the latest news and speculation out of Europe. The market was already down
about 3 percent for the day. Through a strange sequence of events still not fully
understood, the $4.1 billion sell order—which, given the $10 trillion value of
the S&P 500 index, shouldn't have moved markets much—interacted with
ultra-high-speed electronic trading systems to create a massive collapse in the
market.

By 2:47 p.m., the Dow Jones Industrial Average had fallen 1,010 points, a
loss of 9 percent of U.S. stocks' total value. Prices for a share of some major
companies, like consulting firm Accenture and Samuel Adams brewer Boston
Beer Co., fell from double digits to a single penny in a matter of moments. By
shortly after 3 p.m., the market was climbing back to its normal level, and it
closed the day down 3.2 percent, not far from where it had been before what
would soon be known around the world as the Flash Crash.

The episode had more to do with frailties in the U.S. stock market in a
world in which trillions of dollars gush around through automated trades than
anything that the ECB had done. But it wasn't wholly unrelated to the crisis in

Europe. The market had been falling all week as investors fretted about the Greek debt crisis. The Flash Crash was merely one particularly jarring piece of evidence of just how on-edge global investors had become over whether Trichet and his colleagues would intervene to keep Europe together. And given the uncertainty in those early hours (and days) about why it had happened, among the ECB officials themselves, it prompted a particular unhappy reaction: *Did we do that?*

U.S. treasury secretary Timothy Geithner practiced a particularly energetic variety of economic diplomacy. His was a packed schedule, and between meetings he constantly worked the phones to gather information, compare notes, and try to persuade his interlocutors of what they ought to do or say or write. On that Thursday in May, he arrived at his office at 1500 Pennsylvania Avenue NW at 7:30 a.m., and in the fifteen hours that followed would testify at a hearing of the Financial Crisis Inquiry Commission across town; walk next door to the White House three times, once for the senior staff meeting and twice to meet with President Obama; and make at least twenty-six phone calls to a variety of U.S. politicians and White House aides, to journalists from the *Washington Post,* the *New York Times,* and the *Wall Street Journal,* and to his old friends from the world of central banking. There was one call to Ben Bernanke, one to Mervyn King—and two to Jean-Claude Trichet. The last call listed on Geithner's official schedule, with Senate Banking Committee chair Chris Dodd, ended at 10:25 p.m. (Recall that this was during the crucial final days of negotiations over what would become the Dodd-Frank financial reform act.)

Geithner's message to Trichet and other European officials that day and in the days that followed—and, for that matter, in the years that followed—was that the time for half-measures was over. The Flash Crash had only heightened the sense of urgency among the Americans, adding to pressure from around the world—it also came from the British and from Dominique Strauss-Kahn at the IMF—for the Europeans to move more boldly than they had to that point.

About the same time as the Flash Crash, Trichet and his colleagues on the ECB Governing Council gathered to eat at the Palácio da Bacalhoa, a fifteenth-century estate south of Lisbon. At the moment of the crash, a bit before 8 p.m. Lisbon time, many of the central bankers' BlackBerrys started vibrating simultaneously. They couldn't really attend to the confidential business of the ECB during the dinner itself. Their Portuguese hosts were present; so were many of the men's' wives. Nonetheless, in one pointed moment, German Bundesbank president Axel Weber, who was more concerned than most members of the Governing Council that nations like Portugal weren't cutting their budget deficits enough, asked a Portuguese official about what his country was doing to reduce spending. His answer? Portugal was thinking of taxing public employees' thirteenth- and fourteenth-month's salaries, the bonuses that Portuguese workers received just like their Greek counterparts. They'd been tax-free.

Weber was astonished. Forget taxing them. "Why should public employees receive thirteenth and fourteenth payments at all?" he asked. "We got rid of them in Germany years ago."

Trichet waited until dinner was over, about 10 p.m., to convene a secret meeting to discuss the Governing Council's next move. With interest rates spiraling every which way—upward in the GIPSIs, downward in stronger countries like Germany, France, and the Netherlands—the ECB was losing control over monetary policy. Suddenly, ten-year interest rates in Germany (2.79 percent on May 6), were more than three percentage points lower than in Portugal (6.14 percent). The gap with Greece was widening into a chasm. That meant that different European companies and households, even if otherwise identical, were facing dramatically different financial conditions. Trichet asked for the officials to brainstorm ways they might address the crisis.

One spoke up. "We could buy government bonds," he said. The ECB could go into bond markets and buy securities to try to get rates down in the countries where they were climbing skyward. It might not even take much in the way of purchases to change the psychology of the markets. It wouldn't be the printing of money to fund governments *per se*. That was forbidden, after all. It would simply be ensuring that the central bank's monetary policy was working. Ensuring, to use the technical term, the functioning of the "monetary transmission mechanism."

There were people who spoke up against the idea that night in Lisbon, for example, ECB Executive Board member Jürgen Stark, he of the Greek mission earlier in the spring. But the identity of the man who broached the idea of bond buying gave Trichet some inkling that he could make the move with the broad support of his committee?

It was Axel Weber.

Some in the room interpreted his comments as an explicit backing, while others saw it more as a kind of theoretical, academic musing as to the possibility, with no endorsement implied. What they agree upon is that he was the first to explicitly broach the subject, even if they disagree on just how firm his backing was at the time.

Weber was a forceful presence in the ECB's decision-making body. This came in part by virtue of his job as leader of the national bank of the largest eurozone economy, which was also the trading desk that carried out more of the ECB's decisions than any other. It came in part by virtue of his status as heir apparent to Trichet. The Germans had not yet had one of their own occupy the ECB presidency, and Weber seemed the likeliest candidate to take up the job when Trichet's term was to end October 31, 2011. And Weber's stature came in part from his personal manner and background. He was a more accomplished economist than most of his counterparts on the Governing Council, and he wasn't shy about expressing his views. Weber relished the give-and-take of a vigorous debate on economic theory. Big and barrel-chested, with a certain erect Teutonic posture, he looked a little like the television gangster Tony Soprano.

Trichet knew that the Germans would be the biggest obstacle to starting up bond purchases. The prohibition against central banks financing governments was rooted in their experience under Rudolf von Havenstein's Reichsbank in the 1920s, the most vivid illustration of what can go wrong when that practice is carried to extremes. The prohibition against monetization is a foremost principle of the Bundesbank. But if Weber would be comfortable with a limited, strategic use of ECB bond purchases to ease the crisis, Trichet would have more room to move without coming in for criticism from his more hawkish committee members.

But when Weber awoke the next morning, Friday May 7, he reconsidered the idea that he had seemed open to the evening before. Maybe he was reevaluating in the cold light of day something that he'd merely kicked around in a more academic, theoretical way the night before. Maybe he realized how much internal blowback he would face at the Bundesbank if he endorsed even limited bond purchases. Hell, maybe the ghost of Rudolf von Havenstein had visited him in the middle of the night.

Whatever truly drove his shift in thinking, Weber boarded a plane from Lisbon to Frankfurt and began typing out an e-mail during the three-hour flight. He laid out several key ideas. (Sources described the content of the message in detail but wouldn't provide a written copy.) If the ECB were to buy government bonds without the governments themselves having made an ironclad commitment to back each other's' finances, it would make the central bank, not elected officials, ultimately responsible for Europe's financial well-being. Greece was fundamentally insolvent, not just illiquid, and bond buying by the ECB wouldn't change that reality. In any case, such purchases would violate the spirit of the Maastricht Treaty that created the central bank, even if they'd be technically legal. The ECB could perhaps provide more lending to European banks to ensure the financial system is sufficiently liquid, but it was up to political authorities to worry about solvency. It could take a few more days of scary moves in the markets to force the politicians to take action, so if the ECB intervened now, they might not ever make the sort of fundamental changes needed.

If the Governing Council were to begin bond purchases, Weber continued, the Bundesbank president would want his opposition noted publicly, contrary to the ECB's usual practice. If Trichet failed to make that known in his press conference, Weber suggested, he would make it known to the world on his own.

Weber's plane landed in Frankfurt. He hit send, instantly depositing the e-mail in the inboxes of the twenty-two members of the ECB Governing Council. Weber's words made clear that if his colleagues outvoted him and decided to buy the bonds of Greece and other troubled nations, it would come at a cost.

While Weber made his way to Frankfurt, Trichet was bound for Brussels. The heads of European governments were scheduled to meet on the seventh floor of the Justus Lipsius building, a giant glass-and-concrete monument to European unity that looks like a convention center. Trichet's mission was to persuade them that the Greek bailout of the previous weekend wasn't enough. The bond markets were turning on a wide swath of European nations, not just Greece.

Going in, many of the prime ministers and presidents of Europe seemed not to comprehend the degree of risk. Trichet presented a chart showing the selloff of GIPSI bonds that had accelerated over the previous several days. "My main message for the governments was: Some of you have behaved very improperly and created an element of vulnerability for your own country, and by way of consequence for Europe," Trichet later told Bloomberg News. "Now the situation calls for taking up responsibilities."

The responsibilities he had in mind: creating a credible assurance that the governments of Europe would stand behind each other, that they would act collectively to ensure none would become unable to pay its bills. Trichet was confident after the late-night meeting in Lisbon that he had the votes on the Governing Council to begin buying bonds. But that wouldn't offer a permanent solution to Europe's dilemma. He needed to dangle the possibility of ECB bond purchases as a carrot, a reward for government action. At the same time, Trichet didn't want to be explicit about the possibility; after all, the whole point of a central bank is that it makes the decisions it thinks best independently, not as part of a give-and-take with elected officials. So the discussion in Brussels became an exercise in insinuation, a negotiation in which the terms of the talks were unstated—a quid pro quo in which the quid could not be named.

"We will see what we do," said Trichet, his charts looming behind him on a screen. "But we cannot be responsible for ourselves and you. We *need* your action; we have an absolute need for your action," he said according to people present, becoming louder and more animated and his hair more unkempt as he progressed. One of the less financially savvy heads of government tried to pin Trichet down on exactly what the ECB might do; he remained vague and noncommittal. But most of the leaders, over a dinner of asparagus and turbot, understood exactly what he was getting across: The ECB will buy bonds to ease the pressure from markets, but if and only if you do your part as well.

Trichet received an earful from some of the heads of state, particularly Nicolas Sarkozy, who had consistently pressured the ECB to be more activist. But Trichet got their attention. The attendees set their finance ministers to work to try to create a mechanism to guarantee Europe. The ever bombastic Italian prime minister Silvio Berlusconi stopped by the press room after the dinner and told reporters, with excessive confidence, that a rescue deal would come that very weekend. "When a house is burning, it doesn't matter where the water comes from," he said. Unsaid was that he and many of the heads of government were counting on Trichet to lead the fire brigade.

· · ·

They had arrived jet-lagged and bleary-eyed, from all points of the earth, carrying sheaves of paper and emerging from black Mercedes sedans, some with a burly security guard or two in tow. For the central bankers, Basel— pronounced "Bahl" by the cognoscenti and like the name of a fragrant summer herb by everyone else—is supposed to be a place of refuge. They check into their preferred hotels—the Americans favor the Hilton; many of the Europeans the rather more grand Three Kings—and step temporarily into the close camaraderie of people who understand the unique burdens of a central banker. They head to a fortress of a building that might have been designed as a workplace for George Jetson: a cylindrical tower that looks as if someone squeezed it slightly in the middle, with a base that wraps around without a straight line in sight, as if the elegance of the curves can hide the imposing thickness of the blast-protected stone. The building may be steps from the Basel train station, but legally it isn't on Swiss soil. Like the United Nations headquarters in New York, it's an entity without a country, belonging to the world. The sign out front says BANK FOR INTERNATIONAL SETTLEMENTS, but the place might more easily be thought of as the central bank of central banks. This was where Trichet, Weber, and most of the other leading central bankers would spend the fateful hours of decision over how far they were willing to go to save Europe.

Normally, at the Global Economy Meeting, about thirty governors of central banks in Europe, Asia, Africa, Australia, and North and South America, whose countries together account for 80 percent of the world's economic output, enter a conference space and sit around a circular table. In the center are several big-screen TVs, facing outward for presentations. Each governor brings a deputy; they sit one row back, ringing the room. The head of the U.S. Federal Reserve usually starts, offering a briefing on the state of his country's economy, the world's largest, then answering a series of questions: How will U.S. authorities reduce their budget deficit? What exactly is going on with the American housing market? The discussion then pivots to Europe, and then to emerging nations like China and India. The session continues for hours, occupying these elite policymakers for an entire intellectually exhausting morning.

On Sunday evenings, they feast. Think of the groups that peel off for dinner together as concentric circles of influence. On the outside, there are the deputies. Next are the governors of central banks of smaller countries. And finally, the innermost circle. Its official name is the "Informal Dinner for Governors of the Economic Consultative Committee." In reality, it is the most exclusive regular dinner party on the planet. The heads of the world's most important central banks gather to dine together, usually on the BIS's eighteenth floor: the chairman of the Federal Reserve and president of the Fed's New York outpost, the president of the European Central Bank, and the heads of the central banks of Japan, Britain, Germany, France, Italy, Canada, and Switzerland. The group was expanded in 2009 to include the central bankers of China, India, Brazil, and Mexico too, a signal that their countries had arrived on the global stage. The diners eat well, with black-clad waiters delivering a progression of precise, subtle dishes—lobster, duck, lamb—each in a rich, buttery sauce. They drink even better, with generous pours of Bordeaux and Burgundies, which Global Economy Meeting attendees jokingly refer to as "*grand cru* BIS." Early on in his time as chairman of the Federal Reserve, Ben Bernanke, noting that the event is called an informal dinner, remarked to a colleague that "this is one of the four most formal meals I've had in my life."

The Basel club, complete with great food and wine and intimate conversation on Sunday nights, has existed since 1930. "These people have been concerned with their own problems without regard for the rights of anyone else," said an American attendee in 1931. "As they sat down around the table for two days you could almost see their point of view change as they began to realize the effects of their own actions . . . the greatest use of the BIS is not in the specific action it may take but in the opportunity which it may afford for the gathering together of these central bank people and the development, as it were, of social pressure upon them to appreciate the problems of other countries." It was just down the road from the present-day building where, soon after the creation of the BIS in 1930, the central bankers of that day failed to act with the decisiveness and mutual goodwill needed to combat the great panic of that day. And it was in Basel where Trichet would face his own greatest test.

Throughout the 2008 phase of the crisis, the leaders of the Federal Reserve often found themselves scrambling to come up with a major decision on a Sunday night, before financial markets in Tokyo, Hong Kong, and Sydney opened for their morning sessions. It happened so often that Ben Bernanke joked that he would title his memoir *Before Asia Opens*. Now it was the Europeans' turn to race against the clock through a long weekend of talks.

The finance ministers were in Brussels; ECB vice president Lucas Papademos, who would later serve a turn as Greek prime minister, was in there monitoring the talks, reporting back by cell phone to Trichet in Basel. Other ECB officials were in the Eurotower in Frankfurt. An open-line conference call connected finance ministries and central banks in capitals including London, Washington, and Tokyo to the action. Geithner made a series of private calls to European officials, attempting to apply whatever weight came by virtue of his being an experienced crisis manager and the finance minister of the world's largest economy. Early in the conference call, there was discussion of putting together an emergency fund of perhaps €60 billion. Geithner, flabbergasted at the paltry amount, suggested that it wasn't nearly enough. To persuade markets they were serious, the officials would need ten times as much, something on the order of the U.S. government's TARP bank bailout during 2008. The Europeans reluctantly came to agree and set to work on a bigger package.

Geithner was also in frequent touch with Trichet, speaking with him once at 1:30 p.m. Washington time Friday and again at 9:55 a.m. Sunday. Neither Geithner nor Trichet would discuss the substance of those calls. But other officials said that by the weekend it was well known within the U.S. government, among those who worked for or with Geithner, that the ECB had all but decided to begin buying bonds and was holding off any decision in order to push the governments toward action. Indeed, the Americans played an odd role of helping ensure that European finance ministers properly understood the coded messages Trichet had sent them. Did Trichet tell Geithner explicitly what he had planned? Only the two men know. But it is the case that Trichet and Geithner had a great deal in common as noneconomists who were nonetheless among the most important economic policymakers of their generation, immensely skilled at economic diplomacy and bureaucratic maneuvering. They'd spent countless dinners together in Basel during Geithner's time at the New York Fed. Between two men who understand each other so well, a great deal can be said without very many words at all being exchanged.

Bernanke had dispatched his vice chairman, Donald Kohn, to represent the Fed in Basel while the chairman gave a commencement speech at the University of South Carolina, in his home state (topic: The Economics of Happiness). Around the time Bernanke was finishing his speech that Saturday, at 12:55 p.m. on the East Coast, he received an e-mail from an aide about a pressing message from Italy's central bank governor, Mario Draghi, who was among the more respected and influential of the European central bankers. "Governor Draghi asked me to forward this to the chairman with suggestions that a statement like the following be issued jointly late Sunday or early Monday morning by the Fed, ECB, SNB, BOE, BOJ, BOC." That is, the central banks of Switzerland, Britain, Japan, and Canada. "Major central banks stand ready to supply the financial system with adequate and immediate liquidity in the days ahead. Let's work together to address foreign currency funding shortages." The Europeans were looking for the Americans to step up and show their commitment to keeping the financial system from again coming unglued.

On one hand, Bernanke and Kohn were eager to do whatever they could to help ease the financial pressures in Europe and signal the joint resolve of the global central banks to combat the crisis, but they also were in a delicate spot. They viewed the problems as fundamentally Europe's to solve, with any globally coordinated steps as much symbolism as substance. And it came at a supremely delicate time politically, as the Senate was set to vote on a series of amendments in the following week on key aspects of the Dodd-Frank Act that affected the Fed. Headlines about the Fed offering billions of dollars in new loans to foreigners would hardly help things. Bernanke couldn't even very well make a round of calls to key lawmakers in advance of a decision either, in hopes of receiving their blessings; the very principle he was fighting for was that the Fed must make its decisions separate from politics, away from interference by elected officials.

Bernanke called a meeting of the Federal Open Market Committee for Sunday morning, by videoconference; the Washington-based Fed governors gathered in the "Special Library," an intimate but ornate conference room down the hall from the chairman's office, and the rest of the Fed officials joined in from their respective cities. Kohn, from Basel, explained the state of play among the Europeans. The committee agreed with Bernanke and Kohn's recommendation: that the Fed reopen swap lines, but if, and only if, the Europeans could agree on a sweeping response of their own.

Essentially, all the actors in the crisis were linking hands and agreeing to jump at the same time: the European governments, the ECB, and the global central bankers. They each refused to go unless the others would do their part as well.

After the FOMC call ended, Nathan Sheets, the Fed's top international economist and the staffer who had joined Kohn in Basel, went around to the offices set aside for use of visiting central bankers, to see which of them would join in the announcement of swap lines. He was a door-to-door salesman, and his product was billions of dollars.

As the finance ministers gathered in Brussels that Sunday, the day began with misfortune. Wolfgang Schäuble, the German finance minister, who had been confined to a wheelchair ever since being shot in a 1990 assassination attempt for his role in the reunification with East Germany, fell ill on his way to the meeting and was taken to a hospital in Brussels. Europe's largest economy would initially be represented by a relatively junior official, Jörg Asmussen, state secretary at the finance ministry. Chancellor Merkel quickly dispatched a plane to pick up her interior minister, Thomas de Maizière, in Dresden and fly him to Brussels. Asmussen wasn't in a position to negotiate on behalf of the government, so the hours it took to get Maizière to the meetings were essentially wasted.

The basic dispute to be resolved among the finance ministers was over how a rescue fund would be organized. France and most of the other European nations wanted to create a new entity controlled from Brussels and funded by the members of the eurozone. It would stand ready to lend money to countries that fell into trouble—by issuing "eurobonds," new debts ultimately backed by all European governments—and enforce conditions attached to the aid. Germany, Austria, and Finland preferred an approach that would leave them with greater power to influence the details of any aid packages and the strings attached. They saw the French solution as one that would require them to send checks to Brussels but have little power over how their money was deployed. This division was crystal clear by the afternoon of Sunday, May 9, and it would take many hours, an implied threat by Trichet to withhold any ECB aid, and the deadline of the Asian markets opening to force a resolution.

Sunday evening, Trichet again assembled the Governing Council, some in person in a conference room at the Bank for International Settlements in Basel, some in Frankfurt, and a few in their respective countries around Europe. It was time to make a formal decision on the idea they'd been discussing off and on since Thursday night in Lisbon. Would the ECB engage in some targeted purchases of Greek, Irish, and Portuguese bonds in order to push rates in those countries down a bit, ease the sense of crisis, and ensure that it maintained control over monetary policy? Or would it stick with a more doctrinaire view of its powers and avoid violating the spirit of its treaty in order to keep all the pressure on elected officials to rescue Europe? Trichet argued forcefully for the former.

He proposed that even as the ECB bought government bonds on the open market, it should withdraw an identical amount of money out of the eurozone economy through other tools, so the purchases would be "sterilized"—that is, not increase the overall number of euros in existence. Weber and Stark argued with equal vehemence against the move, using logic similar to that Weber had expressed in his e-mail two days earlier. The ECB should intervene in the bond market only if things got even worse—bad enough to force government leaders into more decisive action than anything they were cooking up over in Brussels that weekend.

In the end, the council was overwhelmingly in favor of buying bonds—but also of keeping that a secret from the finance ministers and heads of state until they'd reached their own deal. If they found out that the ECB had decided to intervene, it would remove the pressure on them to act. The vote was a triumph of pragmatism over principle. Weber and Stark led the opposition, joined by Nout Wellink of the Dutch central bank.

Less controversial were steps the Governing Council agreed to take to pump money into the European banking system—making six-month loans available to banks and reactivating the swap lines with the Federal Reserve that had proved so useful in combating the 2008 crisis.

The ECB had decided. It would buy bonds under what it called the Securities Markets Programme, or SMP. Early Monday morning, the Rubicon would be crossed. Now the ECB just had to keep quiet until the politicians did their part. If word of the bank's decision leaked in Brussels, after all, suddenly the finance ministers might no longer feel quite the same sense of urgency.

With the ECB in action, the Fed was ready to move on swap lines as well. At 7:46 p.m. Basel time, 1:46 p.m. Washington time, Kohn sent Bernanke an e-mail, with the subject line "Swaps are a go."

In Brussels, the talks had bogged down amid the delay in finding a nego-tiator for the Germans. It was getting late, and no deal would gel. "With all due respect to Australia," French finance minister Christine Lagarde said, "let's forget about Sydney, concentrate on Tokyo, and take a break." In other words, they were going to miss the 1 a.m. deadline before the Australian stock market was to open, so would focus on getting a deal in place by the 2 a.m. opening of the Japanese market. It was a proposal from the Dutch that became the com-promise: The bailout funds would be managed initially by a newly created in-stitution known as the European Financial Stability Facility, backed by the entire European Union and authorized to borrow as much as €440 billion to aid governments in trouble. It was to last only three years, to be replaced at that point by a more permanent "European Stability Mechanism."

The French didn't get their eurobonds, but the Germans won enough con-cessions to feel that they'd made no commitment to write a blank check. The IMF pledged €250 billion, keeping the two-to-one ratio of European to IMF funds that'd been a part of the Greek deal. This helped assure the Germans that there would be tough budget-cutting conditions placed on the recipients of bailout money. It also was something of a mirage: While Dominique Strauss-Kahn pledged the money, he had no authority to actually do so; that would re-quire a vote of the IMF Executive Board, on which countries around the world have representatives. Besides being evidence of how on-the-fly this trillion-dollar bailout package was, it was an example of the supremely confident Strauss-Kahn getting the theater right and worrying about the bureaucratic niceties later.

At 3:15 a.m., the finance ministers had finally finished their hard-fought series of compromises and announced their measures. They missed the Japa-nese market deadline as well, but apparently the sense that European leaders were furiously working toward a deal was enough to assuage the markets. The ECB followed shortly thereafter with its announcement, as did the Fed and the other central banks participating in swap lines. "The Governing Council . . . decided on several measures to address the severe tensions in certain market segments which are hampering the monetary policy transmission mechanism," the announcement said, the first of countless moments in which ECB leaders argued that their action wasn't about rescuing troubled governments at all, but about ensuring it had control over the value of the euro.

For Axel Weber, losing the argument over bond buying wasn't the end of things. The rules under which ECB Governing Council members operate call for them to keep quiet about how they vote. Unlike the Fed and the Bank of England, which release minutes of their meetings that detail how different committee members voted, the ECB keeps such information secret for thirty years. The theory, of course, is that this should make it easier for officials to make decisions that are in the best interest of the eurozone as a whole, rather than represent the interest of their own native countries. Another fundamental principle is that the national banks of Europe—the Bundesbank and Banque de France, for example—would carry out the orders of the ECB Governing Council and buy and sell securities accordingly. Like the twelve U.S. Federal Reserve banks, it is these institutions that actually carry out policy set by the committee.

To Weber, the Governing Council had so thoroughly ignored its own rules and orthodoxies that those principles were now in question.

Shortly after the Governing Council meeting Sunday evening, Weber convened a conference call of the Bundesbank Executive Board. He and colleague Andreas Dombret were still in Basel, the other board members in various locations in Germany. Officially he wasn't supposed to tell anyone of what the Governing Council had just decided, but this was so momentous that he posed a quite serious question to the board members: Should we do it? Should the Bundesbank follow its marching orders from the ECB and buy billions of euros' worth of Greek and Portuguese bonds, violating its long-cherished principle of not using the printing press to fund governments?

If they had answered *nein*, it's nearly certain that the euro would have unraveled within days, the ECB would have lost all credibility, and Germany would have been forced to reinstitute the Deutschmark as its currency. The global financial markets would have entered a tailspin more dramatic than what followed the Lehman bankruptcy. Staring at that precipice, the Bundesbank concluded it was better to hold its nose and violate orthodoxy than to unleash such dangerous consequences. But that the action was discussed at all suggests the world came closer to financial catastrophe that night than all but a few insiders knew at the time.

Weber, as he had threatened in his Friday morning e-mail, decided to ignore the principle of ECB secrecy further still and make his discontent known to the world. Trichet only obliquely acknowledged the internal dissent. "On some decisions there was unanimity," he said in a Bloomberg Television interview on May 10. "On bond purchases we had an overwhelming majority." Weber wanted his opposition known more explicitly than that. His staff arranged a Monday morning interview with *Börsen-Zeitung*. "The purchase of government bonds poses significant stability risks," Weber told the Frankfurt-based financial publication. "And that's why I'm critical toward this part of the ECB council's decision, even in this extraordinary situation."

And Weber was just the most prominent of the German critics. As *Die Welt* wrote the day after the announcement, "What was carved in stone the day before no longer has any validity, and nothing symbolizes this more than the ECB's loss of independence." People who worked with Trichet said that he took the criticism from German economists and journalists that followed the bond-buying decision personally. The consummate European, who had spent a career winning respect as a hard-nosed, German-style central banker, was deeply hurt that his dedication to stable prices would come under doubt.

Trichet was also furious at Weber's open insurrection, people close to him said. To the Frenchman, it was an affront not only to the rules of the ECB and the idea of European unity, but also to the obligations that central bankers, the Boys in Basel, owe to one another.

# FOURTEEN

# The King's Speech

The official name of the gathering is "The Lord Mayor's Banquet for Bankers and Merchants of the City of London." Everyone knows it, however, simply as the Mansion House Dinner, for the official residence at which it occurs, at the intersection of Threadneedle and Lombard Streets. For the grandees of British finance, it's among the most important events of the annual calendar, an evening on which they don tuxedos, drink wine, and hear what the chancellor of the exchequer and the governor of the Bank of England have to say about the state of their world. For the speakers, it's the highest-profile speech of the year, the one they use to broadcast their biggest ideas, ensuring that they're heard not only by the financiers in the room, but also by the many more around the globe who know to pay particular attention to what happens at the lord mayor's Corinthian-columned Georgian palace each June.

So it seemed rather odd, just two days before the 2009 dinner, when Mervyn King's aides told Alistair Darling's that the governor's speech wasn't yet finished. "This I found curious," Darling said in his memoir. After all, King was known for his thoughtful, carefully reasoned speeches. He didn't leave them to the last minute. When Darling finally received a copy of the talk, a couple of hours before it was to be delivered, he saw why King had been keeping it under wraps.

"It has been a quite a year," King began, on a note of understatement. "A year to remember, but not to repeat."

He gave a *tour d'horizon* of the crisis and its aftermath and expressed his view that "fiscal policy too will have to change," to develop a "clear plan to show how prospective deficits will be reduced." He then said a few things about how Britain's regulation of the financial industry ought to change to reflect the lessons of the crisis. Noting that the Bank of England had rather limited powers to oversee the financial sector, a legacy of the Labour government's 1997 reforms, he offered a rather deft metaphor to make his point: "The Bank finds itself in a position rather like that of a church whose congregation attends weddings and burials but ignores the sermons in between," he said with a twinkle in his eye. "Experience suggests that attempts to encourage a better life through the power of voice is not enough. Warnings are unlikely to be effective when people are being asked to change behavior which seems to them highly profitable.

"So it is not entirely clear how the Bank will be able to discharge its new statutory responsibility if we can do no more than issue sermons or organize burials."

The Bank of England, in other words, can't just tell banks what to do. It needs some real power. Got that, Mr. Chancellor?

Darling got it all too well, as he sat on the dais trying with mixed success not to let his annoyance show to the hundreds of bankers staring at him. "Everyone knew what he was getting at," Darling wrote later. "It was a naked attempt to wrest powers from the [Financial Services Authority, created in 1997 to regulate British banks]. As such—and all those present knew it—it was a direct challenge to government policy, and therefore to me."

The British press, always quick to shine a spotlight on conflict among high government officials, didn't disappoint. "King clashes with Chancellor over how to regulate banks" was the headline in the *Independent*. "King launches shot across Darling's bow over City regulation," said the *Guardian*. "Put your books in order, and soon, King warns Darling," blared the Conservative-leaning *Daily Telegraph*, which focused on King's remarks about fiscal policy in its story about the governor's "fiercest rebuke yet to the Chancellor." If King wanted to stick a proverbial knife in Darling's side, he succeeded.

For the chancellor, struggling with the aftermath of a massive financial crisis and working for a wildly unpopular government in what would prove to be its final year in power, King's comments were typical of the governor he'd been working with for years. "This was another occasion on which I felt that Mervyn had decided that, because of the government's weakness, he had license to roam in a way he would never have done if he had thought he would still have to deal with us after the next election," Darling wrote.

"This is dangerous territory for any Bank Governor . . . he was coming perilously close to crossing a line between legitimate comment and entering the political fray."

Central bankers in modern democracies end up playing a role that is bigger than their official responsibilities would suggest. Their job isn't merely to set monetary policy and oversee banks. They are also their nations' economists in chief. Ideally, they should be persuasive voices for sound economic thinking, steering politicians away from bad decisions and guiding them toward good ones. At the same time, they're supposed to stay aloof from politics and leave their countries' major choices to those officials who were actually elected. Threading the needle is among their greatest challenges.

They might simply appear at the side of a finance minister or president, as Ben Bernanke did during the debate over bank bailouts in 2008. They might lend tacit support to a policy, as Alan Greenspan did with George W. Bush's tax cuts in 2001. Or they might take a more assertive role in guiding their nations' policies, as Jean-Claude Trichet did repeatedly starting in 2010. Each of these actions comes at a cost: In each case, the idea of the central banker as a neutral arbiter or member of a high priesthood committed only to technocratic decisions is damaged.

In 2009 and 2010, King, his tongue acid, his elbow sharp, took a consistently aggressive stance toward the politicians—or at least toward the politicians who happened to be in charge. The concerns over deficit spending and bank regulation King expressed in the Mansion House speech put him squarely at odds with the Labour government—and in almost exact alignment with the Conservative Party, which was gearing up for a campaign to return to power in the 2010 general election. The consequences of King's apparent political alignment would shape both Great Britain's economic fortunes and the governor's legacy.

Like the rest of the Western world, Britain emerged from the 2008 panic deeply scarred. After fifteen years of prosperity, during which London had re-emerged as a great center of global commerce, the question haunting Britain was what would come next. Unemployment had risen from about 5 percent just before the crisis to nearly 8 percent by the time of the Mansion House Dinner. The nation's massive banking sector was in shambles, and its government debt was exploding, from 44 percent of GDP in 2007 to 69 percent in 2009. Queen Elizabeth II was sufficiently alarmed that she summoned King for a meeting in March 2009—the first time she'd sat down with a governor of the Bank of England in her then fifty-seven-year reign. After a conversation with the queen, King said later, "one must never breathe a word to another mortal." But in answer to a question she'd posed publicly, of why, if the looming crisis was so big, nobody saw it coming, he suggested that "everyone did see it coming but no one knew when. It's like an earthquake zone. You should be trying to build buildings in ways which are more robust."

The day of the Mansion House speech, Britain could borrow money on global markets for a decade for less than 4 percent. But to King, the nation's finances were more precarious than the bond market made it appear. The market for U.S. Treasury bonds is the largest and most liquid in the world; a pension fund or sovereign wealth fund from the developing world can always buy or sell Treasury bills, even on a massive scale. That has allowed the U.S. government to borrow more money for longer periods than might seem justifiable based on its finances. (In the summer of 2009, U.S. government debt was 90 percent of GDP.) Japanese bonds, meanwhile, are bought primarily by the nation's own citizens as a savings vehicle, almost as a patriotic duty. That allows Japan, too, to borrow on much larger scale than its fiscal situation would seem to justify. (That same summer, Japanese government debt was 210 percent of GDP.)

But the pound isn't the world's reserve currency the way the dollar is, and Britons don't invest in their own government's bonds the same way the Japanese do. Investors would readily dump UK government bonds—or "gilts," for the gilt edges the securities once had—if they concluded that the nation's finances were at the breaking point. The low interest rates that Britain was paying to borrow money were little solace. Market sentiment, as the financial crisis had shown, can shift quickly and unpredictably. The British government would need to borrow £175 billion that year to fund itself, and nearly as much for years to come. If global investors were to suddenly cut off the taps, the result could be disastrous. Parliament, King argued, should act now to prevent Britain from being threatened with a debt crisis down the road.

The governor had come a long way since the earliest days of the crisis, in the second half of 2007, when he led a restrained, even timid response and didn't want to get involved with bank regulation. Like the Federal Reserve and the European Central Bank, the Bank of England had by this time thrown out the rulebook. King had viewed bank supervision as a messy, legalistic job, and his apparent contempt for bankers had only deepened after the industry's failures became more apparent. But it was clear that the Bank of England would need to play a greater role in overseeing the banks. The Financial Services Authority, created in 1997 under then chancellor of the exchequer Gordon Brown, had fallen down on the job in the run-up to the crisis, focused more on dealing with narrow problems like stock market scams than the bigger picture of whether the British financial sector was sound.

In the tumultuous eighteen months that followed the Northern Rock failure, the Bank of England was the only institution with the power and resources to step in as lender of last resort. Yet its institutional knowledge of the inner workings of the banking system had atrophied in the years of King's reign, when the bank focused instead on theoretical macroeconomics. Parliament had passed a law earlier in 2009 stating for the first time that one of the objectives of the Bank of England would be to "contribute to protecting and enhancing the stability of the financial systems of the United Kingdom," though that law included little in the way of new powers.

It had been famously said that the governor of the Bank of England could direct the activities of British banks simply by raising an eyebrow, but King wanted something a little more concrete. If the Bank of England were going to stand behind the banks, it needed some real control over what they might get up to.

A week after the Mansion House event, King went before Parliament's Treasury Select Committee for his regular report on the state of monetary policy—but it was the simmering hostility between him and the government that was on the minds of his audience. King didn't back down from his statements at the lord mayor's dinner. On fiscal policy, he said, "I do not think we can afford to wait until the Parliament after next before taking action to demonstrate credibly that the United Kingdom is going to reduce its deficit and that fiscal policy will be credible."

The Conservative opposition immediately seized on his statements to bash the government. It was "demolition day for Gordon Brown's tax and spending policies," said George Osborne, the shadow chancellor of the exchequer. King's comments, he continued, "demolished for good any claim that this discredited government ever had a credible plan for the recovery."

Darling was in the process of working up the government's plan for financial reform—a white paper outlining the strategy was due out the following week—and signs were pointing to a divided set of regulatory responsibilities, with the Financial Services Authority sharing power with the Bank of England as well as the Treasury. Relations between King and Darling were sufficiently toxic at this point that, asked if he had consulted on the white paper, King replied, "It all depends on your definition of consultation. I have not seen a draft of it, no. . . . I do not know what will be in the white paper. Whether anybody else does, I don't know." (By contrast, during this same period Tim Geithner's staff was making plans for its own financial reform, and Bernanke and the Federal Reserve were heavily involved; some Fed staffers were even detailed to Treasury to help with technical issues.)

"I have a good working relationship with Alistair Darling," King assured the members of Parliament that morning. "There is no problem with that working relationship whatsoever."

Hardly a person present believed him.

When he wasn't trying to use the bully pulpit to guide Parliament, King had his usual job to attend to—even if his working relationship with his own Monetary Policy Committee was also becoming problematic. In March 2009, he and his colleagues had agreed to push their main benchmark of the price of money, known simply as Bank Rate (no "the" please, we're British), down to 0.5 percent, the lowest it had been in the 315-year history of the Bank of England.

They might have gone lower still, except they worried that because many building societies made loans tied to Bank Rate, they would stop lending at all if rates fell too low. Instead, they joined the Fed and the Bank of Japan among those central banks experimenting with quantitative easing, or using newly created funds to buy longer-term government bonds in hopes of pushing more

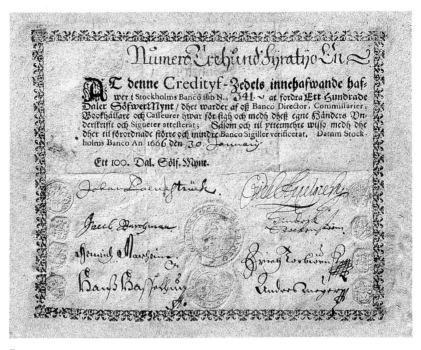

In 1660s Sweden, Johan Palmstruch's Stockholms Banco introduced the first banknotes, shown here, bringing paper money to Europe. The Palmstruch bank collapsed and was replaced by what would become the Swedish Riksbank, the nation's central bank to this day.

Walter Bagehot, editor of *The Economist* in the mid-nineteenth century, wrote about the Bank of England's efforts to combat the financial panic that followed the collapse of Overend, Gurney & Co. in 1866. His lessons add up to Bagehot's dictum, an idea that modern central bankers followed during the crisis that began in 2007.

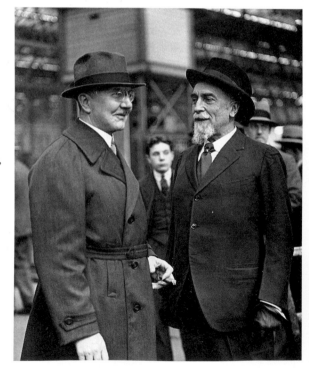

The central bankers of the 1930s, including Hjalmar Schacht (*left*), president of the German Reichsbank, and Montagu Norman, governor of the Bank of England, were unable to contain the great financial crisis of their generation, setting the stage for years of economic depression and, eventually, a global war. Their failures haunted their modern successors.

Arthur Burns, chairman of the Federal Reserve in the 1970s, lacked the willpower—or the independence from the Nixon administration—to take the painful steps needed to contain the burgeoning inflation of that era. Inflation approached 9 percent in his final year in office.

Paul Volcker, chairman of the Fed starting in 1979, aggressively tightened the money supply to stop inflation—causing a deep recession in the short term but laying the groundwork for a generation of prosperity known as the Great Moderation.

European leaders spent the second half of the twentieth century building bonds of unification among their nations, aiming to prevent the kinds of conflicts the continent had experienced in the first half of the century. Here, in February 1992, they gathered in Maastricht, the Netherlands, and agreed to use a common currency. The European Central Bank would be created in 1998 to manage what would become the euro, the most visible symbol of European integration.

By 2007, when the first tremors of panic were felt, the leading Western central banks were led by Mervyn King (*left*), governor of the Bank of England; Ben Bernanke (*center*), chairman of the U.S. Federal Reserve; and Jean-Claude Trichet (*right*), president of the ECB. Their partnership would shape the course of the global economy.

The world's central bankers met regularly at the Bank for International Settlements in Basel, Switzerland, where they had long discussions about economics and bank regulation and shared intimate dinners in the evenings over great food and wine. Between the meetings in Basel, on the sidelines of global economic summits, and economic conferences such as one each August in Jackson Hole, Wyoming, one central banker remarked that he seemed to see the other central bankers more often than his wife.

When Ben S. Bernanke joined the Federal Reserve Board of Governors in 2002 after a long career in academia, he was very much the professor; he envisioned only a brief foray into government service. Four years later, he became one of the most powerful men in the world as chairman of the Fed.

Bernanke led the Federal Open Market Committee, which sets monetary policy for the United States, through a controversial decision to cut interest rates and push money into the flailing U.S. economy through "quantitative easing," or buying bonds using newly created money.

The series of financial bailouts during the crisis exposed Bernanke and the Fed to vociferous criticism from the left and right, and the Fed's long-standing powers and independence came into doubt in Congress in its aftermath. Shown here are Bernanke (*seated*) and Treasury Secretary Tim Geithner (*standing*) at a House Financial Services hearing in 2009 about the AIG bailout.

Bernanke (*left*), Fed governor Kevin Warsh (*center*), and vice chairman Don Kohn (*right*)—here at a coffee break from the annual Kansas City Fed economic symposium in Jackson Hole—formed the inner circle in a series of extraordinary interventions to try to keep the global financial system from coming unglued in 2008.

Despite criticism from all sides during the bailouts, the Fed kept its powers to regulate banks and the independence to set monetary policy. It had support from President Obama, who was in turn influenced by his treasury secretary and former New York Fed president Timothy Geithner, and crucial help from banking lobbyists and presidents of regional Fed banks across the United States, including Tom Hoenig of the Kansas City Fed, pictured here.

Bernanke's stewardship of the economy and crisis management was enough for Obama to nominate him to a second four-year term in 2009—though the Senate confirmation was a closer call than anyone had expected.

B. Bernanke

M. King

Over the course of the crisis, Bernanke and Mervyn King shared a particular bond—a background as academic economists—and had even shared an office suite as young faculty at MIT. King created the modern Bank of England, first as its chief economist in the 1990s and as governor starting in 2003.

King (*right*) sometimes clashed with Alistair Darling (*left*), the chancellor of the exchequer until 2010. They are pictured here in Porto, Portugal, at an international summit on September 14, 2007, the day Britain experienced its first bank run since Overend, Gurney—this time on Northern Rock.

Darling wrote that he was blindsided by King's comments at the 2009 Mansion House dinner, arguing for the Bank of England to be given greater authority over the banking system. But by the 2010 dinner, pictured here, King was on better terms with the new chancellor, George Osborne (*seated*).

Leading central bankers and finance ministers traveled to Iqaluit, Canada, in February 2010 for a G-7 summit. In the Arctic, they developed consensus that after extensive intervention to support economic growth, including fiscal and monetary stimulus, it was time to begin planning an exit. As it would turn out, some of the greatest challenges were yet to come, and the turn to austerity was premature.

Mervyn King took advantage of the demonstration of dog sledding, though the banker's interest in native culture went just so far; only the Canadian officials partook of raw seal meat in Iqaluit.

Jean-Claude Trichet, shown here at the Jackson Hole conference, had made a career helping build a unified Europe through a common currency. The veteran French civil servant was the second president of the ECB, the most vivid testament to European unity, starting in 2003. But by 2010, the economic fallout from the 2008 crisis had left the finances of Greece, and soon other European nations, in such precarious straits as to risk an unraveling of the union.

"Now, Jean-Claude, it is your turn," Bernanke (*right*) told Trichet (*center*) in a private meeting in Frankfurt as the eurozone crisis became more severe.

The ECB's governing council usually met at its headquarters in Frankfurt to set monetary policy for the seventeen-nation eurozone, but in May 2010, as the debt crisis that began in Greece was rapidly spreading to Ireland, Portugal, and Spain, they met instead in Lisbon, shown here. At a dinner later that night, they broached for the first time the possibility of using ECB resources to buy bonds of countries that were under attack from markets.

Axel Weber (*left*), the president of the powerful German Bundesbank, was initially open to bond purchases in that late-night meeting, but by the next day he had changed his mind. He would become the most vocal opponent of the proposal, seeing it as a form of printing money to subsidize profligate governments. He resigned from the Bundesbank in early 2011, after his differences on this question with most others on the ECB governing council made the idea of his succeeding Trichet in the presidency untenable.

The ECB intervention succeeded in easing the sense of crisis in the summer of 2010. But that October, French president Nicolas Sarkozy and German chancellor Angela Merkel went for a walk on the beach at a summit in Deauville, France, where they sketched out a plan to push for private owners of Greek debt to take losses on their holdings. That led to a resumption of the crisis and its spread to Ireland and later Portugal and Spain.

Vice-President

President

Under Trichet (*right*), the ECB became part of the "troika," the group of international institutions that negotiated with the Greek government, and later those in Ireland and Portugal, over the spending cuts and reforms they would need to undertake as a condition of aid. It put the central bank in the uncomfortable position of dictating to democratically elected leaders what policies to enact. In 2011, Lucas Papademos (*left*), the former vice president of the ECB, even became the prime minister of Greece.

In October 2011, days before Trichet's term as ECB president was set to end, an event was held in Frankfurt to honor him. But afterward, instead of remaining in the opera house for a symphony performance, Trichet (*left*), IMF chief Christine Lagarde (*center*), and Merkel (*right*), among others, retreated to a conference room to try to hammer out a new accord to repair Europe.

With no German candidate in line for the job, Trichet's replacement was Mario Draghi (*right*), the top Italian central banker and a savvy economist and market maven. But the question was whether "Super Mario" would be able to succeed where Trichet had failed at using the ECB as a force to preserve the eurozone without undermining the institution's credibility—and the support of the German government.

Jens Weidmann replaced Axel Weber as the head of the Bundesbank. He continued Weber's stance of deep skepticism toward any bond buying by the ECB, even as Draghi pushed to defend the eurozone.

Mario Draghi

With a subtle diplomatic touch and strong background as an economist, Draghi (pictured here at his first news conference in November 2011) guided the ECB governing council to a series of interest rate cuts to try to combat an economic downturn on the continent. He would later announce the Long-term Refinancing Operation, a massive effort to flood European banks with cash, and in September 2012, an unlimited, overarching backstop to try to stand in the way of a eurozone collapse. A united Europe was preserved, at least for the time being.

Zhou Xiaochuan, the governor of the People's Bank of China, was a force for modernization and markets in the ascendant economy of China during this era, but he lacked the independence and power to act on his own accord held by the Western central bankers. As such, the Chinese central bank was not part of the joint efforts repeatedly launched by the other industrialized nations.

money out into the economy. They started with £75 billion; two months later, they increased that to £125 billion.

This early phase of the crisis had been a time of peace on the Monetary Policy Committee, a result of both a clear-cut sense of what needed to be done and a desire to project unity in the face of panic. Even the pre–Lehman Brothers feud between King and Danny Blanchflower died down, in part because the latter was getting his way on cheaper money.

Blanchflower's term on the MPC ended in May 2009. Yet by August, conflict between King and his committee members flared again—with a nearly unprecedented result. The British economy had pulled out of its nosedive over the summer, but it didn't seem to be climbing with any vigor, and the risk of deflation hadn't fully receded. Everyone on the nine-member MPC thought it was time to ease policy more. The question was, by how much?

The committee, following the procedure King had helped create as chief economist more than a decade earlier, first assembled on the Friday morning before the meeting itself, in this case on July 31. This session, which includes dozens of economists and other staffers from across the bank, as well as "bank agents" with business contacts around the United Kingdom, is an opportunity to get a broad interpretation of what is happening with the British and world economies.

The following Wednesday, the afternoon before a decision is to be made, the nine members gather for a much smaller meeting in a Pemberley-worthy room with a huge crystal chandelier and a grand Palladian window overlooking a courtyard. They talk for three hours or so, then reconvene on Thursday to discuss what policy action the bank should take. The final meeting starts at 9 a.m., with a decision due to be announced to the world promptly at noon.

The Bank of England's monthly meetings to set monetary policy are intimate affairs, at least compared to the Fed's, in which seventy or so people are in the room and nineteen people make up the committee itself, or the ECB's, in which there are twenty-three members of the committee. The sheer size of the Fed and ECB policy meetings means they must rely on protocol, with clear dictates of who speaks when and for how long.

The grandeur of the interior aside, MPC meetings aren't dissimilar from the get-togethers of any corporate board in the world, in the sense that they involve a very small group of people debating in a rather informal fashion in order to reach a consensus. For all of Mervyn King's dominance of the Bank of England, this less structured format left him with less power to control the actual decision than his counterparts at the other major central banks. He couldn't, for example, use Trichet's technique of limiting potential dissenters to only five minutes' say. British political culture is one in which people feel free to state views vigorously and disagree openly. Never was that more evident among the members the MPC than on the morning of August 6, 2009.

The session the afternoon before was, as is often the case, relatively free-wheeling, with jokes and interjections. On Thursday, the meeting always began with the governor speaking for five or ten minutes, summing up the discussion of the economy from the previous day and setting a framework for the decision. Then Charles Bean, the deputy governor for monetary policy, would speak for another ten minutes to propose policy options—although a careful listener might have already discerned which one King favored.

The Bank of England's models, Bean explained that day in August, suggested that it would have to make about £50 billion in further bond purchases to keep inflation near its 2 percent target. King then invited the other seven members of the committee to share their views, one at a time. Next, he made explicit his own view: that the risk of deflation taking hold was high enough to warrant even more aggressive easing than the bank's models suggested. He had in mind £75 billion.

This is the kind of thing that committees exist to hash out. According to the bank staff's analysis, the British economy wouldn't have been radically different a year later either way. Whether to authorize £50 or £75 billion was a close call—equivalent to choosing to cut Bank Rate by either 0.5 percentage points or 0.75. The meeting should have been routine.

But for reasons that still mystify some of the participants, it wasn't. Everyone was in a tetchy mood, perhaps burnt out from the long year of crisis fighting and eager to get on with an August vacation. The committee members' irritability might also have been in part a passive-aggressive response to King's high-handed, top-down mode of leadership. King seemed to expect the kind of deference to his views that he received during the worst days of the crisis, when MPC disunity could have rattled markets, even as many of the other committee members wanted to reassert their role as independent shapers of policy.

When King finally went around the table to count the votes, only two committee members, Tim Besley and David Miles, sided with the governor on buying £75 billion in bonds. The other six—among them King's seniormost deputies, Bean and Paul Tucker, who was in charge of financial stability, as well as the bank's chief economist, Spencer Dale, and its markets chief, Paul Fisher— all voted for £50 billion. It was only the third time King had been outvoted in more than seventy meetings of the committee.

Two weeks later, when the minutes of the meeting were released publicly, they contained only the subtlest of references to the verbal warfare at Thread-needle: "There was a range of views amongst the Committee over the precise balance of risks to the outlook for inflation and how much significance to as-cribe to the various arguments about the appropriate policy response to that outlook."

But the document clearly disclosed the outcome of the vote, and the world knew that King had faced a small act of rebellion by his committee.

I n the final months of 2009 and the first few of 2010, the evidence that Brit-ain needed to reckon with its fiscal deficit sooner rather than later was, at least to King, mounting. Debt crises in Greece in October and the Arab city-state of Dubai in November meant that global investors were no longer cavalier about the risks of government bonds. At the G7 meeting in Iqaluit, Canada, in February, King, when he wasn't dogsledding, was joining with other high offi-cials in calling for a move away from high government deficits. If you squinted, you could even see signs that the bond markets were becoming less fond of UK debt: The ten-year gilt yielded 4.02 percent at the end of 2009, up from 3.4 percent in early October. (Never mind that a six-tenths of a percent increase doesn't necessarily signal an imminent debt crisis, or that those rates were quite a bit lower than they had been during the Lehman crisis in late 2008.)

King never made the argument that Trichet did with regard to Greece, that cutting deficits would increase business confidence enough to fully coun-teract the negative impacts of lower government spending and higher taxes. But the Bank of England chief did suggest that fiscal austerity would result in at least some boost to confidence, easing the UK's pain more than conventional economic models might suggest. Asked in a February 2010 press conference whether he agreed with Trichet's view that cutting budget deficits is stimulative, King said it "depends on the circumstances." "I just think it's more complicated than just saying, you know, you must always close the deficit immediately. But what is very important, and why I totally agree with Jean-Claude Trichet, is that at all times governments need to have a clear and credible plan for reducing a structural deficit."

King was essentially splitting the difference between Trichet and Bernanke, the latter taking a more traditional Keynesian view that slashing budgets causes economic suffering with few offsetting benefits in the immediate future. Fundamentally, King wasn't an adherent to Trichet's theory of "expansionary austerity," as some of his critics argued. Rather, he was making an argument for risk management: If a fiscal crisis arose, it would both damage the nation's economy and limit the Bank of England's options for dealing with it. Helping his case was the fact that the bank could ease monetary policy and reduce the value of the pound, helping to some degree to counteract near-term budget cutting.

But no matter how nuanced or substantive King's calls for government debt reduction were, they didn't exactly endear him to the ruling party. "If there were any mobile phones, staplers or printers still intact in 10 Downing Street on Tuesday, it's a good bet they found themselves being hurled towards the nearest cowering staffer that afternoon," wrote *Daily Telegraph* economics editor Edmund Conway in January 2010, "for it was then that Gordon Brown learned of the contents of a speech that the Governor of the Bank of England was about to read out that evening. Despite private remonstrations with the Bank, despite Mr. Brown having thought he had secured Mervyn King's agreement to refrain from barbed economic comments until the election was over, the turbulent Governor had gone and done it again."

Conservatives, meanwhile, took King's comments as independent verification that the Labour government had been feckless in its stewardship of the nation's finances. "This is a decisive moment in the economic debate in Britain," Shadow Chancellor of the Exchequer George Osborne said in February, "a moment when Gordon Brown's argument on the deficit has collapsed and a new consensus for more decisive action emerges."

His relationship with Darling and the Labour government increasingly strained, King sidled ever closer to the men who would soon rule Britain. Six times in the winter and spring of 2010, King met at his office with Osborne, two of them with future Conservative Prime Minister David Cameron as well. Despite efforts to keep the existence of the meetings secret, they only increased the sense that King was advising the Tories. Said Kate Barker, who served on the Monetary Policy Committee from 2001 to 2010, "The cynical view would be that this was Mervyn's effort to get the Bank into a good working relationship with the next regime. The uncynical view is that he was worried markets could lose confidence, which is certainly plausible, so you can argue Mervyn was right to say, 'This can't go on.' But the way he expressed his views on fiscal policy meant they could be interpreted in a political way."

Whatever King's true motivations for becoming so vocal an advocate of fiscal austerity, he seems to have been unimpressed with Osborne and Cameron themselves. On February 16, 2010, King met with Louis Susman, who had recently been installed as U.S. ambassador to the Court of St. James's, assigned with nurturing the "special relationship" between the United States and its former colonial master from the fortress of the U.S. embassy building overlooking Grosvenor Square. Susman reported back to Washington what he had heard from the Bank of England governor. "King expressed great concern about Conservative leaders' lack of experience and opined that Party leader David Cameron and Shadow Chancellor George Osborne have not fully grasped the pressures they will face from different groups when attempting to cut spending."

King indicated that in his meetings with Cameron and Osborne he "received only generalities" when he asked how they would reduce the debt. And he seems to have viewed the two relative youngsters—Cameron was forty-three at the time and Osborne thirty-eight—as lightweights. "King also expressed concern about the Tory party's lack of depth. Cameron and Osborne have only a few advisers, and seemed resistant to reaching out beyond their small inner circle. The Cameron/Osborne partnership was not unlike the Tony Blair/Gordon Brown team of New Labour's early years, when both worked well together when part of the opposition party, but fissures developed . . . once Labour was in power."

These were harsh judgments to share with a foreign power about the men who would soon rule Britain, even if King meant them to remain in confidence.

Britons went to the polls on May 6, 2010, the same day ECB officials gathered in Lisbon and discussed how to rescue the eurozone late into the evening, and the same day the U.S. stock market experienced its Flash Crash. Between the perpetually gloomy Gordon Brown and the dismal economy, things weren't looking good for Labour. All the polls pointed to the party being swept from office. Indeed, the Conservatives picked up ninety-seven additional seats in the 650-seat House of Commons, with Labour losing nearly as many. It wasn't quite the decisive result that Cameron and company had wanted, however. They fell short of a majority and would need to form a coalition with the Liberal Democrat Party, which held fifty-seven seats, to take control of the government.

For once, the third party of British politics had some real negotiating power, as both the Conservatives and Labour competed for the affections of the Lib Dems as coalition partners. King wasn't directly involved in the negotiations, of course—yet he wasn't entirely absent from them either. The deficit, wrote David Laws, a Liberal negotiator, "was the spectre which loomed over our talks. This was the reason that the Governor of the Bank of England stood ready to brief us on his perspective on the risks to the UK." The Tories cited King's support for spending cuts as a lever through which to push the Liberals toward more austerity, faster. Sunday, May 9 (the day Trichet and most of the other central bankers were in Basel hammering out what would be the ECB's controversial bond purchase program), civil service chief Gus O'Donnell is said to have offered to arrange a briefing by King so negotiators could "understand the seriousness of the economic situation."

King was in a curious position, both at the center of momentous events taking place in Basel and London and physically apart from them. He was on a long conference call with the finance ministers and central bankers of the world's leading powers, which stretched over the entire evening of May 9 and into the early morning hours of May 10. (One American official dialed into the international number from home and ended up with an $800 phone bill.) There was a long stretch of silence, as the European finance ministers in Brussels put their phone on mute in order to hammer out some differences among themselves. King, showing his impish humor, entertained the other leaders on the phone by reading off that day's soccer scores, the joke being that this was his only way of staying awake.

When British politicians finally did reach agreement to form a coalition and on immediate austerity, King gave them a sort of reward. "The most important thing now is for the new government to deal with the challenge of the fiscal deficit," he said in a press conference May 13. "It is the single most pressing problem facing the United Kingdom. . . . And I have been told what is in the agreement between the Conservatives and the Liberal Democrats this morning, and I am very pleased that there is a very clear and binding commitment to accelerate the reduction in the deficit." As a government came together, so did the forces that would buffet the British economy under Prime Minister Cameron. Prices for food, energy, and other commodities had soared on global markets in the first part of the year, even as the value of the pound had fallen due to the Bank of England's quantitative easing policies, hiking the cost of imports. Additionally, a stimulus measure that had cut the value-added tax expired, meaning the purchase price of a wide variety of goods increased further still. That added up to 3.4 percent inflation in March, well above the 2 percent the Bank of England aimed for. King and most of his colleagues on the MPC viewed this as a one-time price jump, not the kind of ongoing inflation that might warrant raising interest rates. "In the medium term we expect inflation to come down below the target, given the extent of spare capacity in the economy," King said in a May 12 press conference, while acknowledging "enormous uncertainties around this."

On top of the inflation scare, the eurozone crisis was sending British financial markets on a wild ride. About half of British trade was with nations in the eurozone, meaning their economic downfall could be catastrophic for UK companies. With the coalition not yet formed, Alistair Darling was in Brussels representing Britain that crucial Sunday of May 9 as European finance ministers raced to finalize a eurozone bailout before markets opened in Australia and Asia Monday morning. His last official assignment as chancellor of the exchequer was an especially tricky one: Britain's economic future depended on a eurozone rescue, but Darling had to try to keep too much British money from being committed to the action. Imminent replacement Osborne had even wondered whether Darling could abstain from the negotiations due to purdah, the practice by which an outgoing government avoids binding an incoming one to policy decisions it may not support.

Osborne and Darling didn't support any British underwriting of a eurozone bailout, but were more enthusiastic about austerity. Whatever effort King had made before the election to curtail his overt campaigning for tighter fiscal policy went by the wayside in his press conference of Wednesday, May 12, two days after the coalition had formed. He could hardly have been blunter about what he thought the Conservatives and Liberal Democrats needed to do:

The most important thing now is for the new government to deal with the challenge of the fiscal deficit. It is the single most pressing problem facing the United Kingdom; it will take a full parliament to deal with, and it is very important that measures are taken straight away to demonstrate the seriousness and the credibility of the commitment to dealing with that deficit. . . . I think we've seen in the last two weeks, particularly, but in the case of Greece, over the last three months, that it doesn't make sense to run the risk of an adverse market reaction.

His none-too-subtle message to the new prime minister, in other words: Do what you've promised. No flinching now.

Not long after an MPC policy announcement, the committee members gather again to approve minutes of their decision-making process for public release. The discussion itself might have been lengthy and discursive, taking place over two days and six hours, but bank staffers manage to summarize it with a series of bullet points describing the various views that were expressed and the reasons for the result, all in ten pages or so. The meeting to approve the minutes is usually a speedy and civil affair: The policymakers suggest changes to the draft minutes staff have prepared—add a bit more precision here, a bit more ambiguity there—with agreement to the tweaks made by consensus.

But when it was time to approve the minutes for the May 10 meeting, which had taken place just days after the election and the morning after the European summit, a curious thing happened: The normally collegial process became something quite different.

The draft of the May minutes, prepared by staff directed by King, gave the full approval of the MPC to the fiscal austerity message that the governor had been sending in his own public statements. "A significant fiscal consolidation in the United Kingdom was necessary in the medium term," the minutes said. "A more detailed and demanding path for fiscal consolidation than set out in the March 2010 Budget, upon which the Inflation Report projections had been based, might therefore be needed in order to avoid unnecessary increases in the cost of issuing public debt." It was an attempt to give the imprimatur of the committee to King's theory that Britain could be heading for a debt crisis if it didn't begin austerity measures.

But not everyone at the Bank of England was so sure. With the British economy still in a fragile postcrisis state, and now under threat from the troubles in the eurozone, some of the committee members thought it unwise to advocate so vigorously for rapid deficit cutting—all the more so given that the markets were giving only the faintest signals of losing confidence in UK government bonds and that fiscal policy isn't the job of a central bank in the first place. King was adamant, and they voted on the material's inclusion in the minutes. King won the vote, six to three, with the dissenters including Adam Posen, an American economist who had joined the committee the previous fall, and Kate Barker in her final meeting after a nine-year run on the MPC.

It was a victory for the King of Threadneedle Street—but one that would come back to haunt him.

The coalition government listened to the governor's advice. On May 24, just two weeks after taking office, Osborne announced £6 billion in spending cuts for the fiscal year then already under way. That amounted to only about 0.4 percent of Britain's economy, but given the speed with which the cuts were to be implemented, and the tepid pace of recovery, they were a surprise even to advocates of austerity. The cuts were highly concentrated in symbolic, headline-generating areas: forbidding government workers from buying first-class train tickets on official travel, for example, and freezing more than three thousand vacancies in the civil service to save on bureaucratic salaries. There was a plan to defund "quangos," or quasi-autonomous nongovernmental organizations, such as local development agencies, regulatory commissions, and some museums and art galleries. Even though the Conservatives and Liberal Democrats avoided big-ticket areas of expenditure such as the National Health Service, they sent a clear message: "The age of plenty is over," as Lib Dem leader Nick Clegg put it.

The Mansion House Dinner on June 16 was a rather warmer affair than it had been a year earlier; the governor and the chancellor were, this year, in something of a mutual admiration society.

Osborne proposed a new approach to financial regulation that would undo the structure created by the Labour government more than a decade earlier and put the Bank of England squarely in charge of overseeing Britain's banks— granting King and his successors the very powers the governor had asked for at the same event a year before. "Only independent central banks have the broad macroeconomic understanding, the authority and the knowledge required to make the kind of macro-prudential judgments that are required now and in the future," Osborne told the assembled tuxedo-clad financiers. "And, because central banks are the lenders of last resort, the experience of the crisis has also shown that they need to be familiar with every aspect of the institutions that they may have to support. So they must also be responsible for day-to-day micro-prudential regulation as well." He would give details of the plan to Parliament the next day. It was evident that the chancellor and the governor had coordinated their remarks. Speaking immediately afterward, King said that a priority of the bank was to "accept the challenge of the new responsibilities that you, Chancellor, have asked the Bank to take on. . . . I welcome those new responsibilities."

King also offered his endorsement of the government's fiscal measures—and strongly suggested that if there were negative economic consequences, the Bank of England would come to the rescue. "I do . . . Chancellor, welcome your commitment to put the UK's finances on a sound footing," the governor said. "I know there are those who worry that too rapid a fiscal consolidation will endanger recovery. . . . If prospects for growth were to weaken, the outlook for inflation would probably be lower and monetary policy could then respond."

The £6 billion in cuts that Osborne had put forward in May were only the beginning. A few days after the Mansion House Dinner, the chancellor unveiled his budget for the years ahead. The plan was to slash the deficit by more than 6 percent of GDP by the fiscal year that would begin in April 2014. It included increasing the value-added tax from 17.5 percent to 20 percent, which would increase the price of almost all goods on British store shelves by 2.5 percent and raise about £13 billion in extra revenue for the government. With the health service and international development protected from cuts, all other government departments were to reduce their operational expenses by an average of 25 percent over four years. In one nice touch, Osborne proposed abolishing the Treasury's "Euro Preparations Unit," which had been charged with laying the groundwork for Britain to join the eurozone.

Britain—with encouragement from Mervyn King—was embarking on something that has rarely been attempted. At a time when the British government could borrow money for a decade for only 3.5 percent and unemployment was nearly 8 percent, Osborne and Cameron were cutting spending and raising taxes in a preemptive strike against the risk of a future debt crisis. In the process, they risked stopping a weak economic recovery in its tracks and had to hope that their actions would sufficiently boost confidence among consumers and businesses to ease at least some of the pain—and perhaps that King and the Bank of England would find a way to counteract any damage to the economy with easier monetary policy.

Over the years, the governor has sometimes posed a question to his audience at the start of his annual Mansion House speech, offering his answer at the end. In 2010, he inverted the practice. The answer, he announced to the financiers, was "23." He would tell them the question only at the conclusion of his speech:

> To what question is 23 the answer? Several plausible answers come to mind. First, 23 is the number of players in England's World Cup squad in South Africa. Second, it is of course 23 years since England last won the Ashes "down under." But neither of these are the right answer which is that 23 years is the age difference between the Chancellor of the Exchequer and the Governor of the Bank of England. In case there is any doubt, George is the younger. This age difference is highly desirable because the appropriate incentives are to allocate the responsibility of determining monetary policy to the older generation, which has a real interest in preserving the value of money, and the responsibility for fiscal policy to the younger generation, on whom falls the burden of excessive debt. . . . Given those incentives, Chancellor, I look forward to a harmonious coordination of monetary and fiscal policy.

It's a frustrating reality of economic policymaking that one receives little credit for a crisis prevented. The counterfactual is unknowable. But what's certain is that for the British economy, the harmonious coordination between King and Osborne would prove costly indeed.

By November, the *Financial Times* caught wind of internal dissent over the Monetary Policy Committee's advocacy of austerity. Norma Cohen, Chris Giles, and Daniel Pimlott reported the evening of November 9 that "some senior staff at the Bank of England are uncomfortable with Mervyn King's endorsement of the government's public spending cuts, suggesting he has overstepped the line separating monetary and fiscal policy." The next day, at King's quarterly press conference, Pimlott put a question to the governor, directly and on the record: "Is the MPC unanimous in supporting your strong endorsement of what is essentially the political decision on the scale and size of the fiscal consolidation?" King's response was, at best, disingenuous. "There are different views among the committee on monetary policy, so I'm sure there are probably differing views on fiscal policy," he said. "But we don't sit down and discuss it because it's not the remit of the MPC."

In fact, they had discussed the matter quite explicitly in the vote over the minutes back in May. Posen and Barker, believing their views had been misrepresented by King, went to his press aide with an ultimatum: Unless the governor retracted his statement, they would go public with their objections. He didn't. So they did. In a hearing before Parliament's Treasury Select Committee on November 25, Conservative MP Andrew Tyrie asked Posen about the *Financial Times* article. The American laid out, albeit somewhat obliquely, what had happened with the wording of the May minutes:

> A number of people in the committee, myself plus at least one other . . . were concerned that that statement could be seen as excessively political in the context of the election and the discussion that had gone on. We expressed that point of view. We offered alternative language. The majority of the committee decided that they were comfortable with the language that appeared in the report. . . . It is factually correct, however, that at least one other member plus me were concerned that that language was too political, too much of a statement. That's my personal opinion.

A few days after that, another penny dropped. WikiLeaks, the publishing cooperative led by eccentric Australian Julian Assange and devoted to exposing the world's secrets, began unveiling a trove of diplomatic cables that U.S. embassies around the world had sent to Washington, never meant for public consumption. Among them was Ambassador Susman's write-up of his meeting with King from earlier in the year, showing the governor offering a ruthlessly critical assessment of the men who were now in power. King's old adversary Danny

Blanchflower suggested that the governor resign, writing in the *Guardian* that King had a "thirst for power and influence that has clouded his judgment one too many times. He has now committed the unforgivable sin of compromising the independence of the Bank of England by involving himself in the economic policy of the coalition. He is expected to be politically neutral but has shown himself to be politically biased and as a result is now in an untenable position."

But while the meeting with Susman was an embarrassing disclosure, Blanchflower overstated the degree of King's mistake. Worries about the experience levels of the young Cameron and Osborne were widespread in UK political circles, and the conversation was meant to be a private one. And the cables showed nothing inconsistent with King's public advocacy of budget cuts. Cameron, for his part, played it cool. Speaking to reporters December 1, his spokesman said that King was doing a good job and that "the issue of confidence simply doesn't arise. My experience is the Bank of England governor makes lots of statements on economic policy. That's what you'd expect." The comment seemed to split the difference between dismissing the matter entirely and allowing King to twist in the wind.

Indeed, throughout late 2010 and early 2011, King faced the suspicion that he'd made an implicit deal with the Tories: He would stick with low-interest-rate policies in exchange for their quick shutoff of the fiscal spigot. When confronted, King was adamant that there was no such horse trading. "I have never discussed with [Osborne] propositions of the kind, 'If we tighten fiscal policy, will you loosen monetary policy?'" King told a parliamentary committee in March 2011. "That kind of conversation has never taken place."

As King faced these political difficulties, the British economy was entering a nasty period of stagflation, a central banker's worst nightmare—and the leaders of the Bank of England were all over the map about what to do about it.

British GDP fell 0.4 percent in the fourth quarter of 2010, and while it rebounded at the start of 2011, growth was too slow to bring unemployment down. UK unemployment, 7.8 percent at the end of 2010, started rising above 8 percent again as 2011 progressed. Simultaneously, the weaker value of the pound, higher prices for imported fuel, and the value-added tax increase created another spike in consumer prices. And prices kept rising at a pace well above the Bank of England's 2 percent target—at more than 3 percent in the final months of 2010, and at more than 4 percent at the start of 2011.

It's always a dilemma for central bankers when unemployment and inflation are both high at the same time, and this episode brought out particularly stark divisions on the Monetary Policy Committee. At one meeting, in February 2011, the nine-member committee split four different ways. The differences boiled down to what lessons each member drew from the Great Inflation of the 1970s.

At one extreme, there was inflation hawk Andrew Sentance, who started advocating for raising interest rates in June 2010 and dissented from the rest of the MPC until the end of his term in May 2011. Sentance looked at those rising prices and saw an incipient threat that businesses and consumers would accept high inflation as the new state of affairs, much as Arthur Burns had in the United States four decades earlier. That could allow a vicious cycle of higher prices leading to higher wages leading to higher prices. "Notwithstanding my affection for the rock music of the seventies, the economic turmoil of that period is definitely not something we want to revisit," Sentance said in a February 2011 speech titled "Ten Good Reasons to Tighten." "But one of the lessons from the battles against inflation in the 1970s and the 1980s, was the importance of having credible policies. Statements about the need to reduce inflation need to be backed up by actions to achieve that objective."

At the other extreme was dovish Adam Posen, an accomplished macroeconomist who had been a leading analyst of Japan's stagnation over the previous two decades. By the fall of 2010, he'd seen enough. On September 28, he gave a speech titled simply "The Case for Doing More." Posen warned that the British economy—and, for that matter, the U.S. economy—appeared to be functioning well below its potential, meaning that inflation wasn't nearly as big a threat as recent price increases suggested. If the Bank of England would "see through" the uptick in commodity prices and the hike in the value-added tax, it would discover that, due to the weak economy, the real pressure on prices was downward, not up. The lessons of the 1970s, he suggested, were the wrong lessons to draw in 2010, when the fundamental problem facing Britain and the other major Western powers was idle workers and idle factories:

> Central bankers' fears on this score can be taken to intellectually unjustified extremes, and there is a risk of our doing so now when the damage could be great by so doing. When the overwhelming bulk of

pressures in the economy are disinflationary, and when the level of output and employment is clearly likely to be below potential for an extended period, it is right for central bankers to take the additional negative effects of protracted recession on trend productivity growth and on capacity into account. That is a far cry from 1960s and 1970s monetary policy efforts to push the economy into growth without regard for the limits on, and in fact the decline then in, potential growth.

In other words, let's focus on the problem we're actually facing, not on the problem of our parents' generation. Posen started voting for an extra £50 billion of quantitative easing at the October 2010 MPC meeting, and he became as consistent an advocate for easier money as Sentance was for tighter throughout 2011. Posen actually violated Bank of England etiquette by giving strong suggestions of his policy view before changing his vote; by tradition he should have changed his vote and subsequently explained it. But while at times Posen seemed on the verge of becoming the next Danny Blanchflower–style black sheep on the MPC, he was better at playing by the rules than the Dartmouth professor.

King's views in late 2010 and early 2011 were somewhere between Sentance's and Posen's. He often spoke more pointedly of the risks of inflation than Posen did, but he also argued that it was best for the bank to look past the short-term impacts of higher energy prices, increased taxes, and falling exchange rates. Yet as the British economy muddled along, unemployment and inflation rising together, the Bank of England sat on its hands and left policy unchanged.

If the Tory–Lib Dem coalition thought there was an unspoken agreement with the governor of the Bank of England to offset austerity with more monetary easing, King disappointed terribly. Might there have been a different result under a central banker who didn't have anything to prove about his political independence? Or one who had a less acidic tongue, a better gift for persuading his colleagues, and fewer enemies?

The lesson from Threadneedle Street in the aftermath of the crisis is that even for a king, power isn't limitless.

# FIFTEEN

# The Perilous Maiden Voyage
## of the QE2

The reporters sat nervously in the basement of the Treasury building at 1500 Pennsylvania Avenue in Washington on November 3, 2010, tapping, glancing around, double- and triple-checking that their computers were working. Finally, a fax machine belonging to Dow Jones Newswires spit out a document, two pages containing information that seemingly every trader and money manager on the planet lusted for: the outcome of the latest meeting of the Federal Open Market Committee, the policy arm of the Federal Reserve.

Sandra Salstrom, the young Treasury press staffer in the room, wouldn't, by tradition, read or even touch the document. That, the logic goes, could compromise the vaunted independence of the central bank from the U.S. Treasury Department. Instead, Dow Jones reporter Jeff Bater took it from the fax machine, photocopied it, and with Reuters' Mark Felsenthal placed the copies on a table so the thirty or so journalists who'd piled into a room that usually holds a dozen could make a mad dash for them. The reporters had a mere ten minutes to turn the 482-word statement into a story that would be blasted across the earth.

Salstrom was there as official timekeeper. She used the timer on her Black-Berry, a technological advance over the cheap cartoon-character wristwatch that had served as the timepiece a few years earlier.

"Five minutes," she warned.

"Two minutes."

"One minute—open your lines." The reporters were now allowed to open communication with their editors, giving them sixty seconds to begin transmitting the information.

When the big moment came, at 2:15 p.m., Salstrom rang a large bell. As she had been repeatedly advised when first taking up this duty, she gave the pull a good yank to ensure that everyone could hear.

An instant after Salstrom rang the bell, word was transmitted to every trading floor on earth. The journalists, experienced at parsing Fedspeak, had seen quickly that the real news was buried in the third of seven paragraphs: Over the next eight months, using newly created dollars, the Fed would buy $600 billion of U.S. Treasury bonds.

Within the Fed, the plan was known as "large-scale asset purchases," a strategy to try to increase the supply of money in the economy when short-term interest rates were already near zero. Ben Bernanke could explain all day long how this was different from the "quantitative easing policy" the Bank of Japan had tried a decade earlier. (Both central banks expanded their balance sheets, but the BOJ did so only by buying short-term government debt, whereas the Fed was buying longer-term debt.) To anyone not involved in the rarefied debates that went on inside the Eccles Building, though, it was a distinction without a difference. This being the second round of quantitative easing by the Fed, the approach adopted that November afternoon would soon be known around the world as QE2, whether Bernanke liked it or not.

The reaction was instantaneous—and surprisingly muted. Yes, a vast sum of dollars was about to be unleashed upon the global financial system. But the Fed had succeeded in telegraphing its plan in advance through a mix of public speeches and off-the-record statements to Fed watchers in the media and beyond. The Standard & Poor's 500 stock index ended the day up less than four tenths of a percent, effectively flat. For Bernanke and the Fed, it was a moment of triumph: They'd guided markets to exactly where they wanted them to go. Even a major new policy could be announced without disruption.

The policy itself was hardly revolutionary—the Fed's internal analysis viewed it as the equivalent of cutting short-term interest rates by half to three quarters of a percentage point. But Bernanke could rest easy knowing he'd moved boldly enough to prevent the U.S. economy from the long slog of falling prices and stagnant growth that Japan had experienced for the better part of two decades. And he'd done it with a fair degree of consensus: Only one of eleven policymakers with a vote in that meeting had dissented, and that was Tom Hoenig of the Kansas City Fed, who had been voting against the rest of the committee all year long.

The sense of triumph wouldn't last long. The financial markets may have been well prepared for the decision to launch QE2, but the rest of the world, it soon became clear, was not.

Backlash against the Fed's $600 billion intervention in the economy began that very evening, with Glenn Beck, then near the peak of his influence as an evening conspiracy theorist on Fox News. "I've been telling you that it would be the Weimar Republic moment," Beck, never one to pass up a reference to Nazi-era Germany, told his audience of nearly two million. "It is largely untested and unconventional. I mean, I'm sure Zimbabwe tried it. It's a huge gamble. It is probably the biggest bet in history and the biggest bet in the history of our planet." Failed vice presidential candidate cum media sensation Sarah Palin was comparatively restrained: "We shouldn't be playing around with inflation," she said a few days later, showing her first public sign of interest in monetary policy. "Maybe it's time for Chairman Bernanke to cease and desist."

The criticism from American conservatives extended to a newly energized Republican Party. Just a day before the Open Market Committee's decision, the GOP had prevailed in midterm elections and gained a majority in the House of Representatives. In the Republicans' telling, the easy-money policies of the Fed were aiding and abetting excessive government spending. Opposition to QE2 became a rallying cry.

"Look, we have Congress doing tax and spend, borrow and spend. Now we have the Federal Reserve doing print and spend," said Wisconsin representative Paul Ryan, tapped to chair the House Budget Committee in the new Congress, on Fox News a few days after the announcement. "What the Fed is basically doing is they're trying to bail out the fact that our fiscal policy is so bad. The Fed should focus on keeping our money sound and honest, not on doing this, which I think is going to give us a big inflation problem down the road."

American conservatives had a surprising set of allies overseas. "I don't recognize the economic argument behind this measure," acid-tongued German finance minister Wolfgang Schäuble told *Der Spiegel*. "The Fed's decisions bring more uncertainty to the global economy" and "artificially depress the dollar exchange rate by printing money." As President Barack Obama prepared for a meeting of the Group of 20 in Seoul, South Korea, officials from governments around the globe joined in the fusillade of criticism. The United States "does not recognize . . . its obligation to stabilize capital markets," said Zhu Guangyao, China's vice finance minister. "Nor does it take into consideration the impact of this excessive fluidity on the financial markets of emerging countries." The Chinese government's media campaign against the Fed was so vigorous that the shampoo girl in a Beijing hair salon asked an American customer about it with a tone of accusation.

The Germans and Chinese and South Koreans and Brazilians were arguing that by flooding the market with dollars, the Fed was essentially engaging in a currency war, trying to benefit American exporters by depressing the value of the dollar. It may seem nonsensical that the central bank was simultaneously being accused by U.S. conservatives of undermining the American economy and by foreign governments of giving American businesses an unfair advantage. But those were the strange bedfellows of the great QE2 debate.

In Seoul, Obama found himself in the uncomfortable position of being attacked by foreign leaders for a decision over which he had no power. In Basel—by coincidence, one of the six-times-a-year gatherings of the world's central bankers was scheduled for the weekend immediately following the QE2 decision—Fed vice chairman Janet Yellen and New York Fed president Bill Dudley faced more polite and economically literate criticism from the other central bankers. But in the formal sessions and the intimate dinner high above Basel alike, the accusations of fecklessness flew.

When it wasn't international central bankers pummeling the Fed, it was animated bunnies. In a seven-minute YouTube video created by Omid Malekan, then a thirty-year-old real estate manager, two animated animals with computer-generated voices—whether they were in fact rabbits or bears or pigs or dogs was hard to say—engaged in a Socratic dialogue about "the quantitative easing" that had been launched by "the Ben Bernank" to benefit "the Goldman Sachs." The video went viral; by mid-December, it had been viewed 3.5 million times. That November, after two of Bernanke's closest advisers at the Fed, Gov-

ernor Kevin Warsh and communications chief Michelle Smith, had each been
sent links to the video multiple times, they concluded that they needed to show
it to the chairman. Bernanke found the video funny despite deep flaws in its
economic analysis.

There was even criticism from within the Federal Reserve System itself.
On the Monday after the decision, Warsh published an opinion piece in the
*Wall Street Journal.* "The Federal Reserve," he wrote, "is not a repair shop for
broken fiscal, trade or regulatory policies." The Fed's easing should be reversed,
he said, if "purported benefits disappoint, or potential risks threaten to materialize," and the increased role of the Fed in the bond market "poses nontrivial
risks that bear watching." The wording was all very polite, but anyone who
knows the language of central banking could read between the lines: Warsh
was deeply apprehensive about the action he had voted in favor of five days
earlier. It was Warsh's way to balance his deep respect for Bernanke with his
distaste for the new policy: The chairman would get Warsh's reluctant vote for
QE2; Warsh would publicly explain his reservations a few days later. Bernanke
had even read the piece before it was published.

But Warsh's apprehension was only part of a broader discontent within
the Fed. Tom Hoenig's lone official dissent reflected a quirk of the calendar:
Voting rights rotate among the twelve Fed bank presidents each year, and in
2010 only one of the four officials who were dead set against QE2 had a vote.
Warsh and two or three more policymakers had serious reservations.

The weekend after the decision, the Atlanta Fed held a "Return to Jekyll
Island" conference to mark the hundredth anniversary of the gathering off the
Georgia coast where the First Name Club had plotted out what would become
the Federal Reserve System. In the chilly late fall air that Friday night, as Fed
officials, economists, and reporters made their way from a conference space
that was once J.P. Morgan's indoor tennis court to dinner in the old main hotel
building, then on to the small underground bar where they would order after-
dinner drinks and jockey with a wedding party for elbow room, Charles Plosser,
the president of the Philadelphia Fed and perhaps the most voluble of Fed officials, spoke in increasingly animated fashion with Sandra Pianalto of the
Cleveland Fed, perhaps the least.

"How can you say we've got a consensus?!" he bellowed, within earshot of
reporters. "We don't have anything *close* to a consensus!"

. . .

H ow had it come to this?
    In the spring of 2010, a U.S. economic recovery had seemed under
way. After shedding jobs for twenty-four straight months, the private sector finally began adding jobs that March. The Obama administration launched a
publicity tour it called "Recovery Summer," pointing to projects funded by its
fiscal stimulus program that were presumably contributing to a surging economy. At the Federal Reserve, the words on seemingly everyone's lips were "exit
strategy." On the markets desk at the New York Fed, small-scale experiments
began to test some of the methods of draining liquidity—that is, extra cash—
out of the banking system.

Bernanke and other officials wanted to be sure that when the time came
to tighten the money supply, the Fed had the ability to do so without letting
prices spiral out of control. If they succeeded at persuading the world that that
was the case, it could actually benefit the economy in the near term: If people
expected high inflation in the future, they would demand higher interest rates
on longer-term bonds, which would in turn lead to higher interest rates for
mortgages and corporate borrowing, discouraging growth. The Fed's exit strategy talk could, in theory at least, help keep inflation expectations down, long-
term interest rates low, and the American economy humming.

But such plans began to seem premature as the summer of 2010 progressed. The near implosion of Europe drove the S&P 500 index down 16 percent from April 23 to July 2. And the economic data that was coming out
pointed not to a recovery but to a possible dip back into recession. When the
May 2010 jobs report initially came out at the start of June, it showed a mere
forty-one thousand private jobs created that month, far too few to represent
meaningful growth in the United States, with its 150 million workers. Later
revisions put the number at more like eighty-four thousand, though even that
suggested job growth too weak to drive down the unemployment rate.

At the same time, inflation was low—and falling. Overall prices had gone
on a wild ride in the preceding years as the price of oil and other commodities
soared in the summer of 2008, plummeted at the end of that year with the
global economic crisis, and then rebounded in the spring and summer of 2009.
But by the middle of 2010, fuel prices weren't the problem. There were now

enough jobless workers that few Americans were getting wage increases. And there were so many idle factories and empty office buildings that companies had room to expand without pushing up prices. Fed officials had years earlier agreed that "price stability" means that consumer prices rise around 2 percent a year. In the twelve months ended in June 2010, the consumer price index rose only 1.1 percent, and even less than that when the volatile food and energy categories were excluded.

Perhaps more worrisome, investors and other economic decision makers were starting to conclude that very low inflation would be the new normal. Investors in the bond market were expecting inflation to average only 1.2 percent over the ensuing five years, based on the gap between bond yields that were and were not indexed to inflation.

People may not like it very much when prices for the goods they buy are rising, but if the Japanese experience shows anything, it's that they experience more economic pain when prices and wages are falling. Large debts become even harder to pay off, so households hang on to their money rather than spend it, creating a vicious cycle in which less spending begets fewer jobs begets even less spending. Typically, a central banker could counteract low inflation and high unemployment by cutting interest rates and increasing the supply of money in the economy. But with the Fed's target interest rate already stuck near zero, where it had been since December 2008, the typical tool wasn't available. And that turned what would otherwise have been a simple decision into something rather more complicated.

But even as the data on the economy turned more negative, Bernanke stepped gingerly. Central banks tend to move slowly, not wanting to jar markets by overreacting to the latest economic report. That's all well and good when policymakers have the right basic idea about what's happening in the economy. In the summer of 2010, the Federal Reserve didn't.

The official forecast of Fed policymakers, released that July, predicted the gross domestic product to rise at a 3.5 to 4.5 percent rate in 2011. The actual number turned out to be 1.6 percent. The Fed had underestimated the degree to which overhang from the boom years—the housing market crash, the blows to business confidence, the debts still being paid off—would prevent growth. But that was its projection, and the central bank was sticking to it, even as one data point after another seemed to prove it wrong.

"My colleagues on the Federal Open Market Committee and I expect continued moderate growth, a gradual decline in the unemployment rate, and subdued inflation over the next several years," Bernanke told the Senate Banking Committee on July 21, 2010, in his semiannual testimony on monetary policy. He acknowledged that risks to growth were "weighed to the downside," but, tellingly, spent almost a third of his time discussing how the Fed might exit from policies to support growth. He mentioned a nonexit strategy only when prompted by a senator's question—and then only as a distant possibility. "If the recovery seems to be faltering," Bernanke told Alabama senator Richard Shelby, "then we would at least need to review our options, and we have not fully done that review, and we need to think about possibilities."

There was, among both Fed policymakers and the public, a large measure of "activism fatigue"—a sense that the government, including the central bank, had already done everything it could to try to stimulate growth, so a certain amount of patience was in order. Businesspeople were sitting on piles of cash and had easy access to the debt markets, so they didn't see tightness of the money supply as a constraint on growth and hiring. Consumer spending was the big problem. "I could borrow two billion dollars tomorrow at three and a half percent," David Speer, the chief executive of Illinois Tool Works, a sixty-thousand-employee industrial company, said in August 2010. "But what am I going to do with it?"

Bernanke had in fact weeks earlier urged Fed staff to begin studying subtle ways to ease the money supply. The Fed could cut the interest rate it paid banks to park cash from its already low 0.25 percent to something even lower, for example, or give the world a more explicit pledge to keep its ultra-low-interest-rate policies in place. (At the time, its statements indicated only that rates were expected to stay low for an "extended period.") But at the July 21 hearing, Bernanke remained noncommittal.

"We have not come to the point where we can tell you precisely what the leading options are," the chairman said.

A week in advance of each of the Federal Open Market Committee's eight meetings a year, senior Fed officials around the United States log in to their secure document server. There they gain access to the single most important piece of briefing material they need to review before the meeting. It has, since June 2010, been called the Teal Book. Before then, it was two separate documents, the Blue Book and the Green Book. If the document would be a merger of the two, so, the logic went, would the color.

Prepared under the watchful eye of the chairman, the Teal Book contains charts and narrative descriptions of what the Fed's economics staff in Washington thinks is happening with the labor market, inflation, and so on, as well as what the staff forecasts the economy will do in the future. It also lays out three options for future Fed policy. Option A is invariably the dovish one, focused on trying to encourage growth by easing the money supply. Option C is the hawkish choice, focused on combating inflation by tightening the money supply. And Option B, falling somewhere in between the other two, is the one that the committee almost always ends up approving, albeit sometimes in modified form. After all, it's the chairman and people who work directly for him who put together the options. Inevitably, the range of possibilities reflects both his own preferences and his best guesses as to what the variety of views on the committee might be.

On August 3, 2010, however, the day the Teal Book was to be posted to the secure server and seven days before the FOMC meeting, Fed officials scattered around the country learned of what might be on the agenda through a different means. The front page of the *Wall Street Journal* that Monday morning announced, "Fed Mulls Symbolic Shift." The article, by staff reporter Jon Hilsenrath, said that Fed officials "will consider a modest but symbolically important change in the management of their massive securities portfolio when they meet next week to ponder an economy that seems to be losing momentum."

By long tradition, the small and insular club of journalists who cover the Federal Reserve regularly abide by what are known as "Fed rules." Reporters can use information gained in interviews with high-ranking Fed staffers, but they can't attribute it in any way—not even to "a senior Fed official." Instead, they write what they know in a strangely omniscient voice, giving no hint of how they know it. So even though Hilsenrath's story gave no clue as to where his information came from, it seemed a safe assumption, both to people across the Federal Reserve System and to those in the community of analysts who monitor the central bank, that his main source was either Bernanke or someone with intimate knowledge of the chairman's thinking.

In this case, Fed policymakers around the country suspected they were learning of a new policy move from their morning newspaper. Sure enough, when they logged in to the secure document server to examine the Teal Book, Option B called for the Fed to ease monetary policy a bit, in the manner Hilsenrath had described. In a coffee break at the meeting the following week, some policymakers complained to Bernanke's communications adviser, Michelle Smith, that the press had gotten wind of an imminent policy shift before many of them had.

So what happened between July 21, when Bernanke gave no hint that the Fed would be acting, and August 10, when the FOMC met? There was another weak jobs report in that span—but that was released on August 6, after both the *Wall Street Journal* story and the Teal Book had been issued. What actually provoked the change was new evidence compiled by analysts at the New York Fed of what would happen in the absence of an adjustment to Fed policy. After pushing interest rates to zero at the end of 2008, the Fed took its first step toward unconventional monetary policy with QE1, using newly created money to buy up mortgage-backed securities issued by government-sponsored companies like Fannie Mae and Freddie Mac and funded by ordinary Americans' home loans. It was meant to simultaneously expand the money supply and funnel funds to the cash-starved mortgage sector.

The result was that the Fed owned $1.1 trillion worth of such securities by the summer of 2010. But the bank's policy at the time was that as those bonds matured—as people refinanced or paid off their mortgages—it wouldn't buy new ones to replace them. Instead, it would allow the amount of money it was pumping into the financial system gradually to decline.

But the economy was weakening that summer, and interest rates fell as investors plowed money into the safe haven of mortgage bonds effectively guaranteed by the U.S. government. Lower mortgage rates meant that people who had home loans ultimately funded by the Fed had incentive to refinance their mortgages. When they did, and the central bank didn't buy replacement mortgages, the Fed was in effect sucking money out of the financial system—the exact opposite of what it wanted to be doing when the economy was looking bad. New York Fed president Bill Dudley's staff had initially estimated that the mortgage securities portfolio was on track to shrink by $200 billion by the end of 2011. When it revised that number in light of the drop in rates, it came up with $340 billion—an extra $140 billion that the Fed would be pulling out of the economy at a time when the outlook was getting weaker.

To stop that unintended tightening, the FOMC would need to pull an about-face on its policy. Just before the August 10 meeting, Bernanke changed its start time from 9 to 8 a.m. so the committee would have more time to discuss the possibility.

There were clearly a number of factions among the committee members. One group, including Eric Rosengren of the Boston Fed, Charles Evans of Chicago, and Janet Yellen of San Francisco (who had been nominated as the new Fed vice chairman but not yet confirmed), saw the economy slipping and thought the central bank needed to move aggressively to try to stop it. Changing the mortgage-bonds reinvestment policy, they argued, should be merely the first action in a broader campaign to pump money into the economy. The mainstream of the committee, including Bernanke, Vice Chairman Don Kohn, and a number of governors who tended to follow the leader, saw the change as a necessary measure but didn't believe it should necessarily lead to further moves toward easy money. It was a reverse, certainly, but just a technical one—not really a big deal.

Another set of policymakers, including Bernanke intimate Kevin Warsh and Governor Betsy Duke, had significant reservations but found it hard to argue against the narrow logic of changing the reinvestment policy to avoid a "shadow tightening." Of the four inflation-hawk reserve bank presidents who were dead set against the change, Richard Fisher, Jeffrey Lacker, Charles Plosser, and Tom Hoenig, only perpetual naysayer Hoenig had a vote that year.

So the decision to change the reinvestment policy, announced right on schedule at 2:15 p.m., became a Rorschach test for Fed officials: Those who wanted to begin a major easing of policy could believe it was the start of just that; those who didn't could view it as just a tiny technical change.

That ambiguity may have helped Bernanke build consensus on his committee, but it created nothing but confusion in the outside world. Had the Fed changed its view that the recovery was on track? Was the action the start of something big, or just a one-off tweak? The people whose job it is to analyze what the Fed is up to had no idea, and quirks of the calendar made it hard for them to find out. Many of the policymakers who would typically explain themselves in postmeeting speeches were on vacation. The first to discuss the decision was Minneapolis Fed president Narayana Kocherlakota, the newest FOMC policymaker. He was so new, in fact, that Fed watchers were still unsure of where to place him on the scale from dove to hawk.

On the reinvestment decision, Kocherlakota was among those in the moderately hawkish camp who went along because they viewed the policy change as a one-off. That's what he told the world in an August 17 speech at Northern Michigan University—then added that the decision had a "larger impact on financial markets than I would have anticipated." The next Fed insider to address the issue publicly was St. Louis Fed president Jim Bullard, another relative newcomer and one known for his idiosyncratic views on monetary policy. (He both opposed the pledge to keep interest rates low for an extended period and been warning of the risk of deflation in a paper ominously titled "Seven Faces of 'the Peril.'") He seemed more open to a large-scale, programmatic move toward easier money, saying that new action "may be warranted." After Bullard came Hoenig, who yet again warned of the perils of keeping rates too low for too long.

The people who work in the financial markets and make or lose fortunes on the central bank's every action didn't know which end was up. "The chatter you're getting around policy right now is such a cacophony," said Ethan Harris, an economist with Bank of America–Merrill Lynch. "There's just a bunch of wildly different views being presented from both inside and outside of the Fed, and that is confusing markets."

For clarity, the world had no one to look to but Ben Bernanke.

The chairman's speech at the Kansas City Fed's annual Jackson Hole conference always receives a great deal of attention, from the speechmaker as well as the audience. Bernanke each year pours dozens of hours of both his own time and that of his staff into getting his message just right. (Ironically, for all the extra attention, it's the only speech Bernanke gives that's not broadcast on television; only a text is released.) Earlier in the summer, he'd planned to offer a rather academic talk on current account balances. But that speech was scrapped and a new one, aiming to give the world a thorough explanation of what the Fed was thinking, was hammered out in time for the late August conference.

In the early days of Bernanke's chairmanship, staffers would write the first drafts of his speeches. But he found himself revising so extensively that by

2010 he wrote first drafts himself, then handed them over to staff to check and revise his data and analysis. For the 2010 Jackson Hole speech, he took a much more collaborative approach. His planning involved not just the usual discussions with his closest aides, but a series of meetings that amounted to a framing of their entire strategy for monetary policy. The meetings included Kohn, who was set to step down as vice chairman and leave a forty-year career at the Fed four days after the speech, Warsh, Michelle Smith, and the heads of the Fed's two major economics research departments: Bill English of monetary affairs and David Stockton of research and statistics. In Bernanke's office, the discussion evolved until it wasn't just about how best to communicate to the world what the Fed had done, but also about whether the Fed should do more at all.

In the Federal Reserve System, as in all modern central banks, it is a committee that formally decides how to best steer an economy toward the happy middle ground between inflation and recession. But even though the Fed chairman has only one vote out of twelve, his true power goes far beyond that. He sets the agenda and frames the options on the table. He guides the discussion toward directions he believes useful and away from those he disfavors. And seven of the twelve voters at each FOMC meeting are governors based in Washington, who frequently feel an institutional loyalty to vote with the chairman even if they have reservations. Those deliberations about the Jackson Hole speech were really about Bernanke making up his mind.

Of those in the room for this innermost of circles, Warsh, a onetime investment banker turned White House staffer who had been the youngest Fed governor in history when President George W. Bush appointed him in 2006, most consistently argued against a new program of easing. What was wrong with the U.S. economy, according to Warsh's line of reasoning, wouldn't be fixed by pumping more money into it. There was the overhang of housing from the boom years and a glacially slow process of foreclosures that was preventing the market from clearing, the debts weighing on households, the retrenchment of state and local governments. With short-term interest rates near zero, Americans could already obtain a thirty-year fixed-rate mortgage for an interest rate of around 4.4 percent, far below any longer-term historical average, and creditworthy businesses could borrow at similarly low rates to buy equipment or build a factory.

It wasn't at all clear that injecting an extra few hundred billion dollars into the economy would encourage more economic activity. And it would come with risks, too: If the Fed owned too much of the federal government's debt, it might disrupt the American bond market, the biggest in the world. Would the market function properly if private buyers were essentially pushed out? Would they return once the Fed was ready to back away? Could yet another round of activism by the Fed make the central bank vulnerable to attacks by elected officials who were wary of government involvement in the economy? And could that actually undermine confidence among businesses?

As Warsh mounted those arguments against new action, Bernanke and Kohn countered with a much simpler logic. The Fed's job, as dictated by Congress, is to try to ensure stable prices and maximum employment—the "dual mandate," as it's known. Prices were rising more slowly than the 2 percent that most Fed leaders viewed as stable. And the job market wasn't rebounding anywhere near as quickly as anyone had hoped. Therefore, Bernanke and the Fed's task was to find a way to pump more money into the economy, even if they couldn't be sure just how much of an effect it would have.

Bernanke was in particular a subscriber to a "tipping point" theory of how the economy works. The U.S. economy is capable of growing somewhere around 2 or 2.5 percent each year simply due to an expanding labor force and rising worker productivity. That means that slower growth, if sustained, could create a vicious cycle: more people unemployed, driving down incomes, driving down demand for products, leading to more layoffs, and voilà, an economy back in a recession, or even an outright contraction. If the Fed could give the economy just enough of a push to get it over that 2.5 percent growth hurdle, the reverse might set in: a virtuous cycle of falling unemployment, rising incomes, more demand, and more hiring. One little nudge from the Fed might make a great deal of difference.

The most recent report on growth at the time had shown a 2.4 percent rate of expansion in the spring of 2010—in other words, right on that line where, if Bernanke's tipping-point premise was correct, a little bit of a push in the right direction could go a long way. Yes, cheaper money might not help growth as much as it could without the counterinfluences of mortgage market dysfunction and debt overhang. But it could probably help on the margins.

And if the Fed did squeeze private investors out of the Treasury bond market, he argued, they would have to put their money elsewhere, affecting the economy through what is known as the portfolio balance channel. They might buy corporate bonds, which would mean still more money available for companies looking to expand. They might buy mortgage securities, which would make it cheaper for Americans to buy or refinance a house. Or they might invest in the stock market, pushing up share prices and, in the process, household wealth.

By the end of these sessions—half a dozen in total—Bernanke and his closest advisers had drafted a speech that laid out the decision of whether to do another round of quantitative easing as one of costs versus benefits. "As we return once again to Jackson Hole, I think we would all agree that, for much of the world, the task of economic recovery and repair remains far from complete," Bernanke, yet again standing under the elk-antler chandeliers at the Jackson Lake Lodge, said to the 110 or so people gathered in the ballroom. Many thousands more around the world read the text of the speech as it was published simultaneously online.

Bernanke very much raised the possibility of new action but stopped far short of pledging it. "The committee is prepared to provide additional monetary accommodation through unconventional measures if it proves necessary, especially if the outlook were to deteriorate significantly . . . the issue is instead whether, at any given juncture, the benefits of each tool, in terms of additional stimulus, outweigh the associated costs or risks of using the tool." In other words: QE2 was very much on the table, but it would only be enacted if conditions deteriorated further.

"Fed Ponders Bolder Moves" was the *Wall Street Journal* headline; "Bernanke Pledges Dramatic Steps If Economy Worsens," said the *Washington Post*. That was the public perception. Those who had been privy to the writing of the speech had a different view. The Fed chairman would never have said so explicitly, but from the Jackson Hole speech forward, the task at hand was to figure out how best to pump more money into the economy and build support for drastic action on the committee. The Bernanke that advisers saw in those private sessions was a man who had made up his mind that the Fed was going to do something—and something big. He just had to figure out how to make it happen.

Barely three weeks after the Jackson Hole speech, the FOMC was due to meet again, once more against a backdrop of gloomy economic news. The August jobs report, released September 3, showed another month of anemic private job creation and an unemployment rate that had ticked up to 9.6 percent, yet another sign of a sputtering economic expansion. Around the country, when the presidents of Fed banks logged in to the secure document server in advance of the September 21 FOMC meeting, they found that Option B again tilted toward easier money.

This time, at another rushed one-day (really one-morning) committee meeting, the consensus was that the apparent low inflation and weak growth warranted moving toward looser monetary policy. But there was no agreement on how to pursue it. Bernanke didn't force the issue. Instead, he encouraged the committee members to signal the things they could agree upon in the statement released after the meeting: that inflation was "currently at levels somewhat below" what the committee views as best, and that the Fed "is prepared to provide additional accommodation if needed to support the economic recovery and to return inflation, over time, to levels consistent with its mandate." Translation: We're on the verge of doing something, even if we don't know yet what it is.

Incrementalism proved a useful method for bringing more Fed policy-makers around to Bernanke's point of view. It allowed time for more evidence to mount that the economy was indeed stuck in neutral, as well as for those officials who had reservations about a new policy to believe that their concerns were given a fair hearing. Meanwhile, Bernanke's inner circle was changing: Kohn, the walking institutional memory of the Fed, who had been right-hand man to Alan Greenspan and then vice chairman under Bernanke, had retired on September 1. Obama had appointed Janet Yellen to replace Kohn as vice chairman, and although she wouldn't be confirmed until October 4, she had already moved to Washington. And she was decidedly dovish—one of the committee's strongest advocates for the idea that with the economy underperforming and inflation not much of a threat, greater activism was warranted.

Bill Dudley, who had succeeded Timothy Geithner as president of the New York Fed, also believed that the central bank needed to do more to boost the economy. Even better, he knew the practical, nuts-and-bolts details of how to carry that out, which ensured that any desire to ease policy wouldn't run up against technical problems identified by "traders," as the New York Fed's markets desk calls them, who buy and sell securities in order to carry out Fed policies. Dudley had previously run that operation, so he knew well what challenges awaited in execution. With Kohn gone and Warsh firmly against new monetary easing, Yellen and Dudley became Bernanke's closest collaborators.

On October 1, Dudley gave a speech that left little doubt that something significant was on the way. Speaking to the Society of American Business Editors and Writers, he described how the Fed was failing in both encouraging job creation and in keeping inflation at its target rate, explaining how buying bonds might improve things on both fronts. He even raised a relatively controversial idea that had been often mentioned by academics but rarely by policymakers: that a central bank might respond to inflation that's too low by allowing some period of "catch-up" inflation. He then offered a conclusion that included none of the understatement, jargon, or circumlocution that are standard whenever senior central bankers talk about what they might do. "My assessment is that both the current levels of unemployment and inflation and the timeframe over which they are likely to return to levels consistent with our mandate are unacceptable," Dudley said. "We have tools that can provide additional stimulus at costs that do not appear to be prohibitive. Thus, I conclude that further action is likely to be warranted."

Fed watchers in financial markets often overestimated how much FOMC members coordinate their speeches. Contrary to common assumption, presidents of the reserve banks around the country don't generally run their speeches by Bernanke and his colleagues in Washington, let alone take marching orders. They act on their own. But when Dudley speaks, it's a little different. By long tradition, the New York Fed chief is vice chairman of the FOMC, and with that comes a responsibility to ensure he isn't getting too far out of step with what the majority of the committee—and its chairman—is thinking. For that reason, Dudley's speech came very close to preannouncing QE2.

Bernanke had successfully built a consensus that some sort of easing made sense; he and his allies now set out to shift the discussion toward *how* as opposed to *whether.* As if to underscore that shift, three days after Dudley's speech, his key deputy, Brian Sack, who ran the Fed's markets desk and would be the official charged with carrying out the new easing program, gave a talk of his own. With the intentionally bland title "Managing the Federal Reserve's Balance Sheet," the speech explained the technical challenges of a new round of bond purchases and how the New York Fed markets desk was overcoming them. Although Sack didn't express his own view of whether a new purchase program was warranted the way Dudley had a few days earlier, the simple fact that he was discussing the issues involved at such length gave another hint about where the FOMC was going. After all, why spend hundreds of words explaining a policy that isn't going to be enacted? The hawks on the committee were particularly annoyed; they were forever being told not to front-run the committee by speaking about what it might do; now Dudley and even Sack, not a member of the committee at all but a staff member, were doing just that. "It was quite upsetting to me," said Tom Hoenig, "to have the head of the Reserve Bank of New York—and the money desk guy—out there defining what the moves are going to be." Hoenig and others made their objections known to Bernanke. "By that time I wasn't going to wait until [the FOMC meeting]" said the Kansas City Fed chief. "I'm pissed."

It was a wet, cold, and gloomy New England morning when, promptly at 8:15 a.m., Boston Fed president Eric Rosengren called to order the bank's annual research conference on October 15, 2010. Eleven years earlier, the Boston Fed had brought many of the same economists together in Woodstock, Vermont, to discuss "Monetary Policy in a Low Inflation Environment." There, Princeton professor Ben Bernanke had argued that Japan was failing to ease monetary policy sufficiently out of "self-induced paralysis." Now, revisiting the same topic, the question on the table was whether the Bernanke Fed was stuck in a paralysis of its own. In his keynote address, Bernanke left few doubts of where he stood. "Given the committee's objectives, there would appear—all else being equal—to be a case for further action," the chairman said that morning, his words carried live on all the financial news channels. Acknowledging that there can be downsides to unconventional policy steps, he added that "the Federal Reserve remains committed to pursuing policies that promote our dual objectives of maximum employment and price stability."

Bernanke left the conference soon afterward to fly back to Washington. In the hours that followed, leading academic economists debated the theoretical challenges of easing the money supply when short-term interest rates are already at zero. The challenge of the situation that the Bank of Japan found itself in a decade earlier, and that the Fed now was grappling with, was that it couldn't cut rates to the point where they would be low enough to stimulate investment, below the so-called zero lower bound. Some grappled with the mind-bending question of why rates *can't* go below zero. What if the Fed tried to set a negative interest rate—that is, effectively levying a tax on savings? Said Greg Mankiw, a Harvard economist and former White House adviser, at the Boston conference, "What a depositor is going to do is say, 'Well, if they're going to charge me money to keep my money at the bank, I'm just going to keep my money at home,' and the only thing you'll generate is a demand for safe assets—and by that I mean assets that are safes because they're going to be buying a bunch of safes so people can put their money in their safes rather than in the bank." He added that one way around that problem, suggested by a student, would be to declare currency with certain serial numbers invalid. "I won't say who he was," Mankiw said. "Because he may want to be a central banker one day."

While the academics talked in a conference space next to the Boston Fed's cafeteria, the senior Fed officials in attendance quietly slipped out at around 2:30 p.m. and took an elevator upstairs to Rosengren's office suite. There, they logged in to a secret video teleconference of the Federal Open Market Committee. The regularly scheduled FOMC meeting was still two weeks away, and the idea that there would be a QE2 was fully expected by the market after Bernanke's speech that morning. But the chairman wanted to hold this session to ensure plenty of time to discuss the technical details of how to carry out the program. Should the Fed announce one giant number up-front for the amount of Treasury bonds it would buy, say $500 billion or $800 billion? Or should it revisit it at every FOMC meeting, for example, starting with $100 billion and then either announcing another $100 billion or cutting the number to zero depending on what the economy did in the interim? (This was the approach favored by St. Louis Fed president James Bullard.) A final option, which drew some interest from Bernanke but never took off among fellow committee members, would be to target some particular longer-term interest rate and then buy bonds in whatever amounts necessary to hit that target. The attendees also debated whether the Fed needed to improve how it communicates its goals to the public, such as by making its target for inflation more explicit or having Bernanke begin holding press conferences.

The three-hour conference had the practical purpose of determining which strategies had wide support among committee members and which didn't. But it was also one of the last acts in a strategy that had combined persistence with patience. Between the August and September FOMC meetings, the smaller sessions in Bernanke's office, and this special videoconference, the QE2 decision had been so fully aired that by the time the November 2–3 policy meeting rolled around, no one on the committee could have argued that his or her voice had gone unheard. Bernanke, from that August meeting on, had been constantly pushing toward new easing, even while giving his more recalcitrant colleagues time to come around to his view. Before taking this new plunge into unconventional monetary policy, however, he had a few more people to convince: the finance ministers and central bankers of the twenty most powerful nations on earth.

Located in the southeast corner of South Korea, with no airport of its own, two hours by train from Seoul and an hour by car from Busan, the small city of Gyeongju was, for most of the officials scheduled to meet there for the Group of 20 economic summit on October 22 and 23, 2010, rather difficult to get to. Bernanke had wanted to skip the meeting entirely. With round-trip travel, the two days of meetings occupied five days on his schedule. (The Fed chairman usually flies commercial; if he were to routinely catch a ride on the treasury secretary's Air Force jet, it could be seen as compromising the central bank's independence.) But in the interest of diplomacy, he needed to explain the imminent QE2 to the world.

It was an unwieldy gathering: Each of the twenty member nations sent its finance minister plus its central banker. Each of those forty officials brought a deputy. Some also had interpreters. And there were various "honorary" attendees, ranging from international groups like the International Monetary Fund and the World Bank to larger non-G20 countries like Spain and Vietnam. All told, there were around a hundred people in the room, hardly an intimate gathering.

The South Korean finance minister began, welcoming the attendees and taking care of administrative announcements. Then, by long tradition, the United States was given the floor, asked to explain what was going on with the world's largest economy. Normally, Treasury Secretary Geithner would have dominated this part of the discussion, but this time he gave the prime speaking role to Bernanke, who set out to explain the policy move that by this point it was widely expected the Fed would soon take. He and Kevin Warsh, there as Bernanke's deputy, worried that the briefing could prompt political criticism: Why should the Fed involve the rest of the world in a domestic policy decision? So Bernanke took care to say only that the Fed was likely to consider new asset purchases, without suggesting that it was an absolute certainty. Still, who knew what that might sound like through the filter of a journalist speaking to a foreign official?

The possible move, he said, was about adjusting U.S. monetary policy to properly match U.S. economic conditions. It wasn't about trying to manipulate the value of the dollar, even if a reduced value of the dollar on foreign exchange markets was one likely result. I'm not trying to start a currency war, Bernanke argued, I'm just trying to stop deflation and economic contraction from taking hold in the United States.

Several of the officials in the room—from the same countries who would raise vocal public objections three weeks later—were having none of it. The Germans argued that the Americans were tempting inflation on a mass scale and new financial bubbles, which to Bernanke just sounded like the usual German hard-money fetishism. The Chinese and Brazilians argued that the hundreds of billions of dollars the Americans would soon unleash would find their way into oil markets, driving up energy prices, as well as into stock markets in emerging economies that were already dealing with vast inflows of "hot money" and a risk of bubbles. Bernanke was sympathetic to the Brazilians, though less to the Chinese: All they had to do to avoid importing inflation from the United States was to end their policies of intervening in markets to depress the value of their own currency relative to the dollar, which was exactly what the United States government wanted them to do. The emerging markets' arguments, in Bernanke's view, boiled down to the idea that the U.S. government should do what was best for them, not what was best for the U.S. economy.

As they do eight times a year, the men and women of the Federal Open Market Committee who came to Washington from out of town for the two-day meeting that was to begin on November 2 checked in to the Fairmont Hotel, then piled into vans for the mile-long drive to the Eccles Building. The financial news networks were in full hyperventilation mode, alternating between assessing the impact of massive Republican wins in congressional elections that Tuesday and the QE2 announcement expected the next day. They parked their satellite trucks around the Fed's building in Foggy Bottom; there would be nothing to report until Wednesday afternoon when the meeting concluded, but having the white marble edifice of the Fed's headquarters behind their reporters lent gravity to the broadcast.

"Good afternoon, everybody," Bernanke said a bit after 1 p.m. that Tuesday. He welcomed Sarah Bloom Raskin, a newly confirmed governor, who was participating in her first in-person meeting. To laughter, he noted that Janet Yellen, while newly confirmed as vice chairman, had been to "a few meetings" before. And so the meeting began.

There is always a certain formality to FOMC meetings. Committee members gather in a grand room and follow a rigid agenda: First the briefings from staff, then go-rounds in which each official speaks for a few minutes about his or her view of the economy and policy. The participants, who might be "Ben" or "Bill" over coffee in the hallway, are "Chairman Bernanke" and "President Dudley" when the FOMC is in session. And ever since the 1995 decision to begin releasing transcripts of the meetings with a five-year delay, the gatherings have been somewhat stilted, with officials reading prepared remarks rather than engaging in extemporaneous discussion. Even when there is little controversy over policy, committee members meticulously split hairs over how to phrase their postmeeting statement. Did the U.S. economy grow "modestly" or "moderately" in the previous six weeks? Only the FOMC could spend several minutes debating the distinction.

The QE2 meeting was a little different.

The "Will we act?" question had been more or less resolved at the September meeting, at which the tide shifted toward an answer of "Yes." And the conference call two weeks earlier had been enough to work through the details of the program. All that was left, really, was for the policymakers to make their last, best arguments for the directions they favored. When the transcript is released in early 2016, it will show the strongest advocates of more easing—Yellen and Dudley, plus Charles Evans of the Chicago Fed and Eric Rosengren of Boston—making their case in sometimes moralistic language about the necessity of doing *something* to put more of the then 15.1 million unemployed Americans back to work at a time when inflation was too low.

The inflation hawks—Richard Fisher, Jeffrey Lacker, Charles Plosser, and Tom Hoenig of the Federal Reserve banks in Dallas, Richmond, Philadelphia, and Kansas City, respectively—will come across as even more impassioned. They painted an ugly picture of what QE2 could do: fuel bubbles in the stock market and commodity prices and compromise the Fed's independence by putting it in the position of effectively printing money that would help fund government deficits. The central bank, they said, shouldn't take ownership of an

economic dilemma beyond its power to solve. Warsh, normally Bernanke's closest ally, related his objections with a vehemence that would make his *Wall
Street Journal* op-ed seem reserved. Twice people jokingly called him "Axel" for
his hawkishness—implying that he sounded like German Bundesbank chief
Axel Weber.

It wasn't grandstanding, exactly, on either side of the debate. It was accepting that a decision had been made and ensuring that the historical record
would contain no ambiguity on where each man and woman stood. They went
around the room, voicing their final votes. Of the hawks, Warsh voted with the
majority out of loyalty to Bernanke (and with the knowledge he would spell out
his views in a *Wall Street Journal* op-ed a few days later), and of the rest only
Hoenig had a vote. The decision was made ten to one, the statement hammered
out, and the fax readied for transmission to the press room in the basement of
the Treasury Department.

Glenn Beck, YouTube, and the continued dismay of certain members of
the G20 awaited.

The huge, Florentine palazzo–styled headquarters of the Federal Reserve
Bank of New York, a few steps from Wall Street in lower Manhattan, is an
imposing building. It has thick stone walls and, suitably for a building whose
basement contains the largest stockpile of gold in the world, thick iron grates
guarding the windows on its lower floors. During the 1930s, as ominous clouds
appeared in Europe and Asia foreshadowing a second world war, the governments of the world one by one decided that New York would be a safer place to
keep their gold than at home. The New York Fed was happy to oblige, offering
up its vault, hard against the bedrock of Manhattan Island eighty feet below
street level, as a location for storage. There are 122 cages containing gold stored
for many of the world's governments and central banks—their exact identities a
closely held secret. In total, they hold about $350 billion worth of gold at early
2012 prices, more or less the annual economic output of Thailand.

That's exciting for tourists who want to hold a gold bar (worth about
$600,000 at recent prices, and even heavier than you'd expect) and for movie
producers who want to create an elaborate heist scene (as in *Die Hard: With a
Vengeance*). But for the New York Fed, it's just a sideline business—the equiva-

lent of a local bank branch renting out safe-deposit boxes in an otherwise unused corner of its vault. The real money is two hundred feet above, in a conference room that could be in any office in the world: white walls, a single window, a light-colored wooden table that seats ten. That's where, on a Friday in November 2010, Dina Marchioni and her band of young traders set about executing QE2.

The FOMC can only set the direction for policy. It falls to the staff of the New York Fed to actually intervene in the financial markets, buying and selling securities, to enact that policy. The directive from the committee after the November 3 meeting was to buy $75 billion worth of longer-term Treasury securities each month for eight months, for a total of $600 billion. But what securities exactly, and from whom would they be purchased? The answers on November 12 were: any Treasury bonds maturing between 2014 and 2016, and whoever offered the best price.

Marchioni often brings Danishes or bagels on special occasions, which the start of QE2 certainly was, although it is lost to history what breakfast pastry was on offer that Friday. Three "trader/analysts" sit in Aeron chairs at computer terminals facing the wall. Marchioni sits behind them at the conference table, observing. An IT person sits off to the side, there in case the computers fail. Josh Frost, a slim man in a dark suit and Marchioni's boss, stops by most days to make sure everything goes smoothly. There are a huge flat-screen television airing CNBC, a digital clock, accurate to the second, and, along one wall, three workstations, each with three flat-screen computer monitors, one displaying current market data through Bloomberg's financial information service, the others indicating offers from investors around the globe routed through twenty major financial firms known as "primary dealers."

When the Fed is ready to buy, a special sound emanates from the computers on trading floors at each of the primary dealers. It's a strange, fluttering tone—the musical note F, followed by an E, followed by a D, in rapid succession. F-E-D means that the Fed is in the market. The dealers then have forty-five minutes to put in their offers—the Fed is indifferent as to whether they involve securities the giant banks own themselves or those owned by their clients. Marchioni's staffers monitor the incoming offers, and when one comes in that doesn't make any sense—the bank is offering to sell bonds to the Fed either way above or way below the market price—they press a button on an elaborate phone known as a turret (the one in front of Marchioni has a sticker on it identifying it as the Super Turret) that immediately connects them with the trading floor at J.P. Morgan or Barclays or Goldman Sachs or whichever dealer may have put in the offer.

On that first day of QE2, the offers were piling up: The dealers were ready to sell $29.039 billion in bonds to the Fed. The traders watched as a computer program sorted the incoming offers to find the ones that offered taxpayers the best deal. After all, a bond maturing in October 2014 should have a different price from one maturing in January 2016, so their job is to ensure that they buy the ones in which dealers are offering the best relative price.

With one minute to go, the traders' computers begin flashing red. They watch CNBC and monitor the Bloomberg feed to make sure there is no major market-moving news; in that event, they might delay the end of the auction in order to give the bidders time to adjust their offers accordingly. When the clock expires, the Fed's computer sorts through all the offers to choose the ones that offer the best deals. On November 12, 2010, of the $29 billion being offered on twenty-four different individual securities being offered, the best prices were being offered for sixteen different securities, such as $141 million for a Treasury bond scheduled to mature on February 15, 2015, that when originally issued offered a 4 percent yield.

The traders had bought billons in bonds, which were now owned by the Federal Reserve Bank of New York. The sellers—the banks and their clients—had billions of newly created dollars sitting in their accounts, money that they could lend out or spend to their heart's content. The traders would repeat the practice 139 times over the ensuing eight months, until an extra $600 billion was floating around the world economy. Those dollars would, if Bernanke and Dudley were right, create more lending and investment—or, if the hawks were right, higher prices and bubbles.

As the opposition to QE2 escalated in the days after the decision, Bernanke's Fed was under siege from all sides—from American conservatives, foreign powers, some of his own colleagues, and financial commentators whose views weren't too different from those of the animated talking bears. The tradition of keeping quiet and communicating through formal written statements had ill prepared the Fed for a commensurate response. On the afternoon of the decision, Bernanke's calendar listed two hours of "Calls w/media"—but those were apparently all off the record. Even the efforts to push back were hardly smashing successes.

Bernanke wrote an op-ed for the *Washington Post* that was published the next day, and in December he sat for another of his rare television interviews, again with CBS's *60 Minutes*. "One myth that's out there is that what we're doing is printing money," Bernanke told anchor Scott Pelley. "We're not printing money. The amount of currency in circulation is not changing. The money supply is not changing in any significant way."

Bernanke was being too clever, taking advantage first of the fact that QE2 increased the amount of money in the economy through electronic means, not by literally printing cash. But of course, a hundred dollars in a bank account is just as much money as a hundred-dollar bill in someone's pocket. His second point, about the money supply, was an extremely subtle one: The Fed's purchases would increase "monetary base" or "high-powered money," increasing the number of dollars circulating through the economy only if the banks and individuals with extra dollars in their accounts lent out or spent the cash. This too was disingenuous—the whole action was premised on the hope that they would do just that.

Comedy Central's *The Daily Show with Jon Stewart* was the first to point out the contradiction between Bernanke then and what he'd said on the same show, with the same host, twenty-one months earlier. In March 2009, describing the Fed's earlier round of asset purchases, Bernanke had said that "to lend to a bank, we simply use the computer to mark up the size of the account that they have with the Fed. So it's much more akin to printing money than it is to borrowing."

"You've been printing money?" Pelley asked in 2009.

"Well, effectively," said Bernanke then.

Stewart joked that the Fed wasn't printing money—it was "imagineering" it.

Whatever you call it, by some important measures, QE2 worked. In terms of economic growth and job creation, the next year was stubbornly sluggish. But after a summer in which economic data was pointing to a possible new recession and very low inflation, financial markets responded as quantitative easing shifted from a distant possibility in early August to a certainty in early November. Inflation expectations moved upward from 1.2 percent in August 2010 to right at about 2 percent in early 2011, roughly what the Fed was aiming for. By early 2011, the odds of the U.S. economy slipping into deflation were minuscule, bolstering Bernanke's theory that a central bank need never allow falling prices.

Yet Bernanke and his colleagues were confronting a new variety of criticism. For generations, central bankers had steeled themselves against politicians who argued that money was too tight, interest rates too high. That's what it traditionally meant to be independent—to have the courage to raise interest rates when the economy was overheating and inflation was a threat.

But now, up was down, dark was light, and politicians—at least on the right—were clamoring for tighter money at a time of mass unemployment. The Bernanke committee management strategy, of pushing the action through over the course of three months, three FOMC meetings, and a series of speeches, may have been the best way to get a sprawling group with a wide range of views to come together. But it also served to make the action feel like a giant step toward easy money. Similarly, the decision to announce a single gigantic number surely played a role in the blowback. After the U.S. government had enacted a $700 billion financial bailout and a nearly $800 billion, deficit-financed tax-and-spend package in the recent past, the $600 billion in bond purchases sounded to many critics like more of the same—even though the action likely reduced the budget deficit, because the Fed returns the interest earned on the bonds to the Treasury.

The Federal Reserve, as the Dodd-Frank debate had shown all too well, exists at the pleasure of Congress. To have one of the nation's two major political parties engaged in all-out assault on the idea of "printing money" left many on the FOMC who voted for more easing in the form of QE2 wary of doing so again. The chairman now had a clearer idea of why the Bank of Japan had seemed so timid a decade earlier, when he was urging it toward activism.

"I'm a little bit more sympathetic to central bankers now than I was ten years ago," Bernanke said in a press conference in June 2011, a weary smile on his face.

# Part IV

———⚬⚬⚬———

## THE SECOND WAVE,
## 2011–2012

# SIXTEEN

# The Chopper, the Troika, and the Deauville Debacle

The Irish press called him "the Chopper." At 8:45 the morning of Thursday, November 18, 2010, Ajai Chopra departed the Merrion Hotel in Dublin and walked the fifteen minutes to the Central Bank of Ireland for a day of meetings, trailed by photographers. The deputy director of the International Monetary Fund's European division had suddenly become one of the most famous men in Ireland—and here was a chance to capture an image of the man "ready to rip up the books and offer the country billions" walking past street beggars hoping for some spare change. The symbolic resonance couldn't be beat.

Ireland had been one of Europe's great economic success stories of the previous two decades, emerging from relative poverty to become arguably the eurozone's most dynamic economy. Its free labor markets and low corporate taxes made it a popular destination for international firms looking for a European outpost. Its government was efficient and generally free of corruption, and its public finances before the crisis were impeccable. But when Irish officials decided on September 30, 2008, to give government guarantees to their banks, the nation's financial situation fell apart with remarkable speed. "What's the difference between Iceland and Ireland?" asked a joke that went around in 2009, referring to the tiny Nordic nation whose banking system had imploded the year before. The answer: "One letter and six months."

But while in many ways the joke proved all too prescient, it was the differ-

ences between the two nations that had the Chopper in town. First, Iceland had
its own currency, which collapsed 58 percent against the dollar in 2008, setting
the stage for an economic rebound as exporters became more competitive. That
country's unemployment rate peaked at about 8 percent. Ireland's unemployment rate rose to 14.8 percent in November 2010. Second, Iceland's banking
system was small enough that its institutions could fail without endangering
the entire European or world banking systems. Ireland's couldn't—at least that
was a widespread view among European officials.

"I'm not used to a situation where I'm so recognizable," Chopra said in an
interview on RTÉ television. "People have come up to me, calling me by my first
name as well, but they've done it in a very polite and very gracious way, and
they've always wished me the best. And I think this pluck of the Irish is coming
out in this crisis."

So were the representatives of various international bodies offering bailout loans in exchange for strict concessions from the government. Klaus Masuch, a German economist with a reputation as a tough negotiator and a
proclivity for short-sleeved dress shirts, was in Dublin for the European Central Bank. István Székely, a Cambridge-educated Hungarian who had worked
for his nation's central bank and the IMF, was there on behalf of the European
Commission's Directorate-General for Economic and Financial Affairs. Reporters stationed themselves outside the Central Bank of Ireland and shouted,
"IMF? EU? ECB?" at people exiting because, as the *Irish Independent* dryly
noted, "nobody was really sure what the international officials looked like."

Black humor notwithstanding, the Irish seemed to deal with the coming
era of austerity—and even their loss of economic sovereignty—with greater acceptance than the Greeks had. In the Mediterranean nation that spring, protestors had staged a nationwide strike, tried to storm parliament, and firebombed
a bank, leaving three dead. By contrast, there was no significant violence in the
streets of Ireland, although the chief executive of the low-cost airline Ryanair
upstaged the prime minister by showing up at an event to celebrate the opening
of a new terminal at Dublin's airport with a coffin covered by an Irish flag. He
announced that the terminal amounted to a "nice welcoming lounge" for IMF
officials. It probably helped that the Irish were fast losing confidence in their
own elected officials. As the *Independent* headlined a letter to the editor, "Better Chopra than our hopeless lot."

"I guess older people will be upset or feel a sense of national humiliation," said Niamh Norton, a college student quoted by the *Observer*. "But the truth is that it's the big countries of the world that dictate what's going on. . . . Ireland is a small country."


The cast of international officials may have been a little different, but the small-country script being staged in Ireland had been well rehearsed in Greece a few months earlier. Brought together on the fly in the spring of 2010 and by fall the most powerful partnership in Greek politics, the team of Masuch, Danish economist Poul Thomsen, and Belgian fiscal policy expert Servaas Deroose represented, respectively, the ECB, the IMF, and the European Commission. This was the "troika," suddenly responsible for the economic future of some eleven million Greek citizens.

Over room-service sandwiches and sometimes a Mythos beer in an Athens hotel suite, they talked about what they'd learned that day. Where was the Greek government following through on its promises? Where was it not? How might they steer their discussions tomorrow to have more of the former than the latter? Downstairs in a conference space, their staffers—forty, fifty, or more people—divided into teams, ate catered food, and discussed among themselves their own conclusions and plans for the next day.

In quarterly missions, usually lasting two weeks or so (although a few stretched out to more than a month), the representatives of the troika interrogated midlevel staff at all sorts of government agencies—the tax collectors, the energy regulators, the bank supervisors—to try to figure out whether Greece was living up to the agreements its leaders had made in exchange for the international bailout received in May. The meetings, most of them conducted in English, tended to be civil affairs, with the Greek officials understanding that all present were there to do a job. Some of their interlocutors even seemed pleased to finally have the outside pressure needed to enact reforms they had long sought.

There was more animosity outside the corridors of power, where the citizenry saw the visitors as the reason wages and pensions were being slashed. The faces of Masuch, Thomsen, and Deroose (and later Matthias Mors, who took over as the European Commission's representative), each relatively anonymous at his respective organization, were splashed on newspaper front pages. The men had to travel with a police escort and eventually had to change hotels. At first they'd stayed at the Grand Bretagne. But when sometimes violent protests erupted in the square it overlooks, they moved to the Hilton a few blocks away.

The three officials tried to work out disagreements among themselves—for example, how hard to press on cutting wages for government workers as opposed to encouraging longer-term privatization projects. Ironically, while the IMF became a more visible target of populist ire on the streets of Athens, the organization was more worried than other troika members about the economic impact of immediate austerity. That reflected both the fund's experiences in Asia in the 1990s and Latin America in the 2000s—and the fact that it was led by Dominique Strauss-Kahn, a man of the left who embraced Anglo-American-style Keynesian economics more than many continental Europeans. The ECB and the EC were the greater enthusiasts for steep and immediate spending cuts. Still, the three men—and their bosses in Washington, Frankfurt, and Brussels—managed to keep their disagreements confined to the suite in the Hilton and present a united front.

"It seemed they were very well coordinated with each other so as not to create friction points that were evident to us," said one Greek official who worked across the negotiating table. "I have heard there were disagreements, but they were never able to undermine the collectivity of the troika."

It remains the fact, though, that this was the situation in which Greece found itself in 2010: As the price of a bailout, its central bank was part of a team that was giving instructions to elected leaders on what to do about pensions, taxes, and privatization of state-owned industries.

Democracy had been born in Greece. And democracy, it was said, had died there.

Issues of national sovereignty aside, things were moving in the right direction. The series of interventions hatched over the weekend of May 9, 2010, had succeeded. European institutions—both the governments and the ECB—had shown the resolve necessary to keep the Greek crisis from spiraling out of control. Sure, the European stability fund was more an idea than a reality, but so long as the GIPSI governments carried out what they'd promised, an investor could feel assured that no eurozone nation would be allowed to default on its debts. And the ECB's interventions in the bond market proved surprisingly effective. After an initial burst of purchases of Greek, Irish, and Portuguese debt in May and June, markets were functioning well enough that the buys were allowed to taper off. By the last week of August, the ECB's total bond holdings under the securities-market program added up to only €61 billion.

It was a victory for Jean-Claude Trichet's approach to crisis management. He was a big believer that even small interventions by a central bank, if made at just the right time and in the right way, could cause a significant shift in market sentiment. The start of bond purchases punished those who were betting on a eurozone collapse in the spring and made anyone thinking of selling off bonds wary of betting against the ECB and its limitless balance sheet. Markets eased pressure on the GIPSI countries. Spanish ten-year borrowing costs, for example, fell from 4.9 percent in June to 4 percent at the start of September.

The government of Greek prime minister George Papandreou was even having some success—with prodding from the troika—meeting its ambitious goals of cutting pensions and raising taxes. Finance Minister George Papaconstantinou even approached the Institute of International Finance, an association of giant global banks that are among the major buyers of government debt, to arrange a "non-deal road show"—an occasion for him to go to major financial centers and meet with investors to persuade them of Greece's commitment to repairing its finances, in hopes that they might eventually resume buying its bonds.

The actions of May had bought Europe some time to address its economy's underlying problems. Yet by the fall of 2010, none of its structural defects had been fixed. Greeks were still paid more than their levels of productivity would suggest was sustainable, and German and French banks were still sitting on piles of debt issued by governments with shaky finances. The continent's bank regulators conducted a coordinated "stress test" of their various banking systems to examine potential weaknesses and announced its encouraging results on July 23: Most banks could survive losses totaling hundreds of billions of euros. But the test assumed that the debt of all eurozone countries would be fully repaid, which amounts to begging the question.

There were also early signs of cracks in that sense of common resolve, as the governments of Europe went about figuring out the details of the stability fund they had agreed to. Then came perhaps history's most consequential stroll on the beach.

G erman chancellor Angela Merkel was grappling with competing pressures. Her ability to resolve them would, more than any other factor, determine the future of Europe.

On the one hand, her countrymen were aghast that they were being asked to bail out the Greeks. The very day the bailout package was being negotiated, May 9, her coalition lost massively in regional elections in North Rhine–Westphalia, in part due to discontent over the push to aid Greece, and she would face seemingly constant challenges in Germany's constitutional court as to the legality of the bailout measures to which she had committed the nation. On the other hand, the most powerful woman on the continent was also very much a European, determined to realize the vision of a united continent that her political mentor, Helmut Kohl, had set. "Ladies and gentlemen, let's not talk around it," she said in a speech in Aachen on May 13. "The crisis over the future of the euro is not just any crisis. . . . This test is an existential one. It must be passed. Failing it, the consequences would be incalculable for Europe and beyond. But succeeding, then Europe will be stronger than before."

In the fall of 2010, it was antibailout fervor toward which Merkel was most attentive. Even some within her own government were starting to pose some fair but uncomfortable questions: Why were German taxpayers being asked to aid Greece—what about the people who'd lent the nation all that money in the first place? And wasn't Greece effectively bankrupt? When a company goes bankrupt, its investors lose some of their money. Yet the banks and pension funds that had bought Greek bonds were, under the plan being pursued, not to receive a euro less than they were owed. Why, German politicians asked, shouldn't they suffer the same losses any other unwise investor would? Ironically, this put the questioners in common cause with many Greek politicians, who'd have been more than happy to see their debt burden actually reduced, rather than just restructured.

If that was the mentality in Berlin, the sense in Frankfurt, both at the Eurotower and the Bundesbank, was quite the opposite. European central bankers saw grave risk in forcing losses upon Greek creditors. As Trichet and other ECB officials saw it, if Greek bondholders were forced to take haircuts, it could inspire a dangerous and unpredictable chain reaction. Investors would judge the debt of all the at-risk eurozone nations as riskier and likely dump Irish, Portuguese, Spanish, and Italian bonds. Even France could find itself in the line of fire. German and French banks, major holders of Greek bonds, could find themselves undercapitalized and require a new bailout.

And those were just the knowable effects. Government bonds are the bedrock of the financial system. As with the Lehman Brothers failure, a Greek default could have rippling second-order effects that would be very hard to predict. It was one thing for a nation to stiff bondholders when it had its own currency, as Argentina did in 2001 and Russia did in 1998. But to do so as a member of a shared currency union could cause all manner of unforeseen problems. Bailing out not just the Greek government but also Greek creditors was, in the ECB's view, a small price to pay to prevent them.

On October 18, when the finance ministers of Europe gathered in Luxembourg to try to hash out details of the stability fund they'd agreed to five months earlier, the two most important of their number were not present. Wolfgang Schäuble of Germany and Christine Lagarde of France, representing the largest and most powerful nations of Europe, had dispatched deputies. The ministers themselves were in Deauville, a small tourist town on the coast of Normandy with a star-studded history. Elizabeth Taylor and Coco Chanel had vacationed there. So had the fictional Tom and Daisy Buchanan of *The Great Gatsby*. And Ian Fleming had likely based the setting of his first James Bond novel on the town's casino. Now Schäuble and Lagarde's respective heads of state were about to put the town on the map all over again.

The purpose of the Deauville gathering wasn't to talk economics—it was, rather, a regular meeting of German, French, and Russian heads of state devoted to diplomacy and security issues. But Merkel and French president Nicolas Sarkozy decided to use the occasion to work out, between the two of them, an accord on the path forward for Europe. They met at the Hotel Royal Barrière, and in sight of reporters, Sarkozy gave Merkel a hug and sent an aide to retrieve her coat. Against a stunning late fall sunset, tailed by security guards and with photographers clicking from a distance, the pair strolled along a boardwalk overlooking the English Channel and worked out a deal.

Merkel, responding to domestic political pressure, wanted to ensure that the bailout fund agreed to in May wouldn't be part of a permanent source of funding for nations with weak finances. She insisted that, starting in 2013, any nation needing financial assistance would have to allow haircuts for bondholders. Sarkozy initially resisted, but he agreed to the update in exchange for Merkel's dropping her earlier insistence that governments failing to meet deficit restrictions face automatic sanctions, a measure designed to ensure budgetary restraint in the future.

Shortly after their talk, the French government issued a "Franco-German Declaration" consisting of 391 words in English, most of which would be unintelligible to all but the most knowledgeable student of intra-European economic policy. ("In enforcing the preventive arm of the Pact, the Council should be empowered to decide, acting by QMV to impose progressively sanctions in the form of interest-bearing deposits . . .") Most of the debate within Europe in the days that followed was around what the statement meant for new fiscal rules. But for the investors who buy government bonds, the real news was located near the end of the document. Treaties should be amended, the communiqué stated, "providing the necessary arrangements for an adequate participation of private creditors."

Translation: If there are more bailouts, bondholders will pay.

The finance ministers in Luxembourg first learned of the bargain struck on the beach in Deauville from a news report. At just after 5 p.m., Jörg Asmussen, standing in for Schäuble, printed out an e-mail from his colleagues in Deauville outlining the agreement. Many of the ministers were angry; they'd been trying to hammer out their own arrangement, and the two biggest economies of Europe had just gone off on their own to make a deal that would affect them all. ("We're more or less used to Germany and France cooking things up," said an anonymous diplomat quoted by the *Financial Times*. "But this was really flagrant.") Across the Atlantic, the Americans hadn't even realized that such a major accord was in the offing. If they had, Treasury officials would surely have recommended that President Barack Obama place a call to Merkel and Sarkozy to suggest a different approach.

But no one was angrier at what he'd learned that Monday afternoon than Jean-Claude Trichet.

The plan that Merkel and Sarkozy had agreed upon was the exact opposite of what Trichet and the ECB were recommending. Trichet wanted strict fiscal restraint from countries getting assistance, paired with total protection for bondholders to prevent a new wave of crisis. The bargaining in Deauville had delivered the opposite in both cases. In Luxembourg with the finance ministers, he shouted in French to his home country's delegation, "You're going to destroy the euro!" Ten days later, when the heads of the European governments met in Brussels, he was more pointed still. He aimed to teach the assembled national leaders about the workings of bond markets—and impress upon them just how much the threat of haircuts could endanger the eurozone.

He spoke for only about fifteen minutes, invoking his experience heading the Paris Club for international debt negotiations two decades earlier. Introducing the prospect of losses for creditors was shortsighted, he argued, essentially begging bond investors to shun government debt across the eurozone, making the need for bailouts self-fulfilling. It's one thing if governments do all they can and it turns out their finances are unsustainable. But to warn investors that they'll undoubtedly face haircuts is ludicrous; it just makes the possibility of a default more likely. Spain might be in fine financial shape when it can borrow money for 5 percent, but if bond purchasers believe they will face a loss in any rescue, that rate might rise to 8 or 10 percent, making the bailout necessary. "We must be clear about how the markets work," Trichet said. "If the crisis mechanism involves the private sector, it will be much more vulnerable." Trichet was, in his characteristic style, animated, even enraged, dramatically gesticulating to make sure he got the officials' attention.

The European leader who was the most convinced by Trichet's argument was British prime minister David Cameron. But given that Britain wasn't in the eurozone and wasn't helping to pay for the stability fund, his opinion didn't matter nearly as much as those of Sarkozy and Merkel. Sarkozy had a particularly negative reaction, though his attacks seemed motivated by more than the matter at hand. Sarkozy had often attacked the unelected, Frankfurt-based leadership of the ECB, despite the presence of one of his countrymen at its top. He'd even made the central bank a campaign issue a few years before, when he'd argued that its inflation-focused policies were hurting French business.

Word of Trichet's impassioned opposition to Sarkozy and Merkel's plan soon leaked to the press, even though his public statements were more restrained than what he'd said in Brussels. At a news conference a few days later, the ECB president made his point in a rather more roundabout way, emphasizing that the IMF doesn't announce in advance that bondholders are likely to be punished if the fund comes to a country's aid. "The IMF does not make necessarily the ex-ante working assumption that the relationship with markets, investors, and savers is interrupted," Trichet said on November 4.

His warnings were too late. In the days after Deauville, the bond markets started to behave exactly as Trichet had feared they would. Borrowing rates for Italy, Portugal, and Spain all rose. But most worrisome was Ireland: The day Sarkozy and Merkel went for their walk, the nation could borrow money for a decade for 6.25 percent; by November 11, that had risen to nearly 9 percent. The economic leaders of Europe, in Seoul for a Group of 20 summit on November 11 and 12, issued a statement seeking to ease market pressure, saying that the holders of current bonds would be protected from any haircuts and that losses wouldn't happen until 2013 at the earliest. But that wasn't enough to assuage rising fears about Ireland.

Irish real estate and banking busts had slowed economic activity, which had reduced tax revenues. The country's bank guarantees alone amounted to 40 percent of GDP. In 2010, the Irish government's budget deficit rose to a stunning 31 percent of GDP, from basically nothing three years earlier, putting total debt at 92.5 percent of GDP. When worries about European public finances first emerged in late 2009, Ireland had moved more proactively than Greece or other nations to cut spending and try to reduce deficits. But its monetary policy was set by the ECB based on what was best for all seventeen member nations of the eurozone. The Central Bank of Ireland couldn't work independently to offset the contracting economy with cheaper money. With too-tight monetary policy added to the rest of it, the result was nothing short of an Irish depression.

Still, Ireland wasn't Greece. Even with borrowing costs having skyrocketed, the Irish government actually had plenty of cash on hand, thanks to pension reserves. It had suspended issuing new bonds in hopes that rates would decline again, and it had enough money to last until the summer of 2011, according to internal estimates. But depositors in Irish banks, fearful that questions about the government's solvency meant their deposits could be at risk, started pulling their money out. Irish banks then turned to the ECB—still fulfilling its role as lender of last resort to eurozone banks—to get the cash they needed to cover withdrawals. Because the ECB had lowered its collateral standards for emergency lending programs so that even downgraded government debt could be pledged in exchange for central-bank cash, those Irish banks were able to offer Irish bonds as loan security.

By November 2010, Irish banks were relying on central-bank funding from elsewhere in Europe to the tune of €138 billion—equivalent to 89 percent of the country's annual economic output. Spain, with more than ten times the population and a banking crisis of its own, was relying on about a third as much central-bank support for its banks. All this lending was making central bankers around Europe nervous: The more Irish banks relied on them for funding, the more the Bundesbank and the Banque de France and the others would be exposed if the Irish government ultimately defaulted on its debts.

Trichet wrote a letter to the Irish government that expressed his unease, not so subtly suggesting that the ECB's assistance for Irish banks wouldn't be bottomless. He even said publicly that "it is not a normal situation to have institutions that are 'addicted' [to central-bank funding] and we are continually reflecting on how to deal progressively with this problem." Comments like that made the Irish banking crisis worse, as depositors saw a risk that the ECB would start tightening up its emergency lending standards and leave the banks unable to pay off creditors with central-bank cash.

Trichet proposed to Irish leaders that they restructure their banks, including putting new capital into them, as part of an ECB/IMF/European Commission–overseen program of the sort Greeks had enacted earlier in the year. The ECB mind-set was that the biggest failure of the Irish government had been an unwillingness to slash spending quickly enough to restore confidence among bond buyers. "We took all the opportunities to tell the Irish Government that they had to take bold actions very quickly," said ECB Executive Board member Lorenzo Bini Smaghi in a later interview with the *Irish Times*. "In private conversations, Mr. Trichet mentioned this several times on the margins of the European council or the euro group. . . . In 2009 when the Government announced bold measures, this had a very strong impact on the markets. This kind of boldness was not repeated in 2010."

This is what Bini Smaghi was saying: In the middle of a year in which the Irish unemployment rate would rise five full percentage points in part because of budget cuts already being phased in, he wished that the government had doubled down on spending cuts and tax increases that may or may not have been enough to regain the confidence of bond investors. Clearly, Ireland couldn't do much more on its own.

It was time to call in the troika.

On November 21, the Irish government formally acknowledged what was increasingly apparent: A troika-backed bailout was forthcoming. By November 28, negotiations concluded with an €85 billion assistance package. The IMF was willing to lend Ireland money at 3.1 percent, but European stability funds were at much higher rates, so the price Ireland would pay to borrow money worked out to 5.8 percent, hardly a bargain-basement rate—and a reflection of the ongoing effort to punish those countries receiving help. Britain, with its deep ties to Ireland and particularly to Irish banks, kicked in €3.8 billion, in contrast to its unwillingness to help pay for the Greek rescue.

"I don't believe there were any other real options," Prime Minister Brian Cowen told reporters.

In negotiations with the troika, Cowen's government agreed to €15 billion in spending cuts by 2013—€6 billion of them introduced in 2011—a newly created property tax, a one-euro cut in the minimum wage to €7.65 an hour, and an elimination of twenty thousand public-sector jobs.

But the real flashpoint of the talks was what to do about troubled banks Anglo Irish and the Irish Nationwide Building Society. Both were effectively insolvent and had been nationalized, and the government wanted bondholders who'd lent money to the institutions to share in the losses. Trichet and the ECB, focused on preventing a broader loss of confidence in European banks, wanted those creditors made whole.

As the lender of last resort keeping the Irish banking system afloat as well as a member of the troika, the ECB had the negotiating leverage to largely get its way. Whatever the benefits of Trichet's hard line on overall economic stability, the politics—and even the morality—were terrible: At a time when the Irish economy was in shambles, with public employees being fired, taxes raised, and social welfare benefits slashed, the government was paying billions to investors in bank bonds.

Cowen's party, Fianna Fáil, suffered the worst results in its history in the February 2011 elections, and he was ousted as taoiseach, as the Irish call their head of government, in March. Cowen thus became the first national leader to be swept from office by the eurozone crisis. He wouldn't be the last.

Nine days before Ireland reached its bailout agreement, Ben Bernanke visited Frankfurt to speak at a conference at the ECB. In his remarks to the attendees, he observed that cooperation among international central bankers can be very helpful in addressing crises. "Indeed," he said, "given the global integration of financial markets, such cooperation is essential."

But while cooperation among the major central banks continued as it had since that first breakdown in the money markets three years earlier, the greater part of the burden had now shifted from the Federal Reserve to the ECB. Bernanke and Trichet, by now veteran partners in crisis fighting, met privately earlier that day in the ECB president's office in the Eurotower. The Fed chairman put his finger to the Frenchman's chest and said, "Now, Jean-Claude, it is your turn."

The ECB escalated its aid to Ireland as well as Portugal at the start of December, resuming the "Securities Markets Programme" through which it bought sovereign debt. What had been so controversial in May was now accepted practice. And with an overarching rescue of Irish banks in place, the ECB said it would keep offering unlimited three-month loans to eurozone banks for at least another five months. It was a classic pattern for the wily Trichet: Hold back assistance until other actors—in this case, the Irish government and European authorities—take the steps you believe necessary. Had the ECB acted earlier, it would have reduced the pressure on the Irish to take the bailout, and left the ECB that much more exposed.

At a December 16 European Council, there was a sense of relief, as well as renewed resolve. For all the negative reaction in the markets after Deauville, the Irish rescue and the new ECB interventions had once again eased the sense of panic. The leaders of Europe put together yet another grandiose statement of their mutual commitment, both to the idea of Europe and to the euro currency. "The heads of state or government of the euro area and the European Union institutions have made it clear that they stand ready to do whatever is required to ensure the stability of the euro area as a whole," said the communiqué, which outlined seven key points of agreement. "The euro is and will remain a central part of European integration."

The year to come would test further still how much Europe was prepared to back that idea with more than words. Two of the GIPSI countries were now under the oversight of the continent's central bank. Portugal was next in line, and little that had happened in either Athens or Dublin could have given much reason for hope in Lisbon.

The Eurovision Song Contest is the world's oldest reality TV show. Since 1956, it has pitted singers from the nations of Europe against one another in a broadcast beamed across the continent, with viewers voting for the best performances. It was *American Idol* long before *American Idol*. In the May 2011 edition, Portugal had an unusual entry. Young people upset over their dismal economic prospects had overwhelmed the public voting for the nation's nominee, so the country was represented not by the usual peppy pop number, but by "A Luta é Alegria," an ironic protest song performed by Homens da Luta, a group of self-described "professionals of the struggle" dressed as Latin American revolutionaries.

The song's chorus was a rallying cry for the dispossessed—albeit one that must have mystified viewers who neither spoke Portuguese nor understood why this strange-looking group of singers had been elevated to the Eurovision semifinals. "Night or day / the struggle is joy / And people only go forward / Shouting in the streets," the six members of Homens da Luta sang. It was an expression of frustration by Portugal's *geração à rascal*, a "desperate generation" facing an age of diminished opportunity. "The only work we can get is 'work experience,' the only future we are offered is emigration," said Inês Gregório, a twenty-nine-year-old university graduate turned café worker quoted by the *Financial Times*. One weekend in March, hundreds of thousands of them had taken to the streets of eleven Portuguese cities.

Across the continent, the economic strains of the crisis were becoming social and political strains, tearing at the ideals of European unity. Borrowing costs were again on the rise in the GIPSI countries, and in Portugal, Prime Minister José Sócrates had put forward his plan of what to do about it. On March 23, 2011, with the desperate generation in the streets and the unemployment rate at 12 percent, he lost a crucial parliamentary vote on the plan and promptly resigned pending new elections.

What came next was all too predictable: The troika arrived. Portugal formally requested a bailout package. Negotiations commenced. By May 3, a third nation had its IMF/EU/ECB bailout, along with commitments to imminent and aggressive spending cuts and tax increases. And a second national leader had been forced from office amid the economic despair arising from austerity.

In Greece, on May 11, an estimated twenty thousand people marched through the streets of Athens to protest austerity, some of them throwing rocks and Molotov cocktails. The country's labor unions had called a strike, and the nation's transportation and public services were at a standstill. The unemployment rate was 16.8 percent and climbing—fast. "Enough is enough!" said Litsa Papadaki, a sixty-year-old housewife quoted by the BBC. "They are killing us and our children." It wasn't entirely an exaggeration: The suicide rate in Greece in 2011 was estimated to be double the precrisis level.

The discontent wasn't just on the streets. Tensions between the troika and Prime Minister George Papandreou's government were growing as the lenders found Greece failing to live up to its commitments, particularly in privatizing state-run concerns such as telecommunications firm OTE and the ports of Piraeus and Thessaloniki. Reforms to the labor market designed to give employers greater flexibility to fire or cut the pay of workers were drawn up by representatives of the IMF and the ECB, translated into Greek legalese by an Athens law firm, and delivered to the government as legislation that was to be passed.

That was the situation in the debtor countries of Europe. But social strains had emerged in the creditor countries as well. In Finland, the nationalist True Finns party had shocking success in parliamentary elections on April 17 after campaigning on an anti-EU, anti-immigrant platform. The party, which has long been accused of thinly veiled racism, won 19 percent of the vote and thirty-nine seats in the two-hundred-member Finnish parliament, its strongest ever results. True Finns leader Timo Soini appeared on television denouncing the rescue plan for Portugal, which Finland could potentially veto: "The package that is there, I do not believe it will remain."

Protests on the streets. Clashes in the halls of government. Nationalist fervor in the voting booth. All of these were connected to the strategy pursued by the ECB and Jean-Claude Trichet. But Trichet's time as among Europe's most powerful men was nearing an end, his eight-year term set to end on October 31. Who would follow him?

The chairman of the Federal Reserve is nominated by the president of the United States and must be confirmed by the Senate. The procedure is straightforward. The process for naming a new European Central Bank president is anything but. Theoretically, it's a decision made by a majority vote of the twenty-seven nations in the European Union. In practice, however, only the seventeen EU members that make up the eurozone really matter. Nations that don't use the euro stay out of it. Technically, it's one country, one vote—though few would argue that Malta's view actually carries the same weight as Germany's.

The reality of selecting an ECB president is this: It's a matter of horse trading among the prime ministers and presidents of Europe. Each leader would, all else being equal, most likely prefer one of his or her nationals to run the central bank. But heads of government must weigh their desire to have one of their own countrymen in the job with the "cost" in terms of political capital of making it happen—what they might have to give up in some other negotiation, whether in a directly related area of economic policy or some other area entirely, from agriculture to arms control. Do they even have a candidate who's viewed as capable and credible enough to attract support from other countries? Whose "turn" is it? There could hardly be two Frenchmen serving two consecutive eight-year terms, and often officials from larger and smaller countries alternate in such jobs. Trichet, for example, followed Dutchman Wim Duisenberg.

All of this is considered in utmost secrecy, among the leaders themselves and perhaps a few trusted ministers, and never written down. The general public might not ever discover exactly what horse trading led to a given person's becoming European commissioner or ECB president.

Against that backdrop stood Axel Weber, who at the start of 2011 was considered the most likely successor to Trichet among ECB watchers. Angela Merkel had even seemed to hold off from nominating Germans for other international jobs over the previous couple of years, perhaps clearing the decks for the first German ECB president. But on February 11, Weber shocked the prognosticators when he announced he was resigning as Bundesbank head and removing himself from consideration as ECB president. How that came to be is a case study in the delicate game of intra-European politics.

After Weber made public his dissent to the ECB's bond-buying decision in May 2010, he spent the rest of the year in an uncharacteristically quiet mode.

He was clearly in the minority of the Governing Council on one of the biggest decisions it had ever made, and his going public had made this fact widely known. He still played an important role within the ECB—he led the Bundesbank, after all, which carried out more of the central bank's policies than any other national bank. But he told those close to him that he could never run the ECB so long as he was in a minority position on such a crucial issue. After all, it's hard to be the effective leader of a committee on which you're consistently outvoted. Whatever the public expectations, Weber saw his candidacy as untenable unless the Governing Council reversed course.

He waited nine months before withdrawing. People close to him believe he was biding his time in part to see whether there was a reversal on the bond-buying issue, and in part because he didn't want to be seen resigning from the Bundesbank during a period of acute crisis. He may have also been waiting to see just how aggressively Merkel was willing to act to secure the first German ECB president. For decades, Germany had enjoyed less representation in the top ranks of international organizations than its size and wealth would imply, reflecting a certain reluctance to act on the world stage that stems from the horrors of World War II.

Merkel was eager to redress that imbalance. But she was also a savvy enough tactician to use her political capital carefully. The French government was signaling worry that Weber wouldn't act with enough flexibility to save the eurozone. ("The euro area needs someone who can change his mind when the situation requires, of great intellectual agility," an unnamed adviser to Sarkozy told French financial paper *Les Echos*.) Italian prime minister Silvio Berlusconi was openly endorsing Banca d'Italia governor Mario Draghi, a widely respected central banker who may well have preferred that Berlusconi keep his mouth shut. Other European leaders, Merkel especially, had deep disdain for Berlusconi, known for Mafia ties, "bunga bunga" parties with prostitutes, and a general lack of seriousness. (The crude insult he was reported to have made about her appearance was the least of it.)

The Bundesbank president gave a speech at the German embassy in Paris in November 2010, meeting with (and reportedly impressing) French political and business elites. And at the annual gathering of global elites in Davos, Switzerland, for the World Economic Forum in January 2011, which both Weber and Merkel attended, Weber allies tried to rally support for the Bundesbank chief among the other political leaders present. But as the winter progressed, they saw little evidence that favor for Weber was growing enough among either European politicians or the other central bankers to make for a successful candidacy. They also saw Merkel playing a cagey game, supporting Weber while remaining noncommittal about twisting Sarkozy's arm on his behalf. When Weber's decision to withdraw from consideration leaked to the press before he informed Merkel of it, it came across publicly as nothing short of a rebuke to the chancellor. "Of course she is angry," *Der Spiegel* reported, and the German newspapers painted a portrait of a government in chaos over the matter.

There was still the matter of who would be the new ECB president, if not Weber. Although there were plenty of other capable economists in Germany, Merkel was left with no strong German candidates. Jürgen Stark was credible enough, but the rest of Europe viewed him as more "German"—that is to say, hardline and doctrinaire—than even Weber. And given that he was already near the end of a term on the ECB's Executive Board, it was unclear whether his appointment to a new eight-year term as president was legal. Some dark-horse possibilities from small countries were floated—Erkki Liikanen of Finland, for example, and Yves Mersch of Luxembourg. But there was only one candidate who really had the skills and the credibility in financial markets to take on the ECB presidency in the midst of a crisis: the one preferred by Mr. Bunga Bunga.

Draghi received his economics PhD from MIT three years before Bernanke did, though the two didn't know each other at the time. He'd helped prepare Italy to join the eurozone, ending its chronic high inflation and cementing his position among the most elite of Italian civil servants, the highly capable technocrats who keep their country running amid the seemingly perpetual instability of its elected governments. His fellow central bankers held him in sufficiently high regard that they named him chairman of the Financial Stability Board, a coordinating body for regulating risks to the global financial system.

The blots on his résumé, at least from the vantage point of European leaders weighing whether to name him ECB presidency, were two: He had spent three years as a vice chairman of Goldman Sachs, a politically toxic former employer in the aftermath of a financial crisis caused by giant global banks. (In the matter of the role Goldman played in helping Greece to hide the extent of its indebtedness, Draghi denied any personal involvement, and it began before he joined the firm.) And he was, of course, from one of the is in GIPSI, a nation that could soon find itself negotiating a rescue package. Could an Italian central banker have a hard time winning the confidence of the financially stronger countries that were footing the bill for the bailouts? Would "Super Mario," as the press had taken to calling him, seem so super in Germany, Austria, or Finland?

The initial reaction in Germany was negative. "Please, not this Italian!" said the tabloid the *Bild* in a typically subtle headline. "*Mamma mia,* with Italians, inflation is a way of life, like tomato sauce with spaghetti." The more grown-up *Der Spiegel* engaged in a softer form of national stereotyping by merely observing that the candidates from Finland and Luxembourg, in contrast to Draghi, "both come from orderly nations." But Draghi courted media and political leaders in Germany and beyond, always emphasizing that preventing inflation was his foremost goal.

Given the existential threat to the euro he would inherit as ECB president, it wasn't perhaps the most obvious thing to focus on, but it did the trick. With impressive endorsements from the financial world—twenty-nine of forty-five private economists surveyed by Reuters supported him—Draghi soon became the prohibitive favorite. Even the *Bild* came around to his side, by April publishing an illustration of Draghi wearing a Prussian helmet, writing that "at second glance it is clear that he's rather German, indeed a proper Prussian."

On May 11, Merkel announced that she had come to the same conclusion about Draghi. "He is very much in line with our ideas about stability and economic solidity," she told *Die Zeit.* "Germany could support his candidacy." Unspoken was the reality that she and her advisers didn't really have any better options to put forward, at least none that could garner broad support across Europe. With Germany's endorsement, Draghi sailed through the formal process of going before the European Parliament.

Trichet's successor was in the wings, and the challenges he was to inherit were getting tougher.

O ver the first decade of the euro's history, some things didn't change. Certain countries—Germany, Austria, Finland—were creditors, spending less than they produced and accumulating savings. Others—Greece, Portugal, Spain—were debtors, spending more than they produced and having to borrow to keep their economies going. In Greece, that borrowing funded lavish government spending. In Ireland and Spain, it funded real estate booms. In either case, it meant that a nation's citizens became accustomed to a higher income than would be justified by what they were actually producing. They weren't as rich as they thought they were, and one way or another, their incomes needed to come back in line with reality.

Normally that would happen in large part through currency movements. The Greek drachma would fall against the German mark. And suddenly, workers who were paid 10,000 drachma per week would have a lower real income, even as they received the same number of drachma in each paycheck. The workers might be a bit poorer, with less ability to buy gasoline or imported wine, but their relative income would match their relative productivity. Without government officials needing to do much of anything, competitive balance would have been restored.

With Germany and Greece both using the euro, however, imbalances would need to be righted some other way. One way would be for the ECB to ease monetary policy and aim for higher inflation than usual. If it allowed prices and wages to rise 4 or 5 percent a year in the creditor countries while wages were stagnant in the debtor countries, within a few years their relative wages would come back in line with fundamentals and growth could resume. But the ECB has never seriously entertained this option; it takes its goal of keeping inflation a bit below 2 percent seriously, and anti-inflation Germans would be aghast at seeing their prices rise 4 to 5 percent each year.

That leaves one other option: outright cuts to the pay of workers and pensioners in the debtor countries. That was the strategy Trichet and the ECB pursued. They called it internal devaluation: The debtor countries had to find a way—through cutting state salaries and pensions, renegotiating contracts with unions, and the like—to force wages downward. Within the troika, the ECB was the strongest advocate for wage cuts. Trichet himself broached the issue with senior Greek officials, pointing them to a chart of "unit labor costs" showing that Greek workers were paid too much relative to those in the rest of Europe.

The problem is, economic pain, perceived and actual, is much worse when an imbalance is corrected by cutting people's wages directly instead of through a currency devaluation or inflation. Economists call it nominal wage rigidity.

For reasons that seem deep-seated in the human psyche, people are much less unhappy if their pay stays the same while inflation reduces the value of their paycheck 5 percent than if their employer actually cuts their pay by 5 percent. Moreover, when a country is dealing with an overhang of debt, inflation makes it easier to pay off that debt, whereas deflation and cuts to wages make it harder. A single currency Europe combined with the ECB's unwillingness to entertain higher-than-normal inflation ensured that the GIPSI countries would have to correct long-standing imbalances in the most painful way possible. And because that left them unable to manage their debt loads, it also left the financially stronger countries of Europe on the hook for bailouts.

Given the adjustment they had to make, the best that Europe's more troubled economies could hope for was that the rest of the continent would go on a veritable economic boom. At least then there would be more demand for Greek olives, Italian wine, and Spanish vacation houses. In the spring of 2011, Trichet and the ECB prevented even that possibility.

Prices for oil and other commodities were rising in the early part of the year, partly because demand from China and other developing nations was rising and partly because of geopolitical instability in the Middle East. By March, overall eurozone inflation over the previous twelve months reached 2.6 percent, a bit above the 2 percent the ECB had targeted. Even as the GIPSI countries were grappling with double-digit unemployment, the economies of the more populous core of Europe—Germany, France, the Benelux nations—were actually holding up reasonably well.

Trichet steered the Governing Council at its early March meeting toward signaling an imminent interest rate increase. The group hiked its interest rate a quarter percentage point in April and again in July. At a time when numerous European countries were in what can only be called a depression, the ECB was tightening policy. Asked at his April press conference if the action would increase the stress on the peripheral countries, Trichet was almost dismissive. "I will only say that we are responsible for ensuring price stability for 331 million people, and all the decisions that we have taken since the very beginning of the euro, including today's, have been designed to deliver price stability to 331 million people."

Sorry, Spain, you're out of luck.

In hindsight, those rate hikes in the spring and summer of 2011 might seem to be among the biggest monetary policy mistakes of the modern age. But when regarded in relation to Trichet's negotiating strategy, both within the ECB Governing Council and with other European leaders, they look somewhat better.

From the earliest days of the crisis, in 2007, Trichet had been determined to keep the bold, unconventional steps the ECB undertook to support the financial system distinct from its usual responsibility of monetary policy. Whereas Bernanke treated buying government bonds and interest rate adjustments as different weapons in the same arsenal, Trichet regarded them as designed for wholly different purposes—so much so that in the summer of 2008, as the ECB was lending to European banks with abandon, it was also raising interest rates to combat inflation.

This bought Trichet credibility among his fellow central bankers as well as political leaders. Weber and the Bundesbank, for example, were much more comfortable lending billions of euros to banks when they were confident that the ECB remained hypervigilant about inflation. The spring and summer 2011 rate hikes may have been justified by legitimate research on the risk of inflation, but the real reason for them was one Trichet would never acknowledge, even in private: They were the price he had to pay to maintain the credibility as an inflation fighter that would give him a freer hand to be a crisis fighter.

The votes were even unanimous: The nationals of Greece and Ireland and Portugal on the Governing Council endorsed the hikes. "We felt we needed to send a strong signal, and in that sense, it worked," said one council member. "We felt we could reverse them easily in the fall if we were wrong."

Meanwhile, political fissures within the eurozone were growing. The major fault lines emanated from the proposed European Stability Mechanism and what powers it would ultimately have. Could it buy the debt of a country under attack on the markets, as the ECB had done to this point? Trichet wanted it to—it seemed a more appropriate role for the fiscal policymakers across Europe than the central bank.

But the ugly new politics of the Northern European creditor nations were making their leaders reluctant to sign up for anything that would make them beholden to Southern European debtor countries in financial trouble, the promises of May 2010 notwithstanding. So at the March 2011 Governing Council meeting, the ECB elected to suspend the Securities Markets Programme—to stop buying the bonds of Ireland and Portugal on the open market. Trichet had seen the pattern: Elected leaders were inclined to act on behalf of a united Europe only when markets forced them to. So the ECB was going to sit back and let the markets do their job, however much pain it might cause in the meantime.

Trichet was playing chess, sacrificing his pawns in hopes of saving his queen. But it came at the cost of a European economy even less well positioned to withstand the forces threatening to rip it apart. If Trichet lost, it would be in spectacular fashion.

# SEVENTEEN

# The President of Europe

In early May 2011, Jean-Claude Juncker, the prime minister of Luxembourg, had organized a secret meeting. The finance ministers of the four biggest eurozone countries, plus their counterpart in Athens and Jean-Claude Trichet, were going to meet in his small country to try to figure out what to do about Greece. In his official request for a bailout the previous April, Greek prime minister George Papandreou had described his nation as a sinking ship—and now it seemed to be going under even faster. Over the past year, Greek unemployment had risen from 12.1 percent to 16.8 percent. The ten-year government-borrowing rate had shot from around 9 percent to 15 percent. Public debt had risen from 148 percent of GDP to more than 171 percent. In February, concurrent with a nationwide strike, 100,000 people had taken to the streets of the Greek capital to protest government approval of austerity measures. One banner unfurled outside of parliament read simply, "We are dying."

The hope was that the Luxembourg meeting, with just a few influential decision makers in the room, and none of the public spectacle of formal meetings of the "Eurogroup," with all twenty-seven European Union finance ministers and their staffs present, would be a place where those gathered might truly speak openly, with all possibilities on the table. It helped that the gathering was to take place where few news organizations have a bureau, making the odds of their being spotted coming and going relatively low.

That evening, Friday, May 6, Trichet was in the backseat of a sedan en route to the meeting when an aide's BlackBerry buzzed. There was some bad news: The German news magazine *Der Spiegel* had caught wind of the meeting; just before 6 p.m., it had reported on its Web site that the top finance officials of Europe were gathering to discuss the possibility of Greece's exiting the eurozone and reestablishing its own currency. German finance minister Wolfgang Schäuble, the story said, was going to argue against the idea. He'd come prepared with a ministry study that showed just how dire the risks would be to Greece, Germany, the European Central Bank, and the eurozone as a whole. The move would "seriously damage faith in the functioning of the euro zone" among international investors, the paper reportedly stated. And that "would lead to contagion."

Trichet was furious. He had agreed to come only because the meeting was secret. A publicly announced gathering would create expectation in the markets that some major policy announcement was on the way—and commensurate disappointment and disruption if one wasn't made. Juncker's spokesperson denied to the press that there was any such meeting, later defending the lie by saying that "We had Wall Street open at that point in time," so "there was a very good reason to deny that the meeting was taking place."

In fact, the meeting was more about the touchy matter of reducing Greece's debt load by restructuring its bonds than it was about the nation's potential withdrawal from the eurozone. But the leak was emblematic of a broader problem in Europe's response to the megacrisis. Ben Bernanke and Tim Geithner could speak privately whenever they wanted, with word of their conversations never leaking out. With seventeen finance ministers in the eurozone alone, details of the European talks were forever popping up in one country's newspaper or another. And in an Internet age, what was printed in a newspaper in Berlin was known in the government offices of Paris and on the trading floors of London before the ink was dry.

When the meeting began, Trichet let the assembled officials know in no uncertain terms how irritated he was. "I cannot participate in a meeting advertised as private that then isn't," he said. "I have never seen anything like this in any country." Trichet then refused to take part, left abruptly, and returned to Frankfurt.

The Greek economy, it seemed, wasn't the only thing under strain.

A few days later, another troika higher-up would find his private actions made very much public. At 12:06 p.m. on Saturday, May 14, maid Nafissatou Diallo went into International Monetary Fund managing director Dominique Strauss-Kahn's suite at the Sofitel, a French-owned luxury hotel on West 44th Street in midtown Manhattan. Nine minutes later, she left—after an encounter with Strauss-Khan that she described as a sexual assault and he would later call a noncriminal "moral failure." At 12:26 p.m., Strauss-Kahn left the hotel, briskly making his way to brunch with his daughter and then to John F. Kennedy International Airport for Flight 23 to Paris—he had a meeting with German chancellor Angela Merkel scheduled for the next day.

At 4:40 p.m., Port Authority police approached Strauss-Kahn as his plane idled at the gate, on the pretext of returning a cell phone he'd left at the hotel in his abrupt exit. Instead, they took him into custody for questioning. Rumors of the apprehension began to appear on Twitter less than twenty minutes later. By 7:35 p.m., the *New York Times* Web site had posted what seems to be the first reliable report of the incident. One of the most powerful men in the world, the presumed next president of France, was in a cell at the New York Police Department's Special Victims Unit in East Harlem—and would eventually be charged with multiple felonies, including committing a criminal sex act, attempted rape, and sexual abuse.

Strauss-Kahn soon resigned from the IMF to fight the charges, which were dropped when prosecutors lost confidence in Diallo's credibility as a witness. Strauss-Kahn's sexual appetites had gotten him in trouble three years earlier, when he'd had a brief—and reportedly coerced—affair with a subordinate at the IMF. But now his career was over, both as Socialist presidential hopeful and as one of the key decision makers in the eurozone crisis. The suddenness of his downfall, as well as its sheer tawdriness, stunned his fellow crisis fighters.

More substantively, it left Strauss-Kahn's number two, John Lipsky, in charge of the IMF at what was becoming a crucial time for Greece. Lipsky, an American who was formerly a J.P. Morgan economist, was a thoughtful and respected veteran of managing debt crises. But he didn't have the deep relationships with European leaders that Strauss-Kahn did, and he had already announced that he planned to retire later in the year, making him a short-timer.

It was a particularly bad time for a leadership vacuum at the IMF. Greece was failing to carry out many of the reforms it had promised as a condition of its bailout, and the troika was ready to get tough about it. "The view that seems to be taking hold is that the government program is not working," said Poul Thomsen, the IMF representative in Greece, on May 18. "The program will not remain on track without a determined reinvigoration of structural reforms in the coming months. Unless we see this invigoration, I think the program will run off track." Translation: We will withhold the next installments of aid payments, allowing Greece to go broke, unless the government steps up privatization and austerity.

Prime Minister George Papandreou had done a lot to transform the Greek government. The son and grandson of previous Greek prime ministers, Papandreou was particularly proud of his strategy of using Google Earth to identify houses with swimming pools that hadn't been reported for use in calculating property tax bills. It turned out there were 16,974 suburban homes with swimming pools, not the 324 that had been reported. Tax investigators also wandered the parking lots of Greek nightclubs writing down the registration numbers of luxury cars. They found about six thousand people who drove cars worth more than €100,000 yet had reported implausibly low annual incomes of under €10,000.

But going after affluent tax cheats was the easy part. Even among members of the troika, there was a recognition that Papandreou faced a difficult political task. "Greece has a road ahead, but it is not the autobahn," said a senior European official involved with the troika in June 2011.

Privatization held a special appeal for the troika because it could address many of Greece's problems at once. Should the government comply with demands that it, for example, sell off its majority stakes in the monopoly electrical utility, or the ports of Piraeus and Thessaloniki, two of the busiest in the Mediterranean, it could immediately generate revenue that would help it repay its debts. The action would also help end a cycle of patronage that had kept Greek wages artificially high—politicians maintaining high pay and lavish benefits at state-owned companies in order to secure their workers' votes. That would help Greece's wages become more competitive and improve its longer-run economic prospects. Thus privatization could help achieve Trichet's long-sought goal of cutting Greece's unit labor costs—even more so if the new private owners found ways to make workers more productive. In that case, wages wouldn't need to come down quite as much to make Greece competitive with the rest of Europe.

One irony was that a socialist government was being forced to desocialize the Greek economy. Many of Papandreou's own party members were threatening to defect rather than vote for privatizations that seemed to violate their convictions. The prime minister offered to step down if the opposition center-right party, New Democracy, would agree to form a coalition "unity" government with his Panhellenic Socialist Movement, or PASOK. But New Democracy saw too much political advantage in letting Papandreou twist in the wind and forcing his fellow party members to take a series of wildly unpopular votes for austerity.

"To this demonstrably mistaken recipe I will not agree," its leader, Antonis Samaras, said on May 24, after meeting with Papandreou and declining to cooperate with the plan his government was developing to assuage the troika. The far left was even less cooperative. "I didn't come to discuss the looting of Greek society with Mr. Papandreou. I came to tell him that he must not . . . go ahead with this crime against the Greek people," said Alexis Tsipras, head of the coalition of communist parties.

Papandreou was on his own to try to ram privatization through parliament, so he offered his party a stark choice: Implement the troika-ordered austerity measures or dump me as your leader. He called for a confidence vote, and on June 17 shook up his cabinet, bringing in his old rival Evangelos Venizelos as his new finance minister. Venizelos may not have had the economic expertise of his predecessor, George Papaconstantinou, with his PhD from the London School of Economics, but he was the more experienced politician, a savvy tactician who had led the country's preparations for the 2004 Olympic Games.

Just two days later, Venizelos was dispatched to Luxembourg for a meeting of European finance ministers. French finance minister Christine Lagarde was on track to become Strauss-Kahn's permanent successor at the IMF, but in the meantime, Lipsky took a hard line and stuck to it. Over seven hours of talks that lasted until 2 a.m., he insisted that before releasing the next €12 billion in IMF funds to Greece, he required two things: that the Greek government pass its austerity measures, which Venizelos vowed was imminent, and that the rest of Europe pledge to support Greece's cash needs for a year to come. Lipsky was demanding that the IMF not be left high and dry—and threatening to withhold its resources if he couldn't get assurances it wouldn't be. "We will all require assurances that the program is financed, and that involves assurances from our

Eurogroup partners that adequate finance is available," Lipsky told reporters that night. "That needs to be done before we can move forward and we are hopeful that those conditions will be met with alacrity."

On June 22, Papandreou was able to twist enough arms among members of his party to win his confidence vote. Seven days later, with a narrow 155-vote majority in the three-hundred-seat parliament, Papandreou and Venizelos brought before the reluctant legislature two bills: €50 billion in privatization and €28 billion in budget cuts. Hanging over them was an explicit threat of default. If they were rejected, the troika would withhold its next disbursement and the Greek government would find itself unable to pay its bills. The measures passed—and Papandreou promptly expelled from his party the one PASOK member of parliament who'd voted against them.

In Syntagma Square, immediately outside parliament, thousands of demonstrators assembled. Most were peaceful, but some groups set fire to the finance ministry and threw rocks and Molotov cocktails toward riot-gear-clad police. In response, police flung flash bombs and tear gas canisters into the crowd. Across Athens, ninety-nine people ended up in the hospital as a result of the demonstrations.

Greece had enough money to pay its bills for another day, but a very long and hot summer had only begun.

Once in a while, a country will unilaterally default on what it owes—as Russia did in 1998, when an IMF-backed bailout failed to restore global investors' confidence in the debt-laden nation's government bonds. But more commonly, when a country can't afford its debts, a lengthy series of negotiations with its creditors takes place. Lenders, of course, prefer to be paid every penny of what they're owed, on the terms under which they originally made the loans. But failing that, they want to have a seat at the table to negotiate an orderly restructuring of the debt, not simply to be told how much of their money they'll be getting back and on what terms. For the country involved, the process helps ensure that it will be able to borrow money in the future. For the lenders, it provides a deal that's more favorable to them than if the borrower had just stopped making loan repayments.

In Greece in the spring of 2011, public debt was pushing 160 percent of

GDP. Was this something that could be borne even in the best of circumstances, let alone amid a shrinking economy? International bankers with exposure to Greece were increasingly concluding that they would ultimately have no choice but to accept a debt restructuring, voluntarily accepting losses in exchange for those losses being arrived at as part of an orderly dialogue. Greece, they were concluding, was functionally bankrupt, burdened by debts that it would never be able to repay—and it was time to acknowledge that fact, even if some of the European authorities didn't want to.

The euphemism of choice was "private-sector involvement," which since the early 1980s has meant calling in the Institute of International Finance, or IIF, a Washington-based organization founded by global bankers to represent them in exactly this type of high-stakes negotiation. Soon, another three initials would be joining the IMF, the ECB, and the EU in determining Greece's economic future.

IIF managing director Charles Dallara, a former U.S. Treasury official and J.P. Morgan banker, learned at a gathering of fifty or sixty representatives of his group's members that they were ready to accept some kind of restructuring plan. He called George Papaconstantinou, then Trichet. The ECB president chose his words carefully in speaking to Dallara, whom he had faced across the negotiating table a generation earlier when he worked on issues around restructuring Latin American debt and Trichet was president of the Paris Club. "I respect that your mind is shifting," Trichet said to Dallara, or words to that effect. "But I don't believe this is the way forward and I don't wish to be engaged with you on this matter."

Trichet was as emphatic in public as he was in private: "We are not in favor of restructuring and haircuts," he said in his June 2011 press conference. "We exclude all concepts that are not purely voluntary or that have any element of compulsion. We call for the avoidance of any credit events and selective defaults or default. This is our position, which we have made clear for a long period of time." His reasoning was rooted in fears that a restructuring could destabilize other European nations and set a dangerous precedent. He was ever thinking about the effects of Greek haircuts not just on Greece but on the other finanancially precarious European states, and on the future of the European experiment as a whole.

He also likely had concerns about how private-sector involvement might affect the ECB itself. For one thing, banks in Greece were being kept alive by their ability to pledge the nation's bonds as collateral to the ECB and receive euros in return. If Greek bonds were restructured, the ECB would either have to suffer losses or cut off the banks and allow them to collapse—or both. And it was lost on no one that the ECB, through its bond purchases, was a major owner of Greek debt—€45 to €50 billion worth, according to analyst estimates. That too could mean losses for the ECB in a Greek restructuring, unless the ECB's holdings were given special treatment.

If there were Greek haircuts, in other words, the ECB stood to lose money. If the losses were great enough, the bank could even need to return to the continent's governments to recapitalize. And the minute the ECB needed to raise more capital, the politicians of Europe would have power over what had been an independent central bank—a dangerous thing for central bankers who prize their autonomy. Trichet himself never articulated this set of worries in public, always casting his arguments against private-sector involvement in terms of overall financial stability. Even people close to him don't recall him making the independence case in private. But it helps explain why the ECB was more opposed to any kind of debt reductions than other participants in the talks, including both the IMF and the private bondholders themselves.

Within the IMF, Strauss-Kahn and then Lipsky were generally okay with the ECB view that there need not be debt restructuring. But their staffers weren't so sure. A long-held principle of IMF lending is that it should occur only as part of a sustainable package for the country involved—that is, only when the fund has every reason to believe it will be paid back and the country can come out the other side with a reasonable level of debt at a manageable interest rate. When that's not the case, the IMF is happy to advocate for creditors taking losses. That bondholder losses would likely have bigger consequences for the global financial system if they happened within the eurozone than outside of it was a big complication, but there was a sound logic behind the underlying idea: If a country is broke, better to face up to it rather than send good money after bad.

That's exactly the conclusion IMF officials on the ground in Greece were beginning to reach. The IMF acknowledged the ECB argument that "a sovereign default or disorderly bank failures could send shockwaves through Europe's financial sector and liquidity could well dry up again, with potentially strong and negative global spillovers," according to a July staff report. But while the other two members of the troika believed such negative ripple effects would happen only after a default, the IMF "saw serious risks of contagion, even under a strategy which tries to avoid default."

By the start of the summer of 2011, it was clear that Trichet's passionate opposition was for naught. Where the ECB president saw questions of system-wide risk and moral hazard, just about everyone else saw a math problem with no other solution. That didn't, however, include the Greek government, which had to that point considered any talk of debt restructuring as tantamount to treason. "Any talk of restructuring was a total taboo," an anonymous Greek official told the *New York Times*. "We never even brought it up. If we made this case to Europe, we would have been pariahs forever."

In late June, Dallara traveled to Athens to meet with Papandreou and Venizelos. When he explained that a restructuring seemed inescapable, Dallara later recalled, "There was shock and surprise on their faces. They could not believe it."

The time had come for creditors to cooperate, to work out a voluntary restructuring of Greece's debts as part of the next round of aid to the country. The evening of July 20, Trichet flew from Frankfurt to Berlin to hammer out the outlines of a deal with German chancellor Angela Merkel and French president Nicolas Sarkozy. They agreed that the ECB wouldn't stand in the way of haircuts for bondholders so long as they were voluntary, the central bank received guarantees to guard it against losses, and there would be public assurances that Greece was a unique case and debt restructuring wouldn't happen with other eurozone countries. At about 1 a.m., Trichet, Merkel, and Sarkozy called Brussels with news of the agreement. Then talks between bankers and finance ministers proceeded, in a conference space that became known as the "banker war room."

There, inside the European Council headquarters, a team headed up by Dallara and Josef Ackermann, the chief executive of Deutsche Bank and the chairman of the IIF, led a negotiation that was complex even by the standards of the eurozone. It pitted the European government (which wanted bondholders to take as large a loss as possible) against the banks (which, naturally, wanted to take as small a loss as possible—and had the upper hand, in the sense that they could always walk away from a voluntary agreement). It pitted the countries whose banks had more Greek exposure (like Germany, which wanted the banks to get new, safer bonds to help offset the losses from Greece) against those with less (who preferred that the banks just take their losses outright). And it pitted the ECB against everybody.

In effect, each negotiator was fighting for the other guys to endure more of the burden of restructuring Greek debt. Ironically, the one actor without a major role was Venizelos. By this point, Greece was hardly a shaper of its own destiny.

The agreement that emerged from all that wrangling, announced July 21, 2011, extended the maturities and lowered the interest rates of Greek bonds, giving the government more time to pay back less money, and eliminated some obligations entirely. Overall, the arrangement would save Greece €135 billion through 2020, lengthening the average maturity of its bonds from six to eleven years and reducing what it owed in "net present value" terms by 21 percent. The ECB, meanwhile, would receive both the protection from losses and the public assurance that Trichet had demanded. The IIF was confident that 90 percent of bondholders would accept the deal, preventing the damage to the European financial system that might have resulted had a eurozone member defaulted on its own.

"With this offer, the global investor community is stepping forward in recognition of the unique challenges facing Greece," Dallara said in a statement announcing the deal. True enough—but the global investor community also didn't have any better options.

Following the dramatics over Greece in June and July, markets were jittery. One recurring feature of the eurozone crisis was that authorities seemed to make decisions based on the dilemma immediately in front of them—Greece, say—with seemingly little concern for how their actions would change the behavior of markets with regard to the other GIPSI countries. What seemed like the right thing to do to address Greece might make no sense if it just led bond markets to expect the same for Ireland or Spain or Italy. Trichet was the strongest voice trying to persuade European political leaders of the importance of being sensitive to these effects, with assists at various times from Tim Geithner and Mervyn King, as well as other U.S. and British authorities and, at least until his arrest, Strauss-Kahn. But no matter how many impassioned speeches Trichet gave in some Benelux summit, or how many times his warnings were proved by events, he seemed not to get through.

Indeed, after haircuts were finally negotiated for Greek bondholders, global investors began to look around to wonder what other European countries' bondholders might be stuck taking a "voluntary" loss down the road. Ireland and Portugal were already under agreements that gave them a source of emergency funding, and both countries were fulfilling their bailout obligations more reliably than Greece had, so there was little reason to think they would be cut off from the IMF/EU spigot. Logically, investors shifted their attention to the remaining GIPSIs: Spain and Italy.

If those countries went under, the risk to Europe and the world financial system would be far greater than it had been up to now. Spain and Italy together have about four times the population of Greece, Ireland, and Portugal. Whereas the earlier rescues were easily affordable by the other European countries and the IMF, the cost to rescue Spain and Italy could stretch their resources to the breaking point. The nations were simultaneously too big to fail and too big to save.

At the end of June, the Italian government could borrow money for a decade for 4.25 percent, or about 1.25 percent more than Germany could. On July 14, while the Greek haircuts were being negotiated, the Italian government held one of its regular auctions of bonds, seeking to sell €5 billion worth of five- and fifteen-year securities to pay off older ones that were coming due. But the investors who would normally buy them, in Milan and Frankfurt and London and beyond, didn't place bids in line with anything resembling the bonds' typical cost. With all the uncertainty swirling around the eurozone's future, they would buy the bonds only if they received a higher yield than usual. It was just one of many days that month on which the appetite for Italian bonds fell and their rates rose. By the early days of August, the prevailing interest rate had soared to 5.54 percent.

Italy, and to a lesser degree Spain, was seeing the exact sequence of events that had led Greece and then Ireland and then Portugal to require a rescue— except that now it wasn't at all clear whether a rescue would even be possible. According to calculations by economist and journalist Carlo Bastasin, if France and Germany had to offer backing to Italy on the same scale relative to its debt levels as they had for Greece, Portugal, and Ireland, they would increase their own debt-to-GDP ratios by 23 to 25 percentage points, suddenly putting their own creditworthiness in question. Italy, which was actually running quite small annual deficits but had accumulated a large total debt, needed to find a way out of its problems on its own, or the whole continent could be in trouble.

Making conditions worse on global markets, at the end of July and start of August the United States was in the midst of a standoff between the Obama administration and Republicans in the House of Representatives over raising the nation's debt limit. Failure to do so could have meant that the United States, whose bonds are the bedrock of the global financial system, would begin defaulting on its debt. An accord wasn't reached until July 31, only two or three days from potential suspension of debt payments. On August 5, Standard & Poor's downgraded the U.S. government's credit rating from AAA to AA+, citing political gamesmanship in the wealthiest nation on the planet.

Trichet, speaking with Tim Geithner, said at one point that "this is two thirds our fault and one third your fault." All global markets were moving together. On days when investors could see no end to the megacrisis, they sold off U.S. and European stocks, Spanish and Italian bonds, and futures in oil and other commodities. On days when they believed that global policymakers were starting to get their arms around the problem, they bought those assets and sold off what were considered safer but lower-yielding investments: German and U.S. government debt and currencies like the Japanese yen and the Swiss franc.

Trichet's gambit of ending bond buying and hiking interest rates to force European leaders to act had worked. But suddenly, the very scenario that eurozone crisis fighters had spent two years trying to avoid was starting to materialize, with the panic pivoting to the major economies of Europe and seemingly at risk of getting beyond the capacity of policymakers to solve. The ECB president had just three more months in office, and the whole thing was threatening to spiral out of control. It was time for more decisive action. The alternative—sitting and waiting—seemed to risk the whole European experiment's unraveling, a risk that Trichet could not abide.

At its meeting on Thursday, August 4, the Governing Council decided to reactivate its old Securities Markets Programme, which had been dormant since the spring, and once again go into the market and buy bonds directly.

Trichet played it cagey. In his press conference that afternoon, when Brian Blackstone of the *Wall Street Journal* asked if the bank would resume buying bonds, Trichet replied, "You will see what happens. I would not be surprised if, before the end of this press conference, you would see something in the market. Don't exclude that." Another reporter, apparently having received an e-mail from a colleague or a source, asked, "Mr. Trichet, traders are telling us at the moment that the ECB is on the market for Southern European bonds. Can you confirm or comment on that action?" The president replied, with a bit of a grin, "I commented in advance it seems to me. Thank you very much indeed."

Next question, please.

The markets tanked that day. The ECB, it turned out, had only resumed purchases of Irish and Portuguese bonds, not expanded its program to Italy and Spain. It was an action that didn't seem commensurate with the size of the problem, and the coyness out of Frankfurt had sent a puzzling message. Was Trichet really prepared to do whatever it took to stop the panic enveloping Europe? And if he was, what would he demand in return?

The pressure was on Trichet from all sides. Merkel, Sarkozy, and other European political leaders wanted the ECB to come into the market on a grander scale to ease the pressure on Italy and Spain before it was too late. So did the Americans and the British and Christine Lagarde at the IMF. All argued the case for bond buying privately and delicately, given the tradition that the central bank must make its decisions independently and free of political influence. On the other side were German members of the Governing Council—Jürgen Stark of the ECB Executive Board and Jens Weidmann, who had replaced Axel Weber as head of the Bundesbank—as well as some like-minded leaders of other national central banks. The old debate from May 2010, of principle versus pragmatism, of whether to violate the spirit of the Maastricht Treaty by buying bonds in order to save the eurozone, was back.

There may not have been the resources or the will to put in place a full-scale troika bailout program for the third and fourth largest eurozone economies. But Trichet, the seasoned fighter of economic crises, saw the need to get ahead of the problem—just as much as Trichet the wily strategist of European unity saw the need to attach strings to any promises of help. The day after the Governing Council meeting, August 5, Trichet sent secret letters to the prime ministers of Italy and Spain spelling out what they needed to do to regain the confidence of markets, with the none too subtle implication that if they agreed to the plan described, the ECB would come in and buy bonds to ease the market pressure on them. The Italian letter, addressed to Prime Minister Silvio Berlusconi and signed by Trichet and Mario Draghi in the latter's capacity as head of the Banca d'Italia, laid out in 720 words of English the entire policy agenda that the ECB expected Berlusconi to carry out as the price of receiving the central bank's help. It all boiled down to making the sclerotic Italian labor market better able to adjust to economic realities.

"The full liberalisation of local public services and of professional services is needed," the letter said—and that included "large-scale privatizations." It also demanded "further reform [of] the collective wage bargaining system" that would allow employers to tailor wages and jobs to their needs more easily, as well as changes to the rules on hiring and firing of workers that would allow Italy to achieve smoother "reallocation of resources towards the more competitive firms and sectors." Other demands included laws to enforce deficit reduction plans. It was all to be ratified by the Italian parliament by the end of September. "We trust that the Government will take all the appropriate actions," wrote Trichet and Draghi.

The letter was received with anger by Berlusconi's government. Officials viewed it as one more volley in the long battle between the technocrats who kept the country running and elected leaders. Berlusconi's allies saw the Banca d'Italia as a left-wing, pro-union organization and the letter as primarily written by Draghi. It was an odd reading of the situation, given that much of what the letter demanded was anathema to Italian unions. Central-bank sources say the letter was drafted by Trichet and the ECB, with Draghi and the Banca d'Italia suggesting only modest changes; when they needed help most, Berlusconi's government was grumbling over the details.

The contempt with which Berlusconi's government held its marching orders from the central bankers would have lasting consequences, but the prime minister and Finance Minister Giulio Tremonti saw little choice but to acquiesce. Berlusconi called a press conference and pledged to accelerate deficit reduction and institute other changes to make Italy more competitive. It lifted global markets nicely.

The press conference was a public acceptance of the terms spelled out in the secret letter. Trichet also received private assurances from the Italian government, though given Berlusconi's track record of bombast and unreliability, they didn't count for much in the eyes of ECB officials. "There was private communication, but what counted was what was said publicly," said one senior official who was involved with the confidential communiqué. "You can trust only the public commitment."

It was about six weeks before a Milan newspaper, *Corriere della Sera*, got hold of the Italian letter. The text of the message from Trichet and Banco de España governor Miguel Angel Fernandez Ordóñez to Prime Minister José Luis Zapatero never even leaked. Spain, it seemed, was ready to accept its lot. The deeply unpopular Zapatero had already acknowledged that his Spanish Socialist Workers' Party was done for if he remained at its head and had called for early elections, saying he would step down. Unlike Berlusconi, ever attuned to his own political survival, Zapatero agreed to the ECB recommendations without protest.

With both Italy and Spain having accepted Trichet's conditions, the Governing Council met again on the afternoon of Sunday, August 7. The six members of the Executive Board gathered in Trichet's office on the thirty-fifth floor of the Eurotower in Frankfurt. Others dialed in from their respective capitals or whatever vacation retreats they had made their way to in the three days since their last meeting. Trichet marshaled his arguments: that they had to act to keep the situation from spiraling out of control, that they were merely ensuring their ability to guide monetary policy by keeping different countries' interest rates from getting too far out of whack, that he had pledges from Spain and Italy to undertake reforms and from France and Germany to ramp up the European Financial Stability Facility more quickly. Merkel and Sarkozy put out a joint statement as the ECB was meeting, pledging their commitment to finish setting up a structure for the EFSF so that, they strongly implied, it could take over bond-buying responsibilities from the central bank.

The skeptics on the Governing Council weren't having it. They just saw the ECB abandoning principle yet again and putting its resources at risk to help profligate countries. Jürgen Stark was the most vocal dissenter. He had been even more staunchly opposed to the bond purchases of a year earlier than his fellow German Axel Weber, but he had been more discreet publicly, never making his disagreement known to the world. But Stark was furious that the ECB was set to double down on what he saw as a mistake. He viewed the letters to the Spanish and Italian governments as the ECB going far beyond its mandate, inappropriately setting up the central bank as a European version of the IMF and violating all norms of democratic legitimacy and central-bank independence. After all, if buying Italian and Spanish bonds is monetary policy, then it should be carried out regardless of what those governments did or didn't agree to. If it's fiscal policy, then it isn't the job of the ECB and should be undertaken by the European Commission and the IMF. Stark was vocal and direct, and while he didn't threaten to go public with his objections the way Weber had, some fellow Governing Council members thought it unlikely that Stark would stay at the ECB much longer if he lost on this issue.

After about four hours of deliberation, Trichet held the vote. Stark, Bundesbank president Weidmann, and the heads of the central banks of the Netherlands and Luxembourg held fast—and were soundly outvoted. The next morning, the ECB for the first time started buying up Italian and Spanish bonds. It was enough to push the nations' borrowing costs down by 0.8 and 0.9 percentage points, respectively.

At first, Italy seemed to live up to the budget-cutting and liberalization policies it had agreed to as part of the implicit deal to get bond market relief from the ECB. On August 12, Berlusconi's cabinet agreed to €45 billion in budget cuts that put it on track for a balanced budget by 2013. The package included higher taxes on the affluent, with a 5 percent income tax surcharge on those making more than €90,000 a year, and called for municipalities to cut back on local government expenses. With typical grandiosity, Berlusconi that day blamed Italy's dire financial situation on its earlier participation in the Greek bailout. "Our hearts pour with blood if we think that our point of pride was that we had not put our hands in the pockets of Italians," the prime minister said. "But the global situation has changed and we are facing a planetary challenge."

Soon, Italian tax collectors, stealing a strategy from the Greeks, were noting the registration numbers of Ferraris and Maseratis and checking to see if their owners claimed an implausibly low annual income. "Here's the real problem with Italy," a member of the Italian parliament told the *Washington Post*. "You have people with villas and back yards the size of a park still declaring 15,000 euros a year."

But just three weeks later, Berlusconi backed off under pressure from

members of parliament, dropping the tax surcharge on those making €90,000.
But the ECB wasn't without power as the Italian government seemed to be losing resolve. The yield on ten-year Italian debt reached a low of 4.32 percent in
mid-August, as the ECB bought a total of €22 billion in bonds its first week in
the market and €14 billion the second. But as word that Berlusconi was balking
made its way from Rome, Trichet throttled back on bond purchases. The third
week, the central bank bought only €5 billion in bonds, almost all certainly
Spanish issues rather than Italian. Italian ten-year bond yields rose to 4.92 percent in early September. It was a strange game in which traders in Frankfurt
were using their purchases to reward the Berlusconi government when it behaved and punish it when it didn't. Monsieur Trichet giveth, and Monsieur
Trichet taketh away.

"Who do I call if I want to call Europe?" That line, frequently attributed to
Henry Kissinger (though he doesn't think he said it), reflects the frustration of
American and other global officials over having no single point of contact in
Western Europe, no one person who can act with authority and decisiveness on
behalf of a continent with dozens of countries and languages. But by August
2011, that had changed. There *was* a centralized authority in Europe—a man
with a French accent who worked in Frankfurt, who used his bottomless supply
of euros to direct the actions of prime ministers and parliaments across the
continent. As one analyst said to Bloomberg News that month, "Trichet has
become the de facto president of Europe."

But as would soon become all too clear, there are limits on what even a
president can do.

September and October 2011 were unproductive months for European
unity. Berlusconi, amid his gamesmanship with the ECB and the looming possibility of indictment for corruption, was a joke. The Spanish government was
in flux in the run-up to elections. Markets swung wildly in response to the latest rumor or announcement.

Jürgen Stark, after he had lost the argument over new ECB bond purchases in early August, had begun quietly laying the groundwork for his exit. To
avoid roiling markets, he wanted to ensure that Merkel and the German government had time to line up a replacement on the Executive Board. Technically,
there was no seat officially reserved for Germany, but it was unthinkable that
the six-member board could have no representative from the continent's largest

economy. Stark announced his resignation on September 9. Although the ECB's official statement said he was leaving "for personal reasons," anyone close to Stark knew that those personal reasons were that he thought the ECB's massive purchases of Italian and Spanish bonds were feckless and violated the central bank's rules.

The markets went into a yet another tailspin that day amid fears of a divided ECB. "It's a very bad sign," said an analyst quoted by the *International Herald Tribune*. "It means that the split within the E.C.B. that we thought was far down the road is here now." But the commentary that day missed the real lesson of Stark's resignation. It was quickly leaked that Merkel sought to replace Stark with a close aide of hers, German finance ministry official Jörg Asmussen. Earlier in the year, she had picked Jens Weidmann, another close adviser, to replace Axel Weber as Bundesbank chief. What the two choices had in common was that they didn't represent the hard-line, by-the-book approach traditionally favored by the Bundesbank.

Merkel could have chosen for either job a Bundesbank insider, like Andreas Dombret, its financial stability chief, or any of several hard-money German academics. Instead, she went with economic experts of a more political bent, those who might be expected to show greater flexibility about doing whatever was needed to preserve the eurozone—in the process relieving some of the pressure on Merkel and the German government to shoulder the burden of rescuing Europe. (Weidmann ended up hewing more to the traditional Bundesbank view of things once in office, opposing a reopening of the ECB's bond-purchasing program. But ex-ante he had seemed more inclined to support bailout actions than Weber had been.) Stark's departure was indeed a reflection of a divide within the ECB. But his exit meant the divide was becoming less severe, not more.

The ECB's bond purchases had been buying time, but the governments of Europe still needed to create some lasting, secure structure through which they could stand ready to assist one another. The French remained inclined toward "eurobonds," by which debt would be issued by and guaranteed by the eurozone nations collectively, much as U.S. government debt is guaranteed not just by California or New York but the nation as a whole. That was attractive to the countries facing trouble, but it was viewed unfavorably by Germany and the other creditor nations, which didn't want to be formally put on the hook for the perceived profligacy of the debtors. They would begin to consider such an arrangement only if the nations of Europe gave up a great deal of power over their tax and spending policies to centralized authorities in Brussels.

But that, of course, would mean asking European nations to cede much of what makes them sovereign. And it would even have violated a September 7 ruling of the German Constitutional Court, which often circumscribed Merkel's maneuvering during negotiations over a permanent European stability mechanism. On this occasion, it said that the German government couldn't hand over its power to a central European authority without a treaty governing the arrangement.

There were other, more exotic possibilities floated, such as giving the European Financial Stability Facility a banking license, allowing it to issue bonds on its own and use its resources to buy up European countries' debt as necessary. Trichet hated this idea because it would mean giving the fund access to the ECB's lender-of-last-resort programs, essentially using ECB resources to support individual governments. Tim Geithner argued that the Europeans needed to find a way to place the potentially massive resources of the ECB behind its government rescue fund, much as the Americans had combined the resources of the Treasury and Fed in their rescue of the financial system in 2008. That too struck Trichet as a violation of the spirit of the Maastricht Treaty.

Trichet had bought the political leaders time to develop a new model for European integration—and the political leaders were squandering it.

The Alte Oper, Frankfurt's historic opera house, was built in 1880, leveled by Allied bombs during World War II, and rebuilt in the decades that followed, thanks largely to the tireless exertions of a group of civic-minded local residents. DEM WAHREN SCHOENEN GUTEN, the inscription on the reconstructed neo-Renaissance façade reads: "To the true, the beautiful, the good."

On October 19, 2011, this monument to grand ideals once again became the locus of a European preservation effort. The event that night was meant to be a celebration—an evening to honor Jean-Claude Trichet, now less than two weeks from his retirement from the ECB, for his four decades of dedication to the European idea. But as it turned out, a few of the officials who'd gathered to toast Trichet would spend much of the night not in the Oper's mahogany-paneled Great Hall enjoying the scheduled entertainment, but in an out-of-the-way meeting room trying to hash out the European Financial Stability Facility.

Some eighteen hundred people filed into the opera house that Wednesday evening. One after another, the titans of European integration took the stage, the flags of the European Union behind them: former French president Valéry Giscard d'Estaing, former German chancellor Helmut Schmidt, the presidents of the EU's other major institutions—Herman Van Rompuy of the European Council, José Manuel Barroso of the European Commission, Jean-Claude Juncker of the Eurogroup. Angela Merkel spoke. So did Mario Draghi, soon to be Trichet's successor.

But it was Schmidt, who'd been among the key architects of the euro, whose speech was the most memorable. "The Executive Board of the ECB, led by Trichet, is the only body that has proved itself to be capable of action and effective during the financial and sovereign-debt crisis," raged the ninety-two-year-old former chancellor from his wheelchair. "All the talk of a so-called 'euro crisis' is thus just the idle chatter of politicians and journalists. What we have, in fact, is a crisis of the ability of the European Union's political bodies to act. This glaring weakness of action is a much greater threat to the future of Europe than the excessive debt levels of individual euro area countries."

Trichet then took the lectern, looking as if he'd aged more in one year than in the previous decade. His speech, delivered with his usual self-confidence but more than his usual emotion, evoked the distant past. "The single currency is an ancient idea, which has deep roots in history," he said, invoking the Roman Empire and a fifteenth-century Bohemian king who called for a common European currency. "The major weakness of the Economic and Monetary Union lies in its insufficient governance of the economic union, while the monetary union has delivered according to expectations. The need to strengthen economic governance is the first lesson from the crisis. . . . I have continuously called for a 'quantum leap' in governance."

After the speeches were done and Trichet had basked for a bit in the thunderous applause, he and several of those who'd toasted him retreated to a side room to try to figure out what form that "quantum leap" might take.

Christine Lagarde of the IMF was present. So was Nicolas Sarkozy, who had left the side of his wife, who was in the hospital giving birth, to fly in at the last minute. He had tried to sneak in through a side entrance, but it is exceptionally difficult for the president of France to show up at an event well attended by journalists and not be noticed. The most powerful actors on the European stage were in one room, and the clock was ticking: In four days, they were scheduled to attend what was supposed to be their last debt-crisis summit, the one that would resolve their differences for good.

They called themselves the Groupe de Francfort, and they would even have special badges identifying them as such at an international economic gathering a few weeks later. Sarkozy argued for giving the European Financial Stability Facility a bank charter—and was smacked down by Merkel and Trichet. A complicated plan to use IMF funds was similarly rejected.

The arguing between Sarkozy and Trichet became so intense that they often lapsed into their native French rather than the English that was the primary language of such meetings. The two men had often clashed over what Sarkozy viewed as Trichet's excessively doctrinaire view of monetary policy, and the French president's absence from the speech-giving earlier was no coincidence. There were some minor things they could agree on. But the major question, of how the Frankfurt Group might finally take the quantum leap of integration Trichet had demanded, hung in the night air with no answer.

Draghi soon slipped out to attend the concert already in progress in the Great Hall, a symphonic program cosponsored by the ECB and the Banca d'Italia that was the inaugural event in that year's monthlong "Cultural Days of the European Central Bank" celebration. Bologna's Orchestra Mozart, led by legendary conductor Claudio Abbado, would be performing compositions by its namesake, by Rossini, and by Mendelssohn. The last was represented by his Fourth Symphony, which had been inspired by a trip to Italy the German composer took in the early 1830s. In a letter sent home in 1831, he predicted that the so-called Italian symphony would be "the jolliest piece I have ever done, especially the last movement," which was modeled on exuberant Neapolitan and Roman folk dances.

As Trichet and Merkel and Sarkozy hammered at each other in their back room, no resolution to be found, the notes of Mendelssohn's finale echoed through the building, the music as jolly as the outlook for Europe was looking dismal.

# EIGHTEEN

# Escape Velocity

Rick Perry wasn't merely the governor of Texas; rather, he exuded Texas. The son of a rancher and graduate of Texas A&M University who majored in animal husbandry, he jogged with a loaded pistol, which he claimed to have used to shoot a coyote in 2010. When Perry entered the race for the U.S. presidency in August 2011, he was a popular figure in the nation's second most populous state, had a huge base of donors, and was the kind of rock-ribbed conservative that Republican Party activists had hungered for. He would eventually fade, with commentators gleefully declaring him more "Texas toast" than Texas. But he initially seemed to many astute political analysts like the man to beat for the Republican nomination.

On August 15, two days after Perry announced his candidacy, a man in a blue polo shirt at a meet-and-greet with voters in Cedar Rapids, Iowa, asked him what he thought of the United States' central bank. "Oh, uh, the Federal Reserve. I'll take a pass on the Federal Reserve right at the moment, to be real honest with you," Perry said, barely pausing as he continued, not taking a pass at all. "I know there's a lot of talk and what have you about 'em. If this guy prints more money between now and the election, I don't know what y'all would do to him in Iowa, but we, we would treat him pretty ugly down in Texas.

"I mean, printing more money to play politics at this particular time in American history, is almost treacherous, er, treasonous, in my opinion."

The crowd applauded. Ben Bernanke had steered the U.S. and world economies away from the financial abyss in 2008, preserved the Fed's political independence in 2009, and undertaken QE2 in 2010, quite possibly averting a deflationary spiral and a new recession. Now a major presidential candidate was insinuating that, for doing what central bankers do, he would be due for a whuppin' should he ever find himself in Texas.

At the time of Perry's comment, the U.S. economy was undergoing its second consecutive summer swoon. The first four months of 2011 had been a time of optimism; the nation added an average of 207,000 jobs a month. But from May to August, that average fell to less than eighty thousand. The unemployment rate was 9.1 percent. There were a variety of explanations for the bad economic numbers, including the onset of more financial strains from Europe, as well as some technical kinks in the data that likely exaggerated strength early in the year and weakness over the summer. But the simple truth is that growth seemed to be again falling below a pace that would bring unemployment down over time—and that for all of Bernanke's concerns about what he had' called "escape velocity," the Fed had in recent months done nothing new to help the U.S. economy reach it. Bond purchases under the QE2 program ended on June 30, but the Federal Open Market Committee had shown no inclination to re-open it.

The bank had already bought massive quantities of bonds and pushed short-term interest rates to almost zero. What more could it do? It was one thing to have been bold and proactive in late 2008. Three years later, during what was less a sudden panic than a lingering slump, could the Fed adopt the same kind of inventiveness?

Amid internal uncertainty about what would actually help the U.S. economy and external hostility toward the very idea of central banking, Ben Bernanke, it seemed, had a Texas-sized problem.

It was time for the Fed to look again at all available options. But there were two big differences from a year earlier, when the push toward QE2 had begun. The first was that, mainly due to a run-up in fuel costs earlier in the year, inflation was higher—3.8 percent in the twelve months that ended in August, compared with 1.2 percent in the twelve months previous to that.

The second was that Bernanke and his colleagues had experienced the aftermath of QE2, during which seemingly everyone—from conservatives in Congress to high Chinese and German officials—had attacked them for the

$600 billion in bond purchases. Central bankers, of course, aspire to do what's best for their nation's economy regardless of political attacks or other outside pressure. But in practice, their parameters of what seems wise or acceptable are almost always influenced by the world in which they're operating. And the continued hostility to easy money in the United States in 2011 meant that the world Bernanke inhabited was one opposed to more Fed easing.

There were some voices arguing for much more aggressive action from the central bank, perhaps most prominently Nobel laureate cum *New York Times* columnist Paul Krugman. But within the day-to-day political discussion, there was essentially no debate: Republicans were almost uniformly hostile to loose money policies, while Democrats didn't seem to express any opinion on them whatsoever.

At a July hearing of the Senate Banking Committee, for example, Republican senator Bob Corker—generally a Bernanke supporter—said to the chairman, "I find the activism at the Fed right now a major turnoff, and I am very concerned. And as one person who I think we've had a good relationship, I want to tell that you I'm quickly moving to a camp that wants to clip the wings of the Fed, because I do believe that the activism there is distortive of the market, and I believe that . . . something's causing you to do a lot of things that I think are going to create some long-term damage." At the same hearing, the committee's Democratic chairman, Tim Johnson, merely asked in a neutral tone whether Bernanke was considering QE3, offering no real pressure one way or the other.

Bernanke encouraged his staff to brainstorm new ways to ease policy. The blowback to QE2, in his judgment, had itself made the policy less effective. It lowered market expectations of future rounds of easing, and it may even have made businesses and consumers more wary of spending and investing: When commentators loudly complain that the central bank is being feckless and irresponsible, economic actors can hardly feel confident about the future. Fed staffers thus devoted particular effort to methods that weren't as flashy, that didn't involve announcing hundreds of billions of dollars in bond purchases.

Fed officials have always sorted their options for easing monetary policy into two groups. One set of tools could be used to adjust the size and composition of the assets on the Fed's books. QE2 was a prime example. The other is more indirect: using communication of the central bank's plans and expectations for tomorrow to try to adjust the price of money in the economy today. For example, since late 2008, the Fed had indicated that it expected to keep rates "exceptionally low" for an "extended period." This was the approach the FOMC elected when it gathered for its regularly scheduled meeting on August 9.

To nudge policy a bit more in the direction of easier money, Fed staff, in their confidential "Teal Book" of analysis and policy options, offered the possibility of expanding on that "extended period" of very low rates. Rather than promising something so vague, the FOMC could assign a specific time period to how long it expected to keep rates low. Bernanke and company decided to adjust their statement to tell the world that they expected economic conditions were "likely to warrant exceptionally low levels for the federal funds rate at least through mid-2013." It was hardly revolutionary—analysts already expected rates to stay near zero for nearly that long anyway, so a future of cheap money was already priced into borrowing costs. But it was enough to signal that things had worsened to the point that the Fed was looking for ways to ease policy. It was also enough to anger the hawks on the committee.

Richard Fisher of the Dallas Fed, Narayana Kocherlakota of the Minneapolis Fed, and Charles Plosser of the Philadelphia Fed all voted against the move. It was the first FOMC meeting with three dissenters since 1992, and Bernanke was on notice that any further easing moves would come with significant internal dissent. The action had another potential downside: It seemed to send a pessimistic signal to anyone thinking about making a longer-term investment: *We here at the Fed think that things will be SO BAD that we expect to keep interest rates at zero for two more years.* At the same time, the chairman had become a punching bag in the Republican primary race. It was almost as if other candidates wanted to catch up with Perry in their Bernanke bashing.

"I would fire him tomorrow," said Newt Gingrich in a September 7 debate. "I think he's been the most inflationary, dangerous, and power-centered chairman of the Fed in the history of the Fed. . . . And I think his policies have deepened the depression." During the FOMC's two-day meeting in late September, Republican leaders of the House and Senate even sent Bernanke a letter saying that the Fed "should resist further extraordinary interventions in the U.S. economy," an extraordinarily blatant attempt to apply political pressure to monetary policy.

But if anything, the case for extraordinary interventions was now even stronger, with economic conditions in the United States worsening as the eurozone crisis deepened. Fed staff knocked together another clever tool that would allow the bank to ease policy without all the Sturm und Drang that would come with a QE3 program. The means by which quantitative easing affects the economy is called the portfolio balance channel. When the Fed buys $600 billion in Treasury bonds, as it did in QE2, the investors who would otherwise have owned those bonds have to stuff that money into something else—corporate bonds, for example, or mortgage-backed securities or stocks. According to Fed thinking, wherever the money goes, it helps growth, either by making corporate and home mortgage borrowing cheaper or by boosting the stock market.

There was plenty of evidence that this was true—the stock market inevitably rallied after speeches or comments that suggested more bond buying was likely, for example. The success of the approach suggested an interesting possibility: If the Fed were to shift its portfolio into longer-term bonds and away from shorter-term debt, it might be able to lower long-term interest rates across the economy, encouraging business investment and mortgage borrowing. The action would have the effect of simultaneously raising short-term interest rates, but only negligibly, because the Fed had already committed to keeping them near zero. Theoretically, borrowing would be inexpensive in both the short and the long term.

It's called twisting the yield curve, and a variation had been tried at the central bank in 1961, when it was called Operation Twist, a not terribly sly reference to the dance craze of the time. The Bernanke Fed, with its culture of seriousness, called the strategy a Maturity Extension Program. But to the media, Operation Twist, with its attendant possibility of Chubby Checker-based headline puns, was an irresistible way to describe the policy. In the Fed's analysis, simply selling off $400 billion worth of bonds maturing in less than three years and buying $400 billion of bonds maturing in six to thirty years would a powerful boost for the U.S. economy—nearly as impactful as QE2 had been.

But because the Fed wasn't creating any new money by buying additional bonds—and because the typical politician didn't understand Operation Twist—the maneuver seemed less likely to draw the kind of counterproductive attacks that QE2 had. "Printing money" sounds scary. "Extending the duration of the Federal Reserve System Open Market portfolio" just sounds confusing to most people. It was, in a sense, a stealth form of quantitative easing—which was quite clear to the FOMC hawks. Richard Fisher, Narayana Kocherlakota, and Charles Plosser again dissented.

For the most part, though, public criticism was muted. Major world newspapers used the term "Operation Twist" in ninety-four different stories in the two weeks following the FOMC meeting. In the equivalent period after QE2 was announced, that term appeared in 158. Bernanke had spent his academic career arguing that central bankers, whether in the Great Depression or 1990s Japan, had the power to boost an ailing economy even in the lowest depths of a crisis. He retained that faith in his fifth year as Fed chairman—but he'd become savvier about how to use that power to get the economic benefits of easier money without suffering so many of the political costs.

I f the U.S. economy was recovering slowly from the trauma of the previous few years, the UK economy was recovering not at all. Inflation and unemployment were high, and the eurozone crisis seemed to send a new wave of panic washing over global financial markets every few months. "The euro-area crisis has had more dramatic moments, in which the ultimate resolution seems to be at hand only to be confounded by subsequent events, than there are episodes in *The Killing*," Mervyn King said in his 2012 Mansion House speech, referring to the television police drama that had originated in Denmark and become a domestic hit on BBC Four. "And the Danes aren't even members of the euro area."

Indeed, Jean-Claude Trichet and then Mario Draghi appeared at times to exert greater control over the American and British economies than Bernanke and King did. Trichet and Draghi spoke regularly with their international counterparts, in private phone calls, in Basel, and on the sidelines of their never-ending series of global summits. But except for the rare joint intervention, particularly the reopening of global swap lines at the end of November 2011, they essentially left Bernanke and King trying to do what they could to help their domestic economies and hoping for the best.

There was a feeling of impotence settling over Threadneedle Street. "It felt like every time you checked your BlackBerry," said one official, "there was another nasty headline out of Europe and not much we could do about it." Britain's decision to stay out of the eurozone a decade earlier was very much looking like the right one: Its public finances weren't so different from Spain's, and if British monetary policy were set in Frankfurt instead of London, the nation would almost certainly have been lumped in with the GIPSIs. (Where that would have left the acronym creators is anyone's guess.)

Even without the euro as its currency, Britain faced massive ripple effects from Europe's troubles. Eurozone nations accounted for almost half of UK exports, British banks had considerable exposure to the continent, and British companies' confidence was affected by the latest dispatches from across the Channel in each morning's *Financial Times*. "The fact that we're not in the euro area does not mean we're exempt from the consequences of what happens," as King put it with some understatement in 2012.

Almost too appropriately for that frustrating summer of 2011, the governor sat and watched as Spaniard Rafael Nadal defeated Scot Andy Murray in the men's singles semifinals at that most British of institutions, the All England Lawn Tennis and Croquet Club, better known as Wimbledon. King was in the royal box alongside the newly married Duke and Duchess of Cambridge, as well as others from worlds far more glamorous than that of economic policy, including actor Michael Caine and *Vogue* editor Anna Wintour. It is forbidden to use cell phones in the royal box, a fact that led the *Mail on Sunday* to speculate about whether King was out of touch during matches.

The paper went to great lengths to suggest so. It ran a 1,451-word article on the governor's Wimbledon attendance, asserting that he'd been at the tournament at least six of its thirteen days. A photo that accompanied the story online showed King with his eyes closed above the accusatory caption "FRIDAY JULY 1: Sir Mervyn snoozes during the tense men's semi-final which saw Andy Murray defeated by Rafael Nadal. It was the day on which more gloomy figures on the state of Britain's economic recovery were released."

In truth, the sharp elbows King received from the press and some of his enemies in British politics for afternoons at Wimbledon were a bit unfair. Even his detractors at the Bank of England said that King was among the hardest workers they had known, putting in long hours at night and on weekends. On the days he spent the afternoon watching tennis, he spent both mornings and evenings working on bank business.

But Britain was a nation in need of a scapegoat. The full brunt of the austerity policies King had advocated in 2010 was being felt, with economic growth near zero during the first half of 2011. At the time, analysts, including those at the Bank of England, saw some possible temporary reasons for that: commerce interruptions caused by snowstorms that winter; supply disruptions caused by the earthquake in Japan that March; a drop in productivity due to the extra vacation days taken by many Britons around the time of the royal wedding that spring. But in hindsight, those were mere excuses—the British economy was indeed stagnant.

Unemployment rose over the summer of 2011, from 7.7 percent in March to 8.3 percent in September. Yet inflation remained high—above 5 percent through the spring, due to a combination of higher fuel prices and higher import prices due to a lower value of the pound. Both effects had started to recede by summer, suggesting that inflation would eventually come down. But in 2011, that added up to stagflation, a terrible situation for Britons and an unwelcome dilemma for central bankers.

At the Bank of England, there was a divide. Two of the nine members of the Monetary Policy Committee, Martin Weale and Spencer Dale—the latter the bank's chief economist—saw inflation as the greatest threat facing Britain and voted to hike interest rates through July 2011. On the other side was Adam Posen, who believed that a decelerating economy and rising unemployment was the main risk. He had argued for a new round of quantitative easing, for Britain's own QE2, at every MPC meeting since October 2010. The majority of the committee, led by King, elected for no change.

On the face of it, such indecision may seem like a repeat of the summer of 2008: With inflation high, some on the MPC wanted to tighten policy and others wanted to ease it, with King splitting the difference by standing pat. But both people who were in frequent contact with the governor and a careful reading of his public statements reveal that despite the lack of formal changes to monetary policy, there was a major evolution in King's thinking over the summer and fall of 2011.

With each month that passed, as the leaders of continental Europe seemed ever more adrift, King's alarm increased. In June, testifying to Parliament's Treasury Select Committee, he said that "the reason we would raise interest rates would be in the context of a much stronger economy with unemployment falling rather than rising," thus effectively dismissing the idea that the bank would raise rates as joblessness rose. At the same time, he laid the groundwork for more bond buying by the Bank of England, playing down the idea that quantitative easing is some exotic form of economic sorcery. "I regard QE as a perfectly conventional monetary policy tool," King said. "This is something we can do."

Then in August, when the MPC was putting together its quarterly inflation report—the most detailed regular summary of bank leaders' views of the economic outlook—the committee took an unusual approach. With a eurozone implosion looking increasingly plausible that month, King and his colleagues judged that they couldn't properly factor what might happen into their projections. If a collapse did occur, it would surely make all their forecasts useless, just as the Lehman Brothers bankruptcy had three years earlier. So they made their forecasts for GDP, inflation, and so on as usual, assuming that there would be no great implosion in Europe—which, in any case, would be "almost impossible to calibrate." Then they added what amounted to a one-page asterisk, laying out their view that "the risks emanating from the current euro-area tensions have few obvious parallels" and therefore there would be a chance of major disruptions to the economy not reflected in their forecasts. In other words, the risks from a eurozone collapse were so grave that they had to be accounted for entirely separate from the main forecast.

"The big risks facing the UK economy come from the rest of the world," King said in his press conference on the report. "We must work with our colleagues abroad to tackle the challenge of how to reduce the overhang of private and public debt. But there is a limit to what UK monetary policy can do when large real adjustments are required. And it cannot influence inflation over the next few months. But it can ensure that policy is set in such a way that these adjustments take place against a backdrop of low and stable inflation. And that is exactly what the MPC will do."

At the committee's early September meeting, King and the other members seemed on the verge of instituting new quantitative easing, with wide consensus that the British economy was in grave danger from Europe and that inflation was dissipating. But as much as everyone seemed to be on the same page about what the Bank of England ought to do, King argued for holding off for just one more month. "The attitude seemed to be, 'I'm nervous about the outlook, but let's get one more month of data,'" said a person with knowledge of the deliberations. The financial markets had been so chaotic in August that King wondered whether they might soon render new easing unnecessary. "We were very conscious that there had been significant news in August, particularly in financial markets," King said later, "and it could have been that that was volatility that might reverse itself over the next month. I do not think we felt that the underlying position would improve but there was a possibility that the volatility would dampen down. Basically, we were in a position in September where, if nothing else changed over the following month, we would then implement further asset purchases."

Sure enough, October arrived with no abrupt improvement in financial markets, and the MPC unanimously agreed to buy £75 billion in UK government bonds, or gilts—"shock and awe," as the *Daily Telegraph* put it. It was the equivalent, relative to the size of the respective economies, of the Fed buying $750 billion in bonds; in other words, in relative terms, Britain's QE2 was 25 percent bigger than the United States'. In the months before, even Posen, the most persistent dove on the committee, had been advocating for only £50 billion in bond purchases. But King's strategy—of waiting until there was definitive evidence of a crumbling economy and weaker inflation, then building his case incrementally—meant that even aggressive action was viewed as more acceptable, both inside and outside the bank.

King portrayed the action publicly as a simple response to events. "The world economy has slowed, America has slowed, China has slowed, and of course particularly the European economy has slowed," he told reporters. "The world has changed and so has the right policy response."

B en Bernanke had done the twist in September 2011. Mervyn King had fired up the printing presses in October. Both had carefully laid the groundwork for their moves and thus been able to boost their nations' economies without jarring the markets or hurting their central banks' political standing. In the world of zero-interest-rate policy in which the Fed and the Bank of England were now living, Bernanke and King both had to weigh the costs and benefits of easing more carefully than they would have if there'd been room to simply cut short-term interest rates. And in the fall of 2011, as the Anglo-Saxon economies continued muddling along with no real rebound evident, some began to believe that they were both moving too cautiously—that for all their apparent activism, they were in fact becoming the Masaru Hayamis of the twenty-first century.

These critics, some of them inside the central banks, began dreaming big, imagining ways that the central bankers might encourage their economies to do something better than merely extending the duration of the Fed's portfolio or buying another £75 billion of gilts. Charles Evans, the president of the Federal Reserve Bank of Chicago, who was rapidly becoming the Adam Posen of the United States, took to a stage in London that September to make a case for more aggressive action. "Suppose we faced a very different economic environment," Evans told the European Economics and Financial Centre. "Imagine that inflation was running at 5 percent against our inflation objective of 2 percent. Is there a doubt that any central banker worth their salt would be reacting strongly to fight this high inflation rate? No, there isn't any doubt. They would be acting as if their hair was on fire. We should be similarly energized about improving conditions in the labor market."

The Fed had been persistently overestimating how well the U.S. economy would do over the next several months. For example, in January 2011, the official consensus of FOMC members was that the economy would grow 3.4 to 3.9 percent that year; the actual number turned out to be 2 percent. Evans, hair on fire, advocated a more systematic way of addressing the weakness: Instead of improvising new policies whenever the economy disappoints, he argued, why not lay out specific economic conditions to which the Fed would respond in specific ways. For example, in September 2011, U.S. unemployment was at 9 percent and prices, excluding those in the volatile food and energy sectors, had risen 2 percent over the year. Evans proposed that the Fed announce it would keep ultra-low-interest-rate policies in place until unemployment fell to, say, 7 percent, so long as inflation stayed below 3 percent.

The FOMC discussed this idea, and many variations, at a series of meetings. Even some of the more hawkish leaders of the central bank, like Charles Plosser of the Philadelphia Fed, found the concept attractive. After all, it would give the world a clear and predictable way to understand the Fed's policies. But they were tripped up on the details. While Evans and some of the doves on the FOMC were comfortable allowing inflation to get up to 3 percent or so, many of the other policymakers were reluctant to announce—as they would implicitly be doing—that they had decided to tolerate inflation above their 2 percent target.

Evans's idea got batted around seriously, but the closest the FOMC came into turning it into something concrete was a decision, made at its December meeting, to begin giving the public a summary of what committee members expected monetary policy to be in the future—how many anticipated the first interest rate hikes to take place in 2014 versus 2015 and so on. It was a mere baby step toward offering more clarity for what policy might be in the future.

In his September speech, Evans also mentioned a related idea, one that had advocates outside the Fed, including the economics research group at Goldman Sachs and Berkeley economist and former Barack Obama adviser Christina Romer. In 2011, about $1 trillion fewer goods and services were produced within U.S. borders than would have been the case if the precrisis growth trajectory had held. That was the "output gap" between what the economy seemed capable of producing and what it was actually producing. Why not set an explicit goal of returning GDP to that precrisis path, pledging to keep easy-money policies in place until the nation got there, even at risk of inflation above the normal 2 percent target.

Nominal GDP targeting, as its advocates called the approach, would essentially be a pledge from the central bank to keep the pedal to the floor to try to accelerate the economy until the effects of the crisis wore off. Romer compared the proposal to what Paul Volcker had done in 1979 when he persuaded the FOMC to remake its entire framework for monetary policy, to focus on constricting the money supply to address inflation. "Desperate times call for bold measures," she wrote in the *New York Times*. "Paul Volcker understood this in 1979. Franklin D. Roosevelt understood it in 1933. This is Ben Bernanke's moment. He needs to seize it."

By the time she wrote that, Bernanke had already assigned Fed economists to do an extensive study of how nominal GDP targeting might work, using computer models to examine its potential benefits and pitfalls. The FOMC listened to a detailed staff presentation and discussed the idea at length on the first day of its November 1–2 meeting. In theory, the idea had promise, the staff models suggested. But there were also great weaknesses to the approach. For instance, it would work only if the Fed could credibly deliver on its pledge over a very long time, perhaps ten or fifteen years. If people making economic decisions such as hiring and investing had doubts that the central bank would follow through—and remember that each Fed chairman's term is only four years—nominal GDP targeting wouldn't work.

And following the policy would mean that if growth remained slow, the Fed would not simply accept high inflation, but practically promise it. If, for example, the nominal GDP target were 5 percent and growth only 1 percent, the Fed would aim to set policy to get 4 percent inflation. That would likely mean a world in which financial markets were reacting badly, long-term interest rates were rising to reflect inflation risk, and ordinary Americans were unhappy about rapidly rising prices for gasoline and other goods.

The discussion of nominal GDP targeting and variations thereof took up hours on that November Tuesday. Some FOMC members, particularly those on the central bank's more hawkish wing, viewed it as not worth considering because they saw stable prices and low inflation as the most important goals of a central bank. They simply couldn't abide a policy that would mean tolerating higher inflation. Others had a more nuanced set of views. But at the end of the discussion, not even any of the committee's more dovish members was prepared to endorse such a policy. There would be no Volckeresque sea change in the Fed's approach. Bernanke himself, when speaking privately with colleagues about the topic, would become uncharacteristically animated and strident, apparently annoyed that economists who hadn't analyzed the pros and cons of nominal GDP targeting as carefully as the Fed had would assert with such supreme confidence that it was the policy to pursue. At the same time, he was sensitive to the underlying critique of the Fed's policies—that they would work better if they could strengthen confidence that the United States would return to its precrisis path and that the Fed would not rest until that goal was achieved. The challenge was how to make that happen in a world where every move seemed to be met with attacks, where the tools that might work were risky and untested, and it would take agreement on a committee with wide-ranging views to do much of anything at all.

As 2012 dawned, Bernanke and King each pursued a strategy of continuity. In January, the Fed pushed its expected date for rate hikes to the end of 2014, from the mid-2013 date previously announced. The Bank of England, judging that inflation was falling as economic growth in Britain remained weak, returned to the well of quantitative easing in February, expanding its bond purchases by another £50 billion. The Fed undertook "Operation Twist 2" at its June meeting, swapping out another $267 billion of its shorter-term bond holdings for longer ones, on top of the $400 billion that was part of the first Twist. In July, the Bank of England tacked on *another* £50 billion in QE.

King and Bernanke turned again and again to a relatively narrow set of policies, seemingly reluctant to adopt any that might rewrite the rulebook. Only they and their deities know whether that was because they knew from analysis that more unconventional moves would fail, whether they were constrained by the committees they led, or whether they were driven by a fear of political blowback. There were bolder, riskier tools out there. But in 2012, Bernanke and King held back, hoping that Mario Draghi and company could resolve the eurozone crisis and eliminate its downward pressure on the U.S. and UK economies. If so, there might be no need for yet more risky, unproven actions.

At King's May 2012 press conference, Ed Conway of Sky News noted that the governor had been pushing European officials to respond more resolutely to their crisis for "years and years." "Is it frustrating that no one seems to be listening," Conway asked, "even when you are kind of shouting from the rooftops about this particular crisis?"

"I have," acknowledged King, who seemed almost resigned to the fact that the future of the British economy was outside his control. "I will do no more shouting. I will simply rest where I've made that point; others now have to respond."

# NINETEEN

# Super Mario World

Panagiotis Roumeliotis sat down for lunch in the cafeteria of the International Monetary Fund, a few blocks from the White House in Washington. Roumeliotis was Greece's representative to the IMF, no easy task in the final weeks of 2011. But as one of his country's elder statesmen, he was happy to do the job. His cell phone rang. On the line was George Papandreou. "We need you to come to Athens immediately," the embattled prime minister said. "We would like for you to become prime minister."

Papandreou's position had become untenable. His party, the Panhellenic Socialist Movement, held only a narrow majority in parliament and was losing confidence in a prime minister who'd overseen the nation's descent into depression. Papandreou was in talks with the opposition conservative party, New Democracy, about forming a coalition or "unity" government—to join together to select a nonpartisan technocrat to be his successor as prime minister, someone who could lead Greece through all the unpleasant reforms being demanded by international creditors, then be replaced in a new election down the road.

Roumeliotis called his wife. She was none too pleased by her husband's promotion: "There is no way you can do that! They will kill you!" she said. To Roumeliotis, though, the risk of something awful happening—and just being prime minister of a nation on the verge of economic and political collapse would be awful in its own way—was one he had to take for the sake of his troubled country. He packed his things and made it to Dulles International Airport in time for a 4 p.m. flight to Frankfurt, then on to Athens.

By the time he arrived, however, New Democracy leader Antonis Samaras had apparently changed his mind about Roumeliotis's suitability. It just wouldn't do, Samaras had decided, to have somebody associated with the much-hated IMF as prime minister—even if Roumeliotis had been there representing the Greek government, not working for the fund itself.

So Papandreou kept looking. He next called Lucas Papademos, a retired Greek economist and visiting professor of public policy at Harvard. Papademos, ironically, had until recently been a senior official of another troika member: He was vice president of the European Central Bank until 2010. But for whatever reason, the ECB didn't attract quite the populist ire that the IMF did, so Papademos was viewed as a more politically palatable choice. Two days later, Papandreou resigned and Papademos was set to try to lead his nation away from the abyss.

This strange sequence of events is emblematic of how the most consequential decisions imaginable were being made on the fly as European leaders tried to redirect their flailing crisis response at the start of November 2011. Conveniently, Papademos was already in Europe when his name was called, so he didn't have to cross the Atlantic the way Roumeliotis did. He was scheduled to appear together in a panel discussion in Frankfurt with Mario Monti, another retired wise man of Europe. Both had to cancel: On November 11, Papademos became prime minister of Greece, and on November 12, Monti was named prime minister of Italy. Jean-Claude Trichet had retired less than two weeks earlier, and Spanish prime minister José Luis Zapatero was set to fall on November 20.

The cast of characters was fast changing in Europe's crisis at a time when Europe desperately needed a fresh start. The question was, could the new team get a new result?

When Mario Draghi took over as ECB president on November 1, there was no time for ceremony. Jean-Claude Trichet moved out of the airy thirty-fifth-floor office he had occupied for eight years and Draghi moved in, without even setting up any personal effects. The day he took office was one of the ugliest on global markets in recent memory. The stock prices of European banks plummeted, with shares of French giant Société Générale falling a stunning 16 percent. Yields on Spanish and Italian debt stayed relatively contained—but only because of massive bond purchases by the ECB. As the *Guardian* put it, only somewhat unfairly, "Mario Draghi's first day at work as the head of the ECB was spent buying up unseemly quantities of his own country's debt."

The day before, Papandreou, reeling under the pressure of trying to lead an increasingly dysfunctional nation with the narrowest of majorities in parliament, had announced a bold gambit: He would hold a referendum, asking Greek voters to decide whether to accept the measures required of them as a condition of their bailout—and, implicitly, whether to keep the euro as their currency and remain in the European Union. If they voted yes, Papandreou would be newly empowered to do what had to be done. If they voted no, the country would surely default on its debt and likely spiral into economic chaos. To Papandreou, it was a way to force the issue and end the muddling through. To essentially every other European leader, it was a reckless and desperate measure. As one European diplomat put it to the *Financial Times*, it was "the political equivalent of smashing rare and expensive plates at a restaurant when one is happy. The meaning of this eludes everyone."

As the confusion generated by Papandreou's announcement spread, Draghi led his first meeting of the ECB's Governing Council on November 3. His style was different from that of his predecessor. He was less tolerant of long-winded soliloquies by council members, preferring crisp, focused debates. "The meetings are very well targeted. Rather than philosophizing about things, it's rather concise and analytical," said one person who was in meetings with both men. Trichet, of course, could turn long-windedness to his advantage, using the ticking clock to ensure he got his way; every minute one council member spent explaining his reasoning in detail was a minute that couldn't be used to push the discussion away from where Trichet wanted it to go. And Trichet started meetings by laying out his own view and preferred policy choice, putting implicit pressure on the other twenty-two participants to agree—or at least prepare to be on the defensive should they disagree.

In a change that neatly parallels the one that took place at the Federal Reserve when Ben Bernanke succeeded Alan Greenspan in 2006, Draghi reversed the sequence. He allowed his colleagues each to speak their views first. He then summed up the range of perspectives and set forth his own opinion— in this case, that there was compelling evidence that the eurozone economy was sliding into a new recession, that this would inevitably put downward pressure on prices, and that the ECB should cut interest rates to try to bolster growth on the continent.

Draghi stood before the media in the Eurotower that Thursday afternoon, as Trichet had for the ninety-six months previous, and explained that after his first monetary policy meeting as president, the ECB was cutting target interest rates by a quarter percentage point. After his second meeting, the bank did the same. The two actions reversed Trichet's rate hikes from April and July, which looked even more misguided in hindsight than they had to critics at the time. Although a range of surveys and projections pointed to Europe's being in or near a recession at the time—by this point, the economic evidence was overwhelming—it was nonetheless a bold move for Draghi. The Italian essentially cast aside any fears of looking weak on inflation to Germans who were skeptical of him because of his nationality, and he took decisive, well-reasoned action. It was an early sign of self-confident leadership from the new ECB president.

The slogan France chose for the gathering of the Group of 20 heads of state that year was *Nouveau monde, nouvelles idées:* "New world, new ideas." But as the most powerful men and women on earth descended on the south of France for the two-day summit, their agenda would be usurped by old problems in an ancient center of the Old World.

The G20 had emerged as the preeminent vehicle for coordinating global policy in the depths of the 2008 crisis, as it became clearer to the United States and the great powers of Europe that it would no longer do to discuss global problems only among themselves. The rising powers of the developing world—in particular, China, Brazil, and India—needed to have a seat at the table if world leaders were to truly address their common challenges collectively.

The core idea is indisputable. But the G20, which includes all of the world's major economic powers, as well as some smaller ones that serve as de facto representatives for a region (South Africa for sub-Saharan Africa, for example, and Saudi Arabia for the Middle East) is in reality an unwieldy, indecisive group. Once those twenty heads of state and their respective finance ministers, staffers, and translators sit down with the various other invitees—the secretary-general of the United Nations, the managing director of the IMF, and so on—the whole thing becomes a sometimes grueling exercise in diplomacy for show. The joint communiqués released at the end of the meetings charting a common course for the world tend to be as vague as possible. How could it be otherwise when they must be unanimously approved by a group of nations with such disparate interests?

The 2011 gathering in Cannes was even more grueling than most. It poured rain for almost the entirety of the summit. And some of the diplomacy, no matter how much it was undertaken for the greater global good, seemed akin to bullying, with representatives of the world's economic superpowers leaning on their counterparts from the hapless GIPSIs. Although Greece wasn't an official participant, Sarkozy, German chancellor Angela Merkel, and other members of the Groupe de Francfort summoned Papandreou to Cannes the evening before the G20 was to formally begin and gave him an ultimatum: If you insist on having a referendum, it must be on the larger question of whether Greece is to remain in the eurozone. "The referendum in essence is about nothing else but the question, does Greece want to stay in the euro zone, yes or no?" Merkel reportedly said over a dinner where, as *Der Spiegel* put it, "the food was excellent, clearly the product of a gourmet chef. But the conversation was more on the level of a street corner eatery."

Moreover, they made clear, the next €8 billion in aid wouldn't be dispensed until either the vote was in favor of remaining in the eurozone or the referendum was canceled. "We made Papandreou . . . aware of the fact that his behavior is disloyal," said Eurogroup chief Jean-Claude Juncker later. Papandreou returned to Athens the next morning and embarked on the new strategy of discussing with New Democracy's Antonis Samaras a coalition government between Greece's center-left and center-right parties, led by a technically accomplished but nonpartisan elder statesman. "Papandreou became the punching bag for everything bad in Greek society," said a senior Greek official. "He had honest intentions of navigating the country through a difficult program, but he did not have the skills to convincingly defend it, and he appeared out of touch. What happened in Cannes was humiliating for Greece and for him personally."

United States president Barack Obama was nearly as assertive as Sarkozy and Merkel, shuttling from one closed-door meeting to another at the Palais des Festivals et des Congrès, more commonly the scene of movie-star schmooz-ing than high-stakes negotiation. Obama, taking a page from the role that Tim Geithner and his international affairs undersecretary Lael Brainard had often played through the European crisis, aimed to act as a catalyst, an outside source of pressure for decisive action by eurozone authorities. The evening of November 3, the same long day on which Papandreou had reversed course on his referendum and Draghi had cut interest rates, Obama and top Europeans officials gathered to put pressure on Italian prime minister Silvio Berlusconi. They caught him by surprise, almost ganging up on him for coming to Cannes without a credible plan for getting his nation's finances under control.

What the Italian prime minister agreed to on that rainy night—IMF monitoring of his country's economic management—was technically voluntary. But it came after hours of browbeating. "It amounted to the final stage of the 'waterboarding' sessions to which Berlusconi had been treated in the last months by his partners and by the markets," Italian journalist Carlo Bastasin wrote. "The old leader, who believed himself to be the best Italian political leader ever and one of the most authoritative in the world, was not even able to reply . . . and felt like he had fallen into an ambush."

Italy was one step closer to the kind of intrusive oversight endured by Greece and the other countries where representatives of the troika were installed. And while it was technically Berlusconi's choice to accede to IMF oversight, he did so under an implicit threat: If he refused, the international community's willingness to help Italy through its times of trouble would evaporate. Berlusconi's ability to rally his parliament to his side was already waning, and his credibility with international leaders was nonexistent. Although irrelevant to his country's economic situation, his apparent leering at the backside of Argentinian president Cristina Fernández de Kirchner during an official photo shoot surely didn't help his standing among Merkel and other European leaders.

As the Cannes gathering wound down, the conventional wisdom was that it had been a disaster. While the national leaders had been driven everywhere, their staffers had to walk or take shuttles from hotels, inevitably ending up soaked anywhere their umbrellas didn't cover. It was a wet, dreary gathering at a time when the world's economic prospects looked equally dreary. There was no progress on the longer-term goals of creating a more durable world economy. But that doesn't mean there was no progress. Both Greece and Italy were set on course to bring in new leaders who would be more credible than those they replaced. More important still, at a time when European leaders had started to chafe at American and British officials repeatedly urging them to act, new voices were emerging. Over and over, the other national leaders around the table, from all points on the globe, were applying the same sort of pressure that had become old hat from Obama and British prime minister David Cameron.

The leaders of Brazil, Australia, and any number of other countries blamed Europe for their own economic weakness. Chinese head of government Hu Jintao was particularly assertive, suggesting that his nation wouldn't deploy its massive cash reserves to help Europe until the continent had a credible plan to help itself.

If Merkel, Sarkozy, and Draghi ever had any doubts that the world was waiting for them to move, they knew better now.

The following week, the talks that led to Papademos and Monti taking over from Papandreou and Berlusconi came to a head. Some reports portrayed those appointments as having been made effectively in Frankfurt, Brussels, and Berlin instead of Athens and Rome, suggesting that the ECB, the European Commission, and the German government were dictating to those countries who could lead them. It was subtler than that. Well-placed sources in Greece and Italy said that they didn't receive any specific instructions from European authorities as to who would be an acceptable prime minister. Nor did outsiders meddle in the details of the selection process. But at the same time, the party leaders negotiating over who would succeed Papandreou and Berlusconi did so knowing that the whole point was to put in place a leader who could negotiate credibly with the troika and the other European governments.

More concretely, markets were putting more pressure on Italian government leaders than Angela Merkel ever could: Ten-year borrowing costs for Italy started October at below 5 percent. By November 9, just before Berlusconi's resignation, they reached 6.56 percent. If sustained, rates that high would be enough to render the country insolvent. That spike reflected the influence of Draghi and the ECB: In the week ending November 11, the central bank bought only €3 billion in bonds, compared with €10 billion the previous week. Less ECB buying meant higher rates, which meant more pressure on members of the Italian parliament to dump Berlusconi as their leader. Draghi didn't have to tell the Italian government what to do; the ECB's decision to buy bonds, or not, did it for him.

The appointment of Monti as prime minister of the eurozone's third largest economy gave instant credibility to a country that had been less influential than its size would suggest during negotiations among European leaders, simply because Merkel and Sarkozy didn't particularly respect Berlusconi. With Monti in place, Italy was poised to join France as a counterweight to German sway over Europe. Within two weeks, there were two Italians with significant influence over the course of the eurozone crisis where before there had been none: Monti and Draghi—the Super Mario Brothers, as the press gleefully nicknamed them.

An overwhelming victory for Mariano Rajoy's center-right People's Party in Spanish elections on November 20 completed the sweep: The crisis had now brought down the prime ministers of all five GIPSI countries.

They served white wine from the Pfalz region of Germany, just west of Frankfurt, when the leading bankers of Europe came to lunch with Draghi on a Wednesday not long after he took office. As his guests sipped, they offered more than polite comments on the local viticulture—they offered the germ of a plan that could help quell the panic that had enveloped Europe and the world.

The banks those men led were the key transmission mechanism of the crisis from one country to the next, the institutions that made the difficulties of countries like Greece and Italy big problems for the likes Germany and France. The continental European banks had loaded up on government debt, and as its value fell, their financial stability came into question. Greek debt was to 2011 what subprime mortgage securities were to 2008—a once seemingly ironclad investment that turned out to be nearly worthless. And all sorts of red lights were flashing in November 2011, indicating that the European banks that owned the stuff were in trouble. They faced higher and higher borrowing costs, for example, suggesting that investors were losing confidence in the banks' ability to repay them.

A major way to assuage fears about Europe, then, would be to reassure the world that European banks weren't going to lose access to funding—that the ECB was still ready, willing, and able to serve as lender of last resort. And if the banks had greater assurance that they'd be able to fund themselves in the years ahead, the European bankers told Draghi over lunch, it could help stop the vicious cycle by which a sovereign debt crisis fueled a banking crisis.

At the same time, the leading central bankers outside of Europe were also trying to figure how to stop the never-ending crisis in the eurozone from continuing to sap global economic confidence. They had already deployed trillions of dollars and pounds in an earlier phase of the crisis and now faced new technical and legal limits on what they might do. (Bernanke and the Fed, for example, were subject to new restrictions on emergency lending under the Dodd-Frank Act.) What to do next was a topic that consumed Draghi, Bernanke, and Mervyn King, and they directed their staffs to work together to come up with possibilities. King in particular had become considerably more worried about what the eurozone's problems would mean for the domestic economy than he had been even a few months earlier. He took the lead in engineering a global response, serving as a sort of go-between in helping the Fed and ECB agree on a coordinated approach.

Thursday, November 24, was Thanksgiving Day in the United States, but before Bernanke or New York Fed chief Bill Dudley could turn on football or eat turkey with their families, there was yet another international conference call to attend. Three years after the global central bankers had begun working in tandem to fight the post–Lehman Brothers panic, they had an idea of how to do it again. The swap lines that had been an unsung part of that international response were still open, but were barely being used. European banks were getting dollars through private markets rather than through the central banks, which is typically how it should be. But amid the global economic uncertainty of 2011, private funding was hardly a sure thing. Perhaps the Fed could make its terms more attractive and thus help the Europeans pump liquidity into their frozen banking system?

Bernanke and other Fed officials were more than willing to try. They would lower the interest rate charged on those swap lines to try to make dollars available more cheaply to European and other international banks. And the major central banks of the industrial world—the Fed, the ECB, the Bank of England, the Swiss National Bank, the Bank of Japan, and the Bank of Canada—would all announce the move in tandem. That part was merely theater—Japanese and Canadian banks weren't really under any pressure, and the main purpose of the action was to funnel dollars from the Federal Reserve to banks in the eurozone. But the Lehman crisis had taught the world's central bankers that they have more impact even when they merely appear to be acting in concert, so they all signed on.

The heads of the central banks all agreed verbally to the plan during the Thanksgiving Day conference call, but each had to assemble his policy committee to formally approve the action. That was particularly time-consuming for the Bank of Japan, which under its rules had to hold an in-person meeting rather than a videoconference of the sort the Fed used. The formalities took a few days to finalize, but at 8 a.m. New York time on November 30, the six central banks were able to announce "coordinated actions to enhance their capacity to provide liquidity support to the global financial system."

Substantively, the move cut the cost international banks had to pay to get loans from their central banks by half a percentage point. Symbolically, it was something more. "Finally, global action!" exclaimed an analyst quoted in the *Globe and Mail*. "America rides to Eurozone rescue," was the headline in the *Daily Telegraph*. Every major global stock market soared; the big American, French, and German stock indexes each rose by more than 4 percent.

The next day, Draghi made a prescheduled appearance before the European Parliament. First greeting the officials in Brussels in English, then French, German, and Italian, he then gave a none too subtle hint of what was to come. "What I believe our economic and monetary union needs is a new fiscal compact—a fundamental restatement of the fiscal rules together with the mutual fiscal commitments that euro area governments have made," he said, hinting that the ECB would be cooperative in addressing market volatility. "Other elements might follow, but the sequencing matters," he said. In other words, there would be more help forthcoming from the central bank—but only if a more permanent overarching arrangement for a common fiscal policy was put in place by the continent's governments.

Many analysts thought at the time that Draghi was signaling that more bond purchases by the ECB would be the reward for decisive action by political authorities. In fact, there was by this point some bond-purchase fatigue in the ranks of the Governing Council, even among members who had initially supported them. There was a growing sense that while the purchases of Italian and Spanish bonds had helped alleviate immediate concerns in the markets, they weren't doing anything to foster a long-term solution. Instead, the ECB was taking on risk and giving the politicians greater cover for their own inaction—and the longer the purchases continued, the truer that would be.

That sort of skepticism was, as always, strongest at the Bundesbank—and Draghi was looking for ways to keep Bundesbank president Jens Weidmann and the other German central bankers on his side. The Bundesbank had all along been far more comfortable with taking measures to pump money into the European banks than it had with buying government bonds—recall that in May 2010, Axel Weber was comfortable with new bank liquidity actions even as he vociferously objected to bond buying.

Since August 9, 2007, when the European money markets first froze up, a key to the ECB's strategy had been making money available to the continent's banks on more relaxed terms—with looser collateral requirements, and over a longer period of time. But the longest banks had been able to get ECB cash was for thirteen months. If the European banks could get assurance that they would have access to euros for much longer than that—three years, say—they would feel less need to sell off Italian and Spanish bonds. In effect, if the ECB were to make money available on looser, longer terms to the banks, the banks would do the work of propping up the government bond markets. And the ECB could retain some purity, serving as lender of last resort to banks, but not to governments directly.

Weidmann and the Bundesbank preferred extending the terms to perhaps only two years, and with tighter collateral requirements than what the majority of the Governing Council wanted. They didn't want commercial banks to become too dependent on central-bank financing. But this was a routine disagreement over details, not the kind of matter of deep principle that the dispute over bond buying had been. At its December 8 meeting, the council debated, held a vote, and agreed to announce that the ECB would enact two "longer-term refinancing operations" with looser collateral requirements and a longer maturity of thirty-six months.

Similarly, Germans—including Jürgen Stark, who was in his final meeting as the ECB's chief economist—were reluctant to cut interest rates for the second straight month and fully reverse Trichet's rate hikes from earlier in the year. Stark and a handful of others were inclined to hold off on a rate cut until the ECB had more definitive evidence that the eurozone economies were slowing and inflation was coming down. Indeed, the text for Draghi's press conference had been predrafted under the assumption that there would be no rate cut. But a majority of the Governing Council saw compelling enough evidence to cut immediately, and Draghi allowed the majority to prevail. Trichet and Stark would usually agree between themselves on what the policy move would be in advance, then steer the committee toward that decision. That Thursday, though, Stark had to scramble to revise the text for Draghi's announcement in the two hours between the end of the meeting and the press conference. Draghi even conceded to reporters that "it was a lively discussion—and one should not abuse the word 'lively,' because we are central-bank governors after all"—and that opinions were divided "not in terms of the substance but in terms of the timing."

Draghi's great victory at his second monetary policy meeting as ECB president wasn't merely that the bank introduced both an interest rate cut and a giant new backstop for the European banking system. It was that he pivoted policy away from the divisive bond-purchase program and toward actions that drew support from the powerful Germans on the committee, even when they disagreed with their specifics.

The long-term refinancing operations were a greater success than even ECB insiders had expected. Banks, seeing the opportunity to lock in funding for three years for only a 1 percent annual interest rate, took advantage on a massive scale. During the first operation in December, 523 banks took out a combined €489 billion in ECB financing. In a second operation, eight hundred banks took out another €530 billion.

The technical details were different, but Draghi and the ECB had in essence done exactly what Bernanke and the Fed did during the 2008 phase of the crisis: erected a massive firewall of central-bank money to stand between the world and the flames.

One day after Draghi's bold moves and exactly twenty years after the start of the summit in Maastricht that created the euro, the leaders of Europe once again gathered in Brussels to try to rework the financial architecture of their currency union. It was yet another meeting of only halting progress toward a plan for how the nations of Europe might collectively back each other. The major headlines coming out of the gathering were about clashes between British prime minister David Cameron and Nicolas Sarkozy over financial regulation, with the former wanting to ensure that new rules didn't threaten London's status as a world financial capital. But that was a sideshow. The main event was as unexciting as ever.

The thing is, though, it didn't matter. Thanks to the work of the Super Mario Brothers, the winter and spring were a period of optimism. Yes, the longer-range question of European financial integration was unsettled, but the ECB's wall of money had stabilized the banking system. And Mario Monti was carrying out fiscal reforms in Italy that had been mere empty promises for Berlusconi. The country's ten-year borrowing cost, 6.57 percent on November 25, 2011, was down to 4.19 percent on March 9, 2012. Meanwhile, Ireland and Portugal continued enacting their bailout agreements, painful though they were, with a remarkable degree of political cohesiveness. And Spain, under its new center-right government, went through its own series of painful reforms. Once more, Greece was the outlier.

Papademos was an accomplished economist and central banker, with a doctorate from MIT and the wisdom accumulated over three decades of working in the highest reaches of European policymaking and as a professor at Columbia. He was not, however, a politician. He spoke quietly and without obvious charisma, and he viewed the challenges his country faced mainly as complicated technical problems. Typically for a central banker, Papademos made decisions with cold analysis rather than a politician's instinctive sense for public opinion. His job, though, was one that would challenge even the most skilled of politicians: He had to assemble a cabinet on the fly in December 2011, taking care to bring together leaders from both of the parties that had formed the coalition, then lead a group of ministers who were normally at each other's throats.

That made the January and February 2012 negotiations over a "second memorandum"—a revised set of conditions for Greece to fulfill in order to receive its bailout money—particularly onerous. That Papademos had personal credibility didn't suddenly make the Greek political system more accepting of troika-ordered pay cuts and privatization. Neither did it make the European Commission and the ECB more flexible in their demands. And with Dominique Strauss-Kahn out of the picture, the IMF was less inclined to move slowly on tightening fiscal policy. Papademos and his team first had to negotiate with the troika over what unpleasant wage cuts and unpopular privatization measures would take place, then turn around and bargain with the two coalition parties to get them both on board. The talks often went until four or five in the morning.

The eventual result was two documents totaling eighty-two pages and spelling out the newest round of Greek concessions. The government got its bailout deal and would be able to meet its financial obligations come March. But it had to pay a terrible political price.

Some eighty thousand people took to the streets of Athens on February 13, protesting the wage and pension cuts the nation's parliament had just agreed to. There were 150 stores looted, 45 buildings burned, and 104 police officers injured. "It felt like war," a doorman named Dimitris Arvanitis told the *New York Times*. "I could not believe I was in Athens. I have never seen this in my almost 60 years of life, and I have been working here all my life." One Greek newspaper, *Dimokratia,* published on its front page a photo of Angela Merkel manipulated so she appeared to be dressed like Nazi official, swastika and all.

It was the beginning of the end for the unity government, then just three months old. The right-leaning New Democracy party saw its opening and demanded new elections—after all, the left-leaning Panhellenic Socialist Movement, or PASOK, was widely loathed, blamed for an unemployment rate that was at 21.7 percent and climbing as well as the various austerity measures the Greek populace had already endured. It was a startlingly shortsighted decision. With more economic pain to come, it would have made more sense to allow Papademos—who had no political ambitions of his own—to remain in power and endure popular discontent, and then call for elections once the worst was over.

But Papademos wasn't the only Greek official who had trouble with political calculus. Antonis Samaras and New Democracy were too eager to be back in power. Elections there would be.


The success of the ECB's wall of money didn't mean that all was well. Huge chunks of the continent were in recession that spring, and even those that continued to grow did so at a glacial pace. Italy's economy contracted at an annual rate of 3 percent in the first half of 2012, Spain's by about 1.5 percent. France's economic growth flatlined. Of the large countries, only Germany's economy was growing, and at a tepid 1.5 percent annual rate. There was unemployment on a mass scale—in April 2012, 10.1 percent in France, 10.5 percent in Italy, 14.9 percent in Ireland, and a shocking 24.4 percent in Spain. In countries with stronger economies—Germany, the Netherlands—the rate was a bit above 5 percent, and even lower in Austria.

It was a bifurcated continent, with those living in a handful of nations experiencing either mild economic growth or mild recession while millions of their neighbors were in dire straits. And the ECB could set only one interest rate policy for all of them, which meant that the great fear of the Euroskeptics of the 1990s had come to pass.

What was increasingly clear that spring was that even against the backdrop of more stable financial markets, the status quo couldn't endure. With the GIPSI countries going through with their agreed-upon austerity, their economies were shrinking without the benefit of a countervailing force such as dramatic ECB rate cuts. Across the continent, the conversation started to shift from austerity to growth. How might countries like Italy and Spain find their way back to a path of expansion that would make their fiscal problems all the more manageable?

Draghi in particular emerged as a voice urging governments to focus not merely on reforms that would save money in the present, but also those that would strengthen economic growth in the future. Governments, he told the European Parliament on April 25, "must undertake determined policy actions to address major weaknesses in the fiscal, financial and structural domains," adding that steps already under way "need to be complemented by growth-enhancing structural reforms to facilitate entrepreneurial activities, the start-up of new firms and job creation. Here, governments should be more ambitious."

Translation: Given that we at the ECB (1) can't tailor our monetary policy for the various countries of Europe individually and (2) aren't willing to accept the high inflation in stronger European countries that might help the GIPSI nations get out from under their heavy debt loads, it's on you elected officials to find policies that will get European growth going. It was quite a shift in tone from the ECB, which under Trichet had emphasized the urgency of governments cutting their deficits above all else.

But nowhere was the shift in emphasis from austerity to growth more dramatic than in France. Its presidential election, held in two rounds on April

22 and May 6, pitted Sarkozy against François Hollande, who had emerged as the Socialist Party standard-bearer after Strauss-Kahn's arrest in New York. Sarkozy had spent the previous three years attached at the hip to Merkel—"Merkozy," the headline writers enjoyed calling them—and their partnership had significantly shaped Europe's response to the crisis.

Within that partnership, the French president frequently argued for greater European unity and more generous accommodation of the countries in need of help. But Sarkozy often seemed more committed to maintaining good relations with Merkel than to any specific policy. And he could give the impression of being more attuned to coming up with a splashy announcement than coming up with the right answer.

Offering more than just the appearance of activism, Hollande campaigned on a promise to raise taxes on the wealthy to cut budget deficits while maintaining social welfare benefits. In the end, he won, and then he began swiftly to deliver. Significantly for Europe as a whole, he was skeptical of Germany's all-austerity-all-the-time model for how Europe ought to fix itself. Combined with the emergence of Monti in Italy, his election left Merkel an isolated advocate of an approach that had, to that point, been failing.

It also marked a near-complete ejection of the national leaders who'd fought the earlier stages of the global crisis, with only Merkel still in place. In some countries (Britain, Spain, Portugal) voters ousted parties on the left in favor of those on the right, in others (France and arguably the United States in 2008) on the right in favor of those on the left. It was a matter of who was in power. It's no coincidence that Merkel not only survived politically, but also received high approval ratings in mid-2012: Germany's economy had been performing better than that of any other large Western nation. Voters elsewhere didn't know exactly what they wanted in their elected leaders—they just knew they wanted something different from what they'd had.

In this volatile political climate, voters in Greece seemed to want something very different. On May 6, the same day Hollande prevailed over Sarkozy, Greeks went to the polls to choose the parliament that would replace Papademos's coalition government. The results stunned the world—or at least that portion of the world that hadn't tracked the growing discontent on the streets of the Hellenic Republic.

According to Greek opinion polls, voters overwhelmingly objected to the agreement with the troika to which their government had agreed. But they also by wide margins wanted to keep the euro. These were, practically speaking, irreconcilable views. If the nation rejected the bailout deal, it would rapidly run out of money to pay its bills—not just what it owed international creditors, but also salaries for government employees and payments to hospitals, the military, and so on. Unlike a nation with its own currency, Greece couldn't simply print money to fund those obligations, inflationary consequences be damned. The decision to reject the troika's demands would almost certainly have to be accompanied by a decision to convert to a new drachma or other uniquely Greek currency.

The new currency would surely plummet in value against the euro, in expectation of high inflation. That would crush the savings of any Greeks who hadn't already moved their euros to a Swiss or German bank or stashed them in cash somewhere in their homes. It would also make all Greeks' paychecks lower in real terms, accomplishing in one fell swoop the reduction in wages that the ECB had so eagerly sought. And it would make Greek exports and tourism much more competitive, potentially laying the groundwork for a return to growth. Suddenly, the vacationer trying to decide whether to spend his or her holiday in Greece or Italy would see the former as a bargain.

The invented word for a Greek exit from the eurozone, "Grexit," became commonplace not just in newspaper headlines but also among high government officials discussing what to do next. The possibility of Greece leaving the eurozone had in just two years gone from something so unthinkable that European leaders were dismissive of any commentators who dared mention it to something openly discussed.

Syriza, an alliance of communist and other far-left parties, won 17 percent of the vote in the May 6 Greek election. It had won 5 percent in the previous race. Golden Dawn, the country's neo-Nazi party, went from 0.3 percent of the vote in the previous election to 7 percent. A large proportion of the Greek electorate had looked at the economic despair that the parties of the center had brought it and rejected them for the extremes. New Democracy didn't win enough seats for a majority, even in a coalition formed with PASOK. After days of fruitless negotiations with smaller parties, no coalition came together and new elections were scheduled. In the next round on June 17, New Democracy and PASOK had just barely enough votes combined to form a new and fragile coalition. The center had held, but by a thread.

I n July 2012, Draghi used an unusual metaphor to describe the work that lay ahead in fixing the eurozone's deep structural problems. "The euro is like a bumblebee," he said. "This is a mystery of nature because it shouldn't fly but instead it does. So the euro was a bumblebee that flew very well for several years. And now—and I think people ask 'how come?'—probably there was something in the atmosphere, in the air, that made the bumblebee fly. Now something must have changed in the air, and we know what after the financial crisis. The bumblebee would have to graduate to a real bee. And that's what it's doing."

In that same speech, Draghi pledged that "the ECB is ready to do whatever it takes to preserve the euro. And believe me, it will be enough." But could the bank accomplish this so far impossible task before the economic schisms of the summer of 2012 transformed into the bloody political schisms of the old Europe? Six decades of European integration had been all about ridding the continent of political extremism and intolerance, the forces that had led to the twentieth century's great upheavals. That had been the ultimate ideal of postwar Europe, the animating force behind the European Union and the euro, the "life compass" of Jean-Claude Trichet, the crowning achievement of a generation of prime ministers and presidents.

One Monday evening in late May 2012, on the rooftop terrace of the Grand Bretagne hotel in Athens, tourists speaking a variety of languages—German, Finnish, English—laughed, photographed themselves with the Parthenon lit in the distance, and enjoyed €14 gin and tonics. Drumbeats sounded in the distance, and almost simultaneously police in white helmets and riot gear streamed out of the parliament building, forming a series of defensive lines. A crowd of perhaps five hundred made its way around Syntagma Square, several people waving giant Greek flags, others waving lit flares and ominously evoking villagers charging a castle.

They were from Golden Dawn, the neo-Nazi party, the bartender explained, as the demonstrators shouted a series of chants in Greek and then went on their way. "They come through every few nights." The night had offered two contrasting Europes: one lively, cosmopolitan, and content, the other austere, insular, and full of fury.

The work of central bankers often seems a dry and technical affair. But Draghi's job was really about something bigger than bond markets and bailouts. His task, five years after the crisis first began, was to try to rid the Aegean twilight of angry extremists. It was to bring back a world of economic possibility that would again suppress the ugliest instincts that lurk in the hearts of men.

# TWENTY

# Governor Zhou's Chinese Medicine

Amid purple neon lights, the sixty-two-year-old man with a round face and graying hair stepped up to address the crowd, on a stage that could have been set for a rock concert rather than a speech by a central banker. Everything was big and splashy: A chandelier the size of an elephant hung from the ceiling; the event's sponsors included BMW and the Boston Consulting Group. It could have easily been in Las Vegas or Dubai.

But this was Beijing, at the base of the city's tallest skyscraper, the China World Trade Center Tower III. When Zhou Xiaochuan, the governor of the People's Bank of China, spoke at the Caixin Summit economic conference on that November day, he couldn't have contrasted more with the usual image of Chinese leaders, who typically make public appearances against a red backdrop of faded solemnity. When Zhou walked onstage, he was also setting foot into the new China, a world of big buildings, big money, and, if Zhou does his job well enough, a big imprint on the financial life of people across the globe.

The rise of a great world power almost always goes hand in hand with its rise as global financial powerhouse. And behind the scenes of every great financial power is an effective central bank. London was the financial capital of the world during Britain's reign as a nineteenth-century imperial power, which was made possible in no small part by the Bank of England. New York supplanted London as the world's financial capital after World War I as the United States emerged as the great global power of the twentieth century. It's no coincidence that the Federal Reserve System was created in 1914.

China's ascent is perhaps the most remarkable economic trend of the last generation. The nation produced $330 worth of goods and services per person in 1991, adjusted for inflation. In 2011, that figure had reached $5,430. Behind those numbers are hundreds of millions of people who can now feed themselves reliably, endure less backbreaking work, and enjoy more of the comforts of the modern age than their parents' generation could have dreamed of. China passed Japan to become the world's second largest economy in 2010, and with a population four times that of the United States', will almost certainly become the world's largest within a generation.

But whether Shanghai can become a great center of global commerce on the order of New York or London—and if so, what this twenty-first-century financial capital will look like—is very much in question. The tasks for Zhou and his successors at the People's Bank of China aren't easy ones. They must wrest power and influence away from the nation's political leaders to build a financial system that takes full advantage of all the lessons learned by Western central bankers over the centuries. Yet they must ensure that the system they build suits a Chinese culture and economy that are quite different from those of the United States and Western Europe.

That Friday in 2010, on that neon-lit stage in Beijing, Zhou offered a fitting metaphor for the differences between Chinese and Western economic policy. "A drug from Western medicine, which is based on theory and clinical trials, usually contains one ingredient and has a quick effect, while a prescription of Chinese medicine includes various ingredients that work together to treat a disease," he said. "A Chinese doctor will adjust the composition of the treatment according to the patient's condition, removing herbs, adding new ones and adjusting the dosage of some ingredients. Overall, the adjustment is based on the feedback from the patient.

"Chinese medicine probably is not as comprehensive or logical as Western medicine," he added. "Some drugs with large side effects may be removed, or reduced through trial and error. This is learning through experience, with endless adjustments." In other words, Chinese economic policy is forever a work in progress, an effort to use a wide range of tools in concert to maintain good health—or, more literally, a prosperous and peaceful nation. The global crisis that erupted in 2007 in the United States and spread to Europe repeatedly threatened China's booming economy, endangering the "harmonious society" that has been the foremost goal of current Chinese leadership.

In a narrow sense, Zhou's job was to make the Chinese renminbi as central to global commerce at the U.S. dollar. But his greater challenge was to shape an economy more resilient, a prosperity more durable than those of the crisis-stricken nations of the Western world. And he had to do it all without the authority that central bankers in the more advanced industrial nations have.

But then nobody ever said that taking center stage would be easy.

The chairman of the Federal Reserve is easily among the half dozen most powerful U.S. public officials, and arguably number two behind the president. The president of the European Central Bank at times seems like the most powerful person in all of Europe. But the governor of the People's Bank of China is, by most accounts, not even among the couple dozen most powerful Chinese officials. This fact is often lost on Westerners. *Forbes* listed Zhou as number fifteen on its list of the "World's Most Powerful People," and *Foreign Policy* placed him number four on a list of global thinkers, one spot below Barack Obama and one above Ben Bernanke, rankings that make China experts scoff. To understand why, one must know how the People's Bank of China differs from central banks in the West.

Created in 1948, the PBOC in its early decades wasn't China's central bank so much as its *only* bank, the state-owned financial institution responsible for making credit available to state-owned companies. Starting in 1983, as China was beginning its shift toward a hybrid economy of liberalized markets and state control, four different state-owned banks were spun off from the PBOC. In 1995, the institution was formally made the nation's central bank in its modern form. Like its counterparts in most countries, the PBOC carries out a wide range of tasks for the Chinese government, including printing and circulating cash, executing the government's interest rate and foreign exchange policies, and backstopping banks. The trillions of dollars in reserves that the Chinese government holds to guard itself against ups and downs of the global economy are held in accounts at the PBOC.

But while the PBOC does many of the same jobs as central banks in the West, that doesn't mean it has the same power. In the Chinese system, the concept of an independent central banker—the central-bank governor as an independent actor who can make whatever decisions he believes best for the nation—simply doesn't exist. Zhou and his predecessors were technicians, functionaries charged with carrying out the policy directives that come down from higher up. The nine members of the Politburo Standing Committee, led by Chinese paramount leader Hu Jintao (until late 2012) and Xi Jinping (his successor), make the biggest decisions. Zhou had status as one of thirty-five members of the State Council, the administrative arm of the government. But his was only one voice, alongside those of officials representing many other interests—manufacturing, agriculture, the military, and so on. Zhou is said to have briefed the State Council on the condition of the economy every two weeks and make recommendations as to whether interest rates should be raised or lowered. But the decisions are authorized by a small, more exclusive group within the State Council and, ultimately, the Standing Committee.

"I was in a museum one day when I realized it's just like the imperial era, when the emperor received draft edicts from his advisers," said one Chinese central banker, "If the emperor approved, he would stamp them with the imperial seal. Today, the PBOC sends guidance upwards. But nothing happens without that stamp from the top."

Even among people who devote their lives to studying Chinese policymaking—analysts, diplomats, academics—the details of how the central bank's decisions actually get made are murky. It is presumed that Zhou and PBOC staffers have at least some say. "I think they're part of the intellectual debate, but I don't think they're part of the power structure," said an academic with deep relationships within the PBOC. As a U.S. official experienced in dealing with China matters put it, a Chinese diplomat to Washington can learn more about how decisions are made at the highest levels of the U.S. government by reading a few days' worth of the *New York Times* and the *Washington Post* than a U.S. diplomat to Beijing can from years of assiduously cultivating government sources.

This secrecy has created an atmosphere of fevered speculation and even distrust around the PBOC. In August 2010, there was a strange rumor circulating in Asian financial circles and redistributed by the political analysis firm

Stratfor: The PBOC had suffered massive losses on its portfolio of U.S. Treasury bonds and Zhou had defected to the United States to escape punishment from Chinese authorities. One particularly implausible detail was that Fed vice chairman Donald Kohn had threatened to retaliate against any punishment of Zhou by disclosing the Swiss bank account holdings of some five thousand Chinese officials. China dealt with the rumor by shutting down Web sites repeating it and publishing indications of support of Zhou in state-run media. It was all nonsense, but the absence of the kind of transparency that's standard in Western democracies means there are no reliable independent arbiters of fact. By contrast, when there was a rumor in financial markets that Alan Greenspan had been gravely injured in a car accident when he was Fed chair, his spokesman was able to shut it down by simply confirming to news services that Greenspan was sitting unhurt in his office.

To understand the PBOC's policies throughout the crisis, then, one has to understand the political system and political culture in which it operates. Every government has a wide range of tools it can use to influence the economy—most significantly, taxing and spending, regulation, domestic monetary policy, and international currency policy. The major Western democracies have delegated those different tools to different arms at the state: Taxing and spending is the province of elected officials. Regulation is generally carried out by executive agencies. And monetary policy, experience has convinced the Western nations, is best left in the hands of independent technocrats who are largely separate from politics.

The Chinese system essentially puts all these tools of state power over the economy in the same hands, at the highest levels, aiming to use them in concert to realize the government's overarching goal. And that goal, more than anything, is self-preservation. Communist Party leadership in China has an implicit deal with the country's 1.2 billion citizens: Leave us in power, and we will maintain rapid growth that will result in steadily rising standards of living.

In the fall of 2008, when the world financial system was convulsing in the ugly aftermath of Lehman Brothers' bankruptcy, the advantages of the Chinese method of making economic policy were evident. As the Western economies collapsed, so did demand for the clothing made in Zhejiang Province, the toys made in Wenzhou, the dishwashers made in Foshan. The implied deal between the Chinese government and its citizens was at risk of ripping apart. How many unemployed factory workers would it take for the masses to hit the streets to make their dissatisfaction known?

On November 5, the government announced a new fiscal stimulus of ¥4 trillion, or about $587 billion—or about 12.5 percent of Chinese GDP that year. (The U.S. stimulus package enacted in February 2009 was not only much later coming, but also only 5 percent of that year's GDP.) But more remarkable than the scale of China's response was the way it deployed every tool of government power at once. Zhou's PBOC, which just a few months earlier had been fretting about high inflation and an overheating real estate sector and trying to tighten the availability of credit in the economy, abruptly reversed course. It slashed the required ratio of reserves held by Chinese banks as well as the interest rate on deposits. Local governments were ordered to ramp up their spending on public infrastructure. The PBOC relaxed quotas that had held back bank lending, and so the four giant state-owned banks happily loaned money to those local governments and state-owned companies on a mass scale.

"They had a red rubber stamp, stamping on every project that they came across," said Northwestern University professor and veteran China watcher Victor Shih, at a conference. "Once you have this paper from the [National Development and Reform Commission], you'd take it to the bank and say give me money."

Compare that to the crisis response in the United States. In both countries, monetary policy was loosened to try to combat the economic downturn. Both countries enacted fiscal stimulus, though with the messy realities of democracy, the American Recovery and Reinvestment Act became a contentious partisan issue. And because banks are under direct government control in China, the nation's leaders were able to force them to lend, whereas the privately owned banks of the United States, reeling from crisis, were pulling back at the time the economy needed them most. Another difference: In late 2008, when experts and scholars began criticizing the U.S. stimulus package for funding wasteful projects, Chinese media were ordered to stop publishing negative coverage. The U.S. effort was vociferously and repeatedly attacked in the American media.

It all worked. The Chinese economy bottomed out in the fourth quarter of

2008, six months earlier than the U.S. economy did, and it returned to its pre-crisis growth path of nearly 10 percent almost immediately. Democracy and free speech are among the greatest achievements of Western civilization, but in moments of financial panic, authoritarianism has its advantages.

Zhou and the PBOC were good soldiers in this initial phase of responding to the crisis, even at the risk of the banking system becoming overextended and inflation rearing its head. "From other countries we've already learned this lesson: We'd rather act quickly and decisively," Zhou said in an interview with a Chinese publication in March 2009. But later that year, with the Chinese economy having decisively rebounded, the opposite problem was starting to afflict the nation: There was too much bank lending, with a great potential that many of those loans were going to unworthy projects that would leave the banks with big losses in the future. Banks were doing as they were told, making loans to local governments on a mass scale, comfortable that the national government would cover any losses, but in the process they were creating longer-term risks for the Chinese economy, very likely starting to inflate the next bubble.

Wu Xiaoling, a former vice governor of the PBOC who left the bank in 2007 and has thus been able to speak more freely on recent events than Zhou, said that in July and August of 2009, "astronomical lending" levels were "masking catastrophe." The PBOC started quietly tightening its regulatory policies over the second half of 2009. On January 18, 2010, the central bank was sufficiently alarmed by the latest numbers on lending that it reportedly gathered senior bank executives together for an hour and a half to issue a "stop order" demanding that they cease making loans. The PBOC backed up the words with penalties: Banks that failed to comply would face higher reserve requirements, essentially making them less profitable and choking off the flow of money into the economy.

The Chinese government, including the PBOC, had accomplished something remarkable. First, it had shielded its nation from the ripple effects of the Western financial crisis, to the extent that the global downturn caused only temporary damage domestically. And then, as its excesses of stimulus started to threaten new bubbles and inflation, it had immediately turned off the spigot.

Harmoniousness had been preserved.

. . .

Zhou Xiaochuan was born in 1948, as Mao Zedong's armies were starting to overwhelm Chiang Kai-shek to conquer what would soon become known as the People's Republic of China. Zhou's father, Zhou Jiannan, was a top official in the Ministry of Machine Building and elsewhere in the Chinese government, and, crucially for his son's political career, was a mentor of Jiang Zemin, the nation's leader from 1993 to 2003. The younger Zhou is a "princeling," the vaguely derogatory term for the sons of top Communist Party officials under Mao who have emerged as members of China's new ruling class.

Being a child of privilege of his generation came with costs as well as benefits. During Mao's Cultural Revolution of the 1960s and '70s, Zhou and many other young, educated urbanites were dispatched to the countryside to do hard labor. Zhou, who spent four years at a construction-materials factory in northeastern China, has given no hints that it was as brutal an experience for him as it was for many others. "Besides laboring," he once told an interviewer, "I was exposed to other things, like telephone technology, and I got to improve upon carrier-wave broadcast technology, and also updated some machine tools." Zhou's interest in engineering persisted, and he studied at Beijing Chemical Institute in the early 1970s as a "worker-farmer-soldier-student," then earned a PhD in economic systems engineering from Tsinghua University's Machine Building Research Institute. His dissertation was on how the engineering concept of "control theory" could apply to price reforms in migrating a centrally planned economy to a market-based one.

In 1986, Zhou joined a government economic think tank, where his engineering studies proved surprisingly relevant to analyzing economies—particularly those in crisis. Control theory deals with how to keep a system stable through sensors that constantly adjust themselves based on conditions. Its uses can be mundane—allowing a car to drive using cruise control or a washing machine to adjust its cycle depending on the load it contains—but it is also a crucial technology behind communications satellites and advanced weapons systems. Borrowing from control theory, Zhou said in a 2009 speech, "In a complicated system, there are usually many feedback loops. . . . A positive feedback loop enlarges amplification, tends to create oscillation like

boom and bust pro-cyclicality. . . . while a negative feedback loop can reduce
amplification. . . . In economic and financial systems of recent years, we have
too many positive feedback loops. Thus the system shows a strong pro-
cyclicality. What we need to do is not to totally rebuild the system, but to add a
few negative feedback loops."

As a young economic researcher in the 1980s, Zhou worked with some of
China's reformers, people committed to building a system with less corruption
and more reliant on markets. One of them, the prominent economist Wu
Jinglian, to this day speaks out against "old-style Maoists"; another, onetime
premier of the People's Republic of China Zhao Ziyang, was purged for opposing the 1989 massacre of demonstrators in Tiananmen Square. In the aftermath of Tiananmen, Zhou lost his job as an assistant minister of foreign trade
and was forced to leave China, maybe because of his ties to Zhao. He went to
the United States, where he spent two years on a fellowship at the University of
California at Santa Cruz, publishing papers and writing a book. He seems not
to have made a great impression on his U.S. colleagues during his time in Santa
Cruz: A quarter century later their recollections of him were faint to nonexistent.

Zhou's political career in China had seemed finished after Tiananmen
Square. But as his father's old protégé Jiang Zemin rose to the top ranks of the
Chinese government and those of a reformist bent ascended more generally in
the 1990s, opportunities in his homeland reopened. Whatever one thinks of
the revolving door between the financial sector and economic policymaking
in the West (Exhibit A: Hank Paulson serving as chief executive of Goldman
Sachs, then as U.S. treasury secretary), it's nothing compared to the interconnection of the major Chinese banks and the government agencies that shape
China's policy. Steps toward privatization notwithstanding, the big banks remain tools of the state, responsive to directives on what companies to lend
money to and on what terms. Their executives have deep political connections,
and the career paths of senior economic policymakers inevitably wind through
the worlds of both banking and public service.

Zhou is a prime example. In the early 1990s, he was a vice president of the
Bank of China (not to be confused with the People's Bank of China). Next, he
spent two years as deputy governor of the PBOC, then two years at the China
Construction Bank, then two years at the China Securities Regulatory Com-

mission, the nation's equivalent of the U.S. Securities and Exchange Commission. He was appointed to the governorship of the PBOC in 2002, where he would serve for a decade. Throughout, his economic sensibility was different from that of most Chinese government officials. On taking the job as China's chief securities regulator in 2000, he said, "Whatever the market can solve, let it solve it. As regulators, we should only be referees, not athletes, not coaches."

The People's Bank of China is a curious mix of old-school Chinese bureaucracy and Western-style economic thought. It is headquartered just over two miles west of Tiananmen Square in central Beijing, in a semicircular building meant to evoke a Chinese ingot, the currency of the imperial era. As at many government agencies, workers gather for communal meals according to a strict schedule, at 8 a.m. for breakfast, noon for lunch, and 6 p.m. for dinner; many take a break after lunch for a walk or a nap. Low- and midlevel employees gather at long tables, eating rice and bony fish unappealing to the typical Western palate; higher-level officials and visitors eat in an executive dining room that serves food that could be found in any business hotel in the world.

The organization Zhou inherited didn't have high-performing economic research departments. "Most of their researchers are not trained as proper economists," said a former PBOC official. "They don't do academic research. The reports are more like case studies or policy papers. They are not as technically trained." There are few of the vigorous internal debates on economic theory that one finds at the Western central banks. Instead, researchers carry out projects assigned by Zhou and other higher-ups.

Zhou has aimed to change that culture and make the PBOC a more typical central bank. He has disproportionally hired *haigui*, or "sea turtles"—Chinese nationals who left for the West and then returned. (The term is a pun: *Gui*, the word for "return," sounds like the word for "turtle.") Zhou himself, despite having spent only a brief time overseas, is deeply connected to Western culture: He drinks good French wine, enjoys European classical music and opera, and in his office at the PBOC sometimes listened to Voice of America radio broadcasts in English. Like Tim Geithner, Mervyn King, and many other economic policymakers in the West, he plays tennis. In a doubles match against then White House economic adviser Larry Summers in 2009, Zhou and Summers jokingly bet that the winner could set the renminbi-to-dollar exchange rate. Zhou's partner was so good that the Americans suspected he was a ringer, perhaps an accomplished college player picked from the PBOC staff. The Chinese won.

In Zhou's decade as governor of the Chinese central bank, there was remarkable progress made toward creating a more liberal, market-oriented national financial system. In the early 2000s, China was at a crossroads. It didn't want to get stuck being merely the factory for the rest of the world and providing only middling wages for its citizens (a situation known as the middle-income trap). A modern financial system would be required to fund the industries of the future and allow China to assert its influence across Asia and the world. The nation's old system, however, had worked marvelously to bring hundreds of millions of people out of dire poverty since the 1980s. It's difficult to turn away from a system that's working, whatever its limitations.

In the debate over China's economic future, Zhou and the PBOC pushed for a freer flow of capital across borders, interest rates set by markets rather than by the government, and less intervention in global currency markets to lower the value of the renminbi and hence advantage Chinese exporters. The Chinese government set as a goal making Shanghai a global financial center by 2020, and work by Zhou and the PBOC would be essential if that were to come true.

Part of being a great financial power is having a deep and liquid bond market—a place where savers can put large amounts of money and channel it to companies or governments that have useful things to do with it. Bond markets, when fully developed, grease the wheels of commerce and support a wide range of other transactions, setting market interest rates across the economy. And a vibrant bond market ensures that companies have access to capital outside the channels of state-controlled banks; it funnels money to the businesses that the market decides have the best prospects, not just those favored by politicians. China's bond market is breathtakingly underdeveloped, with total corporate bonds outstanding of about 9 percent of its GDP in 2012, compared with more than 50 percent in the United States. Zhou and the PBOC long advocated for developing a more vibrant bond market, and in recent years had some success.

In 2005, the PBOC created a loophole allowing Chinese companies to start issuing short-term commercial paper on financial markets after completing a streamlined registration process, in contrast to the lengthy, politicized process that securities regulators had in place for companies to issue longer-term corporate bonds. In 2008, seizing on the need for Chinese municipalities to borrow money amid stimulus spending to combat the financial crisis, the PBOC prevailed in creating a market for medium-term local government debt. The central bank successfully argued, as part of the campaign to make the renminbi a more international currency, for loosening capital control rules to allow "dim sum bonds"—that is, bonds traded in Hong Kong but denominated in the Chinese currency—starting in 2010. And in 2012, the PBOC and securities regulators relaxed rules to make it easier for corporations and municipalities to issue debt for even longer periods of time.

Zhou and the PBOC, in other words, were persistent and opportunistic in pushing for the development of the Chinese bond market, using loopholes, the need for stimulus spending amid the crisis, and Chinese financial nationalism to get his way. The PBOC has also been one of the most consistent promoters of renminbi internationalization, the idea that China's currency should one day stand alongside the dollar, the euro, and the yen as an important currency of global trade. In an essay published in early 2009, Zhou openly pondered what "kind of international reserve currency we need to secure global financial stability and facilitate world economic growth," suggesting that the supremacy of the dollar was a major factor in the world financial crisis.

The statement reflected a general angst among Chinese leaders—evident after the Fed's QE2 announcement—that their massive holdings of U.S. debt had left them uncomfortably exposed to the vicissitudes of the American economy. Unspoken but unmistakable was the conviction that a greater role for the renminbi would be an inevitable part of some new global currency regime. In October 2009, the PBOC created a new department, the "Monetary Policy 2" division, to study renminbi internationalization. It is headed by a consummate sea turtle, a Stanford PhD and Harvard Law graduate named Li Bo.

In recent years, the PBOC has created swap arrangements with many other central banks of the Pacific Rim, including those in South Korea, Indonesia, Thailand, and Australia. "The main purposes of the swap agreement are to support trade and investment between Australia and China, particularly in local-currency terms, and to strengthen bilateral financial co-operation," the Reserve Bank of Australia said in its announcement. There was talk in 2012 that other advanced nations' central banks, such as the Bank of Japan and even the Bank of England, might soon enter similar arrangements. That should allow banks in those countries access to Chinese currency should they need it, part of a deliberate effort to smooth the process by which more global trade happens in the renminbi rather than the dollar.

In public communications, Zhou and the PBOC soft-pedal the idea that they're trying to make the renminbi a major global currency. In official documents, the phrase used for the phenomenon is not "RMB internationalization," but rather what would be translated as "the RMB going out"—which is to say going out into the world beyond China. Zhou in a 2012 interview said that renminbi internationalization was "the will of the market rather than a government-backed move."

But there is clearly a deliberate effort under way, even if it's a reversal of the usual sequence by which nations ascend to great financial power. Typically, as prominent Chinese economist Gang Fan put it, internationalization of a currency begins with a flexible exchange rate system, followed by a liberalization of capital flows that makes the nation an attractive place for international investment, which leads to widespread use of the currency. China is supporting the use of the renminbi in international transactions before fully liberalizing other aspects of its economic policy. Zhou, in one interview, was blunt about why. "If some areas need to be reformed, but it is impossible to do, we can first reform other aspects, and then push forward reform of those aspects which are difficult to advance."

There's a more cynical way to cast the same idea, a theory of what Zhou and other Chinese reformers are up to that's widely accepted among Western China watchers and policymakers—even if Chinese officials dismiss it, as one central banker put it, as a "conspiracy theory." Zhou and the PBOC face steep political resistance to liberalizing Chinese finance and wresting more power for the technocrats at the central bank for its own sake. But when they cast their arguments in terms of China's national greatness, when the question isn't about the petty battles of this bureaucracy versus that one but making Shanghai to the twenty-first century what New York was to the twentieth and London was to the nineteenth, their political masters are more likely to listen.

The question is, are they? Zhou's Western tastes and academic background may have limited his influence outside the central bank. "Within the PBOC, Zhou Xiaochuan has a very high authority," said one former official of the central bank. "But outside the financial system, he lacks—I wouldn't call it 'ability,' but the 'style' of how traditional Chinese bureaucrats take care of things in the process of interfacing with other ministries and crafting policy. Sometimes, with such a strong academic background, it's unavoidable that you get a little more academic. But to be a bureaucrat, you not only have to be technical, but you have to be able to work together with people while reaching your own goals."

A t 6 a.m. New York time on November 30, 2011, the PBOC published an announcement that hit the financial wires like a bolt of lightning: It was cutting by half a percent the proportion of their assets that Chinese banks must hold in reserve. At a time when Europe was struggling with its crisis response and the global economy seemed to be slowing, China had elected once again to open the throttle of growth.

Traders weren't the only ones who were surprised. So too were the leaders of the other global central banks. That very day, just two hours after the PBOC statement, the leaders of the U.S., European, British, Japanese, Canadian, and Swiss central banks issued their joint announcement of cutting rates on swap lines, which they had developed through weeks of conference calls and coordination. Leaders of those banks had no idea that Zhou and the PBOC were poised to make a move of their own. It was a happy coincidence that the move happened on the same day and was in the same direction toward easier policy. In financial markets, there was a sense that a cavalry of the world's central bankers were all galloping to the rescue together.

But the reality is that the PBOC had done its own thing, in its own way, without involving its counterparts outside of China. Zhou and his predecessors have long attended Bank for International Settlements gatherings and met with their international colleagues in other global settings. Since 2009, Zhou was even included in the private Sunday night dinner in Basel with the other top central bankers. He speaks excellent English and was viewed as a thoughtful economist and a jovial presence. More importantly, Zhou's fellow central bankers saw him as part of a reformist wing of the Chinese leadership that, if it eventually prevails, will bring China more fully into the club of global leaders and help create a more peaceful and prosperous world.

But as of 2012, there remained a measure of distance and doubt between Zhou and the other central bankers. A big part of it was that they knew he didn't have the power to act on his own the way they did, that his actions had to be approved by his nation's high political authorities. He couldn't commit to a co-ordinated policy even if he wanted to. On October 10, 2010, during the annual meetings of the International Monetary Fund and the World Bank, Zhou said that China wouldn't be raising interest rates within the year. Nine days later, the PBOC hiked its benchmark interest rates by a quarter percentage point. Some in the media accused Zhou of "trickery," but more likely, he simply hadn't yet been told of the decision by the Standing Committee. Similarly, knowledge-able sources say, the PBOC wasn't informed of a June 7, 2012, interest rate cut until very shortly before it was to be announced, possibly even the same day.

One senior official of a Western central bank said that while there's im-plicit trust among counterparts at the likes of the Bank of England or Federal Reserve that news of an upcoming policy change won't leave their close-knit community, they worry about sharing information with a representative of the surveillance state that is China. Might information about an upcoming policy move told to the PBOC governor make its way to the portfolio managers who oversee China's vast reserves? There has been no evidence that it has happened, but some Western central bankers don't have total confidence it couldn't.

Zhou's speech at the purple-lit Caixin Summit in 2010 showed his delicate balancing act of trying to maintain strong bonds both with the Boys in Basel and within the Chinese government. Addressing the Fed's decision to under-take QE2 a few days earlier, which his own government was fiercely criticizing, Zhou mentioned that he had discussed the matter extensively with Ben Ber-nanke at BIS meetings, and that "in the communication process, we felt that many of their comments were actually understandable." He then explained the rationale for the move in language that tracked almost precisely with how Ber-nanke had talked about it: "The Fed has the mandate to create jobs and main-tain low inflation in the United States. Given the fragile economic recovery, relatively high unemployment rate, low inflation rate, and the U.S. federal funds rate close to zero, it is understandable that the Fed has adopted the quantitative easing monetary policy."

Then Zhou explained the Chinese position: that because the dollar is the international reserve currency, the United States has a special responsibility, one that it hadn't upheld in the run-up to the megacrisis. "The U.S. dollar has global impacts," Zhou said. And even if QE2 is in the best interest of the United States, "it may not necessarily be optimal for the world, and may have some side effects." Rather than staking out a strong position, allying himself with either his friend Ben from Basel or the Chinese political leaders who were openly using QE2 as a cudgel to throw at the United States, Zhou finished up with this bold statement: "To sum up, multiple angles are needed in the comprehensive analysis of the QE2's global impacts."

Zhou's term as governor for the PBOC was set to expire in December 2012, after a decade in office. China economy watchers spent the better part of the year trying to read the tea leaves as to whether he would enjoy a comfortable retirement or be promoted to a higher office in the new government coming in, with the conventional wisdom on this question going back and forth several times over the course of the year. He ultimately was not tapped to receive a promotion in the new government. But though his run at high levels in the Chinese government appeared to have come to an end, Zhou's legacy was shaping the course of modern China, even despite limited authority. He helped avert a deep economic downturn. He helped persuade his political overlords to reverse easy-money policies as a bank lending bubble emerged. He made great strides in encouraging the development of China's financial markets and the freer flow of capital across his nation's borders. At a time when the Western economies were flailing, their entire philosophical underpinnings coming into question, China was an unlikely source of strength for the global economy. And that success, at least through 2012, was vindication for Zhou and his band of *haigui* technocrats.

But the nation still has deep-seated economic problems and risks that may curtail its emergence as a preeminent economic power. The boom of the past decade was rooted in investment, particularly in infrastructure and housing. Might billions of yuan have gone toward projects that weren't in fact economically justified and will never pay off, leading to bank losses and a new crisis? Might the run-up in housing prices have gone far beyond what's justified by fundamentals, as it did in many Western countries in the mid-2000s? And while large, state-owned enterprises have had easy access to bank lending, small and medium-sized businesses, at least those without deep political connections, have had a much harder time gaining access to capital. Zhou spent his time as a senior official trying to change that, with only mixed success.

Beyond this is the question of how far China's financial system can take the nation. It was quite effective through the years of global crisis. But as messy as market capitalism can be, the system that evolved in the Western powers over the centuries has created more wealth than any other. Even after its great recession, in 2011, the United States had a per capita economic output that was nearly six times that of China's. The crisis certainly exposed the weaknesses of free-market capitalism. But as reformers like Zhou try to create a new economic and political system in China, they face a great challenge: They must grapple with the reality that for the most complicated medical problems—and the Chinese economy at the start of the twenty-first century is nothing if not complicated—herbal medicine usually doesn't cut it.

What Zhou spent his decade at the PBOC doing—and his successor and other reformers will now take up—wasn't as simple as trying a few traditional remedies. His accomplishment, rather, was to take the best lessons of his own tradition and merge them with the lessons of the West, of cancer treatments and heart stents and gene therapy. Can the unique aspects of China's culture, politics, and economic system be merged with the pieces of financial infrastructure that have helped create untold prosperity for people who live in the more advanced industrial nations, such as a market-based system for allocating capital and a powerful, independent central bank? The economic future of billions depends on the answer.

# Afterword:
# Back to Jackson

On August 30, 2012, seven years after they had toasted Alan Greenspan and five years to the day after they had gathered in the Grand Tetons to discuss housing finance amid the first ripples of megacrisis, the world's central bankers returned once again to the Jackson Lake Lodge to consider the world they had created. Both the tributes of 2005 and the warnings of 2007 seemed very far off indeed.

For the first time since the creation of the European Central Bank, no member of its Executive Board had made it to the conference: Mario Draghi and his colleagues were too busy back in Frankfurt developing their newest plan to combat the eurozone crisis. The officials who did make the voyage seemed exhausted, worn down from their many years of late-night decision making. Even the scene in the Blue Heron Lounge in the evenings was subdued, without the usual tables full of attendees shrugging off their jet lag to enjoy a little backslapping camaraderie.

The Friday night entertainment, too, seemed somehow less vibrant. In 2007, the horse whisperer had demonstrated how to break a wild mare. The same technique, he had said, could be applied to inspire trust and confidence in nonequines, too—which prompted one audience member to quip, "What about the commercial-paper market?" This year, local ranchers brought in artificial cattle made of wood and cloth and taught the central bankers how to lasso them. One Fed official yanked the rope so hard after successfully roping one of the "bulls" that its plastic horns came off. If there was an economic analogy here, no one wanted to joke about it.

Each of the major central banks had taken steps beyond any it would have considered possible a few years earlier. The ECB had bought the bonds of eurozone states, violating the spirit if not the letter of its founding treaty, and inserted itself deeply into the budget, tax, and regulatory decisions of several democracies. The Federal Reserve had rescued investment banks and insurance companies, maintained zero interest rates for four years and counting, and bought $2 trillion in bonds through quantitative easing. The Bank of England had joined the ECB in becoming uncomfortably entangled in politics and the Fed in vastly expanding its balance sheet.

And all for what? The economies of the major Western powers were a shambles, with the United States, Britain, and all but the strongest European nations producing well below their potential. In the summer of 2012, there were thirteen million more people jobless in the European Union and the United States than there would have been if pre-2007 trends had continued. A generation of young people faced poor career prospects; a generation of retirees saw its life's savings damaged by the crisis. In some European countries, extremists were on the march, most dramatically in Greece. By the fall, members of the neo-Nazi Golden Dawn party would be launching violent attacks on immigrants and other non-Greeks with chilling frequency. The streets of Spain and Portugal and Italy similarly roiled with discontent, though of a more peaceful variety.

In Jackson Hole, Michael Woodford, a Columbia University economist who was among the most esteemed academic monetary theorists in the world, took the stage underneath the lodge's elk-antler chandeliers to deliver a presentation with the dry title "Methods of Policy Accommodation at the Interest-Rate Lower Bound." Without quite saying so explicitly, the owlish-looking Woodford suggested that the Fed and the BOE's approach to interest rate policies during the crisis had been all wrong.

"The results that we have do not imply that the task of a central banker under current conditions is an easy one," he said. "There seem to me to be fewer options that are likely to be effective, and that are likely to be attractive on other grounds, than central bankers sometimes suggest when seeking to reassure the public." Over the course of thirty-nine thousand words, Woodford noted that central bankers again and again had taken discrete policy actions, but done little to shape expectations for the future more broadly.

All the quantitative easing in the world, he argued, would have little effect in isolation. People across the American, British, and, to some degree, European economies were convinced that the minute there was some improvement, their central banks would cease their stimulative monetary policies. Without knowing exactly what policies their banks would enact as a next step, they had no reason to believe that their economies would ever really take off and grow. And the Fed's "guidance policies" of stating an expectation of low interest rates until some future date were equally problematic: The central bank had essentially said that it expected the economy to be so lousy that it would keep rates low for years—hardly the kind of prediction to inspire confidence.

Think of the central bank as the driver of a car who pushes the accelerator all the way to the floor, and then lifts his or her foot every time the car goes a bit faster. The key to getting up to highway speed isn't just to put the pedal to the metal, but to keep it there for a while even after the car starts speeding up.

"It does not make sense to suppose that *merely expressing* the view of the economy's future path that the central bank would currently wish for people to believe will automatically make them believe it," Woodford said. "If speech were enough, without any demonstrable intention to *act* differently as well, this would be magic indeed."

Among Woodford's audience of weary and frustrated modern-day alchemists, there must have been more than one who wished, just for a moment, that the wave of a wand could make it all disappear.

I never plan my holidays ahead and I only ever go away for a few days," Mario Draghi said in a July interview. "One thing is certain: I will not be going to Polynesia. It's too far." So was Wyoming, it turned out.

Draghi had decided that it was time to force an ultimate reckoning with Europe's woes. There'd been nearly three years of halfhearted and timid responses, of kicking the can down the road over and over again. The ECB had tried twice to restore the economy to health with its Securities Markets Programme of bond purchases and twice more with its "long-term refinancing operations," which funneled hundreds of billions of euros into the continent's banks. But each had been more painkiller than cure, simply delaying the kinds of hard choices facing Europe. Draghi wanted a more permanent answer to the questions of what the eurozone of the future would look like and what the ECB could do to ensure that it came to be.

Since June, Draghi had been directing ECB staff and key allies on the Executive Board, Jörg Asmussen and Benoît Cœuré, to begin developing plans for how the central bank might defend the European idea in a more systematic way. At the same time, he began a deft diplomatic campaign. He briefed German finance minister Wolfgang Schäuble and top aides to Chancellor Angela Merkel about the evolving plans, hoping to ensure that he could count on having the German government's support. He met with some of the central bankers who had been opposed to the previous bond-buying efforts, such as those from Finland, the Netherlands, and Austria, in hopes of persuading them to come around on a more all-encompassing program. Private dinners, solicitous phone calls, visits on the sidelines of summits and international meetings— whenever he had a chance to buttonhole someone whose support might be helpful for the plan he had in mind, Draghi took it.

While he pursued those efforts privately, he stuck a marker in the ground publicly. The setting was the Lancaster House, a grand mansion in London's West End overlooking Green Park. Draghi's speech to the Global Investment Conference there on July 26 had been drafted as a thorough overview of the European economy and its challenges, largely without laying out any new ideas. But Draghi scribbled an extra couple of sentences onto his typed script. They weren't included in the version of the speech handed out to reporters, so the ECB later had to publish the updated speech on its Web site as "Verbatim of the remarks made by Mario Draghi."

Draghi essentially took it upon himself to preannounce that something big was on the way. Without having discussed with his Governing Council colleagues, he made the audacious pledge that "the ECB is ready to do whatever it takes to preserve the euro. And believe me, it will be enough." He led every interested party—the financial markets, the political leaders, his own colleagues—to count on a major new action by the ECB. The outcome was preordained, he was effectively saying.

The ECB had already intervened with hundreds of billions of euros, but without any overarching strategy, only at the last possible moment, and constantly pulling away whenever conditions seemed to be improving. The central bank would be better off, Draghi argued, setting clear criteria as to what it would do and under what conditions. Once those rules were set, it would be willing to deploy potentially unlimited funds.

Most of the press coverage of the London speech focused on the "whatever it takes" line. But the speech had a coda that was in many ways more important, if much harder to parse. If some countries' bonds carry higher interest rates because their governments have a higher risk of defaulting, that's simply the market at work, assigning risky nations higher "risk premia," Draghi argued. But if those higher rates are due to a risk of "convertibility," or fears that the euro could implode, it's a different matter. "To the extent that these premia do not have to do with factors inherent to my counterparty—they come into our mandate," Draghi said. "They come within our remit."

In other words, if investors are selling off Spanish or Italian bonds not because they fear they won't be repaid, but because they fear the eurozone will collapse, it is the ECB's job to intervene.

"So we have to cope with this financial fragmentation addressing these issues," Draghi said. "I think I will stop here; I think my assessment was candid and frank enough."

When Merkel appointed Jens Weidmann president of the Bundesbank a year earlier, he had seemed to have a more flexible approach to central banking than his predecessor, Axel Weber. He'd spent his career in public policy navigating between the doctrinaire, hard-money sensibility of the German central bank and the more adaptable approach of the nation's government. Within Merkel's government and beyond, he was expected to be a different kind of Bundesbank leader, one who would simultaneously honor its traditions and find ways to do whatever was required to rescue the eurozone.

But once ensconced in the brutalist concrete headquarters of the Bundesbank fifteen minutes north of the Eurotower in Frankfurt, Weidmann quickly made clear that he was just as committed to principle and purity as his forerunners. And he was livid over Draghi's apparent promise to print up a potentially unlimited amount of euros. "This is a political problem that in my view needs a political solution," Weidmann told Draghi that July day in a phone call, according to one report.

At a dinner on August 1, the evening before a Governing Council meeting, over baked goat cheese, roast beef, and caramel mousse, Draghi laid out his ideas. It would, of course, violate the founding treaty of the ECB for the central bank to monetize debt, he said. The ECB must not print money to fund governments. But when interest rates rise in a country like Spain or Italy because investors are betting against the continued existence of the euro, would it not be appropriate for the bank to intervene to get interest rates in that country in line with its target rate? Would that not be consistent with the ECB's mandate—all the more so if the central bank eschewed longer-term bonds, those whose prices most reflect markets' views of a nation's fiscal prospects? For good measure, the ECB could insist that before buying any bonds, the nation involved formally request the assistance and submit to conditions from the IMF.

Draghi found his colleagues in a more receptive mood than he might have expected, given the multiple dissents to previous ECB interventions. Only Weidmann was dead set against the notion. Even as he voiced his reservations, opinion was shifting against him, with central bankers from the Netherlands, Finland, and Austria all supportive of Draghi's argument that it was within the ECB's mandate to deploy euros to combat speculation that the eurozone will fall apart. Draghi had asked German finance minister Wolfgang Schäuble to back the ECB's proposed bond buying publicly, which he did. Angela Merkel's government was essentially giving Draghi cover in Germany. Through some skillful diplomacy, Draghi succeeded in isolating Weidmann and the Bundesbank.

The morning after the dinner, the ECB had its usual interest-rate-setting meeting, and after a quick lunch, Draghi again stood before the press. Although the night before had made it clear that there was widening support for a new bond-buying program, the bank needed another month to prepare the details. Markets were initially disappointed that there was no grand announcement, falling worldwide. And then traders took another look at Draghi's statement to the press. The ECB "may undertake the open market operations of a size adequate to reach its objectives," he'd said. The details would be decided "over the coming weeks."

As Draghi and his allies worked on their plan, Weidmann was on the outside looking in. The German made the voyage to Jackson Hole, traveling eighteen hours each way from Frankfurt at the very time the ECB's inner circle was sorting out what to do. He gave an interview to *Der Spiegel*, published on August 29: The framework for European unity, Weidmann said, "has been stretched and, in some cases, disregarded," and bond buying by the central banks was "too close to state financing via the money press for me." The cover of Germany's most influential magazine featured Weidmann staring out, his fists clenched together, under the headline "Aufstand der Bundesbank"—"Rebellion of the Bundesbank."

It didn't matter. Draghi's campaign had succeeded. The next Governing Council meeting, on September 6, was almost anticlimactic. Draghi and Asmussen presented the plan they'd spent the previous weeks cooking up. Weidmann again stated his objections. Then a vote was held. It was twenty-two to one.

Draghi took the stage in Frankfurt that Thursday afternoon amid a bit more press corps murmuring than usual, and with the central banker's standard practice of understatement he announced that "the Governing Council today decided on the modalities for undertaking 'Outright Monetary Transactions' in secondary markets for sovereign bonds in the euro area." It was yet another new abbreviation, OMT, replacing the SMP of the earlier Securities Markets Programme.

The program would focus on medium-term securities of nations in trouble—three- to five-year bonds, not longer-term securities. The theory was that this would ensure that markets continued to exert pressure on profligate countries by demanding high interest rates for longer-term debt. Governments receiving the help would also be subject to strict fiscal conditions. Asked if the decision to enact the program was unanimous, Draghi impishly told reporters, "There was one dissenting view. . . . It is up to you to guess."

Less than two weeks later, Weidmann spoke at an institute devoted to financial history in Frankfurt. He started at the beginning, telling the story of money from its ancient origin as shells or salt or furs used as a means of exchange to its present-day status as a "social convention" no longer backed by tangible assets and issued on paper by central banks. Speaking in the hometown of Goethe, Weidmann examined *Faust* as an allegory of economics. "Mephistopheles stirs up the general elation even further," he said, "by saying, 'Such paper's convenient, for rather than a lot / Of gold and silver, you know what you've got. / You've no need of bartering and exchanging, / Just drown your needs in wine and love-making.' Those concerned are so overjoyed by this apparent blessing that they do not even suspect that things could get out of hand."

Weidmann didn't mention the ECB's new program explicitly, but given the timing and location of the speech and his open opposition to bond purchases, there was no escaping the obvious metaphor: Mario Draghi was Mephistopheles, and Europe had just made a deal with the devil.

But Weidmann's opposition was confined to words. He and his colleagues at the Bundesbank were unwilling to take the ultimate step of refusing to follow the ECB's orders to carry out the program, an action that would put him at odds with the German government and likely create a constitutional crisis. At his press conference announcing the new plan, Draghi was asked about the pressure placed on him by Weidmann. "I think that, in my job as president, I have been blessed by almost having unanimity on the very important and fundamental decisions that we have taken in the last few months. There is nothing I would wish more than to have total unanimity, of course. So I am looking forward to having that," Draghi said.

"I am what I am, really," the Italian said. "I think one thing that is required for this job . . . is that you have to think with your head, and external pressures do not really have a role to play in your decision making."

Three hours before Woodford presented his paper in Jackson Hole, Bernanke spoke. As always, his speech was more carefully considered than most that he gave, calibrated with the knowledge that the world was looking to the Explorers Room for guidance.

Quantitative easing and the other tools the Fed had been using since the end of 2008 to support growth had helped, Bernanke argued, and the downsides some had warned of hadn't materialized. But the U.S. economy was growing too slowly, unemployment was too high, and inflation seemed barely a threat. "We must not lose sight of the daunting economic challenges that confront our nation," the chairman said. "The stagnation of the labor market in particular is a grave concern not only because of the enormous suffering and waste of human talent it entails, but also because persistently high levels of unemployment will wreak structural damage on our economy that could last for many years."

Against that backdrop, Bernanke continued, "Taking due account of the uncertainties and limits of its policy tools, the Federal Reserve will provide additional policy accommodation as needed to promote a stronger economic recovery and sustained improvement in labor market conditions in a context of price stability."

And that was it.

The speech was notable for what it didn't say. Bernanke set the table for new easing, but he didn't reveal exactly what dish would be served. Would the Fed start yet another round of bond buying, a QE3? Would it expand Operation Twist to longer-term bonds, or pledge to keep interest rates even lower for even longer than previously promised?

Bernanke's lack of specificity was no accident.

Privately, the chairman had decided weeks earlier that the Fed needed to do more than continue its series of temporary, one-off measures. In the days after Jackson Hole, Bernanke began trying to steer his fellow members of the Federal Open Market Committee toward the same conclusion. He placed phone calls, sent e-mails, and, in the case of his colleagues on the Fed Board of Governors in Washington, arranged in-person meetings.

The FOMC had a number of members already committed to decisive action, among them Bernanke's inner circle of Janet Yellen and Bill Dudley and emerging thought leaders such as Charles Evans of the Chicago Fed and John Williams of San Francisco. Then there was the committee's more hawkish wing, the people who couldn't be swayed to vote for more monetary easing no matter what, including Jeffrey Lacker of the Richmond Fed and Charles Plosser of Philadelphia. Bernanke concentrated instead on the swing voters. They weren't the flashier members of the committee, whose public utterances attracted the most attention. But if he could bring all or most of them on board with a new policy, he knew that it would have staying power.

Bernanke spoke with Dennis Lockhart of the Atlanta Fed and James Bullard of the St. Louis Fed and e-mailed with Narayana Kocherlakota of Minneapolis. He met with Jeremy Stein and Jay Powell, two new Fed governors who were still feeling their way around the organization and wary of some of the risks attached to unconventional easing. He worked with Governor Elizabeth Duke, a banking expert with an independent streak who was a reluctant proponent of new easing, to adjust the language of his proposal with an eye toward reaching a compromise with any holdouts. In these conversations, Bernanke was partly seeing what his colleagues might be willing to do, partly trying to persuade them that the FOMC need not simply look at its options in isolation but make a Woodford-style commitment to boosting the U.S. economy until it returned to health.

On September 12, less than two weeks after the Jackson Hole speech, the committee gathered around its mahogany table in the Eccles Building where the results of Bernanke's handiwork were evident. The group agreed that it would be a good idea to do something like what Woodford had advocated, pledging to keep easy-money policies in place until a specific unemployment or inflation rate had been reached.

But there was disagreement on, among other things, what those numbers would be. So the committee settled on buying more bonds—$40 billion of them a month, initially. Combined with the Twist policy already in place, that meant the Fed would be pumping an extra $85 billion into the financial system every thirty days. And, the FOMC pledged, "If the outlook for the labor market does not improve substantially, the Committee will continue its purchases of agency mortgage-backed securities, undertake additional asset purchases, and employ its other policy tools as appropriate until such improvement is achieved in a context of price stability." It added that it expected that "a highly accommodative stance of monetary policy will remain appropriate for a considerable time after the economic recovery strengthens."

Translation: We'll keep pushing money into the system until the job market really starts to improve or inflation starts to become a problem. And we will act on whatever scale we need to until we achieve that goal. We're not going to take our foot off the gas, that is, until some time after the car has reached cruising speed.

Markets had been eagerly speculating about the possibility of QE3. Instead, they got something bigger: QE infinity.

Bernanke didn't stop there, however. For more than a year, he and the committee wrestled with the notion, first advocated by Charles Evans, of pledging to keep pushing money into the economy until either unemployment fell to some specific level or inflation rose above some specific level. Bernanke and many others on the FOMC saw the theoretical appeal of Evans's approach. It would clearly tie the future of the Fed's interest-rate policies to what happens in the economy. Perhaps the mere act of offering clarity of what levels of unemployment would coax the Fed to start raising rates—and how much inflation it could tolerate in the course of getting there—would make businesses and consumers more confident about the future. It was a practical way to apply the Woodford critique of Fed policy. There were quite a few things standing in the way. Fed leaders didn't want to send a signal that they were making policy based only on two numbers and didn't want people to confuse their "thresholds," as the strategy was known internally, for their longer-term targets for inflation and joblessness.

On December 12, 2012, following another FOMC meeting, Bernanke held his usual press conference. "The conditions now prevailing in the job market represent an enormous waste of human and economic potential," he said that Wednesday afternoon. The FOMC said it would keep ultra-low-interest-rate policies in place as long as the unemployment rate remained above 6.5 percent, so long as its forecast for inflation does not surpass 2.5 percent. Bernanke had pulled another rabbit from his hat, guiding his committee toward yet another novel tool to try to help bring the U.S. economy out of its doldrums. He had come full circle. The professor who preached to the Japanese more than a decade earlier about the need for experimentalism and resolve in the face of economic catastrophe was now making it happen, for better or worse. His was a lifelong war against economic policy defeatism. And in 2012, he was winning it.

Mervyn King was feeling Shakespearean when he took the stage at the South Wales Chamber of Commerce in October 2012. He discussed the state of the "sceptered isle," a reference to *Richard II*, acknowledging that given the global forces walloping the British economy, "this precious stone set in the silver sea seems more like a storm-tossed vessel."

But while the ECB and the Fed had undertaken bold new policies late in the summer of 2012 to try to combat those waves, the Bank of England had once more chosen inaction. The British economy was by many measures in worse shape than the United States, in part because of the tightening of fiscal purse strings that had started in 2010. King estimated that economic activity in Britain was 15 percent lower than it would have been had its pre-2007 trajectory held. The U.S. economy, by contrast, was functioning at about 6 percent below its potential.

Two weeks earlier, King had in another speech cited an exchange between John Maynard Keynes and Josiah Stamp, a great British industrialist. "Is not the mere existence of general unemployment for any length of time an absurdity, a confession of failure, and a hopeless and inexcusable breakdown of the economic machine?" asked Keynes in 1930, soon after the onset of the Great Depression. "Your language is rather violent," replied Lord Stamp. "You would not expect to put an earthquake tidy in a few minutes, would you? I object to the view that it is a confession of failure if you cannot put a complicated machine right all at once."

As King surveyed the British economy that autumn day in Cardiff, he saw a broken machine—but also one that was in the process of slowly repairing itself. "After a period of lopsided expansion, with growing trade deficits and debt levels, and a collapse of their banking systems, advanced economies across the world are facing a huge adjustment. Such is the scale of the global adjustment required that the generation we hope to inspire may live under its shadow for a long time to come," King said. He didn't rule out a return to quantitative easing, should conditions warrant it. But his tone was a far cry from that of Draghi or Bernanke, who offered open-ended pledges to return their economies to stability.

"Printing money is not . . . simply manna from heaven," King said. "There are no shortcuts to the necessary adjustment in our economy. . . . We shall have to be patient."

Every reign must end, and for the King of Threadneedle, that day was approaching. His term was to end in June 2013, and on November 26, 2012, chancellor George Osborne stood up in parliament to announce King's successor. Betting was so strong that Paul Tucker, King's respected deputy governor for financial stability, would get the job that bookmakers had stopped taking wagers. Osborne instead shocked the world, however: The 120th governor of the Bank of England wouldn't be British at all. Canadian Mark Carney, who headed the Bank of Canada, was the government's pick to follow King. Over twenty years, King had been a dominating force at the bank, and in the British economy. The selection of Carney was the clearest sign yet from the government that it was time for a rethinking.

. . .

T he fifth year of the crisis, then, looked a lot like the first. The Bank of England again stood by as others went into action as Mervyn King was convinced that the economy was finding its own way forward, difficult as that might be.

The ECB launched a bold intervention, aiming directly at the financial markets. Under Draghi, the central bank had become, if anything, even more creative and interventionist than anyone could have predicted in August 2007, when Jean-Claude Trichet received his vacation-interrupting telephone call about BNP Paribas. Trichet was by now ensconced in a gigantic office suite at the Banque de France overlooking the Jardin du Palais Royal, giving occasional speeches, influencing world events from the sidelines, and enjoying his time at Saint-Malo undisturbed.

The Federal Reserve, the first of the major central banks to cut interest rates to counter the wider economic damage of the financial crisis in 2007, again went a step further than any of its counterparts in easing monetary policy in 2012. The quiet, cerebral professor from Dillon, South Carolina, had become a savvy Washington power broker. Whether Bernanke's policies would succeed in getting the U.S. economy back on track was an open question, but his academic training told him that cheaper money was the best way to do so, and he made it happen.

The men who guided the world's leading central banks through the megacrisis had different assumptions, challenges, and approaches to leadership. But their common legacy is this: As ugly as the global economy looked five years after the onset of crisis, no war had broken out among the great global powers. Europe remained united. There had been no confidence-shattering hyperinflation or, outside of perhaps Greece and Spain, economic depression. None of this was a certainty. Peace and prosperity are never as deeply entrenched as they may seem at times when things are going well. Rather, they require people like Bernanke, King, and Trichet to safeguard them, often by doing things that are wildly unpopular. It may seem like damning by faint praise, but a catastrophe averted is no small thing.

The central bankers' judgments were far from perfect, and their mistakes—

allowing the collapse of Lehman Brothers, endorsing early fiscal austerity in Britain, moving with such hesitation and delay in the face of the eurozone crisis—will do lasting economic damage. Each will be leaving his institution a very different place from the one he inherited, more deeply entrenched in the vagaries of politics, more thoroughly intertwined in the workings of high finance, with so many Rubicons crossed that there can be no hope of going back. No one can say that the Fed will never bail out an investment bank, or that the Bank of England will never try to preach to Parliament about how to manage its books, or that the ECB will never prop up government finances.

Adam Posen, on his final day as a member of the Bank of England's Monetary Policy Committee, responded to Michael Woodford's Jackson Hole paper with a stirring rebuttal of the idea that central banks should let precedent or politics stop them from doing what they need to do to keep their economies healthy. "It is . . . quite literally a prehistoric argument in monetary terms to assert that central banks are engaged in experimental, unprecedented, or somehow scandalous and dangerous policy maneuvers today—we should stop giving such trumped-up rhetoric any credence," said Posen. "The idea that there are somehow pristine, virgin central banks, expected by the public to be like a vestal priesthood, that will be tainted forever by intervening in a given financial market, is . . . a truly primitive and antirational way of thinking about both economics and the beliefs of the general public."

Ben Bernanke, Mervyn King, and Jean-Claude Trichet learned from the failures of Rudolf von Havenstein and Montagu Norman, of Arthur Burns and Masaru Hayami. Their successors will learn from their failures. Democratic societies entrust central bankers with vast power because some things are so important yet so technically complex that we can't really put them to a vote. We're wrong to expect perfection. But we must demand progress. The story of central banking is also the story of civilization: discovering in fits and starts how to manage a just and prosperous society, forever taking small steps toward a better world.

## ACKNOWLEDGMENTS

Almost any book is the work of many people, and that is true of this one—which covers events that happened in nearly every corner of the world and in a span of 350 years—more than most. Howard Yoon of the Ross-Yoon Agency played a crucial role in refining the concept for this book; I also owe a great debt to his colleagues Gail Ross and Anna Sproul. Leonard Roberge, a terrific freelance editor, provided essential help in shaping this narrative and removed more unintelligible sentences and clunky metaphors than I prefer to admit. Scott Moyers and Mally Anderson at The Penguin Press were marvelous partners in shaping the book you hold in your hands. I also owe a great debt to Ann Godoff for taking a chance on a first-time author with an ambitious idea.

Lea Yu, a talented Beijing-based journalist, made major reporting contributions from China toward Chapter 20. The primary researchers on the book were, at various times, Anna Rose Bianco, Amanda Ruth Reynolds, and Jeniece Howe. Others who contributed research, translation, or other assistance were Athena Korlira and Elinda Labropoulou in Greece; Alessandra Pugliese in Italy; Catarina Nilsson in Sweden; and Caroline Huot in France.

I am greatly indebted to a number of people who read chapters and offered me advice; their work helped make the book more accurate in its factual details and smarter in its analytical conclusions. They include Liaquat Ahamed and Nicholas Lardy, along with several others who prefer not to be named, but know who they are. Final fact-checking was done by Lisa Bonos, Ylan Q. Mui, and Nathan Willis. Of course mistakes and weaknesses that remain are solely the fault of the author.

Many of the world's central bankers are represented by first-rate communications staff. They have a sometimes unpleasant job, being the public representatives of organizations that are inherently secretive, but many do their job with wisdom, good humor, and a genuine desire to help the public understand their institutions. I cannot list them all here, but will single out four to whom I owe a particular debt. Michelle Smith at the Federal Reserve Board has been among the closest advisers to a treasury secretary and two Fed chairmen for good reason; working with her is one of the great pleasures of the Fed beat. Diane Raley of the Kansas City Fed plays a crucial role in making the Jackson Hole Economic Symposium perhaps the hottest ticket in the world of economic policy. Regina Schüller and Eszter Miltenyi of the European Central Bank extended great kindness to this American in Frankfurt. These and other central bank public affairs staff around the world (and their bosses) will dislike parts of what is written here, but it is more accurate and thorough thanks to their assistance.

*The Washington Post,* my professional home since 2000, made this project possible in many ways: first, by teaching me to write and report, and then by putting me on the economics beat that, starting in 2007, gave me a front-row seat to one of the great stories of our age. I am particularly indebted to former executive editor Marcus Brauchli and financial editor Greg Schneider for allowing me to take an extended leave to report and write this book, and to chairman Don Graham and publisher Katharine Weymouth for their stewardship of one of the world's great journalistic entities. The financial desk at the *Post* has a long history of collegiality and warmth, and I have been lucky to make it my professional home. Steven Pearlstein has been a wise and generous mentor, and one could not hope for better colleagues than those who were friends and collaborators during the years of covering the crisis and its aftermath: Binyamin Appelbaum, Lisa Bonos, David Cho, Brady Dennis, Dina ElBoghdady, Zachary A. Goldfarb, Michael A. Fletcher, Kelly Johnson, Lori Montgomery, Steven Mufson, Ylan Q. Mui, Maralee Schwartz, Michael Shepard, Alan Sipress, Sandy Sugawara, Nancy Trejos, and Jia Lynn Yang. Since returning from book leave, I have worked with the superb Wonkblog team: Ezra Klein, Suzy Khimm, Sarah Kliff, Dylan Matthews, and Brad Plumer. *Post* colleagues who offered particular advice on reporting parts of this book include Anthony Faiola, Keith Richburg, and Howard Schneider. During a long stay in London for reporting, Michael Bogdan and Elizabeth Holt-Bogdan, Cassandra Vinograd and Adam Cohen, and Todd Rothman provided great company. And I could not have written this book without important assistance from Lauren Fish, Toan Luong, and Mary Pat Strasser.

I have benefited throughout from wonderful friendships, including with Amy Argetsinger; Margaret Chadbourn; Daniel Drum; Jon Finer; Justin Gillis; Steve, Tara, and Luca Goldenberg; Jay and Elysia Hulings; Jenna Johnson; Nicholas, Erin, and Lena Johnston; Emma Kristensson; Jack Massey; Ellen McCarthy; Bill McQuillen; Matt Vogel; and the marvelous Sarah Halzack. My parents, Co and Nancy Irwin, supported and encouraged me from my earliest days. My uncle Christopher Hicks nurtured my interest in words and ideas. And my siblings Molly Irwin and Nicholas and Ellerbe May and cousins Margaret and Amelia Hicks are the best a guy could hope for. My late grandparents, William Pinckney Irwin III, Walton "Skip" Hicks, and Nancy Jo Hicks, were inspiring examples for how to live a life.

# A NOTE ON SOURCES

I became the *Washington Post*'s beat reporter covering the Federal Reserve on August 16, 2007, one week after the European Central Bank launched the first major intervention of what is now known as the global financial crisis. I intensively covered events from that point forward, focused initially on the work of the Fed and then, when the crisis pivoted to Europe in 2010, with a more global dimension. It was a ringside seat for some of the defining events of our age, and this book is primarily based on the hundreds of interviews I conducted with key central bankers and other policymakers who directed the policy response to the crisis from 2007 on.

Reporting conducted specifically for this book took place in twenty-seven cities in eleven countries, between January 2011 and October 2012. I interviewed many of the senior central bankers whose actions are described here, as well as many more people close to them and other firsthand participants in the events described. The overwhelming majority of sources spoke on a condition of "deep background," meaning that I was free to use their information and insights, but could not attribute it to them by name or affiliation without further permission. Material that appears in this volume without attribution in the notes that follow was based on those interviews.

In most cases, U.S. economic data is drawn from FRED, the database of economic statistics from the Federal Reserve Bank of St. Louis. European economic data is usually from Eurostat, a service of the European Commission. Most financial market data is from Bloomberg.

This book has benefited from the work of generations of economists, historians, and journalists who have written more deeply on several of the historical episodes covered in this volume. Here are some particular recommendations for further reading on areas explored here—and an acknowledgment that I am indebted to these writers for their work.

David Wessel's *In Fed We Trust* and Andrew Ross Sorkin's *Too Big to Fail* are exhaustive journalistic accounts of the 2007–2008 phase of the crisis, from the vantage point of the Federal Reserve and Wall Street titans, respectively. Carlo Bastasin's *Saving Europe,* published in 2012, is the most detailed treatment to date of the eurozone crisis. Dan Conaghan's *The Bank* captures the work of the Bank of England before and during the crisis. Memoirs by two key finance ministers of this period, Hank Paulson (*On the Brink*) and Alistair Darling (*Back from the Brink*), are important pieces of the historical record as well.

Turning to the history of central banking included in this book, on the creation of Sweden's Riksbank, Gunnar Wetterberg's magisterial history of the institution, *Money and Power,* is a detailed and reliable guide. On the Bank of England's work in nineteenth-century Britain, Walter Bagehot's *Lombard Street: A Description of the Money Market* remains surprisingly engaging and understandable to the modern reader. Geoffrey Elliott's *The Mystery of Overend & Gurney* tells the detailed story of the proto–Lehman Brothers. Robert F. Bruner and Sean D. Carr tell the story of the financial crisis that led to the creation of the Fed in their *The Panic of 1907,* and H. W. Brands's *The Money Men* is a brief history of American central banking up to that point.

Ben Bernanke once wrote that "to understand the Great Depression is the Holy Grail of macroeconomics," and fortunately there is a wealth of both popular and scholarly efforts to do just that. Liaquat Ahamed's *Lords of Finance* covers the era through the window of its leading central bankers. Adam Fergusson's *When Money Dies* is a brisk and accessible account of the hyperinflation, and Gerald D. Feldman's *The Great Disorder* an exhaustive and authoritative version. On the economics of the Great Depression, *A Monetary History of the United States* by Milton Friedman and Anna Jacobson Schwartz is hard to surpass, and Charles Kindleberger's *The World in Depression* and Barry Eichengreen's *Golden Fetters* offer similarly rich pictures of the period.

On the creation of the eurozone, David Marsh's *The Euro* and Ottmar Issing's *The Birth of the Euro* are essential reading, and Kenneth Dyson and Kevin Featherstone's *The Road to Maastricht* is a richly detailed scholarly account. John Maynard Keynes's *Economic Consequences of the Peace* was written in 1919, yet is essential reading for anyone wishing to understand European history in the century since.

# NOTES

## INTRODUCTION: OPENING THE SPIGOT

2   **"Trust was shaken today"**: Vikas Bajaj and Mark Landler, "Mortgage Losses Echo in Europe and on Wall Street," *New York Times*, August 10, 2007, A1.

6   **"a welcome development"**: Bank of England, August 2007 inflation report, press conference transcript, August 8, 2007.

## CHAPTER 1: JOHAN PALMSTRUCH AND THE BIRTH OF CENTRAL BANKING

17   **"*snork, pork,* scolding and swearing"**: Gunnar Wetterberg, *Money and Power: From Stockholms Banco 1656 to Sveriges Riksbank Today* (Stockholm: Sveriges Riksbank, 2009), 44.

19   **So in 1619 the king and members of the merchant class got together**: Ibid., 21.

20   **"chief inspector of the banking system"**: Ibid., 33.

20   **A ten-daler plate**: Rodney Edvinsson, "Swedish Monetary Standards in Historical Perspective," Stockholm Papers in Economic History No. 6, Department of Economic History, Stockholm University, 2009, http://www.historia.se/SPEH6.pdf.

20   **"good convenience"**: Wetterberg, *Money and Power*, 32.

20   **the equivalent of $76 million in today's dollars**: Adjustment made using workers' wages to U.S. minimum wage.

24   **"no understanding of the matter"**: Wetterberg, *Money and Power*, 48.

## CHAPTER 2: LOMBARD STREET, RULE BRITANNIA, AND BAGEHOT'S DICTUM

26   **"We regret to announce"**: Geoffrey Elliott, *The Mystery of Overend & Gurney: A Financial Scandal in Victorian London* (London: Methuen, 2006), 180.

26   **There was the plantation in Dominica**: Ibid., 3–4.

27   **The bank's partners**: Ibid., 177–78.

27   **"One unlucky man"**: "London Letters," *Friend of India* (Calcutta), June 21, 1666.

27   **"The doors of the most respectable banking houses"**: "If anything can justify a suspension of the Bank," *Times (London)*, May 12, 1866.

27   **"It is impossible to describe"**: Elliott, *The Mystery of Overend & Gurney*, 181.

29   **"When a private person"**: Walter Bagehot, *Lombard Street: A Description of the Money Market* (London: Henry S. King & Co., 1873), 45–46.

29   **In 1873**: Ibid., 155–56.

32   **"The peculiar essence"**: Ibid., 78.

32   **On the morning of Black Friday**: Elliott, *Mystery*, 181.

32   **"The bankers . . . went wild with fright"**: "London Letters."

32   **"by every possible means"**: Bagehot, *Lombard Street*, 96.

33   **"Banking is a very peculiar business"**: Ibid., 81.

33 **"that no one may borrow":** Ibid., 94.

33 **businesses of all types are forced to pull back on their activity:** Elliott, *The Mystery of Overend & Gurney*, 185–86.

34 **Economic statistics for this era:** B. R. Mitchell, *British Historical Statistics* (Cambridge: Cambridge University Press, 1988).

34 **"mulcted for the unthrifty":** Elliott, *The Mystery of Overend & Gurney*, 184.

34 **"the most mischievous doctrine ever broached":** Thomson Hankey, *The Principles of Banking, Its Utility and Economy: With Remarks on the Working and Management of the Bank of England* (London: Effingham Wilson, 1887).

34 **Legislation to empower the bank:** John H. Wood, "Bagehot's Lender of Last Resort: A Hallowed Tradition," *Independent Review* (Winter 2003): 343–51.

## CHAPTER 3: THE FIRST NAME CLUB

35 **One of the men:** Nathaniel Wright Stephenson, *Nelson W. Aldrich, a Leader in American Politics* (New York: Charles Scribner's Sons, 1930), 373.

36 **"What was it drove our forefathers to this country?":** Matthew St. Clair Clarke and David A. Hall, *Legislative and Documentary History of the Bank of the United States* (Washington, DC: Gales & Seaton, 1832).

37 **Nicholas Biddle:** Phil Davies, "The Rise and Fall of Nicholas Biddle," *Federal Reserve Bank of Minneapolis, Region 22*, no. 3 (September 1, 2008).

37 **he could either tighten or loosen credit conditions:** Tim Todd, *The Balance of Power: The Political Fight for an Independent Central Bank, 1790–Present* (Kansas City: Federal Reserve Bank of Kansas City, 2009).

38 **"the Bank is neither a Jackson man":** Reginald C. McGrane, ed., *The Correspondence of Nicholas Biddle Dealing with National Affairs, 1807–1844* (Boston: Houghton Mifflin, 1919).

38 **"Both the constitutionality and the expediency":** Andrew Jackson, "First Annual Message," speech, United States Congress, Washington, DC, December 8, 1829.

38 **"the titles and estates of our future nobility":** 8 Reg. Deb. 141 (1831).

39 **The downturn was so severe:** Todd, *Balance of Power*, 9.

40 **In San Francisco itself, deposits were unavailable:** Robert F. Bruner and Sean D. Carr, *The Panic of 1907: Lessons Learned from the Market's Perfect Storm* (Hoboken, NJ: John Wiley & Sons, 2007), 24.

41 **Bank officials standing:** Ibid., 78.

42 **"A more incongruous meeting place":** Thomas W. Lamont, *Henry P. Davison: The Record of a Useful Life* (New York: Harper & Row, 1933), 81.

42 **"It is evident":** Nelson Aldrich, "Monetary Commission," address, Economic Club of New York, New York, November 29, 1909.

44 **Carter Glass:** Todd, *Balance of Power*, 12.

45 **"The great political power which President Jackson saw":** "He Uses a Tombstone to Bolster Argument: Grewsome Exhibit Made in the House by Congressman Smith in Opposing Money Bill," *Atlanta Journal-Constitution*, September 14, 1913, 4.

45 **"radical and revolutionary":** "As Bryan's Child Aldrich Attacks Money Measure," *Atlanta Journal-Constitution*, October 16, 1913, 1.

46 **"If, as most experts agree":** Channing Rudd, "How Money Makes Money," *Sun* (London), December 25, 1913, A2.

## CHAPTER 4: MADNESS, NIGHTMARE, DESPERATION, CHAOS: WHEN CENTRAL BANKING GOES WRONG, IN TWO ACTS

48 **"jealousy and ill-will toward our economic flowering":** Gerald D. Feldman, *The Great Disorder: Politics, Economics, and Society in the German Inflation, 1914–1924* (Oxford, London: Oxford University Press, 1993), 32.

48 **"The precondition for this continuation":** Ibid., 32.

48 **"took on a patriotic and fetishistic quality":** Ibid., 33.

49 **The resulting Treaty of Versailles:** Ibid., 148.

50 **"thin and pink-eyelidded":** Harold Nicolson, *Peacemaking, 1919, Being Reminiscences of the Paris Peace Conference* (Bethesda, MD: Simon Publications, 1933).

50 **The catalog of strange anecdotes:** Adam Fergusson, *When Money Dies: The Nightmare of the Weimar Collapse* (London: William Kimber, 1975), 140.

50 **Communities developed ersatz barter systems:** Ibid., 113.

51    For longer-term savings: Feldman, *The Great Disorder*, 583.

51    "made work much slower": Bernd Widdig, *Culture and Inflation in Weimar Germany* (Berkeley: University of California Press, 2001), 45.

51    "that money wouldn't buy four bottles of champagne": Ernest Hemingway, *By-Line Ernest Hemingway: Selected Articles and Dispatches of Four Decades*, ed. William White (New York: Scribner, 1967).

51    "in well-furnished houses": Feldman, *The Great Disorder*, 548.

51    But whatever workers saved on rent: Widdig, *Culture and Inflation in Weimar Germany*, 47.

51    "You could see mail carriers": Pearl S. Buck with Erna von Pustau. *How it Happens: Talk about the German People, 1914–1933* (New York: John Day Company, 1947).

52    "The Reichsbank . . . today issues": Fergusson, *When Money Dies*, 171.

52    "The running of the Reichsbank's note-printing organization": Ibid., 175.

52    "People just didn't understand what was happening": Adam Smith [George J. W. Goodman], *Paper Money* (New York: Dell, 1982), 57.

53    "not so much suffering as a sort of horrified incredulity": Edwin Lefevre, "The Little Fellow in Wall Street," *Saturday Evening Post*, January 4, 1930.

55    "an imperialist seeking the domination of the world": Liaquat Ahamed, *Lords of Finance: The Bankers Who Broke The World* (London: Penguin Press, 2009), 260.

55    "stupid, obstinate, devoid of imagination": Ibid., 260.

55    "short, squat, and bald": Ibid., 259.

57    "inexpedient to exhaust at the present time": Allan H. Meltzer, *A History of the Federal Reserve*, vol. 1, 1913–1951 (Chicago: University of Chicago Press, 2003), 294.

57    "Undoubtedly for a time we were in a serious condition": Charles S. Hamlin, address, Dinner in Honor of Visiting Journalists, Washington, DC, May 26, 1930.

57    But the slumping global economy: Charles Kindleberger, *The World in Depression: 1929–1939* (Berkeley: University of California Press, 1973), 131.

58    "have ample reserves": Meltzer, *A History of the Federal Reserve*, 323.

58    In December, it was 352 more: Milton Friedman and Anna Jacobson Schwartz, *A Monetary History of the United States, 1867–1960* (Princeton, NJ: Princeton University Press, 1963), 308.

59    On July 9, 1931, Luther boarded a private plane: Ahamed, *Lords of Finance*, 415.

59    "made the central banker into a kind of archpriest": Andrew Boyle, *Montagu Norman: A Biography* (New York: Weybright & Talley, 1967), 281.

59    "a spiritual home away from home": Ibid., 281.

59    The absence of jet travel: Barry Eichengreen, *Golden Fetters: The Gold Standard and the Great Depression, 1919–1939* (New York: Oxford University Press, 1992), 263–64.

59    The U.S. government, always skeptical: Ralph A. Young, memorandum to William McChesney Martin, August 25, 1961, http://fraser.stlouisfed.org/docs/historical/martin/21_04_19610825.pdf.

59    "too big for the central banks": Ahamed, *Lords of Finance*, 418.

60    "I declare to you": Robert Skidelsky, *John Maynard Keynes, 1883–1946: Economist, Philosopher, Statesman* (London: Penguin, 2003), 448.

60    "Sorry we have to go off tomorrow": Ahamed, *Lords of Finance*, 430.

60    "chuckling like a boy": Skidelsky, *John Maynard Keynes*, 449.

61    "Grain was being burned": Studs Terkel, *Hard Times: An Oral History of the Great Depression* (New York: New Press, 1970), 218.

## CHAPTER 5: THE ANGUISH OF ARTHUR BURNS

62    "This could be the most important weekend": William Safire, *Before the Fall: An Inside View of the Pre-Watergate White House* (New York: Belmont Tower Books, 1975), 510.

63    "Mr. President": Ibid., 517.

64    "My efforts to prevent closing of the gold window": Robert H. Ferrell, ed., *Inside the Nixon Administration: The Secret Diary of Arthur Burns, 1969–1974* (Lawrence: University Press of Kansas, 2010), 49.

64    "invariably courteous": Milton Viorst, "The Burns Kind of Liberal Conservatism," *New York Times*, November 9, 1969.

64    "I respect his independence": Eileen Shanahan, "Nixon Aide Sees Price Rise Relief," *New York Times*, February 1, 1970.

64    "When you gentlemen get up in the morning": Stephen H. Axilrod, *Inside the Fed* (Cambridge, MA: MIT Press, 2009), 62.

65    "I knew that I would be accepted": Ferrell, *Inside the Nixon Administration*, 47–48

65   **Charles Colson . . . spread the story:** Wyatt C. Wells, *Economist in an Uncertain World: Arthur F. Burns and the Federal Reserve, 1970-1978* (New York: Columbia University Press, 1994), 73.

65   **Another rumor spread by the White House:** Ferrell, *Inside the Nixon Administration*, 48.

65   **"Time is getting short":** Burton A. Abrams, "How Richard Nixon Pressured Arthur Burns: Evidence from the Nixon Tapes," *Journal of Economic Perspectives* 20, no. 4 (Fall 2006).

65   **By the end of 1970, *Time* had published a cover:** *Time*, December 14, 1970.

65   **In a contract negotiated in 1970:** "Business: 1970: The Year of the Hangover," *Time*, December 28, 1970.

66   **"that steakhouse menus arrived":** David Frum, *How We Got Here: The 70's* (New York: Basic Books, 2000), 291.

67   **He also put out a** THANK YOU FOR NOT SMOKING **sign:** William Greider, *Secrets of the Temple* (New York: Simon & Schuster, 1989), 66.

67   **"as a diversified conglomerate":** Donald F. Kettl, *Leadership at the Fed* (New Haven, CT: Yale University Press, 1986).

68   **The son of a town manager:** Eric Gelman et al., "America's Money Master," *Newsweek*, February 24, 1986, 46.

68   **"I used to say that I never":** Greider, *Secrets of the Temple*, 86.

68   **On an air force jet:** Ibid., 116.

68   **"The Anguish of Central Banking":** Arthur F. Burns, "The Anguish of Central Banking," lecture, Per Jacobsson Foundation Lectures, Belgrade, September 30, 1979.

69   **"Scylla and Charybdis have now come together":** "Meeting of the Federal Open Market Committee," transcript, Board of Governors of the Federal Reserve System, Washington, DC, October 6, 1979.

69   **"I said he would remember the press conference":** Joseph R. Coyne, "Reflection on the FOMC Meeting of October 6, 1979," *Federal Reserve Bank of St. Louis Review* 87, no. 2 (March/April 2005): 313.

70   **"Burns smoked a pipe":** Peter T. Kilborn, "Already a New Look at a Legend," *New York Times*, January 24, 1988.

70   **"The Credit Crunch Is On":** David Pauly et al., "The Credit Crunch Is On," *Newsweek*, March 31, 1980, 52.

70   **In 1981, one man who said he was upset:** Joseph B. Treaster, *Paul Volcker: The Making of a Financial Legend* (Hoboken, NJ: John Wiley & Sons, 2000), 6.

71   **"premeditated and cold-blooded murder":** Ibid.

## CHAPTER 6: SPINNING THE ROULETTE WHEEL IN MAASTRICHT

73   **"probably one of the world's most unsuccessful diplomatic missions":** Gilbert Kaplan, "Mad about Music," June 6, 2004, radio broadcast, transcript, http://www.wqxr.org/#!/programs/mam/2004/jun/06/.

73   **"Go for the jugular":** Sebastian Mallaby, *More Money Than God: Hedge Funds and the Making of a New Elite* (London: Penguin Press, 2010), 161.

73   **"Massive speculative flows":** Larry Elliott, Will Hutton, and Julie Wolf, "Pound Drops Out of ERM," *Guardian*, September 17, 1992, 1.

74   **In the first century AD:** Otmar Issing, *The Birth of the Euro* (Cambridge: Cambridge University Press, 2008), 3.

74   **"The solidarity in production thus established":** "The Schuman Declaration—9 May 1950," European Union, http://europa.eu/about-eu/basic-information/symbols/europe-day/schuman-declaration/index_en.htm.

75   **"Not all Germans believe in God":** Ibid., 23.

76   **"Today, as far as I know":** Mary Elise Sarotte, *1989: The Struggle to Create Post–Cold War Europe* (Princeton, NJ: Princeton University Press, 2009), 37.

76   **At 10:30 p.m.:** Ibid., 43.

77   **"destiny today is that Germany can only exist in a united Europe":** Karl Jaspers and Hannah Arendt, *Correspondence, 1926–1969* (New York: Mariner, 1993), 17.

77   **On December 3, 1991:** Kenneth Dyson and Kevin Featherstone, *The Road to Maastricht: Negotiating Economic and Monetary Union* (Oxford: Oxford University Press, 1999), 202.

77   **"It's done now":** Sarah Lambert, "Mozart Ushers in New Dawn at Maastricht," *Independent* (London), February 8, 1992, 9.

78   **"It can't happen":** Rudiger Dornbusch, "The Euro Controversy," MIT Department of Economics Editorial, 2001.

78  **In 2005, Alabama paid:** "Federal Taxes Paid vs. Spending Received by State," Tax Policy Center, October 19, 2007, http://taxfoundation.org/tax-topics/federal-taxes-paid-vs-spending-received-state.

79  **The bailout of savings and loans:** Timothy Curry and Lynn Shibut, "The Cost of the Savings and Loan Crisis: Truth and Consequences," *FDIC Banking Review* 13, no. 2 (December 2000), 26–35.

79  **Losses in Texas:** FDIC Division of Research and Statistics, *History of the Eighties, vol. 1, An Examination of the Banking Crises of the 1980s and early 1990s*, 183, http://www.fdic.gov/bank/historical/history/vol1.html.

79  **In 2007 . . . 787,000 more Americans relocated from the Northeast to the South:** Michael Keegan and Stephen Rountree, "Map: U.S. Migration Flows," *Pew Research Center*, December 17, 2008, http://www.pewsocialtrends.org/2008/12/17/u-s-migration-flows/.

79  **Barry Eichengreen:** Barry Eichengreen, "One Money for Europe? Lessons from the U.S. Currency Union," *Economic Policy* 5, no. 10 (1990): 117–87.

80  **"In the beginning there would be important disagreements":** Martin Feldstein, "EMU and International Conflict," *Foreign Affairs*, November/December 1997, 60.

80  **"Here's how the story has been told":** Paul Krugman, "The Euro: Beware of What You Wish For," *Fortune*, December 1998.

80  **"The European Commission did invite economists":** Eduardo Porter, "A Tempting Rationale for Leaving the Euro," *New York Times*, May 16, 2012, B1.

81  **On November 3, 1997:** Lionel Barber, "The Euro: Single Currency, Multiple Injuries: Lionel Barber Recounts the Race for the ECB Presidency and the Price of Chirac's Insistence on a Frenchman," *Financial Times*, May 5, 1998, 2.

82  **"Who is this man":** Alastair Campbell, *The Blair Years: Excerpts from the Alastair Campbell Diaries* (London: Hutchinson, 2007), 299.

82  **"the most difficult hours I have experienced in Europe":** Katherine Butler, "Blair Seals Backroom Deal over Presidency of Central Bank but Experts Fear Ferocious Row Could Ruin Currency's Credibility," *Independent (London)*, May 4, 1998.

## CHAPTER 7: MASARU HAYAMI, TOMATO KETCHUP, AND THE AGONY OF ZIRP

84  **"Extreme policy mistakes were the primary cause":** Ben S. Bernanke, "Comment on America's Historical Experience with Low Inflation," *Journal of Money, Credit, and Banking* 32, no. 4 (November 2000, Part 2), 995.

85  **It was calculated that the garden around the Imperial Palace:** Richard Werner, *Princes of the Yen: Japan's Central Bankers and the Transformation of the Economy* (Armonk, NY: M. E. Sharpe 2003), 89.

85  **Loan officers would even show up:** Ibid., 96.

86  **"He was called Pope":** Ibid., 62.

86  **"Japan does not need any more steel":** Ibid., 61.

88  **In one story that made its way around the Bank of Japan:** Richard C. Koo, *The Holy Grail of Macroeconomics: Lessons from Japan's Great Recession* (Hoboken, NJ: John Wiley & Sons, 2009), 237.

88  **Bernanke acknowledged this reality in a 2002 speech:** Ben S. Bernanke, "Making Sure 'It' Doesn't Happen Here," remarks, National Economists Club, Washington, DC, November 21, 2002, http://www.federalreserve.gov/BOARDDOCS/SPEECHES/2002/20021121/default.htm.

90  **"Purchasing Japanese government bonds can't be an option":** Alexander Urquhart, "BOJ Resists Government Bond Fund Scheme," *South China Morning Post*, February 12, 1999, 5.

90  **"To this outsider":** Ben S. Bernanke, "Japanese Monetary Policy: A Case of Self-Induced Paralysis," paper, ASSA Meetings, Boston, January 9, 2000.

90  **"We are getting closer to the stage":** "End to Deflation Fears Nearing, BOJ Chief Says," *Japan Times*, May 20, 2000.

90  **"The decision to end the zero-interest-rate policy was not wrong":** "BOJ Adopts Quantitative Monetary Easing Policy," *Daily Yomiuri* (Tokyo), March 20, 2001, 1.

91  **"It was a very difficult decision to make":** Mayumi Negishi, "Hayami Says Jesus Guided Him through Five-Year Ordeal," *Japan Times*, March 20, 2003.

91  **"Does an economy with a zero nominal interest rate":** Alan S. Blinder, "Monetary Policy at the Zero Lower Bound: Balancing the Risks," *Journal of Money, Credit, and Banking* 32, no. 4 (November 2000), 1093.

92    **"I promise":** Kazuo Ueda, "Japan's Experience with Zero Interest Rates," *Journal of Money, Credit, and Banking* 32, no. 4 (November 2000), 1107.

## CHAPTER 8: THE JACKSON HOLE CONSENSUS AND THE GREAT MODERATION

94    **"It's a very unusual day for an economist":** "Queen Knights Fed Chairman Greenspan," *Associated Press*, September 26, 2002.

96    **"What time of year are you going to hold it?":** Tim Todd and Bill Medley, *In Late August* (Kansas: Federal Reserve Bank of Kansas City, 2011).

96    **Volcker quickly became a regular:** Eric Gelman, "America's Money Master," *Newsweek*, February 24, 1986.

96    ***New York Times* columnist Paul Krugman:** Paul Krugman, "Pre-reading for Jackson Hole," *Conscience of a Liberal* (blog), *New York Times*, August 25, 2011.

97    **Don Kohn Death March:** Jon Hilsenrath, "The Path of Kohn: Crisis Changes a Fed Vet," *Wall Street Journal*, April 11, 2009.

97    **At Jackson Hole, two top academic economists:** Charles R. Bean, with Alan Blinder and John Taylor, "Monetary Policy After the Fall," paper presented and remarks, 2010 Economic Policy Symposium, Jackson Hole, WY.

99    **"South Florida is working off a totally new economic model":** Motoko Rich and David Leonhardt, "Trading Places: Real Estate Instead of Dot-Coms," *New York Times*, March 25, 2005.

100   **On the sunny Mediterranean coast of Spain:** "In Come the Waves," *Economist*, June 16, 2005.

100   **In 1980 . . . By 2005:** Federal Reserve Statistical Release, accession number Z.1.B.100.eB.100, http://federalreserve.gov/releases/z1/; Bureau of Economic Analysis, "Gross Domestic Product," http://bea.gov/national/index.htm#gdp.

101   **In Spain, for example:** Ricardo Gimeno and Carmen Martinez-Carrascal, "The Interaction between House Prices and Loans for House Purchase: The Spanish Case," working paper, Banco de España, 2006, http://ideas.repec.org/p/bde/wpaper/0605.html.

102   **"global savings glut":** Ben Bernanke, "The Global Saving Glut and the U.S. Current Account Deficit," remarks, Sandbridge Lecture, Virginia Association of Economists, Richmond, VA, March 10, 2005.

102   **In the United States alone:** SIFMA database (U.S. corporate issuance data), http://www.sifma .org/research/statistics.aspx.

103   **There were, by 2007, $202 trillion in financial assets on earth:** Charles Roxburgh, Susan Lund, and John Piotrowski, *Mapping Global Capital Markets 2011*, McKinsey Global Institute, August 2011, 2, http://www.mckinsey.com/.

104   **"elements of buoyancy":** Jean-Claude Trichet, interview with *Financial Times*, May 14, 2007, http://www.ecb.eu/press/key/date/2007/html/sp070518.en.html.

104   **"It's pretty clear there is an unsustainable underlying pattern":** Edmund Andrews, "Greenspan Is Concerned about 'Froth' in Housing," *New York Times*, May 21, 2005.

104   **The joke that went around London financial circles:** "Old Lady Is Dazed and Confused," *Guardian City Pages*, August 18, 2005.

104   **"Hardly a day goes by":** "Meeting of the Federal Open Market Committee," transcript, Board of Governors of the Federal Reserve System, Washington, DC, June 29–30, 2005.

104   **"Neither borrowers nor lenders appear particularly shaky":** Ibid.

105   **"Not in the United States":** Ibid.

106   **"I offer one more piece of evidence":** "Meeting of the Federal Open Market Committee," transcript, Board of Governors of the Federal Reserve System, Washington, DC, December 13, 2005.

107   **"the apparent consequence of a long period of economic stability":** Alan Greenspan, "Opening Remarks," Federal Reserve Bank of Kansas City Economic Symposium, Jackson Hole, WY, 2005.

107   **Raghuram Rajan:** See, for example, the documentary *Inside Job*.

107   **"I'd like to tell you about the Millennium Bridge in London":** Hyun Song Shin, "Commentary: Has Financial Development Made the World Riskier," Federal Reserve Bank of Kansas City Economic Symposium, Jackson Hole, WY, August 2005.

## CHAPTER 9: THE COMMITTEE OF THREE

112   **"It does not appear possible":** Robert J. Shiller, "Understanding Recent Trends in House Prices and Homeownership," Federal Reserve Bank of Kansas City Economic Symposium, August 31, 2007.

112   **"I am convinced":** Jean-Claude Trichet, "Europe: Cultural Identity," speech, Center for Financial Studies, Frankfurt, March 16, 2009.

113 **"It was . . . a very emotional moment"**: Corinne Lhaik, "Interview with Jean-Claude Trichet," *L'Express*, September 29, 2004, http://www.ecb.int/press/key/date/2004/html/sp041009 .en.html.

114 **By late afternoon:** Jack Ewing, "A Fight to Make Banks More Prudent," *New York Times*, December 20, 2011, B1.

114 **"Crisis is part of his DNA":** Krista Hughes, "How Jean-Claude Changed the ECB," Reuters, November 9, 2010.

114 **"With slightly condescending flattery":** David Marsh, *The Euro: The Battle for the New Global Currency* (New Haven, CT: Yale University Press, 2009), 220.

115 **"My life compass":** James G. Neuger and Simon Kennedy, "Trichet Life Compass Points to Euro at Center of European Unity," Bloomberg News, June 7, 2010.

116 **"there were Jews up in Boston":** David Wessel, *In Fed We Trust: Ben Bernanke's War on the Great Panic* (New York: Crown Business, 2009), 70.

116 **"If you had known Ben Bernanke as a student":** Rich Miller and Jennifer Ryan, "Europe Crisis Rescue Begins with MIT Men as a Matter of Trust," Bloomberg News, January 12, 2012.

117 **"he would look at the numbers":** Ben White, "Bernanke Unwrapped," *Washington Post*, November 15, 2005.

118 **He talks baseball with Lenny Gilleo:** Kai Ryssdal, "The Man Who Makes Ben Bernanke Look Good," *Marketplace*, American Public Radio, April 17, 2012, http://www.marketplace.org/topics/ life/final-note/man-who-makes-ben-bernanke-look-good.

121 **"incredibly stubborn . . . exasperating":** Alistair Darling, *Back from the Brink: 1000 Days at No. 11* (London: Atlantic Books, 2011), 14.

121 **"as an autocratic fiefdom of the Governor":** Ibid., 70.

122 **"Before the crisis":** Chris Giles, "The Court of King Mervyn," *Financial Times Weekend Magazine*, May 5–6, 2012, 17.

122 **"fusse[d] . . . about who has turned up":** Ibid., 17.

123 **"I think the role of conductor":** "Mervyn King," *Mad about Music*, WQXR, June 6, 2004, http:// www.wqxr.org/#!/programs/mam/2004/jun/06/.

## CHAPTER 10: OVER BY CHRISTMAS

125 **"You don't want to be the ones in the end of the queue":** "Customers queue at Northern Rock," YouTube, accessed April 15, 2012, http://www.youtube.com/watch?v=EyVk8EI6asQ.

125 **"They're behaving perfectly rationally":** Alistair Darling, *Back from the Brink: 1000 Days at Number 11* (London: Atlantic Books, 2011).

126 **Known before 1997 as the Northern Rock Building Society:** "Run on the Rock," *Treasury Select Committee of the House of Commons Report I*, January 24, 2008.

126 **When Northern Rock needed cash:** Ibid., 48.

127 **"During the conference call":** Darling, *Back from the Brink*.

127 **"febrile and fevered atmosphere":** "Run on the Rock," 63.

128 **"Your guy Mervyn has a high pain threshold":** Darling, *Back from the Brink*, 28.

129 **As economist Hyun Song Shin . . . explained:** Hyun Song Shin, "Global Banking Glut and Loan Risk Premium," paper, 12th Jacques Polak Annual Research Conference, International Monetary Fund, November 10–11, 2011.

131 **The list of those borrowing substantial amounts:** "Term Auction Facility lending details," Federal Reserve Board, December 1, 2010, http://www.federalreserve.gov/newsevents/reform_taf.htm.

131 **"We think it is a right way to cooperate":** European Central Bank Press Release Database, bond purchase data, http://www.ecb.int/press/.

134 **"What appears to be in substance":** John Brinsley and Anthony Massucci, "Volcker Says Fed's Bear Loan Stretches Legal Power," *Bloomberg News*, April 8, 2008.

135 **"Television dramas":** Jean-Claude Trichet, "President's Address," speech, ECB and Its Watchers IX Conference, Frankfurt, Germany, September 7, 2007, http://www.ecb.int/press/key/date/2007/ html/sp070907.en.html.

137 **"We exchanged many opinions":** Jean-Claude Trichet, press conference, June 8, 2008, http:// www.ecb.int/press/pressconf/2008/html/is080605.en.html.

137 **"We are solemnly telling all economic agents":** Jean-Claude Trichet, press conference, July 3, 2008, http://www.ecb.int/press/pressconf/2008/html/is080703.en.html.

140 **To Geithner, the proposal seemed "gimmicky":** Anton R. Valukas, *Lehman Brothers Holdings Inc. Chapter 11 Proceedings Examiner Report* 8 (2010): 12.

140 **"raise significant concerns":** Scott Alvarez, "Re: Lehman Good Bank/Bad Bank idea discussed last

night," e-mail message to Kieran Fallon, July 15, 2008, obtained by Financial Crisis Inquiry Commission, http://fcic.law.stanford.edu/resource.

141 **"That's not to imply":** Patrick M. Parkinson, "Re: Fw: Our Options in the Event of a Run on LB," e-mail message to Scott Alvarez et al., July 21, 2008.

141 **"If we think that the run had progressed too far":** Joseph Sommer, "Re: another option we should present re triparty," e-mail message to Jamie McAndrews et al., July 13, 2008.

142 **"We thought a year ago":** *Treasury Committee Hearing on Bank of England, August 2008 Inflation Report* (Sept. 11, 2008), http://www.parliament.the-stationery-office.co.uk/pa/cm2007 08/cmselect/cmtreasy/uc1033-i/uc103302.htm.

143 **"financial-market correction":** Jean Claude Trichet, speech, 2008 Eurofi Conference, Nice, France, September 11, 2008, http://www.ecb.int/press/key/date/2008/html/sp080911_2.en.html.

## CHAPTER 11: A WALL OF MONEY

146 **"The failure of AIG":** Ben Bernanke, lecture, George Washington University, Washington, DC, March 27, 2012, transcript by Federal News Service.

147 **a more apt comparison was with popcorn:** Edward P. Lazear, "The Euro Crisis: Doubting the 'Domino' Effect," *Wall Street Journal*, October 31, 2011.

149 **"We came very, very close":** Michael Grunwald, "Person of the Year 2009," *Time*, December 16, 2009.

151 **"conjured up trillions of new dollars":** Ibid.

152 **"Irish bank deposits are not in any danger":** Aine Hegarty, "Don't Panic! Finance Minister Moves to Allay Savings Fears of Bank Customers," *Mirror*, September 20, 2008.

154 **The Fed also pumped dollars into individual foreign banks:** Bloomberg News database, lending data, http://www.bloomberg.com/data-visualization/federal-reserve-emergency-lending/.

157 **"I don't really understand":** Andrew Ross Sorkin, *Too Big to Fail: How Wall Street and Washington Fought to Save the Financial System—and Themselves* (New York: Viking, 2009), 526.

157 **The TARP was among the most unpopular programs . . . ever undertaken:** Karlyn Bowman and Andrew Rugg, "TARP, the Auto Bailout, and the Stimulus: Attitudes about the Economic Crisis," American Enterprise Institute, May 2010, http://www.aei.org/files/2010/04/22/Economic Crisis-2010.pdf.

158 **"You must save your banks":** "Trichet orders Lenihan 'Save your banks at all costs,'" YouTube, http://www.youtube.com/watch?v=WDN7NiEdNJO.

158 **Hurley called Trichet at 6 a.m.:** Shane Ross, *The Bankers: How the Banks Brought Ireland to Its Knees* (Dublin: Penguin Ireland, 2009), 196.

158 **Alistair Darling found out about it on the BBC morning news:** Alistair Darling, *Back from the Brink: 1000 Days at No. 11* (London: Atlantic Books, 2011), 143.

158 **"an impossible position":** Ibid., 143.

159 **"What were they doing screwing around in the United States?":** Craig Whitlock and Ed Cody, "Europe Beginning to Realize Its Lenders Share the Blame," *Washington Post*, October 2, 2008, A12.

159 **"To put it mildly":** Marcus Walker, Joellen Perry, and David Gauthier-Villars, "EU Is Divided on Crisis Measures," *Wall Street Journal*, October 2, 2008.

159 **"If we cannot cobble together a European solution":** Carlo Bastasin, *Saving Europe: How National Politics Nearly Destroyed the Euro* (Washington, DC: Brookings Institution Press, 2012), 15.

160 **people were withdrawing 500-euro notes:** Ibid., 55.

164 **"If two people always agree":** Paul Wiseman, "Bernanke Nonplussed by Dissenters," *Associated Press*, September 19, 2011.

164 **"I felt after going for a walk down the hall":** David Wessel, *In Fed We Trust: Ben Bernanke's War on the Great Panic* (New York: Crown Business, 2009), 258.

## CHAPTER 12: THE BATTLE FOR THE FED

172 **A Gallup poll in the summer of 2009:** Michael Mandel, "Behind Bernanke's Charm Offensive," *BusinessWeek*, July 30, 2009.

172 **"You never want a serious crisis to go to waste":** Gerald Seib, "In Crisis, Opportunity for Obama," *Wall Street Journal*, November 21, 2008.

173 **"giving his son a bigger, faster car":** Neil Irwin and Binyamin Appelbam, "Lawmakers Balk as Administration Tries to Redefine Central Bank's Role," *Washington Post*, June 19, 2009, A1.

175 **"absolutely bizarre":** *Semiannual Monetary Policy Report to the Congress, Before the House*

*Financial Services Committee,* 111th Cong., February 24, 2010, statement of Ben Bernanke, Chairman of the Federal Reserve.

177  **"Mr. Chairman, I understand your objectives here":** *Confirmation Hearing, Before the Senate Banking Committee,* 111th Cong., December 3, 2009, statement of Ben Bernanke, Chairman of the Federal Reserve.

177  **"If the Fed were running for reelection":** Brady Dennis and David Cho, "Fed Losing Support on Bank Oversight," *Washington Post,* November 7, 2009, A18.

182  **He'd won the confidence of Wall Street:** Phil Izzo, "Economists Call for Bernanke to Stay, Say Recession Is Over," *Wall Street Journal,* August 11, 2009.

183  **"I believe that Ben Bernanke deserves substantial credit":** *Executive Session to Vote on Nominees,* Senate Banking Comm., 111th Cong., December 17, 2009.

189  **"Massachusetts was kind of a wake-up call":** Neil Irwin and Lori Montgomery, "Populist Backlash Puts Bernanke under Siege," *Washington Post,* January 23, 2010, A1.

198  **"The time is now that we have got to end secrecy at the Fed":** "Senate Session, Part 1," U.S. Senate, (Washington, DC: C-Span, May 11, 2010), http://www.c-spanvideo.org/program/293440-1.

198  **"I had to make a political decision":** Bernie Sanders, Federal News Service press conference transcript, Washington, DC, May 11, 2010, http://www.fednews.com/.

## CHAPTER 13: THE NEW GREEK ODYSSEY

206  **"It is very important":** Jean-Claude Trichet, press conference, European Central Bank, Frankfurt, Germany, Jan. 14, 2010, http://www.ecb.int/press/pressconf/2010/html/is100114.en.html.

207  **"I do not comment myself on absurd hypotheses":** Ibid.

208  **"Confident":** Howard Schneider and Anthony Faiola, "Hesitation by Leaders Drove Cost of Europe's Crisis Higher," *Washington Post,* June 16, 2010.

209  **"We have spent considerable effort":** *Federal Reserve's exit strategy, Before the House Committee on Financial Services,* 112th Cong., February 10, 2010, statement by Ben S. Bernanke, Chairman of the Federal Reserve.

209  **"The global economic situation has . . . improved":** Jim Flaherty, "G7 Chair's Summary," remarks, G7 Meeting of Finance Ministers and Central Bank Governors, Iqaluit, Canada, February 6, 2010, http://www.g7.gc.ca/news-nouvelles-eng.html.

211  **"Is Greece making the German banks bankrupt?":** Carlo Bastasin, *Saving Europe: How National Politics Nearly Destroyed the Euro* (Washington, DC: Brookings Institution Press, 2012), 183.

211  **"It is the intention of the ECB's Governing Council":** Jean-Claude Trichet, "Introductory statement before the Plenary of the European Parliament," speech, European Parliament, Brussels, Belgium, March 25, 2010, http://www.ecb.int/press/key/date/2010/html/sp100325.en.html.

212  **"the IMF's technical assistance is very important":** Jean-Claude Trichet, press conference, European Central Bank, Frankfurt, Germany, March 4, 2010.

212  **"I never said myself":** Jean-Claude Trichet, press conference, European Central Bank, Frankfurt, Germany, April 8, 2010.

212  **"the mechanism decided today":** Stephen Castle and Matthew Saltmarsh, "Europeans Reach Deal on Rescue Plan for Greece," *New York Times,* March 25, 2010.

214  **Here's a by-the-numbers summation:** International Monetary Fund's World Economic Outlook Database, GDP and other indicators, http://www.imf.org/.

215  **"It is a national and imperative need":** George A. Papandreou, "Imperative Need to Activate the Support Mechanism," speech, Castelorizo, Greece, April 23, 2010, http://www.papandreou.gr.

215  **"frontloaded multiyear adjustment effort":** George Papaconstantinou and George Provopoulos, e-mail correspondence with Dominique Strauss-Kahn, May 3, 2010, http://www.greekembassy.org/Embassy/files/GREECE%20%E2%80%94%20MEMORANDUM%20TO%20IMF%20ON%20ECONOMIC%20AND%20FINANCIAL%20POLICIES14-05-20100.pdf.

216  **"We were also asked by the Heads of State and Government":** Jean-Claude Trichet, press conference, Lisbon, Portugal, May 6, 2010, http://www.ecb.int/press/pressconf/2010/html/is100506.en.html.

217  **The streets of Athens erupted in protests:** Dan Bilefsky, "Three Reported Killed in Greek Protests," *New York Times,* May 6, 2010, A6.

217  **"Better breaking the rule-book":** "The ECB's Last Option: Bring out the Hank Paulson Bazooka," *Business Insider,* May 5, 2010.

218  **"Is the purchase of government bonds an option:** Trichet, press conference, May 6, 2010.

218  **The market was already down:** "Findings Regarding the Market Events of May 6, 2010," *Report of*

*the Staffs of the CFTC and SEC to the Joint Advisory Committee on Emerging Regulatory Issues,* September 30, 2010, http://www.sec.gov/news/studies/2010/marketevents-report.pdf.

219 **At the moment of the crash:** Bastasin, *Saving Europe,* 201.

222 **"My main message for the governments was":** James G. Neuger and Simon Kennedy, "Trichet Life Compass Points to Euro at Center of European Unity," *Bloomberg News,* June 7, 2010.

223 **The ECB will buy bonds:** "How the Euro Rescue Package Came Together," *Der Spiegel,* May 17, 2010.

223 **"When a house is burning":** Ibid.

225 **"These people have been concerned with their own problems":** Gianni Toniolo, *Central Bank Coordination at the Bank for International Settlements, 1930–1973* (Cambridge: Cambridge University Press, 2005), 198.

225 **It happened so often:** David Wessel, *In Fed We Trust: Ben Bernanke's War on the Great Panic* (New York: Crown Business 2009), 1.

226 **Geithner was also in frequent touch with Trichet:** Calendars of the Treasury Secretary, http://www.treasury.gov/FOIA/Pages/calendars.aspx.

228 **As the finance ministers gathered in Brussels that Sunday:** "How the Euro Rescue Package Came Together," *Der Spiegel.*

229 **"With all due respect to Australia":** Ibid.

231 **"On some decisions there was unanimity":** David Tweed and Simone Meier, "Trichet Indicates ECB Decision to Buy Bonds Wasn't Backed by All Members," *Bloomberg News,* May 10, 2010.

## CHAPTER 14: THE KING'S SPEECH

233 **"This I found curious":** Alistair Darling, *Back from the Brink: 1,000 Days at Number 11* (London: Atlantic Books 2011), 254.

234 **"It has been a quite a year":** Mervyn King, Speech at the Lord Mayor's Banquet for Bankers and Merchants of the City of London at the Mansion House, June 17, 2009.

234 **"Everyone knew what he was getting at":** Darling, *Back from the Brink,* 254.

234 **"Put your books in order":** Edmund Conway, *Daily Telegraph,* June 18, 2009, 1.

236 **Queen Elizabeth II was sufficiently alarmed:** Dan Conaghan, *The Bank: Inside the Bank of England* (London: Biteback Publishing, 2012), 219.

236 **"everyone did see it coming":** Charles Moore, "We Prevented a Great Depression, but People Have the Right to Be Angry," *Daily Telegraph,* March 5, 2011, 4.

237 **"contribute to protecting and enhancing the stability":** Banking Act of 2009, http://www .legislation.gov.uk/ukpga/2009/1/part/7/crossheading/bank-of-england/enacted.

237 **"I do not think we can afford to wait":** Treasury—Minutes of Evidence: Bank of England May 2009 Inflation Report, http://www.publications.parliament.uk/pa/cm200809/cmselect/cmtreasy/ 763/09062401.htm.

242 **"I just think it's more complicated":** Mervyn King press conference, Quarterly Inflation Report, February 10, 2010, http://www.bankofengland.co.uk/publications/Documents/inflationreport/ conf100210.pdf.

242 **"If there were any mobile phones":** Edmund Conway, "Watch Out: The Governor's About; Mervyn King's Latest Criticism of the Handling of the Recession Was a Body Blow to the PM, Says Edmund Conway," *Daily Telegraph,* January 21, 2010, 23.

242 **"This is a decisive moment":** Daniel Bentley, "Top Economists Call for Rapid Deficit Cut," *Independent* (London), February 14, 2010.

242 **Five times in the winter and spring of 2010:** Conaghan, *Back from the Brink,* 241.

243 **"King expressed great concern":** U.S. Embassy London, "Bank of England Governor: Concern about Recovery," Cable 10LONDON364, http://wikileaks.org/cable/2010/02/10LONDON364.html.

244 **"was the spectre which loomed over our talks":** David Laws, *22 Days in May: The Birth of the Lib Dem-Conservative Coalition* (London: Biteback Publishing, 2010), 109.

246 **"The most important thing now":** Bank of England, Quarterly Inflation Report Q&A, May 12, 2010, http://www.bankofengland.co.uk/publications/Documents/inflationreport/conf120510.pdf.

247 **"The age of plenty is over":** James Kirkup, "First Swing of the Axe: Osborne £6 Billion 'Taste' of Where the Axe Will Fall," *Daily Telegraph,* May 24, 2010, 1.

248 **"I do . . . Chancellor, welcome your commitment":** Mervyn King, Speech at the Lord Mayor's Banquet for Bankers and Merchants of the City of London at the Mansion House, June 16, 2010, http://www.bankofengland.co.uk/publications/Documents/speeches/2010/speech437.pdf.

251 **"thirst for power and influence"**: David Blanchflower, "Mervyn King Must Go," *Guardian*, December 1, 2010, http://www.guardian.co.uk/commentisfree/2010/dec/01/mervyn-king-bank-of-england.

251 **"the issue of confidence simply doesn't arise"**: Jennifer Ryan and Thomas Penny, "Cameron Backs King as Wikileaks Cites BOE Chief's Concern on Inexperience," Bloomberg News, December 1, 2010.

251 **"I have never discussed with [Osborne]"**: Bank of England 2011 Inflation Report, Transcript of Treasury Select Committee, March 1, 2011, http://www.publications.parliament.uk/pa/cm201011/cmselect/cmtreasy/798/11030102.htm.

252 **"Notwithstanding my affection for the rock music of the seventies"**: Andrew Sentance, "Ten Good Reasons to Tighten," speech before the Ashridge Alumni Business Briefing at the Institute of Directors, London, February 24, 2011, http://www.bankofengland.co.uk/publications/Documents/speeches/2011/speech476.pdf.

252 **"Central bankers' fears on this score"**: Adam Posen, "The Case for Doing More," speech to Hull and Humber Chamber of Commerce, Industry, and Shipping, Hull, September 28, 2010, http://www.bankofengland.co.uk/publications/Documents/speeches/2010/speech449.pdf.

CHAPTER 15: THE PERILOUS MAIDEN VOYAGE OF THE QE2

256 **"I've been telling you"**: *Glenn Beck*, transcript, Fox News Network, New York, November 3, 2010.

256 **"We shouldn't be playing around with inflation"**: Robert Costa, "Palin to Bernanke: Cease and Desist," *National Review Online*, November 7, 2010, http://www.nationalreview.com/corner/252715/palin-bernanke-cease-and-desist-robert-costa.

256 **"Look, we have Congress doing tax and spend"**: *Fox News Sunday with Chris Wallace*, transcript, Fox News Network, New York, November 7, 2010.

256 **"I don't recognize the economic argument behind this measure"**: "Interview with German Finance Minister Schäuble," *Der Spiegel*, November 8, 2010.

257 **"does not recognize . . . its obligation"**: Christopher Bodeen, "China Knocks U.S. Plan to Pump Money into System," *Associated Press*, November 8, 2010.

257 **In a seven-minute YouTube video**: David Weigel, "The Man behind the Quantitative Easing Cartoon Speaks!" *Slate*, November 22, 2010.

258 **"The Federal Reserve . . . is not a repair shop"**: Kevin M. Warsh, "The New Malaise and How to End It," *Wall Street Journal*, November 8, 2010.

261 **Bernanke had in fact . . . urged Fed staff**: Neil Irwin, "Federal Reserve Weighs Steps to Offset Slowdown in Economic Recovery," *Washington Post*, July 8, 2010.

274 **"Good afternoon, everybody"**: "Board of Governors of the Federal Reserve," redacted transcript, March 7, 2012, 491, http://www.federalreserve.gov/foia/files/2007-2010-draft-fomc-transcript-excerpts.pdf.

279 **"Calls w/media"**: Chairman's Calendar, November 2010, obtained through Freedom of Information Act request to Federal Reserve Board of Governors.

279 **"One myth that's out there"**: *60 Minutes*, transcript, CBS News, December 5, 2010.

280 **"I'm a little bit more sympathetic to central bankers now"**: Ben Bernanke, press conference, Federal Reserve, Washington, DC, June 22, 2011.

CHAPTER 16: THE CHOPPER, THE TROIKA, AND THE DEAUVILLE DEBACLE

283 **"ready to rip up the books"**: Fiach Kelly, "The Day 'Chopper' Rolled into Town," *Irish Independent*, November 19, 2010.

284 **"I'm not used to a situation where I'm so recognizable"**: Declan Lynch, "Paddy Gets His Answer to the Only Question That Matters," *Sunday Independent*, December 5, 2010.

284 **"nobody was really sure what the international officials looked like"**: Kelly, "The Day 'Chopper' Rolled into Town."

284 **"nice welcoming lounge"**: Finbarr Flyn, "Ryanair CEO Says $823 Million Dublin Terminal Explains Why Nation 'Broke,'" *Bloomberg News*, November 19, 2010.

284 **As the *Independent* headlined a letter to the editor**: Walter Naugton, "Better Chopra Than Our Hopeless Lot," *Irish Independent*, November 22, 2010, http://www.independent.ie/opinion/letters/better-chopra-than-our-hopeless-lot-2429998.html.

285 **"I guess older people will be upset"**: Henry McDonald, Elena Moya, and Andrew Clark, "From Defiance to Capitulation: Six Days That Humbled Ireland," *Guardian*, Nov. 20, 2010.

287 **By the last week of August:** "Consolidated financial statement of the Eurosystem as at 27 August 2010," press release, European Central Bank, Frankfurt, Germany, August 27, 2010, http://www .ecb.int/press/pr/wfs/2010/html/fs100831.en.html.

288 **"Ladies and gentlemen, let's not talk around it":** Angela Merkel, "Laudatio der Bundeskanzlerin der Bundesrepublik Deutschland," speech, Aachen, Germany, May 13, 2010, translated by Carlo Bastasin in *Saving Europe: How National Politics Nearly Destroyed the Euro* (Washington, DC: Brookings Institution Press, 2012), 219.

289 **They met at the Hotel Royal:** Bastasin, *Saving Europe*, 236.

290 **"providing the necessary arrangements":** "Franco-German Declaration: Statement for the France-Germany-Russia," summit, Deauville, France, October 18, 2010, http://www.euo.dk/ upload/application/pdf/1371f221/Franco-german_declaration.pdf.

290 **At just after 5 p.m.:** Charles Forelle, David Gauthier-Villars, Brian Blackstone, and David Enrich, "As Ireland Flails, Europe Lurches across the Rubicon," *Wall Street Journal*, December 27, 2010, A1.

290 **"We're more or less used to Germany and France cooking things up":** Joshua Chaffin and Peter Spiegel, "Franco-German Bail-out Pact Divides EU," *Financial Times*, October 24, 2010.

291 **"You're going to destroy the euro!":** Forelle et al., "As Ireland Flails."

291 **"We must be clear about how the markets work":** Bastasin, *Saving Europe*, 239.

292 **"The IMF does not make necessarily the ex-ante working assumption":** Jean-Claude Trichet and Vitor Constancio, "Introductory statement with Q&A," speech, Frankfurt, Germany, November 4, 2010, http://www.ecb.int/press/pressconf/2010/html/is101104.en.html.

293 **By November 2010:** Universität Osnabrück, Euro Crisis Monitor, http://www.iew.uni-osnabrueck. de/en/8959.htm.

293 **"it is not a normal situation":** Trichet and Constancio, "Introductory statement."

293 **"We took all the opportunities":** Arthur Beesley, "Ireland's Meltdown Is the Outcome of the Policies of Its Elected Politicians," *Irish Times*, January 15, 2011, 11.

294 **"I don't believe there were any other real options":** James G. Neuger and Simon Kennedy, "Ireland Gets $113 Billion Bailout as EU Ministers Seek to Halt Debt Crisis," *Bloomberg News*, November 29, 2010.

295 **"The heads of state or government of the euro area":** "European Council 16–17 December 2010 Conclusions," transcript, Brussels, Belgium, January 25, 2011, http://www.consilium.europa.eu/ uedocs/cms_data/docs/pressdata/en/ec/118578.pdf.

296 **"A Luta é Alegria":** Susana Morela Marques, "Portugal's Eurovision Protest," *Guardian*, May 2, 2011.

296 **"The only work we can get is 'work experience'":** Peter Wise, "Portugal's 'Desperate Generation' Cries Out," *Financial Times*, March 11, 2011.

297 **"Enough is enough!":** "Greece: Clashes in Athens between Police and Protesters," *BBC News*, May 11, 2011, http://www.bbc.co.uk/news/world-europe-13356923.

297 **The suicide rate in Greece in 2011:** Erik Kirschbaum, "Suicides Have Greeks on Edge before Election," Reuters, April 28, 2012.

297 **Tensions between the troika and Prime Minister George Papandreou's government:** Bastasin, *Saving Europe*, 275.

297 **"The package that is there":** Jussi Rosendahl and Terhi Kinnunen, "Populist Party Surges in Finn Poll, EU Aid at Risk," Reuters, April 17, 2011.

299 **"The euro area needs someone who can change his mind":** Jean-Philippe LaCour, Karl Meyer, and Dominique Seux, "BCE: Conflit Paris-Berlin en vue sur la succession de Trichet" [ECB: Paris-Berlin Conflict for the Succession of Trichet], *Les Echos*, January 18, 2011, 8.

300 **"Of course she is angry":** Veit Medick and Philipp Wittrock, "Weber's Departure Undermines Merkel's EU Clout," *Der Spiegel*, February 11, 2011.

301 **"Please, not this Italian!":** Quentin Peel, "Draghi Wins Over German Newspaper," *Financial Times*, April 29, 2011.

301 **"both come from orderly nations":** Hans-Jürgen Schlamp, "Europe's Next Top Banker May Be Italian," *Der Speigel*, February 23, 2011.

301 **"at second glance it is clear":** Peel, "Draghi Wins Over German Newspaper."

301 **"He is very much in line with our ideas":** Stephen Castle and Jack Ewing, "Merkel Signals Support for Italian to Lead ECB," *New York Times*, May 11, 2011.

303 **"I will only say that we are responsible for ensuring price stability":** Trichet and Constancio, "Introductory statement."

CHAPTER 17: THE PRESIDENT OF EUROPE

**306** **"We are dying":** Renee Maltezou, "Greek Police Clash with Anti-austerity Protesters," Reuters, February 23, 2011.

**307** **"seriously damage faith in the functioning of the euro zone":** Christian Reiermann, "Greece Considers Exit from Euro Zone," *Der Spiegel*, May 7, 2011.

**307** **"We had Wall Street open at that point in time":** Charles Forelle, "Luxembourg Lies on Secret Meeting," *Real Time Brussels* (blog), *Wall Street Journal*, May 9, 2011, http://blogs.wsj.com/brussels/2011/05/09/luxembourg-lies-on-secret-meeting/.

**308** **At 12:06 p.m. on Saturday, May 14:** Christopher Dickey and John Solomon, "The Strauss-Kahn Timeline," *Newsweek*, July 24, 2011.

**308** **At 4:40 p.m., Port Authority police:** Dan Bilefsky, "The French Reaction to IMF Chief's Arrest," *Lede* (blog), *New York Times*, May 15, 2011, http://thelede.blogs.nytimes.com/2011/05/15/the-french-reaction-to-i-m-f-chiefs-arrest/.

**308** **Strauss-Kahn's sexual appetites had gotten him in trouble three years earlier:** Landon Thomas Jr., "Woman in 2008 Affair Is Said to Have Accused IMF Director of Coercing Her," *New York Times*, May 16, 2011.

**309** **"The view that seems to be taking hold":** George Georgiopoulos and Harry Papachristou, "IMF Says Greece Must 'Reinvigorate' Reform Drive," Reuters, May 18, 2011.

**309** **Papandreou was particularly proud of his strategy of using Google Earth:** Daniel Steinvorth, "Greek Government Hauls Billions in Back Taxes," *Der Spiegel*, August 2, 2010, http://www.spiegel.de/international/europe/.

**310** **"To this demonstrably mistaken recipe I will not agree":** Elena Becatoros, "Greek Opposition Party Rejects New Austerity Plan," *Associated Press*, May 24, 2011.

**310** **"I didn't come to discuss the looting of Greek society":** Ibid.

**310** **"We will all require assurances":** Stephen Castle, "IMF Gets Tough with Europe; Aid to Greece Withheld for Now," *International Herald Tribune*, June 21, 2011, 3.

**311** **In Syntagma Square:** Renee Maltezou and Harry Papachristou, "Greek Police Battle Rioters as Austerity Bill Passed," Reuters, June 29, 2011.

**312** **"We are not in favor of restructuring and haircuts":** Jean-Claude Trichet, press conference, European Central Bank, Frankfurt, Germany, June 9, 2011, http://www.ecb.int/press/pressconf/2011/html/is110609.en.html.

**313** **"a sovereign default or disorderly bank failures":** Antonio Borges and Aasim Husain, "IMF Country Report No. 11/184," working paper, Staff Report for the 2011 Article IV Consultation with Member Countries, European Department, Washington, DC, July 1, 2011, http://www.imf.org/external/pubs/ft/scr/2011/cr11184.pdf.

**314** **"Any talk of restructuring was a total taboo":** Landon Thomas Jr. and Stephen Castle, "The Denials That Trapped Greece," *New York Times*, November 5, 2011.

**314** **"There was shock and surprise on their faces":** Thomas Jr., 2011.

**314** **At about 1 a.m., Trichet, Merkel, and Sarkozy called Brussels:** Carlo Bastasin, *Saving Europe: How National Politics Nearly Destroyed the Euro* (Washington, DC: Brookings Institution Press, 2012), 294.

**314** **"banker war room":** Klaus C. Engelen, "Ackermann's Banker War Room," *International Economy* Summer (2011): 62.

**315** **"With this offer":** "Greece Financing Offer: Statement by IIF Board of Directors," official statement, Institute of International Finance, Brussels, Belgium, July 21, 2011, http://www.iif.com/press/press+198.php.

**316** **According to calculations by economist and journalist Carlo Bastasin:** Bastasin, *Saving Europe*, 287.

**319** **"The full liberalisation of local public services":** "Trichet e Draghi: un'azione pressante per ristabilire la fiducia degli investitori," *Corriere della Sera*, September 29, 2011, http://www.corriere.it/economia/11_settembre_29/.

**320** **the Governing Council met again on the afternoon of Sunday, August 7:** Peter Müller et al., "Breaking Taboos: Concerns Mount in Germany over ECB Bond Buys," *Der Spiegel*, August 15, 2011.

**321** **"Our hearts pour with blood":** Giulia Segreti, "Rome Orders €45 Billion in Cuts and Taxes," *Financial Times*, August 12, 2011.

**321** **"Here's the real problem with Italy":** Anthony Faiola, "Amid Crisis, Italy Confronts a Culture of Tax Evasion," *Washington Post*, November 24, 2011.

**322** **as the ECB bought:** European Central Bank Press Release Database, bond purchase data, http://www.ecb.int/press/.

322 **"Who do I call if I want to call Europe?":** Vanessa Gera, "Kissinger Says Calling Europe Quote Not Likely His," *Associated Press*, June 27, 2012.

322 **"Trichet has become the de facto president of Europe":** Jeff Black and Jana Randow, "Trichet Turns 'President of Europe' as Debt Crisis Stuns Political Leaders," *Bloomberg News*, August 9, 2011.

323 **"for personal reasons":** "Jürgen Stark resigns from his position," ECB Press release, European Central Bank, Frankfurt, Germany, September 9, 2011, http://www.ecb.int/press/pr/date/2011/html/pr110909.en.html.

323 **"It's a very bad sign":** Jack Ewing and Nicholas Kulish, "Key German Resigns from Leadership of ECB," *International Herald Tribune*, September 10, 2011, 14.

325 **"The Executive Board of the ECB":** Helmut Schmidt, "Farewell event for Jean-Claude Trichet," speech, European Central Bank, Frankfurt, Germany, October 19, 2011, http://www.ecb.int/events/shared/pdf/speech_schmidt_111019_en.pdf?9e56ea646c3197e7a7b08fa78e70a276.

325 **"The single currency is an ancient idea":** Jean-Claude Trichet, speech, European Central Bank, Frankfurt, Germany, October 19, 2011, http://www.ecb.int/press/key/date/2011/html/sp111019.en.html.

326 **They called themselves the Groupe de Francfort:** "A Crisis? Call the F-Team," *Economist*, November 4, 2011.

## CHAPTER 18: ESCAPE VELOCITY

329 **"I find the activism at the Fed right now a major turnoff":** Senate Committee on Banking, Housing, and Urban Affairs, transcript of hearing, July 14, 2011, CQ Transcriptions.

330 **"I would fire him tomorrow":** Transcript of September 7, 2011, debate of Republican Presidential Candidates at Ronald Reagan Presidential Libary, Federal News Service.

332 **"The euro-area crisis has had more dramatic moments":** Speech by Mervyn King at the Mansion House, June 14, 2012, http://www.bankofengland.co.uk/publications/Documents/speeches/2012/speech587.pdf.

333 **"The fact that we're not in the euro area":** Mervyn King, Quarterly Inflation Report Q&A, May 16, 2012, http://www.bankofengland.co.uk/publications/Documents/inflationreport/conf120516.pdf.

333 **King was in the royal box:** Matt Sandy and Amanda Perthen, "Crisis? What Crisis," *Mail on Sunday*, July 3, 2011.

334 **"the reason we would raise interest rates":** Sean O'Grady, "No Interest Rate Rise before Unemployment Falls, Says King," *Independent* (London), June 29, 2011.

335 **"almost impossible to calibrate":** Bank of England Inflation Report, August 2011, 38, http://www.bankofengland.co.uk/publications/Documents/inflationreport/ir11aug.pdf.

335 **"The big risks facing the UK economy":** Mervyn King, Inflation Report Press Conference, Opening Remarks by the Governor, August 10, 2011, http://www.bankofengland.co.uk/publications/Documents/inflationreport/irspnote100811.pdf.

336 **"We were very conscious":** Examination of Witnesses, Treasury Select Committee, http://www.publications.parliament.uk/pa/cm201012/cmselect/cmtreasy/1576/11102502.htm.

336 **"shock and awe":** Philip Aldrick, "Shock and Awe Could Be QE's Biggest Asset," *Daily Telegraph*, October 7, 2011.

336 **"The world economy has slowed":** Allistair Osborne, "Bank Pins Hopes on QE2 to Keep Economy Afloat," *Daily Telegraph*, October 7, 2011.

337 **"Suppose we faced a very different economic environment":** "The Fed's Dual Mandate Responsibilities and Challenges Facing U.S. Monetary Policy," September 7, 2011, http://www.chicagofed.org/webpages/publications/speeches/2011/09_07_dual_mandate.cfm.

338 **"Desperate times call for bold measures":** Christina D. Romer, "Dear Ben: It's Time for a Volcker Moment," *New York Times*, October 30, 2011, 6.

340 **"Is it frustrating":** Bank of England Quarterly Inflation Report Q&A, May 16, 2012, http://www.bankofengland.co.uk/publications/Documents/inflationreport/conf120516.pdf.

## CHAPTER 19: SUPER MARIO WORLD

343 **"Mario Draghi's first day at work":** "George Papandreou: An All Too Final Stand," *Guardian*, November 1, 2011, http://www.guardian.co.uk/commentisfree/2011/nov/01/george-papandreou-final-stand-editorial.

343 **"the political equivalent of smashing rare and expensive plates":** Joshua Chaffin and Quentin Peel, "Papandreou's Gambit Sparks Eurozone Alarm," *Financial Times*, November 2, 2011.

345 **"The referendum in essence is about nothing else":** Stefan Simons, "Merkel and Sarkozy Halt Payments to Athens," *Der Spiegel*, November 3, 2011.

345 **"We made Papandreou . . . aware":** Ibid.

346 **"It amounted to the final stage of the 'waterboarding' sessions":** Carlo Bastasin, *Saving Europe: How National Politics Nearly Destroyed the Euro* (Washington, DC: Brookings Institution Press, 2012), 338.

347 **In the week ending November 11:** Derived by the author from weekly ECB balance sheet announcements at http://www.ecb.int/press/pr/wfs/2011/html/index.en.html.

348 **They served white wine from the Pfalz region:** Ralph Atkins, "Eurozone Crisis: A Deft Way to Buy Time," *Financial Times*, February 7, 2012.

350 **"coordinated actions to enhance their capacity":** Federal Reserve Press Release, November 30, 2011, http://www.federalreserve.gov/newsevents/press/monetary/20111130a.htm.

350 **"Finally, global action!":** Kevin Carmichael, "Central Banks in Bid to Pull Europe from Doldrums," *Globe and Mail*, December 1, 2011, B1.

352 **"it was a lively discussion":** Mario Draghi, press conference December 8, 2011, http://www.ecb.int/press/pressconf/2011/html/is111208.en.html.

354 **"It felt like war":** Niki Kitsantonis and Rachel Donadio, "Athens Shaken by Riots after Vote for Austerity," *New York Times*, February 14, 2012, A8.

354 **One Greek newspaper:** "'Memorandum Macht Frei': How One Greek Paper Views the Second Bailout," *Journal*, http://www.thejournal.ie/memorandum-macht-frei-how-one-greek-paper-views-the-second-bailout-351455-Feb2012/.

355 **"must undertake determined policy actions":** Hearing at Committee on Economic and Monetary Affairs of the European Parliament, introductory statement by Mario Draghi, April 25, 2012, http://www.ecb.int/press/key/date/2012/html/sp120425.en.html.

358 **"The euro is like a bumblebee":** Speech by Mario Draghi, Global Investment Conference, London, July 26, 2012, http://www.ecb.int/press/key/date/2012/html/sp120726.en.html.

## CHAPTER 20: GOVERNOR ZHOU'S CHINESE MEDICINE

361 **"A drug from Western medicine":** Speech by Zhou Xiaochuan at Caixin Summit, November 5, 2010, official English translation at http://www.pbc.gov.cn:8080/publish/english/955/2010/20101228160916958752023/20101228160916958752023_.html. Author's translation differs from official translation. Original Chinese at http://www.pbc.gov.cn/publish/hanglingdao/2950/2010/20101119164544386735148/20101119164544386735148_.html.

362 *Forbes* **listed Zhou as number fifteen:** Nicole Perlroth and Michael Noer, "The World's Most Powerful People," *Forbes*, November 2, 2011, http://www.forbes.com/powerful-people/.

362 *Foreign Policy* **placed him number four:** "The FP Top 100 Global Thinkers," *Foreign Policy*, December 2010.

363 **In August 2010, there was a strange rumor circulating:** Jason Dean, "Markets Ignore China Rumor (for a Change)," *China Realtime Report* (blog), *Wall Street Journal*, August 31, 2010, http://blogs.wsj.com/chinarealtime/2010/08/31/markets-ignore-china-rumor-for-a-change/.

365 **"They had a red rubber stamp":** "Carl Walter and Victor Shih on the Chinese Banking System," Gerson Lehrman Group High Table Video, May 21, 2012, https://www.hightable.com/china/video/video-carl-walter-victor-shih-chinese-banking-pt-1.

366 **"From other countries we've already learned this lesson":** *21st Century Business Herald*, March 6, 2009, http://www.21cbh.com/HTML/2009-3-9/HTML_5DFC2OOESWSQ.html.

366 **"astronomical lending" . . . "masking catastrophe":** Ru Guo, ["Wu Xiaoling: Astronomical loans mask catastrophe, central bank must return to hedging measures"], July 23, 2009.

367 **"Besides laboring . . . I was exposed to other things":** Chenjing Xu, ["Zhou Xiaochuan: We can't let the common people's money become frayed"], [*Global People Magazine*], November 30, 2010, http://people.huanqiu.com/Exclusive/2010-11/1303775_5.html.

367 **"In a complicated system, there are usually many feedback loops":** Zhou Xiaochuan, "Changing pro-cyclicality for financial and economic stability," March 26, 2009, http://www.bis.org/review/r090421b.pdf.

368 **"old-style Maoists":** David Barboza, "China's Mr. Wu Keeps Talking," *New York Times*, September 26, 2009, http://www.nytimes.com/2009/09/27/business/global/27spy.html?_r=1&pagewanted=all.

369 **"Whatever the market can solve":** Chenjing Xu ["We can't let the common people's money become frayed."]

369 **In a doubles match against . . . Larry Summers:** Bob Davis, "Political Overlords Shackle China's Monetary Mandarins," *Wall Street Journal*, April 15, 2011, A1.

370 **China's bond market is breathtakingly underdeveloped:** Henry Sanderson, "China Bond Market Ready for Takeoff after Bold Moves," Bloomberg News, June 11, 2012.

371 **"kind of international reserve currency we need:** Zhou Xiaochuan. "Reform the International Monetary System," March 23, 2009, http://www.pbc.gov.cn/publish/english/956/2009/20091229 104425550619706/20091229104425550619706_.html.

371 **In October 2009, the PBOC created a new department:** Tao Li ["PBOC confirms the establishment of a second monetary policy division"], Caixin Media, October 30, 2009, http://www.caijing.com.cn/2009-10-30/110299012.html.

371 **"The main purposes of the swap agreement":** "Bilateral Local Currency Swap Arrangement with the People's Bank of China," Reserve Bank of Australia, March 22, 2012, http://www.rba.gov.au/media-releases/2012/mr-12-08.html.

372 **In official documents, the phrase used:** http://www.fx168.com/fx168html/20120514/20120514 134396080.htm; http://www.chinascopefinancial.com/news/post/11212.html.

372 **"the will of the market":** "RMB internationalization is market's choice," *China Daily*, June 5, 2012, http://www.china.org.cn/business/2012-06/05/content_25566200.htm.

372 **"If some areas need to be reformed":** "Reform Is a Big Systematic Transformation and Needs Reasonable Arrangements," Emerging Markets Insight, Mirae Asset, July/August 2012.

374 **"trickery":** Peng Yi ["How did Zhou Xiaochuan become a trickster with the interest rate hike"], *Economic Observer*, October 21, 2010, http://www.eeo.com.cn/2010/1021/183192.shtml

## AFTERWORD: BACK TO JACKSON

377 **"What about the commercial-paper market?":** "Tangled Reins," *Economist*, September 6, 2007. http://www.economist.com/node/9767718.

378 **"The results that we have do not imply":** Michael Woodford, "Methods of Policy Accommodation at the Interest-Rate Lower Bound," paper presented at the Jackson Hole Symposium "The Changing Policy Landscape," August 31, 2012, http://www.kansascityfed.org/publicat/sympos/2012/mw.pdf?sm=jh083112-4.

379 **"I never plan my holidays ahead":** Mario Draghi, interview with *Le Monde*, July 21, 2012, http://www.ecb.int/press/key/date/2012/html/sp120721.en.html.

381 **"This is a political problem":** Brian Blackstone and Marcus Walker, "How ECB Chief Outflanked German Foe in Fight for Euro," *Wall Street Journal*, October 2, 2012, A1.

382 **At a dinner on August 1:** Paul Carrel, Noah Barkin, and Annika Breidthardt, "Special Report: Inside Mario Draghi's Euro Rescue Plan," Reuters, September 25, 2012.

383 **"has been stretched and, in some cases, disregarded":** "Too Close to State Financing via the Money Press,'" *Der Spiegel*, August 29, 2012, http://www.spiegel.de/international/europe/spiegel-interview-with-bundesbank-president-jens-weidmann-a-852285.html.

383 **"Mephistopheles stirs up the general elation even further":** "Money Creation and Responsibility," speech at the 18th colloquium of the Institute for Bank-Historical Research (IBF) in Frankfurt, September 18, 2012, http://www.bundesbank.de/Redaktion/EN/Reden/2012/2012_09_20_weidmann_money_creaktion_and_responsibility.html.

384 **"I think that, in my job as president":** Mario Draghi, press conference, September 6, 2012, http://www.ecb.int/press/pressconf/2012/html/is120906.en.html.

387 **"this precious stone set in the silver sea":** Mervyn King, Speech to the South Wales Chamber of Commerce, October 23, 2012, http://www.bankofengland.co.uk/publications/Documents/speeches/2012/speech613.pdf.

388 **"Is not the mere existence of general unemployment":** Mervyn King "Twenty Years of Inflation Targeting," Stamp Memorial Lecture, London School of Economics, October 9, 2012, http://www.bankofengland.co.uk/publications/Documents/speeches/2012/speech606.pdf.

# IMAGE CREDITS

# INDEX